Iran and the Challenges of the Twenty-First Century

Mohammad-Reza Djalili

Iran
and the Challenges of the Twenty-First Century

Essays in Honour of
Mohammad-Reza Djalili

Edited by
H. E. Chehabi
Farhad Khosrokhavar
Clément Therme

MAZDA PUBLISHERS   Costa Mesa, California   2013

Mazda Publishers, Inc.
Academic publishers since 1980
P.O. Box 2603
Costa Mesa, California 92628 U.S.A.
www.mazdapublishers.com
A. K. Jabbari, Publisher

Copyright © 2013 by Mazda Publishers, Inc.
All rights reserved. No parts of this publication may be reproduced or transmitted by any form or by any means without written permission from the copyright holders except in the case of brief quotations embodied in critical articles and reviews.
Mazda Publishers books may be purchased for educational, or sales promotional use. For information please write to the address above.

Library of Congress Cataloging-in-Publication Data
Iran and the Challenges of the Twenty-first Century : Essays in Honor of Mohammad-Reza Djalili / edited by H. E. Chehabi, Farhad Khosrokhavar, and Clément Therme.
pages cm

ISBN 13: 978-1568592978
ISBN 10: 1-56859-297-3

1. Iran—Politics and government—21st century. 2. Iran—Foreign relations—21st century. 3. Iran—Economic conditions—21st century 4. Iran—Strategic aspects. 5. Djalili, Mohammad Reza. I. Djalili, Mohammad Reza, honoree. II. Chehabi, H. E., editor of compilation.
DS318.9.I7269 2013
955.06—dc23
2013006977

Major funding for the publication of this volume
was provided by a grant from
The A. K. Jabbari Charitable Trust
and by a contribution from
The Graduate Institute of International
and Development Studies in Geneva

CONTENTS

Publisher's Note		*xi*
Acknowledgements		*xiii*
Foreword	Beyond Boundaries, the Passion for Knowledge Alessandro Monsutti	*xv*
Introduction	Mohammad-Reza Djalili: Between the East and the West. H. E. Chehabi, Farhad Khosrokhavar, and Clément Therme	*xvii*
Tabula Gratulatoria		*xxv*
Bibliography of Mohammad-Reza Djalili Compiled by Clément Therme		*xxix*
Chapter 1	The Green Movement: Social Innovation in an Authoritarian Regime Farhad Khosrokhavar	1
Chapter 2	The Shah's Two Liberalizations: Re-Equilibration and Breakdown H. E. Chehabi	24
Chapter 3	The End of a Beautiful Friendship? Mahmoud Ahmadinejad and the Principalists Walter Posch	50

Chapter 4	'Human Rights' by Any Other Name: Iranian Activism in an Authoritarian State Arzoo Osanloo	79
Chapter 5	Inter-Confessional Relations in Iran: Conflicts and Transfers in the Aftermath of 9/11 Stéphane A. Dudoignon	96
Chapter 6	Political Culture, Use of History, and Democracy in Iran. Firouzeh Nahavandi	111
Chapter 7	Nationalism, Myth, and History in Modern Iran Ali Ansari	129
Chapter 8	The Short-Term Society: A Comparative Study in the Problems of Long-Term Political and Economic Development in Iran Homa Katouzian	144
Chapter 9	How to Transform a Rent-seeking Economy: the Case of Iran Thierry Coville	165
Chapter 10	Energy Subsidies in Iran Narsi Ghorban	181
Chapter 11	The Role of Ideology in Iranian Foreign Policy Mehdi Mozaffari	189
Chapter 12	Iran's Cultural Diplomacy Nadia von Maltzahn	205

Chapter 13	'Dialogue' in the Foreign Policy of the Islamic Republic of Iran Clément Therme	222
Chapter 14	France and Iran: Between Tensions and 'Critical Dialogue' Denis Bauchard	239
Chapter 15	Iran's Asian Strategy: The Importance of Economic Ties Thierry Kellner	245
Chapter 16	Iran and Syria: An Enduring Alliance Jubin M. Goodarzi	266
Chapter 17	Iran and the Twenty-First-Century 'Persian World': A Tajik Perspective Frédérique Guérin	285
List of Contributors		303

Publisher's Note

When Prof. Houchang Chehabi called me several months ago and said that he has co-edited a manuscript and is looking for a publisher, at first I was curious. Once he mentioned that this volume of essays is dedicated to Professor Mohammad-Reza Djalili, my initial reaction turned into excitement.

Although my knowledge of the French language is next to none, over the course of the last thirty-three years since I established Mazda Publishers, I have come cross numerous references to and citations of Professor Djaili's research and writings. Without hesitation, I accepted to publish this volume—the eighth festschrift to be published by my press.

In the *Foreword* and the *Introduction*, the authors have eloquently acknowledged the contribution that Prof. Djalili has made to the field over his long and illustrious career and there is no need for me to elaborate further. I just wanted to remind the readers, once again, that I have taken it upon myself to continue publishing similar volumes as a tribute to those scholars who have dedicated their careers to the study of Iranian culture and civilization.

The first volume in this series, published in 2000, was dedicated to Nikki R. Keddi; it was followed by six other volumes, dedicated respectively to Hafez F. Farmayan (2002), Hanns-Peter Schmidt (2003), posthumously to Arthur Upham Pope and his wife and collaborator, Phyllis Ackerman (2005), Peter J. Chelkowski (2007), Amin Banani (2012), and Gernot Windfuhr (2012). There are other scholars whose contributions to the field of Iranian studies ought to be recognized, and as a tribute to them, I shall continue to make such volumes of essays available to the scholars of Iranian studies.

A. K. Jabbari,
Publisher

Acknowledgements

This collective book was the prolongation of the international conference organized in June 2010 at the Graduate Institute of International and Development Studies in Geneva. We thank the Director, Professor Philippe Burrin, for his support in the organization of this gathering of scholars of Iran coming from many countries. Valérie von Daeniken of the International History and Politics section of the Graduate Institute contributed to making this international conference a success. We would also like to acknowledge the help of Professor Jussi Hanhimäki, the director of the International History and Politics section of the Graduate Institute. Finally, we express our profound gratitude to the Fonds national suisse de la recherche scientifique (FNS) for its financial support, without which the June 2010 conference would not have taken place.

Foreword

Beyond Boundaries, the Passion for Knowledge

Alessandro Monsutti

How to be European? This was the facetious question posed by the Persian traveller invented three centuries ago by Charles-Louis de Secondat, baron de Montesquieu. A century later, Hajji Baba of Ispahan, James Justinian Morier's character, picaresquely demonstrated how one could be Persian. Are these fictional accounts eloquent efforts to change perspectives, so that readers question their own beliefs, or a prelude to orientalism, which today is universally discounted without having been totally discarded? We know that power and knowledge, the creation of stereotypes and the discovery of the Other, evolve together, just like an old couple whose members can neither stand each other nor live without each other.

Can one be both European and Persian simultaneously? Can one be passionately cosmopolitan yet remain deeply attached to one's country of origin? This is indeed the question that Mohammad-Reza Djalili poses to himself and to us. Born in Tehran when the world was under the deathly shadow of the Second World War, Mohammad-Reza Djalili travelled to Belgium—in his own words, transported by his love of the French language—to obtain his doctorate. He returned to Iran only to depart once again at the time of the Islamic Revolution—this time for what would become a long and painful exile. He settled in Geneva and joined the faculty of the Graduate Institute of International Studies, where his teaching career developed and grew over the years, nurtured by his ever-present popularity with the students. His passion for knowledge, his good-naturedness towards those under his charge, his courtesy towards his peers, and a certain ironic distance towards the powerful, in a word his humanity, are all elements which have contributed to his success. The subtleties of *ta'arof*, the Iranian code of politeness where amicable rivalry is often manifested in the form of self-effacement, does not hinder the full expression of critical thought in its most strident form.

Following on from an already impressive list of publications, *Diplomatie islamique: stratégie internationale du khomeynisme* (jointly published by the Institut universitaire de hautes études internationales and Presses universitaires de France in 1989) provides a detailed and lucid analysis of the evolution of Iranian foreign policy during the decade following the fall of the Pahlavis. Mohammad-Reza Djalili uses discourse analysis and the sociology of power networks to show how 'Islamic diplomacy' challenges the dominant conception of State sovereignty and the moral primacy of human rights.

Combining Islamism, Third Worldism, and nationalism, the ideology of Ruhollah Khomeini sought to disrupt the international world order while ultimately remaining unable to establish an alternative political system. This striking line of reflection remained strong in Mohammad-Reza Djalili's work thereafter. Although successive waves of pragmatism and dogmatism continued to sweep through Iran, the revolutionary ideal was progressively eroded by the action of the group of clerics that had taken over the core of the country's institutions, as demonstrated in *Iran: l'illusion réformiste* (published by Presses de Sciences Po in 2001).

Insatiably curious, considering history in its *longue durée*, Mohammad-Reza Djalili did not limit his research to Iran. His expertise and knowledge of Central Asia, the Caucasus, and Turkey enabled him to situate his analysis in the broader and deeper context of the 'Turco-Persian world', in reference to Robert Canfield. A vast heterogeneous area, which nonetheless provides a rich canvass for analysis, the Turco-Persian world covers political areas with different if not opposite destinies, spanning the laicism of Kemalist Turkey, the rigorous Islamism of the Taliban, the Soviet experiences, and the quests for identity in Kurdistan and Ferghana.

Passion is inexorably linked to knowledge when one turns to the ample horizons of this region. Beyond his academic work, Mohammad-Reza Djalili is above all an aesthete open to the universal beauty of a poem, a photographic image, the proportions of a palace. What would academic research be worth if it were not grounded in humanism? Having had the privilege and honour of teaching with Mohammad-Reza Djalili, I recall classes which continued over meals, where discussions would meander from the latest headlines to the origins of the Safavid dynasty, from Bonaparte's expedition to Egypt to the subtleties of Turkish cuisine, from the joys of becoming a father to the anxiety of watching one's children grow up. And when discussion would turn to a student's grade, generosity would always trump severity. Friendship, in Iran and elsewhere, is measured by the services which one renders to one another but also, and perhaps above all else, by the time spent sharing the apparently futile. Yes, one can be both Persian and French, Belgian and Swiss, one can be attached to the country of one's childhood while seeing through cosmopolitan eyes. The various contributions in this publication are tributes to a person who has never ceased demonstrating such attributes throughout his career.

Introduction

Mohammad-Reza Djalili: Between the East and the West

H. E. Chehabi, Farhad Khosrokhavar, and Clément Therme

More than thirty-three years after its establishment, the Islamic Republic of Iran is confronted with the most serious political crisis in its history. These unforeseen circumstances have led to a renewed scholarly interest with regards to the challenges that the country is facing at the beginning of the twenty-first century. The first challenge touches upon the problem of cultural and social division, with the relative failure of the regime to translate its Islamicization project into a socio-cultural reality for the nation, especially in the domains of human rights, education, and the general attempts to create *homo islamicus*. The resilience of the Iranian domestic cultural sphere constitutes one of the main obstacles encountered by the Islamic Republic in its aim to export its revolutionary model on the international scene. The second challenge is economic, as Iran is confronted with numerous problems: high inflation, the need for transfer of technology, the weaknesses of foreign investment, particularly in the energy sector, brain drain, and the sanctions imposed by the United States and others. Despite the above challenges, the Iranian economy still has a high potential that could be developed if long-term policies were implemented to replace the current clientelist and short-term strategies. Finally, the revolutionary diplomacy of Tehran is in contradiction with the defence of national interests. Despite elements of continuity with the international positions of the old regime, the revolutionary changes implemented by the Islamic continue to limit the ability of the Iranian authorities to transform Iran into a truly emerging country. Given its long history, geopolitical advantages, and wealth of natural resources, Iran could aim for the status of an emerging power in the absence of such limitations.

During the last thirty-three years, the teaching and research of Professor Mohammad-Reza Djalili have enabled Geneva's Graduate Institute of International Studies and Development to make significant and original contributions to the study of contemporary and historical developments in Iran, contributions that have had tremendous influence on both the regional and international stage. The thirty-first anniversary of the Islamic revolution coincided with the thirty-first year of Djalili's outstanding career in Geneva.

Djalili's legacy comprises a collection of major academic works not only in the field of international relations but also in Iranian studies. Without any doubt, his students will miss a strict but attentive professor focused on their intellectual development. In his teaching approach, Djalili always favoured dialogue and humour over confrontation and a supercilious respect for his authority. Those fortunate enough to have been his students will remember his seminars as a place of high-level intellectual exchanges, in which it was possible to have a contradictory dialogue and to voice disagreements with the professor openly. This spirit of openness is also found in the wide range of his research, for Djalili is interested not only in international politics and geopolitics but also in history in general and Persian culture in particular.

Born in 1940 in Tehran, Mohammad-Reza Djalili, a Swiss and Iranian national, received a bilingual education in Iran and Belgium. After attending the French Lycée in Brussels, he studied at the Université Libre de Bruxelles (ULB), where he obtained his PhD in diplomatic and political sciences in 1971. Like the majority of Iranian students abroad, he decided to return to Iran in order to use his education and expertise to contribute to the development of his country. At that time, the Iranian economy was booming even if structural problems such as increased social inequalities and an autocratic political system remained. In parallel to an academic career in the field of international relations, which led him to teach at the University of Shiraz between 1972 and 1974 and then at the Faculty of Law and Political Sciences of the University of Tehran until 1978, he assumed high-level administrative responsibilities, notably as chief of staff to Iran's minister of development, Houchang Nahavandi, and as the secretary-general of the 'Centre des hautes études en relations internationales' at the University of Tehran.

It was during this period that Mohammad-Reza Djalili founded *La revue iranienne des relations internationales*, becoming its editor-in-chief. The journal was published in the Persian language, French, and English by the University of Tehran until the Islamic revolution in 1979.[1] During the 1978–79 academic year, he was on sabbatical leave at the Graduate Institute in Geneva. This marked the start of his longstanding collaboration with the Institute. During the 1980s, he also taught at the University of Paris II.

An Original Vision of International Relations

In his two main academic works regarding the theories of international relations, *Relations internationales*[2] and *Tiers Monde et relations internation-*

---

[1] For example, see the October 1976 issue on different dimensions of Iranian and French foreign policy, edited in partnership with the *Centre d'études de politique étrangère de Paris*.

[2] Philippe Braillard and Mohammad-Reza Djalili, *Les relations internationales*, Que sais-je ?, Paris: Presses Universitaires de France, huitième édition mise à jour, 2006.

ales,³ Mohammad-Reza Djalili approaches existing theories critically in the sense that for him no explanatory paradigms of international relations (realist, Marxist, liberal, etc.) can be ignored, despite the theories' mutual contradictions. To understand the complexity of international phenomena, one has to use the complementary dimensions of all the paradigms. Mohammad-Reza Djalili and Philippe Braillard summarized their thinking in their work *Les relations internationales* as follows:

While recognizing the primacy of states in international life and the disparate and contradictory characteristics of the international system, we have sought to consider the richness of various paradigms that currently structure the study of international relations, by integrating into our vision of these relations not only the dynamics of interdependence and cooperation but also the effects of the asymmetric nature of certain aspects of international relationships. This vision of international relations seeks to show the profound forces and structural elements of international life through various perspectives and approaches: the identification of actors, the study of foreign policy, the analysis of the structure of the international system and the study of interactions (conflicted and cooperative). This perspective is based on the belief that understanding international life requires a sociological approach that goes beyond a simple reading of events as a series of international phenomena. Contrary to the views of many political scientists and sociologists, this approach does not lead to the construction of a general theory of international relations.⁴

In addition to this global approach, the two authors were also interested in the emergence of Third World countries on the international scene during the Cold War period.⁵ This research shed new light on how a significant group of Third World countries contested the dominant international world order, notably through their original vision of international relations. This perspective is particularly relevant given that, during this period, analyses of international relations were mainly centred on the Western world. The second part of Djalili's research, which is part of this theoretical framework, focuses on a regional approach based on his analysis of the Middle East region.

At the Crossroads of a Regional Approach: Iran

Djalili's first academic work was his doctoral dissertation dealing with the relationship between Iran and the Indian Ocean, and in the 1970s, Djalili's works were limited to the Persian Gulf and the Indian Ocean.⁶ However, after the fall of the Soviet Union his regional focus expanded in the 1990s to in-

---

³ Philippe Braillard and Mohammad-Reza Djalili, *Tiers Monde et relations internationales*, Fribourg: Masson, 1984.
⁴ Braillard and Djalili, *Les relations internationales*, pp. 122–23.
⁵ See 'Avant-propos', in Braillard and Djalili, *Tiers Monde et relations internationales*.
⁶ Mohammad-Reza Djalili, *L'océan indien*, Que sais-je ?, Paris: Presses Universitaires de France, 1978.

clude Central Asia and the Caucasus. While Djalili's research horizons broadened, this was not at the expense of his genuine interest for his country of origin, despite the dramatic changes that had occurred in Iran since 1978. The Islamic Revolution and the subsequent establishment of an Islamic Republic in Iran inspired Djalili to write two books. The first, published in 1981, was a pioneering study on the relations between religion and politics in Iran.[7] In it he emphasized the emerging process of a theocratic Shiite state, a completely new phenomenon at the time. This was followed at the end of the 1980s by a book on Islamic diplomacy that remains the most complete and insightful reflection in the French language on the foreign policy of the Islamic Republic of Iran. Its impact was felt beyond the Francophone world, for *Foreign Affairs* greeted this book as follows: 'It would be difficult to find a better analytical study of Iranian foreign policy over the decade of the Khomeini regime.'[8] In 1989, Djalili had already understood that:

The Islamic Revolution is not a revolution like any other and its foreign policy is not merely an attempt to assert its presence on the international stage [as an act of] revolutionary necessity or to consolidate the legitimacy of the new regime. [The revolution] also harbours an unusual set of ideas on the sovereignty of the state, diplomatic status and immunity, international hierarchy, human rights, war, peace etc., ideas which question international relations as a whole.[9]

Regarding Iranian issues, several books followed, including one on internal politics during the reformist era,[10] and another that deals with the geopolitics of Iran.[11] Most recently, Djalili has published two more general books on Iran, one an alphabetical glossary of issues affecting Iran,[12] the other a comprehensive synthesis of contemporary Iranian history.[13]

At the end of the 1990s, Djalili was one of the first scholars in Switzerland to adopt a geopolitical approach to the contemporary history of Central Asia and the Caucasus. After 1991, his intuition was particularly pertinent in light of the considerable political, economic, and social mutations that both regions have been undergoing since the fall of the Soviet Union. The first book regarding this area was a co-edited volume dealing with Tajikistan.[14] Since

---

[7] *Religion et révolution : l'islam shi'ite et l'Etat*, Paris: Economica, 1981.
[8] See John C. Campbell, *Foreign Affairs* 68/3 (Summer 1989), p. 183.
[9] Mohammad-Reza Djalili, *Diplomatie islamique: Stratégie internationale du khomeynisme*, Paris: Presses Universitaires de France, 1993, p. 13.
[10] Mohammad-Reza Djalili, *Iran : l'illusion réformiste*, Paris : Presses de Sciences Po, 2001.
[11] Mohammad-Reza Djalili, *Géopolitique de l'Iran*, Bruxelles: Editions Complexe, 2005.
[12] Mohammad-Reza Djalili, *L'Iran de A à Z*, Paris: André Versailles Editeur, 2010.
[13] Mohammad-Reza Djalili and Thierry Kellner, *Introduction à l'histoire contemporaine de l'Iran*, Paris: La Découverte, 2010.
[14] Mohammad-Reza Djalili, Frédéric Grare, and Shirin Akiner (eds), *Tajikistan: The trials of Independence*, Richmond: Curzon, 1998.

then, Djalili has co-edited two books, one dealing with Central Asia,[15] the other with the Turko-Iranian world.[16] The books filled a vacuum regarding topics neglected by too many scholars and are testimony to his capacity for teamwork.

Mohammad-Reza Djalili has indeed produced a large academic set of works. These writings were not done at the expense of his teaching activities. He never said 'no' to his students' request for assistance in their professional projects. For more than three decades, he always remained a professor at the disposal of Graduate Institute's students. His colleagues will remember him as 'a man of a rare indulgence, and of a courtesy rarely found in today's world', to quote Professor André Liebich, a Faculty member since 1989 and an eminent specialist of the history of communism and post-communism, history of international relations and the issue of minorities.

Djalili's academic work has had considerable international influence, as evidenced by the numerous translations of his books and academic articles over the last forty years. At first sight, it might seem paradoxical that a laïc (in the French sense of the word) like Mohammad-Reza Djalili should dedicate a significant part of his career to the study of a theocratic political regime. But this paradox is only apparent. Indeed, 'Iran cannot be reduced to its regime,' as a former French ambassador to Iran put it.[17] The immemorial character of Iran, its cultural singularity as well as a tormented contemporary history, surely play a role in Djalili's passion for Iran. He has always been the proponent of a certain idea of Iran. This idea may have been perceived as disconnected from the image of a revolutionary Iran that the Islamic Republic advertises worldwide, but after the events following the June 2009 presidential elections this idea of Iran seems more present than ever.

Homage to a Teacher, Colleague, and Friend

The present volume is mainly based on the presentations made at a two-day international conference organized at the Graduate Institute in Geneva in June 2010, one year after the contested election of June 2009, to honour Professor Mohammad-Reza Djalili on the occasion of his retirement. Sociologists, anthropologists, economists, political scientists, and historians from Iran, the United States, the United Kingdom, Switzerland, Denmark, Belgium, and France gathered in Geneva to shed light on the complex political, social, economic, and cultural evolution of Iran since the Islamic Revolution, drawing a comprehensive picture of what is at stake in the transformation of the internal

---

[15] Mohammad-Reza Djalili and Thierry Kellner, *Géopolitique de la nouvelle Asie centrale*, Paris–Geneva: Presses Universitaires de France/IUHEI, 2003. This book has been translated into Spanish, Arabic, and Turkish.
[16] Mohammad-Reza Djalili, Alessandro Monsutti, and Anna Neubauer (eds), *Le monde turco-iranien en question*, Paris–Geneva: Karthala/The Graduate Institute, 2008.
[17] See François Nicoullaud, 'L'Iran n'est pas réductible à son régime', *Le Monde*, 1 January 2010.

political situation in Iran. This new internal situation is decisive not only for the future of the Middle East but also for the maintenance of the international non-proliferation regime and the security of Western energy supplies. Finally, we wish to acknowledge two internationally renowned scholars of Iran who accepted to contribute to this book despite not participating at the conference: Thierry Coville and Walter Posch.

This book addresses two aspects of Iran's contemporary history. Part One focuses on Iran's internal challenges, examining various social, political, cultural, and economic issues facing the authorities at the beginning of the twenty-first century. Part Two addresses the revolutionary, cultural, nationalist, and economic dimensions of Iran's foreign policy.

Farhad Khosrokhavar presents the historical background of the Green Movement, going back to the Constitutional revolution of 1905–1911. He analyses the innovative nature of this new social movement, and explains its relative failure to undermine the theocratic nature of the Islamic Republic in light of the contemporaneous Arab Spring. In the second chapter, H. E. Chehabi puts the failure of the reformists to effect a genuine liberalization of the Islamic Republic's political regime in perspective by providing a comparative analysis of the two liberalizations that occurred under Mohammad Reza Shah: that of 1960–63, which ended in a reconsolidation of the Shah's rule, and that of 1977–78, which ended in revolution. Walter Posch then shifts the focus to factionalism within the Islamic regime and points out the momentous consequences of the emergence of a new 'principalist' political faction before and after the presidential election of 2009. The fourth chapter, by Arzoo Osanloo, draws our attention towards an understudied question, namely the activities of legal reformers inside the Islamic Republic. Osanloo shows how difficult it became, in the aftermath of the 2009 election, to defend women's rights and human rights in Iran. Nevertheless, the author's main argument is that activism continues in innovative forms as part of a dialogical response to the new constraints. In the next chapter, Stéphane A. Dudoignon delves into the hitherto neglected topic of the Sunni question in the Islamic Republic of Iran and introduces the world vision and strategies developed by the religious and political leaders of the Sunni minority of Iran. Against the background of a relatively low level of interconfessional confrontation in Iran since the emergence of the Islamic Republic in 1979, Dudoignon analyses the appearance of Sunni-Shiite violence in 2009. In the next contribution, Firouzeh Nahavandi explores the manipulation of Iranian political culture by both the Pahlavi monarchy and the Islamic Republic. Nahavandi observes that in the social construction of the past, 'democracy is rarely mentioned' and that one of the main challenges of the twenty-first century in Iran, if it is to become a real democracy, is to switch to a new political culture based on the rights of the people and not the past. Continuing the discussion of the myths that inform Iranians' views of their past, Ali Ansari discusses the recent rise of nationalism that challenges the official ideology of the state. He persuasively demonstrates that the change within Iranian society, towards a renewed interest for Iran's pre-Islamic past, will inevitably affect the political class. This can already be seen in President Mahmoud Ahmadinejad's enthusiasm for integrating Iran's pre-Islamic past into the official discourse of the Islamic Republic. Homa Katouzian then offers a *long-term* historical analysis of Iran *short-term* society. Regarding the most recent period of the history of the Islamic Republic, he challenges the forecasts which promise the imminent fall of the Islamic regime because, according to his view, there is at the moment no major external threat to the regime. He concludes outlining the unpredictability of Iran's future given its definition as 'the country of possibilities'. The last two chapters of Part One consider the economic situation of Iran. First Thierry Coville uses the case of the Iranian economy to illustrate the difficulties of transforming a rent-seeking economy. He emphasizes that Iran needs to focus on economic development in order to fulfil its quest for power on the regional and international scene. This chapter notably examines the main options facing the Iranian leadership to solve the structural problems of the Iranian economy. More particularly, the author outlines the positive effect that increasing trust between the state and civil society would have on economic behaviour, which would be of capital importance for the future economic development of Iran. In the second chapter, Narsi Ghorban persuasively demonstrates that one of the main challenges of the Iranian economy for the twenty- first century is the reform of energy subsidies. Ghorban acknowledges the widespread consensus among experts both inside and outside Iran regarding the need to reform the price of energy. Nevertheless, he also recognizes that the Iranian leadership is facing two main hurdles: first, the government needs to be efficient and wise in implementing the subsidies reform bill in order to limit the political and social costs of the reform, and second, outside political and economic pressures are complicating the reform policy started in 2010 after many years of inaction.

Part Two considers the revolutionary and regional aspects of Iran's foreign policy. This part is introduced by Mehdi Mozaffari, who was, together with Mohammad-Reza Djalili, one of the first scholars of Iran to outline the defining role of Khomeinist ideology in the decision-making process of Iran's foreign policy. Mozaffari focuses on a specific aspect that is missing in the literature regarding this otherwise widely studied topic, i.e., the fact that Iranian foreign policy is guided by a totalitarian ideology rather than by national interest. In the next chapter, Nadia von Maltzahn focuses on Iran's cultural diplomacy. She explains the institutional framework of Iran's cultural apparatus and the efforts of the Islamic Republic leaders to improve the coordination between different institutions dealing with Iran's cultural activities abroad. She also analyses the flexibility of Iran's cultural diplomacy: at the regional level, Tehran attempts to strengthen its cultural reach by promoting the Persian language, whereas in Southeast Asia, Iran's cultural discourse focuses more on Islamic matters. In the following chapter, Clément Therme explains that for the Islamic Republic, the idea of dialogue is first and foremost conceived to guarantee the survival of the Islamic revolutionary state in the context of the Cold War as well as in an international system in which the United States is the dominant power. He then explores the historical background of

Khatami's diplomatic discourse of dialogue of civilizations, noting the decisive intellectual work of Dariush Shayegan. Denis Bauchard's chapter provides new insights into the troubled diplomatic relationship between Iran and France, notably after the Islamic revolution of 1979. What distinguishes this contribution from the rest of the literature is the Bauchard's experience as a former diplomat, in which capacity he has dealt with the diplomats of the Islamic Republic of Iran as a representative of the French state. Thierry Kellner then offers a new perspective on Iran's policy in Asia. He shows that Iran's strategy in Asia took shape after the death of Ayatollah Khomeini and notes that Iran's Asian foreign policy has remained unchanged under the successive presidential administrations of Rafsanjani, Khatami, and Ahmadinejad. After reviewing the historical background of the political and economic connections between Iran and Asia, the author concludes that this aspect of Iran's foreign policy cannot be ignored by Westerners, given their long-term nature. Jubin Goodarzi offers a new interpretation of the alliance between Iran and Syria, showing that, contrary to the view of many analysts who insist on the short-term dimension of this astonishing alliance between a religious theocracy and a secular autocracy, it is of enduring nature. The last chapter, by Frédérique Guérin, is a useful and timely study of the Tajik perspective on the Persian world. Guérin shows that the shared cultural legacy between Iran, Tajikistan, and Afghanistan is a soft-power tool of Iran's contemporary foreign policy, used to increase its regional influence. She concludes that the three countries' shared history and culture notwithstanding, the Persian world is fragmented.

We hope that this collection constitutes not only an original contribution to the study of contemporary Iran, and in particular the challenges it faces at the beginning of the twenty-first century, but also a worthy homage to the diversity and scholarly significance of Mohammad-Reza Djalili academic work.

Tabula Gratulatoria

Ali Ansari, Professor, University of St. Andrews, St. Andrews.

Bruno Arcidiacono, Professor, Graduate Institute of International and Development Studies, Geneva.

Gopalan Balachandran, Professor, Graduate Institute of International and Development Studies, Geneva.

Ladan Boroumand, Research Director, Abdorrahman Boroumand Foundation for the Promotion of Human Rights and Democracy in Iran, Washington DC.

Denis Bauchard, Special Adviser, French Institute of International Affairs (IFRI), Paris.

Philippe Braillard, Honorary Professor, University of Geneva, Geneva.

Stéphane Buissard, Journalist, *Le Temps*, Geneva.

Philippe Burrin, Director and Professor, Graduate Institute of International and Development Studies, Geneva.

Houchang Esfandiar Chehabi, Professor, Boston University, Boston.

Vicken Cheterian, Director, CIMERA, Geneva.

Shahram Chubin, Non-Resident Senior Associate, Carnegie Endowment for International Peace, Washington DC.

Yves Corpataux, Director of the library, Graduate Institute of International and Development Studies, Geneva.

Thierry Coville, Research Fellow, Institut des Relations Internationales et Stratégiques (IRIS), Paris.

Pierre Drion, Board Member of various companies.

Stéphane A. Dudoignon, Associate Professor, University of Amsterdam and Research Fellow, Centre National de la Recherche Scientifique (CNRS), Paris.

Pierre-Marie Dupuy, Professor, Graduate Institute of International and Development Studies, Geneva.

Gilbert Etienne, Honorary Professor, Graduate Institute of International and Development Studies, Geneva.

Shaloma Gauthier, PhD Candidate, Graduate Institute of International and Development Studies, Geneva.

Narsi Ghorban, Director of Research, International Institute for Caspian Studies, Tehran.

Jubin Goodarzi, Professor, Webster University, Geneva.

Frédérique Guérin, Research Fellow, Geneva Centre for Security Policy; Geneva.

Jussi Hanhimäki, Professor, Graduate Institute of International and Development Studies, Geneva.

Homa Katouzian, St Antony's College and the Oriental Institute, University of Oxford, Oxford.

Florence Hellot-Bellier, Research Fellow, UMR Mondes iranien et indien, CNRS, Paris.

Thierry Kellner, Lecturer, Political Science Department Université Libre de Bruxelles (ULB), Brussels.

Fereydoun Khavand, Maître de conférences, University René Descartes, Paris.

Farhad Khosrokhavar, Professor, Ecole des Hautes Etudes en Sciences Sociales (EHESS/CADIS), Paris.

Matthew Leitner, Lecturer, Graduate Institute of International and Development Studies, Geneva.

André Liebich, Professor, Graduate Institute of International and Development Studies, Geneva.

Nadia von Maltzahn, Orient-Institut Beirut.

Antoine Maurice, Journalist, *La Tribune de Genève*, Professor, University of Geneva, Geneva.

Serge Michel, Deputy Chief Editor, *Le Monde*, Paris.

Delphine Minoui, Middle East correspondent, *Le Figaro*, Beirut.

Alessandro Monsutti, Professor, Graduate Institute of International and Development Studies, Geneva.

Mehdi Mozaffari, Professor, Department of Political Science, Aarhus University, Denmark.

Firouzeh Nahavandi, Professor, ULB, Brussels.

Arzoo Osanloo, Associate Professor, Law, Societies, and Justice, University of Washington, Seattle.

Walter Posch, Research Fellow, Stiftung Wissenschaft und Politik (SWP), Berlin.

Pierre de Senarclens, Honorary Professor, University of Lausanne (UNIL).

Mohsen Sohrabi, Businessman, Geneva.

Clément Therme, Associate Fellow, EHESS/CADIS, Paris.

Valérie von Daeniken, Graduate Institute of International and Development Studies, Geneva.

Özcan Yilmaz, PhD Candidate, Graduate Institute of International and Development Studies, Geneva.

Ariane Zevaco, PhD Candidate, Social Anthropology and Ethnology, EHESS, Paris.

Bibliography of Mohammad-Reza Djalili

Compiled by Clément Therme

Books and Books Chapters

L'Iran de A à Z, Brussels: Edition André Versailles, 2010.
Histoire contemporaine de l'Iran, Paris: La Découverte, 2010 (Turkish translation, forthcoming, Ed. Bilge Kultur Sanat, 2010), with Thierry Kellner.
Yeni Orta Asya Jeopolitigi, SSCB'nin bitiminden 11 Eylgl Sonrasina (Geopolitics of Central Asia. From the fall of the USSR to the aftermath of 9/11), Turkish translation, Ed. Bilge Kultur Sanat, 2009, with Thierry Kellner.
'L'Iran dans ses frontières et au-delà', in *Les frontières dans tous leurs états: les relations internationales au défi de la mondialisation*, Pierre de Senarclens (ed.), Brussels: Bruylant, 2009, pp. 241–258.
Les relations internationales, Paris: PUF, 126 p. (Ninth Edition), 2009, with Philippe Braillard.
'L'Europe et l'Asie centrale: de la redécouverte à la coopération', in *Construire l'Europe. Mélanges en hommage à Pierre du Bois*, Andre Liebich, Basil Germond (eds), Paris/Geneva: PUF/IHEID, 2008, pp. 197–235, with Thierry Kellner.
Le monde turco-iranien en question, (co-edited with Alessandro Monsutti and Anna Neubauer), Geneva/Paris: Graduate Institute/Kathala, 2008.
Les relations internationales, Greek translation, Athens: Editions Lambrakis Press, 2008.
'L'Organisation de coopération de Shanghai: nouveau Léviathan eurasiatique ou colosse aux pieds d'argile?', in *Conflits, sécurité et coopération. Conflicts, security and cooperation, Liber Amicorum Victor-Yves Ghebali*, Vincent Chetail (ed.), Mélanges, No. 45, Brussels: Editions Bruylant, 2007, pp. 193–221, with Thierry Kellner.
'Le Caucase dans la stratégie eurasiatique de l'Iran', in *Religion et politique dans le Caucase post-soviétique*, Bayram Balci, Raoul Motika (eds), Paris: Maisonneuve & Larose, 2007, pp. 53–69.
Les relations internationales, Paris: PUF, 126 p. (Eighth Edition, updated), 2006, with Philippe Braillard.
Géopolitique de l'Iran, Brussels: Editions Complexe, 2005, 144 p.

'New Foreign Policies for New States: Transcaucasia and Central Asia in the International Arena', in *The OSCE and the Multiples Challenges of Transition*, Farian Sabahi, Daniel Warner (eds), London: Ashgate, 2004, pp.13–36.

Géopolitique de la nouvelle Asie centrale. De la fin de l'URSS à l'après-11 septembre, Paris: PUF, 2003, 585 p. (Spanish translation: *La nueva Asia Central : Realidades y desafios*, Biblioteca del Islam Contemporaneo, No. 21, Barcelona: Edicions Bellaterra, 2003, 660 p.), with Thierry Kellner.

'Réflexions après l'attentat', Interview with Alain Joxe, Pierre Hassner and Mohammad-Reza Djalili, in *11 septembre un an après*, Paris: Edition de l'Aube/Le Monde Editions, 2002, pp. 101–119.

Iran: l'illusion réformiste, Paris: Presses de sciences po, 2001, 126 p.

Géopolitique de la nouvelle Asie centrale, Paris: PUF, 2001, 311 p. (Arabic translation, Beirut: Editions Daralistiklal, 2001), with Thierry Kellner.

'Changements stratégiques en Méditerranée orientale', in Victoria Curzon Price, Hasni Abidi (eds), *Le partenariat euro-méditerranéen. Un projet, des enjeux*, Geneva: Institut Européen, 1999, pp. 71–76.

L'Iran en transition. Entre espoir et incertitude, Problèmes politiques et sociaux, No. 813, 18 December 1998, 76 p.

Tajikistan: the Trials of Independence, (co-edited with Frederic Grare and Shirin Akiner), London: Curzon, 248 p.

La Caspienne, une nouvelle frontière, (co-edited with Anne de Tinguy), Paris: CEMOTI, No. 23, January–June 1997.

Al-eslam al-shiye va dowula, (Arabic translation by Ali Al-Khatib of *Religion et révolution l'islam shi'ite et l'Etat*), Beirut: Edition Dar al-Maktab, 1997.

Le Caucase postsoviétque: la transition dans le conflit, Brussels: Edition Bruylant, 1995, 264 p.

Le Tadjikistan à l'épreuve de l'indépendance, (co-edited with Frédéric Grare), Geneva: HEI Publications, 1995, 203 p.

'Dar Al-Harb', in *The Oxford Encyclopaedia of the Modern Islamic World*, John L. Esposito (ed.), Vol. 1, New York: New York University Press, 1995, pp. 337–338.

'International Law', in *The Oxford Encyclopaedia of the Modern Islamic World*, John L. Esposito (ed.), Vol. 1, New York: New York University Press, 1995, pp. 337–338.

'Iran: vers un nouveau rôle régional?', Problèmes politiques et sociaux, No. 720, 28 January 1994.

Moyen-Orient: migrations, démocratisation, médiations, (co-edited with Riccardo Bocco), Paris: PUF, 1994, 405 p.

Diplomatie islamique: stratégie internationale du khomeynisme, Paris: PUF, 1989, 241 p.

Les relations internationales, Paris: PUF, 1988, with Philippe Braillard.

The Third Word and International Relations, London / Boulder Colorado: Frances Pinter: Lynne Rienner, 1986, xii–301 p. (updated, English translation), with Philippe Braillard.
Tiers Monde et relations internationales, Paris: Masson, 1984, 304 p., with Philippe Braillard.
Religion et révolution: islam shi'ite et l'État, Paris: Economica, 1981, 69 p.
Le golfe Persique: introduction bibliographique, Geneva:Graduate Institute of international studies, Asian Centre, 1979, 92 p.
L'océan Indien, Paris: PUF, 1978, 127p.
Le golfe Persique: problèmes et perspectives, Paris: Dalloz, 1978, 252 p.

Articles

'Mort d'un dissident islamiste', *Telos*, December 2009, available: http://www.teloseu.com/fr/article/montazeri_la_mort_d_un_dissident_islamiste (Accessed 13 September 2011).
'Double défi pour la puissance régionale iranienne: crises internes et nouvelle politique américaine', *Maghreb-Machrek*, No. 201, Autumn 2009, pp. 45–56, with Clément Therme.
'L'Iran en Amérique latine: la République islamique dans le pré-carré des Etats-Unis', *Maghreb-Machrek*, No. 197, Autumn 2008, pp. 115–126, with Clément Therme.
'Le flanc Est de l'Iran: opportunités et vulnérabilités', *Politique étrangère*, No. 3, 2008, pp. 601–661, with Clément Therme.
'La politique arabe de l'Iran', *A contrario*, Vol. 5, No. 2, 2008, pp. 134–146.
'L'Iran en Asie centrale, politique régionale d'un voisin proche', *Les cahiers de l'Orient*, No. 89, March 2008, pp. 57–68.
'Le croissant chiite: mythe ou réalité?', in *Les Etudes de la Documentation française*, Afrique du Nord et Moyen-Orient, 2007–2008, pp. 103–116.
Irán: fortalezas y debilidades de una potencia regional, Madrid: Casa Árabe e Instituto International de Estudos Arabes y del Mundo Musulman, Documento de trabajo, No. 1, September 2007.
'Iran en el escenario internacional', *Minerva*, No. 6, 2007, pp. 108–114.
'L'Iran sur la scène international', *Questions internationales*, No. 25, May-June 2007, pp. 32–41.
'L'Iran d'Ahmadinejad: évolutions internes et politique étrangère', *Politique étrangère*, No. 1, 2007, pp. 27–39.
'Asie centrale. Un terrain de rivalités', *Courrier des pays de l'Est*, No. 1057, September-October 2006, pp. 4–16, with Thierry Kellner.
'L'émergence d'un arc chiite?', *Questions internationales*, No. 21, September-October 2006, pp. 19–21.
'Intégration régionale en Asie centrale', *CEMOTI*, No. 39–40, 2005, pp. 53–69.

'La politique étrangère de l'Iran à l'épreuve d'Ahmadinejad', *Caucaz.com*, 23 April 2006.
'Le golfe Persique: au cœur de la géopolitique pétrolière mondiale', *Outre-Terre. Revue française de Géopolitique*, No. 14, Winter 2006, pp. 341–376, with Thierry Kellner.
'La Chine, l'Iran et la crise du nucléaire', *The Middle East Review of International Affairs* (MERIA), Vol. 1, No. 1, Spring 2006, pp. 1–33, available: http://meria.idc.ac.il/journal_fr/2006/jv1no1a2.html (accessed 13 September 2011), with Thierry Kellner.
'Paradoxe iranien', *Enjeux diplomatiques et stratégiques 2005*, Paris: Economica, pp. 150–164.
'Regímenes políticos de Asia Central: crisis de legitimidad, violencia política y perspectivas inciertas', *Revista d'Afers Internacionals*, No. 70–71, October 2005, pp. 35–68, with Thierry Kellner.
'Iran, regard vers l'Est: la politique asiatique de la République islamique', *Les Rapports du GRIP*, 2005/2, 35 p., with Thierry Kellner.
'L'Iran entre échec du réformisme et reconfiguration géopolitique', *Géopolitique*, No. 88, October-December 2004, pp. 12–20.
'Les États-Unis et l'Asie centrale de l'après 11 septembre à la guerre d'Irak', *Revue française de géopolitique*, No. 3, 2005, pp. 333–347, with Thierry Kellner.
'La problématique de la souveraineté vue des pays du Sud', *Swiss Political Science Review*, 10 (1), 2004, pp. 109–114.
'Le laboratoire iranien' in 'Les nouveaux penseurs de l'islam', *Le Nouvel Observateur* (Hors-Série), April-May 2004, pp. 84–86.
'Une porte à peine entrouverte : l'Iran et l'Asie centrale (1991–2002)', *Cahiers d'études sur la Méditerranée orientale et le monde turco-iranien (CEMOTI)*, No. 35, 2003, pp. 109–121.
'L'après-Saddam: espérances et incertitudes iraniennes', *Politique étrangère*, No. 3–4, 2003/4, pp. 567–582.
'Géo-économie des hydrocarbures de la Caspienne', *Risques & Management International*, No. 2, 2003, pp. 61–94, with Thierry Kellner.
'Les régimes politiques d'Asie centrale: illusion ou réalité des réformes?', *Les cahiers de Mars*, No. 177, Second trimester 2003, pp. 20–29.
'Les États-Unis et l'Asie centrale après le 11 septembre 2001', *Revue Française de Géopolitique*, No. 1, 2003, pp. 242–269, with Thierry Kellner.
'Images de l'Amérique vues du monde de l'islam', *Quaderni*, No. 50/51, Spring 2003, pp. 265–278.
'Géopolitique de l'Iran au seuil du XXIe siècle', *La Revue Nouvelle*, No. 11, tome 151, November 2002, pp. 38–50.
'Iran and Caucasus: Maintaining Some Pragmatism', *Connections. The Quarterly Journal*, Vol. 1, No. 3, July 2002, pp. 49–58.
'Asie centrale ex-soviétique 1991–2002: la Grande transformation', *Géopolitique*, July-September 2002, pp. 54–61.
'L'Asie centrale un an après le 11 septembre', *Le courrier des pays de l'Est*, No. 1027, August 2002, pp. 4–13, with Thierry Kellner.

'Un monde iranien aux multiples identités', *Boèce. Revue romande des sciences humaines*, No. 3, June 2002, pp. 33–46.
'Conseguenze regionali della prima guerra del secolo', *il Mulino*, No. 401, May-June 2002, pp. 538–545.
'L'Afghanistan et ses voisins après le 11 septembre', *Afghanistan Info*, No. 50, March 2002, pp. 9–13.
'Canaux et canalisations. La Caspienne dans la nouvelle configuration géopolitique de l'après-11 septembre', *Outre-Terre Revue française de géopolitique*, No. 2, May 2002, pp. 115–148, with Thierry Kellner.
'L'Asie centrale après le 11 septembre. Incidences géopolitiques de la crise afghane et facteur islamique', UNHCR, Centre for Documentation and Research, *WriteNet paper*, No. 07/2001, January 2002, 67 p., with Thierry Kellner.
'Républiques méridionales de l'ex-URSS: nouveaux Etats du Sud?', *Nouveaux Cahiers de l'IUED*, October 2001, pp. 71–84.
'La République islamique d'Iran : exacerbation des contradictions et émergence de la société civile', in *Civilisations*, Firouzeh Nahavandi, Paul Claeys (eds), Vol. XlVIII, No. 1–2, August 2001, pp. 51–68.
'Asie centrale: nature et évolution des régimes politiques', *Défense nationale*, No. 7, July 2001, pp. 101–113.
'La Russie et la "nouvelle" Asie centrale', *Géostratégiques*, No. 1, January 2001, available: http://www.strategicsinternational.com/asiecentral.htm (accessed 13 September 2011), with Thierry Kellner.
'L'Asie centrale dix ans après l'indépendance, étude de géopolitique', *Sécurité et stratégie*, Brussels: Institut Royal Supérieur de Défense, June 2000, 84 p., with Thierry Kellner.
'Moyen-Orient, Caucase et Asie centrale: des concepts géopolitiques à construire et à reconstruire?', *Central Asian Survey*, Vol. 19, No. 1, March 2000, pp. 117–140, with Thierry Kellner.
'L'armée et la politique: le cas de L'Iran', *Cahiers d'études sur la Méditerranée orientale et le monde turco-iranien (CEMOTI)*, No. 27, 1999, pp. 95–113.
'La mondialisation de la corruption et de la criminalité', in 'Monnayer les pouvoirs. Espaces, mécanismes et représentations de la corruption', *Nouveaux cahiers de l'IUED*, No. 9, January 2000, pp. 87–98.
'Le rapprochement entre la Turquie et Israël: conséquences pour les relations turco-iraniennes', *Cahiers d'études sur la Méditerranée orientale et le monde turco-iranien (CEMOTI)*, No. 28, 1999, pp. 163–169.
'Nouvelle géopolitique du Caucase: entre turbulences et périls', *Bulletin de la SSMOCI* (Société Suisse Moyen-Orient et civilisation islamique), No. 11, October 2000, pp. 4–10.
'Iran: une approche géopolitique', *Géopolitique*, No. 64, January 1999, pp. 57–64.
'Aux origines des conflits du Moyen-Orient', in Actes du Symposium international. Tome I, *Guerre civile- guérilla - terrorisme*, Pully: Centre d'histoire et de prospective militaire, 1999, pp. 75–82.

'Pétrole et gaz de la Caspienne, entre mythe et réalité', *Transitions*, 1998, pp. 121–158, with Thierry Kellner.
'The Persian Gulf: an Iranian Perception', *World Affairs*, Vol. 3, No. 2, April-June 1999, pp. 36–42.
'La redécouverte de l'Asie centrale par la communauté internationale: du discours à la réalité', *Les pays de la CEI*, 1997, Paris: La documentation française, 1998, pp. 55–91.
'In Search of New Friends: Iran and Central Asia', *World Affairs*, Vol. 1, No. 1, January-March 1997, pp. 102–115.
'La politique extérieure de l'Iran durant les années 1990: une approche critique', *Le trimestre du monde*, First trimester 1996, pp. 19–33.
'La politique afghane de l'Iran prisonnière d'une logique confessionnelle', *Les Nouvelles d'Afghanistan*, No. 68, Second trimester 1995, pp. 7–8.
'Asie centrale', *Département fédéral des affaires étrangères*, Unpublished report, Berne, October 1995.
'Caucase et Asie centrale: entrée en scène et recomposition géostratégique de l'espace', *Central Asian Survey*, Vol. 13, No. 1, 1994, pp. 7–17.
'Iran, une puissance régionale empêtrée', *Politique internationale*, No. 64, Summer 1994, pp. 177–188.
'Téhéran face à l'Asie centrale', *Nouveaux mondes*, Spring 1994, No. 4, pp. 175–190.
'The political Modernisation of Iran', *Iran Nameh*, Vol. XI, No. 2, Spring 1993, pp. 209–219.
'Les Etats-Unis et leur rôle dans le monde: le temps des incertitudes', *Studia diplomatica*, Vol. XLVI, No. 2, 1993, pp. 37–72, with Philippe Braillard.
'L'Iran face aux développements en Transcaucasie et en Asie centrale', *Cahiers d'études sur la Méditerranée orientale et le monde turco-iranien (CEMOTI)*, No. 16, 1993, pp. 245–255.
'L'Iran face au Caucase et à l'Asie centrale', *Le Trimestre du monde*, Fourth trimester 1992, pp. 181–190.
'L'Iran sans l'URSS', *Politique internationale*, No. 56, Summer 1992, pp. 363–373.
'Unilateral Policies in the Field of Disarmament and Arms Limitation', in *Disarmament and Limitation of Armaments: Unilateral Mesures and Policies*, News York: United Nations/Unidir, 1992, pp.49–57.
'Analyse des conflits du Tiers monde: éléments d'une typologie', *Revue internationale des sciences sociales*, No. 127, February 1991, pp. 171–179. (translated in English, Spanish, Arabic and Chinese).
'Guerre et paix dans le golfe Persique', *Le trimestre du monde*, No. 14, Second trimester 1991, pp.161–167.
'Le golfe Persique 1971–1991: de l'ordre colonial à un nouvel ordre mondial?', *Relations internationales*, No. 66, Summer 1991, pp.199–209.
'L'Europe à la recherche de sa sécurité: les acquis de Rome et de Maastrich', *Studia Diplomatica*, No. 5, 1991, pp. 25–44, with Philippe Braillard and Fred Tanner.

'Dimensions internationales de la révolution islamique', in *Révolution et droit international*, Paris: Ed. A. Pedone, 1990.
'Regard sur la politique étrangère de la République islamique', *Civilisations*, Vol. 28, No. 2, 1990, pp. 197–206.
'Conceptions non-occidentales de l'ordre mondial et théories des relations internationales', *Le trimestre du monde*, No. 9, First trimester 1990, pp. 149–161.
'Territoires et frontières dans l'idéologie islamiste contemporaine', *Relations internationales*, No. 63, Autumn 1990, pp. 305–312.
'Une diplomatie dans l'impasse', *Les Cahiers de l'Orient*, First trimester 1989, pp. 57–64.
'The International Dimensions of Fundamentalism', *Word Link*, March 1988 ,pp. 56–57.
'Du bon usage des ayatollahs', *Politique internationale*, No. 38, Winter 1987–1988, pp. 119–133.
'Le Liban à l'épreuve du khomeynisme', *Les Cahiers de l'Orient*, No. 5, First trimester 1987, pp.69–80, with Annie Laurent.
'Les organisations non gouvernementales et le Tiers Monde', in Mario Bettati and Pierre-Marie Dupuy, *Les ONG et le droit international*, Paris: Economica, 1986, pp. 41–49.
'Le colonel, l'ayatollah et les autres', *Politique internationale*, No. 33, Autumn 1986, pp. 39–47.
'Pékin -Téhéran: les paradoxes d'une alliance', *Politique internationale*, No. 28, Summer 1985, with Harish Kapur.
'Les organisations internationales du Tiers Monde: vers l'élaboration d'un nouveau cadre d'analyse', *Etudes internationales,* No. 3, September 1985, pp. 493–504, with Philippe Braillard.
'Problèmes du transport du pétrole et détroit d'Ormuz à l'époque actuelle', *Relations internationales*, No. 44, Winter 1985, pp. 413–424.
'D'un Iran à l'autre: de la politique étrangère du Shah à celle de Khomeyni', *L'Afrique et l'Asie modernes*, No. 140, Spring 1984, pp. 27–39.
'Cinq voisins spéciaux de l'URSS', *Studia Diplomatica*, No. 1, 1984, pp. 79–111, with D. Kappler.
'L'axe Téhéran-Damas', *Politique internationale*, No. 24, Summer 1984, pp. 261–270.
'Iran-Irak : an V de la guerre', *Politique étrangère*, No. 4, 1984, pp. 57–73.
'Iran-Irak: radioscopie d'une guerre ambiguë', *Politique internationale*, No. 21, Autumn 1983, pp. 21–35.
'Le Conseil de Coopération du Golfe: quelques problèmes d'ordre structurel', *Studia Diplomatica*, No. 6, 1983, pp. 625–637.
'Ormuz: un détroit d'importance mondiale', in *Sur l'état de la société internationale*, Paris: Economica, 1982, pp.181–196.
'Reflections on a Typology of Conflicts in the Third Word', in *Unesco Year Book on Peace and Conflict Studies*, 1982, pp. 3–12.
'La communication inégale: la revendication du Tiers Monde', *Le Monde diplomatique,* January 1979.

'La dimension culturelle des puissances moyennes', *Revue iranienne des relations internationales* , No. 13–14, Summer 1979, pp. 71–83.

'Der Persische Golf - Parallelen und kontraste', *Aussenpolitik*, No. 2, 1978, pp. 227–234, with D. Kappeler.

'L'impérialisme culturel entrave à l'épanouissement de l'humanité', *Le Monde diplomatique*, March 1977.

'La situation militaire de l'océan Indien', *Politique étrangère* , No. 5, 1977, pp. 517–530

'Les cinq voisins non communistes de l'Union soviétique', *Studia Diplomatica*, No. 6, 1976, pp. 687–730, with D. Kappeler.

'The Indian Ocean Seen from Iran', *IDSA Journal* (New Delhi), October-December 1976.

'Evolution de la politique iranienne de l'océan Indien', *Revue iranienne des relations internationales*, No. 8, Autumn 1976, pp. 185–196.

'L'Iran et l'océan Indien', *Annuaire des pays de l'océan Indien*, Vol. 3, 1976, pp. 65–72.

'Le rapprochement irano-irakien et ses conséquences', *Politique étrangère*, No. 3, 1975, pp. 273–291.

'Les relations culturelles internationales de l'Iran', *Revue iranienne des relations internationales*, No. 2, Winter 1974–1975, pp. 107–126.

Chapter 1

The Green Movement: Social Innovation in an Authoritarian Regime

Farhad Khosrokhavar

The Green Movement (GRM) is a challenging social movement that developed in Iran during and after the presidential elections of June 2009. It made the democracy within the Islamic regime a major issue. It presented new dimensions: social, technological (in particular in communication technologies), and cultural. Long before the Arab Spring in 2011, it raised the question of democratization in an authoritarian context within the Muslim world. Whereas the Tunisians and the Egyptians succeeded in toppling their autocracies, in Iran the Green Movement failed to shake off authoritarian rule. Still, it shattered the legitimacy of the Islamic theocracy within Iran.

The Historical Setting

In order to understand the Green Movement in Iran, one has to put it into historical perspective. This movement is the consequence of the development of the Iranian society after the Islamic Revolution of 1979. The latter was the pinnacle of an anti-democratic movement that developed in Iran in the last decade of Mohammad Reza Shah's rule. The core of the Islamic Revolution's ideology was Third-Worldist, anti-imperialist, Islamist, and autocratic. It was in reaction to the failure of the preceding movements (mostly the nationalist, secular and proto-democratic movement led by Mosaddeq in the early 1950s). In regard to content, modern social movements in Iran come in three types:

- proto-democratic movements
- anti-democratic movements
- democratic movements[1]

---

[1] To be coherent, one should introduce the notion of 'proto-anti-democratic movements' as well. But this would make the typology more complex. Proto-democratic

By proto-democratic movements I mean those that propound an open political system in an ambivalent manner; they juxtapose ideas and concepts that are contradictory and incoherent. Still, the major thrust is towards political pluralism. As to democratic movements, they propose democracy as their ideal political system through a framework within which a minimum of secularization and the distinction between the religious and political realms are explicitly made. Anti-democratic movements aim to establish 'pure' societies through a 'virtuous' political system that creates a harmonious community in which a leader or a small political or religious elite implements the policies of virtue (Islamic purity and fraternity as well as the social justice for the 'oppressed', *mostaz'afin*, in the Islamic Revolution in Iran). Over the course of the last century, Iran has experienced all three types of movements: proto-democratic, anti-democratic, and democratic, in that order. The first major social movement with proto-democratic features was the so-called Constitutional Revolution of 1906.[2] This movement demanded a 'House of Justice' (*'adalat khaneh*) in order to put an end to royal arbitrary rule and the unruly aristocracy that was repressing peasants and the new fragile middle classes that started emerging in the late nineteenth century. One can single out three main protagonists in it. The first group, the radical secularists, consisted of those who believed that one should cut off the ties with Islam and engage in Western-style political change that would result in the marginalization of religion and its confinement to the private sphere. The second group, the Islamic reformists, thought that genuine Islam is not inimical to social justice and freedom and that democracy can be subsumed under authentic Islam. These people were mainly influenced by Jamaleddin al-Afghani and some other Islamic thinkers. Still, the major religious authorities that supported the Constitutional Revolution had at best a sketchy view of democracy and its implications, mainly towards religious minorities, women, non-Muslims in general, and social justice, necessarily defined in democracy independently of religion. The third group was made of those who rejected democracy in the name of Islam. Their major leader was Sheykh Fazlollah Nuri who was hanged in 1909 for treason. In the Constitutional Revolution, the second group won the upper hand for some time and a parliament was established that promulgated a constitution, ratified by the dying Mozaffareddin Shah. His son Mohammad Ali Shah, in theory a constitutional monarch, overthrew the parliament in 1907 with the help of the Russians. Iran, by and large, was a backward society in

---

movements have some 'proto-anti-democratic' dimensions as well. For the sake of simplicity, proto-anti-democratic movements will be subsumed under the heading of anti-democratic movements.

[2] The literature on the Constitution Revolution is vast. See Mangol Bayat, *Iran's First Revolution: Shi'ism and the Constitutional Revolution of 1905 – 1909*, Oxford: Oxford University Press, 1991; Janet Afary, *The Iranian Constitutional Revolution, 1906–1911*, New York: Columbia University Press, 1996; Ahmad Kasravi, *History of the Iranian Constitutional Revolution: Tarikh-e Mashrute-ye Iran*, Volume I, translated into English by Evan Siegel, Costa Mesa, CA: Mazda Publishers, 2006.

which tribes and a large peasantry were tied to the land by the landed 'feudals', consequently it was not prepared for democracy. The rule of the law through a parliamentary system was achieved due to the weakness of the Shah as much as the dynamics of the new political actors who regarded parliamentary monarchy as a means to limit the semi-colonial rule of imperialist Britain and Russia as well. The ambivalence of the new democratic system toward religion, concretely embodied in the question of how to reconcile Islamic law and people's sovereignty, opened up the path to future movements that were preoccupied by the same major concern, namely, how to articulate Islam and political pluralism.

The second major proto-democratic movement that occurred in Iran was the nationalist movement for the nationalization of oil, under the leadership of Mohammad Mosaddeq in the 1950s. The nationalist sentiment was ignited by the British way of underpaying for Iranian oil while American oil companies offered far better terms to the Saudis. The movement had a democratic content, though the question of Islam remained significant through the participation of Ayatollah Abolqasem Kashani in the movement. Moreover, the participation of the anti-democratic Tudeh party in the movement raised the question of communism. These twin components made the entire movement ambivalent in many respects, and it therefore deserves to be called 'proto-democratic'. The populist side of the movement added to its ambivalence regarding democracy. The movement was overturned in 1953 by the monarchist forces with the direct assistance of the American and British governments.[3]

The overthrow of the Mosaddeq government had deep consequences for the Iranian society, in particular its intellectuals. Up to then, Western democracy had been regarded as a model to follow by most of the new middle classes, religious or not. The active contribution of the American and British democracies to rescinding the legal government of Mosaddeq and the American support for the autocratic rule of the Shah, combined with the ideological influence of Communism and the extreme left resulted in presenting democracy as a screen that hid Western imperialism and its will to hegemony. For the new Islamist forces, democracy became the Trojan Horse of the West to destroy Islam through secularism and exploitation. Third-Worldism, Maoism, Guevarism (Che Guevara's model), in brief, different variants of leftism, went hand-in-hand with the discredit of democracy as a 'bourgeois' regime aiming at domineering the Third World and exploiting its mineral and human resources. For the radical Islamists who became conscious of their strength through the reinterpretation of Islam, democracy meant the illusion of social justice and people's rule, only Islam being able to promote 'real' democracy. Western models of political power, so they thought, meant the denial of dignity to Muslims and their oppression through atheistic worldviews. Many in-

---

[3] See Mark J. Gasiorowski, 'U.S. Foreign Policy Toward Iran During the Mussadiq Era', in *The Middle East and the United States: A Historical and Political Reassessment*, David Lesch (ed.), Fourth Edition, Boulder, CO: Westview Press, 2007, pp. 51–65.

tellectuals of a Marxist bent of late embraced militant Islam and became protagonists of Shiite extremism: Jalal Al-e Ahmad, Ahmad Fardid (after the Islamic Revolution) and many activists of lesser stature (Sadeq Qotbzadeh and Mostafa Chamran, among others) turned Islamic radicals; some of them went to Lebanon to hone their skills in the fight against imperialism.[4] Leftism and Islamic radicalism had more than convergences; they shared, in the years before the Islamic Revolution, the same motives against the Shah's authoritarianism. But they were even more anti-democratic and more autocratic in their tenets than the Shah, whose despotism was not based on a cogent ideology (pre-Islamic Iranian glory was a vague reference, not an ideology). Extremist Islamism in its Shiite version borrowed from radical communism its major arsenal, crystallized in three major concepts: imperialism, which became 'World Arrogance', *estekbar-e jahani*, in the Shiite jargon; the dichotomy exploiter/exploited, which was named *mostakbar/mostaz'af*; and the characterization of the Shah's regime as an illegitimate, exploitative, and unjust government for which they adopted the term *Taghut*, an Islamic concept connoting 'idol', to signify that it was an idolatrous government. In this way, Shiite radicalism was armed to promote a revolution under the guise of Islam, translating leftist notions into an Islamic idiom. The top intellectual who transformed Shiism from a quietist worldview into a revolutionary ideology was Ali Shari'ati. He made of Shiism the equivalent of eschatological communism: the rule of Ali (656–661), the fourth caliph after the death of the Prophet, was presented as the herald of communist egalitarianism; Islam was the unity of God accomplishing the unity of all classes by suppressing them and establishing a classless society (*jame'eh-ye bi tabaqeh-ye towhidi*); Hoseyn, the third Shiite Imam who was massacred with 72 of his companions in 680 in an unequal war against the army of the Umayyad Caliph Yazid, became the revolutionary who spread the message of 'Red Shiism' *(tashayyo'-e sorkh)* in spite of his military weakness; *Taghut*, idolatry, became the political regime in which the Islamic justice of a classless society was not established. Even though Ayatollah Ruhollah Khomeini, the leader of the Islamic Revolution, did not believe in this leftist version of Islam, for the sake of propaganda and in order to attract the leftist intellectuals and their middle-class followers, he did use himself this terminology without adhering to it. The Islamic Revolution of 1979 promoted the ideology of martyrdom in its Marxist version, in which Hoseyn died for the sake of social justice and against the repressive government of Yazid, defined itself in a modernized fashion as identical to the Shah's regime. As a result, the Islamic movement that ended up in the Islamic Revolution was by far more anti-democratic than the Shah's autocratic regime. The latter alienated the middle classes that it contributed to build up through its modernizing policies, destroying every middle-class political

---

[4] For details see H.E. Chehabi, 'The Anti-Shah Opposition and Lebanon', in *Distant Relations: Iran and Lebanon in the last 500 Years*, H.E. Chehabi (ed.), Oxford: Centre for Lebanese Studies, in association with I.B. Tauris, 2006, pp. 180–98.

structure and organization and leaving a gap that greatly facilitated the Islamic Revolution, which was based on clerical connections through mosques, the bazaar's informal organizations, and the leftist groups that fought against the Shah's regime. Social discontent and a mobilizing anti-democratic ideology that had a *two-pronged* communist and radical Islamic dimension were used to legitimize the movement and discredit the Shah, regarded as the representative of the godless and imperialist West in the region. The cycle of anti-democratic movements had been previously opened by the Islamic movement that begun in 1963 in Qom under the leadership of Ayatollah Khomeini, against the land reform of the Shah. The movement was anti-Western, anti-feminist, and anti-imperialist, in the sense that it opposed the granting of diplomatic immunity to US military personnel in Iran, a move that reminded Iranians of the nineteenth-century capitulations and thus deeply hurt Iranian nationalism.[5] The Shah's regime chose in the 1970s a suicidal attitude against the anti-democratic opposition of the extreme left and the Islamic radicals. Instead of rallying the middle classes, it alienated them by heightening despotism, establishing a caricature of a single-party system, and denying the political institutions in Iran (the parliament, the judiciary, and all the intermediary bodies) any autonomy. The result was an autocracy that discredited the imperial regime and with the economic crisis of the second half of the 1970s, totally isolated it. Against this background, the Islamic radicals, under the leadership of Ayatollah Khomeini, gained momentum.

The New Era of Democratic Movements

The success of the Islamic Revolution was in part due to its anti-democratic and radical ideology cherished not only by the extremist Muslims but also by the leftists, in part in consequence of the political blunders of the Shah. The Shah had already become self-absorbed and sexually obsessed in the last decade of his reign,[6] turning more and more paranoid, narcissistic, physically ill, and despotic, being cut off from the social realities of his country. But the way was paved also for the revolution due to the economic conjuncture of Iran, and last but not least, the failure of authoritarian nationalism in the region (the fate of Nasser's Arab nationalism was sealed with the 1967 defeat against Israel), opened up new vistas for political Islam.

The theocratic regime that came to power in Iran was not homogeneous in regard to its social supporters: secular leftists, Islamic radicals, Islamic liberals like Mehdi Bazargan and Ebrahim Yazdi, and fundamentalist Muslims who joined the movement in its last months did not share the same views of the social, political, and cultural (religious) priorities of the revolution. The state had remained intact during the revolution and the regime could build up

---

[5] See Richard Pfau, 'The Legal Status of American Forces in Iran', *Middle East Journal*, 2(2), 1974, pp. 141–53.
[6] See Asadollah Alam, *The Shah and I: The Confidential Diary of Iran's Royal Court, 1969–1977*, New York: St. Martin's Press, 1991, passim.

a theocracy through the new political forces, strengthened by the war against Iraq (1980–88) and the occupation of the American embassy (from 4 November 1979 to 20 January 1981) that legitimized the extremists and eliminated the revolutionary movement's weak liberal wing: the provisional government of Mehdi Bazargan government resigned on 6 November 1979. These events opened the road for Islamic radicalism and gave free rein to Ayatollah Khomeini to shape the regime against the will of some of his allies, the liberals who wanted a democratic Islamic regime and the leftists who wished a religious republic tinged with socialism. Theocracy, under the guise of *velayat-e faqih* (the government of the Islamic jurist) became the official regime in Iran. All in all, Iran's revolutionaries differed with each other on the nature of the state but for one thing, with the exception of the tiny minority of the liberals who mainly were the remnants of the Nationalist Movement of the 1950s, the others were all anti-democratically-minded, many for religious reasons, others due to their leftist leanings.

The paradox, as we shall see, is that in the next two or three decades, the new generations made of young girls and boys who had acceded to primary, secondary, and higher education, put into question the theocracy in the name of the rule of law; the universities became the foci of new generations of democratically minded intellectuals and students who peacefully changed their mindset in the third decade of the Islamic Revolution, directly challenging the theocratic nature of the regime.

The Anthropological Revolution in Iran

By anthropological revolution I mean a threefold change: a major shift within the family structure and mental attitudes within it, the transformation in the urban/rural relationships, and the attitudinal change within the urban world. These three developments happened at the same time in Iran, and they were happening under a political theocracy that was ideologically opposed to them. They mainly began in the beginning of the 1990s, that is, at least a decade after the Islamic Revolution, before the election of the first reformist president, Mohammad Khatami, in 1997.

The Islamic regime imposed the family laws of traditional Islam, based on gender inequality, on Iran: a man's inheritance is twice that of a woman; the man is the head of the family and can divorce his wife easily while enjoying custody over his children and the right to engage in polygamy (although subsequently restrictions were imposed on the exercise of polygamy); before a tribunal a man's testimony is worth twice a woman's. In the next decades, a new generation of young women came to the fore who were much better educated than their mothers and fathers. They attended school and university on parity with men, and their cultural world was closer to that of men than ever. During the Shah's regime, gender inequality was by far less prevalent than under the Islamic regime, in spite of the large cultural differences and women's educational inferiority to men. At present, women and men share the same cultural universe, they are educated in the same way, and they are modernized through the same mechanisms. In spite of this, the juridical system that rules over them gives an unbearable advantage to men. The new self-awareness of women in Iran through the democratic movement of the Campaign for One Million Signatures claiming legal equality between men and women is the result of their common sharing of the same cultural orientations.

The new gender relations expressed themselves among others through the sharp decrease in the birth rates in the late 1990s and the first decade of the twenty-first century:[7] between 1976 and 1986 the population increased from 33.7 million to 49.4 million with an annual increase rate of 3.9 per cent; from 1986 onwards, the annual rate of increase declined to 2 per cent, the population attaining 68.2 million in 2003, the fertility rate falling to 2.1 per cent. The age of the first marriage among women went up: in 1976 it was 19.7 years, in 1986, 20.1 years, in 1996, 22 years, and in 2006, 23.7 years. At the same time, the use of contraceptives reached the highest rate in the Muslim world, concerning 74 per cent of the women aged between 15 and 49 years in the year 2000.[8] The age differential between husband and wife also declined: in 1976 it was 4.4 years, in 1986, 3.6 years, in 1996, 3.1 years and in 2006, 2.8 years.[9] The gap between rural and urban zones narrowed as well. The average age of the first marriage of urban women was 1.1 years higher than rural women in 1976; in 1986, the interval was reduced to 0.4 years (20.1 years in urban against 19.7 in rural areas) and since 1996, there is an inversion of this differential: the average age of the first marriage among rural women in 2006 is higher (23.8 years) than in urban zones (23.7 years).

The Emergence of Women as New Social Actors

Another major factor contributing to the change in the mentality of men and women is education. In 1976, 28 per cent of women between the ages of 15 and 49 were literate and the gap was wide between the urban and rural areas (50 per cent in the cities and only 8 per cent in the rural zones).[10] In 2006 the proportion of literate women in the same age group sharply increased to 87.4 per cent and the gap narrowed between village and town: respectively 92.1 per cent and 76.5 per cent. The schooling years lasted on average 8.9 years (10 years in urban zones and 6.2 years in rural zones).[11]

---

[7] See *World Population Prospects*, the 2004 Revision, March 2005, The United Nations.
[8] See Farzaneh Roudi-Fahimi, *Women's Reproductive Health in the Middles East and North Africa*, Population Reference Bureau, Washington, December 2005.
[9] See the major works of Marie-Ladier Fouladi, *Iran, Un monde de paradoxes*, Nantes: L'Atlante, 2009; *Population et Politique en Iran*, Paris: INED, 2003; Thierry Coville, *Iran, La Révolution Invisible*, Paris: La Découverte, 2007.
[10] See *The General Population Census of 1976*, The Statistical Center of Iran, 1980.
[11] See *The General Population Census*, The Statistical Center of Iran, 2006.

The high number of women in the schools and their access to universities (in 2006–2007, 52.4 per cent of Iran's 2.8 million university students were women) made their cultural universe close to that of men. Never have men and women been as close culturally to each other and never has their juridical situation been as dissymmetrical and disadvantageous to them as now, compared to the Pahlavi era. During the Pahlavi regime, most of the girls in the rural and tribal areas were not allowed by their parents to go to school, the latter being regarded as the place of corruption and depravation for girls, due to their secular setting. After the Islamic Revolution, with the Islamicization of the school system, not only in the rural areas, but also in many urban conservative families, girls were sent to school by their parents who became confident about the sound Islamic values of the educational system. The curriculum for boys and girls is entirely the same and the shared values about the sciences and other topics are by and large similar. While textbooks tend to ascribe different roles to women and men, this has only marginally affected the general spread of knowledge and enlightenment through the school system. Teaching science and related topics and introducing social sciences and other topics have opened up new vistas for women, in particular discussing, arguing, debating, and contesting the views authority figures. This includes parents, and young women today demand the freedom to choose their own husbands and increasingly reject pre-arranged and imposed marriages. Still, the change in the cultural universe of girls and boys and their increasing closeness has not translated into a commensurate share of women's access to the labour market. The discriminatory laws and the government's reluctance and sometimes active administrative opposition make women's access to employment very hard: in 2006 only 12 per cent of women aged between 15 and 64 were officially employed (12.3 per cent in urban zones and 11.2 per cent in the rural areas). This heightens the frustration of young women, who are as educated as men (if not more so), and yet are held back by the obstacles of a social and political system that remains patriarchal and is backed by a religious gerontocracy (the ayatollahs and major power holders have an average age of more than 70 years) that denies them access to the public sphere in the name of traditional Islam. The new 'readings' of religion under the influence of the reformist thinkers are rather silent on women, and in some cases, when the clerical protagonists publicly proclaimed women's demand for more social justice, they were either prosecuted or simply ignored.[12]

Due to the denial of justice, sharing the same worldview as men, women are becoming the new social force that challenges the Islamic Republic in its claim to maintain the disparity between men and women in the name of Islam. The new generation of young women is conscious of its fundamental equality with men, having had the same achievements in schooling and higher educa-

---

[12] The cleric Mohsen Sa'idzadeh who asked for more freedom for women by giving less weight to the traditional Islamic law (*feqh*) was 'defrocked', sentenced to prison, and reduced to silence during the first Khatami presidency by the special court for the clergy (*dadgah-e vizheh-ye ruhaniyat*) in the Islamic Republic.

tion and having bitterly experienced the strong support given to the patriarchal tendency within society by the Islamic theocracy. A few major tendencies can be highlighted:

The secular young women, mostly of the old middle classes of the Shah's regime who have resisted the Islamicization brought about by the theocracy have played a role as the leaders of the feminist movement in Iran, representing the generation of the mothers—one can mention Mehrangiz Kar or the Nobel Prize winner Shirin Ebadi. They are found in the middle-class districts of the large cities, such as Tehran's northern residential areas and Isfahan's southern neighbourhoods.

Another tendency is made up of the young generation of women of Islamic origin who, at the university and outside their home, have distanced themselves from the religious universe of their parents, particularly in middle-sized towns. In Qom, for example, young women and men who went to Tehran or other cities to study at the university (the competitive examination system sends people to different towns according to their grades) experienced a liberation from the straightjacket of Islamic traditions, and, once back home, adopted a more secular and critical attitude towards the ways and customs of their parents. In particular, they denounced the restrictions imposed on women in the name of religion and the 'hypocrisy' of the clerics and the older generation who acted immorally by keeping a pious façade. Still, these young women have an ambivalent attitude towards religion: many of them experience deep guilt feelings by transgressing the patriarchal religious norm. What is noteworthy is that these guilt feelings have not inhibited them: instead, they have allowed them to violate the traditional tenets while still maintaining their ties to a religion that has imperceptibly undergone secularization. Instead of playing a negative role, ruefulness and remorse have played the role of a security valve for their action, upholding their ties to Islam and promoting their Self as a Muslim Self.[13] This attitude is also promoted by the new religious intellectuals who have argued for an open interpretation of Islam: Abdolkarim Sorush, Mohammad Mojtahed Shabestari, Mostafa Malekian, Mohsen Kadivar, HasanYusefi Eshkavari, thinkers whose narrative has had a major impact on the youth from the 1990s onward.

In sum, the new generations of Iranian men and women are better educated than ever, having had better access to school and university. The restrictions imposed on them by the Islamic regime in the name of decency, modesty (for women), and Islamic norms pushes them either towards the rejection of Islam (in the large cities) or overstepping the boundaries of traditional religion in the name of a new Ego, which is both religious and in quest of personal freedom.[14] They are prone to discussion and open dialogue, they refuse the

---

[13] See the analyses of these girls' secularization through ambivalence in Farhad Khosrokhavar and Amir Nikpey, *Avoir Vingt ans au pays des ayatollahs, la vie quotidienne dans la ville sainte de Qom*, Paris: Robert Laffont, 2009.

[14] See for the specific case of music (considered as impure and forbidden by ultra-orthodox Shiites) the case of young women who deny the religious authorities the right

rigid hierarchy of the Islamic theocracy, and they are wary of any authoritarianism based on a sacred view. Their experiences in the last decades have made them sympathetic towards open political and cultural attitudes rather than the inflexible and rigid norms of Islamic theocracy.

The Urbanization Process

Iran's secularization process not only did not stop with the Islamic Revolution but somehow accelerated its pace in a paradoxical manner after it. The more the theocratic regime increased its hold on education (mainly school education) and set up Islamicization programmes through textbooks[15] and the official media (TV and radio), the more the new generation distanced itself from the official version of politics and religion. In the meantime, not only the rush to the city kept up its pace, but because of the road network built by the *Jehad-e sazandegi* (Construction Jihad, which started as a foundation and became a ministry) between villages and towns and cities, rural people became more and more like citizens, especially the young, male and female, who frequented the school and became more and more literate. Many moved to the towns to pursue their higher education. The change in the relationship between towns and villages has been qualitative as well as quantitative. In Iran, every settlement with more than 5,000 inhabitants is considered a town in administrative terms. Below that, it is a village. The building up of roads and trails connected towns and villages in a way that had never happened before, and resulted in the importation of consumer habits from the towns into the villages and a decrease of the birth rate akin to that observed in towns. The war period (1980–88) caused a massive exodus from rural areas in the southwestern Iran, and many who went to the cities outside the war zone did not return back after the war, preferring to stay in the cities where they sent their children to school and attempted to find jobs. As for those who remained in the rural areas, the electrification of the rural zones gave them access to radio and television and, more widely, to urban culture. Water conveyance projects, a massive school building programme, adult literacy projects, the setting up of programmes for the preventive treatment of illnesses, the establishment of care centres, all contributed to the rise of awareness in the rural areas.

The Islamic Republic, feeling the threat of the modernized middle classes, aimed to mobilize rural areas in its favour, if necessary against the secular middle classes that were against it, be it in street demonstrations or in major elections. At the same time, there was an ideological movement for the betterment of the conditions of the 'oppressed' (*mostaz'afin*), a motto of the Iranian Revolution that continued to have a mobilizing effect. Indeed, many rev-

---

to decide for them, although their parents belong to these groups, Farhad Khosrokhavar, 'The New Religiosity in Iran', *Social Compass*, 54(3), 2007, 453–63.

[15] See Saeed Paivandi, *Religion et Education en Iran, L'échec de l'islamisation de l'école*, Paris: L'Harmattan, 2006.

olutionary actors put them into practice in the rural zones in the first two decades of the Islamic Republic.

The result of these actions was the importation of consumer habits of the town into the rural areas and the birth of a new culture in which, with the decrease of the birth rate and the access to education and schooling, many middle-size villages came to resemble small towns, with the same aspirations and the same demands for modern goods and comfort.[16] Not only with the migration to the cities, but also within the rural zones urban culture made inroads and new habits in matters of sport (especially football) and hobbies (in particular movies, which were viewed mainly through video cassettes) introduced new behaviour patterns. The change also affected the migrants from the villages to the towns, like university students or those whose family had ties to the village but continued to live in towns, who intermittently returned to the villages and brought back urban youth culture.[17] Three decades after the Islamic Revolution, what has happened is not the 'ruralization of the cities' but the 'urbanization of the villages' in terms of the consuming habits and close ties with the towns and cities in terms of urban attitudes towards education and patterns of behaviour.

The Intellectuals and the Reappraisal of the Islamic Theocracy

In the 1990s a silent ideological revolution took place in Iran. The 1960s and 1970s had been the era of Islamic radicalism, mainly in the Shiite world. Many Islamic ideologues, influenced by Marxism and Third Worldism, translated their radical tenets into a religious idiom. In the Sunni world, secular nationalism was rejected by Sunni radicals such as Sayyid Qutb and Abul Ala Mawdudi. In the Shiite world, especially under the aegis of Ali Shari'ati, a new version of Islam was put forward that questioned the legitimacy of capitalism, imperialism and secular autocracy. These interpretations of Islam shared one major feature: their rejection of democracy and political pluralism as equivalents of idolatry (*taghut*, the worshipping of the people as the new idol) and a regression from the Golden Age of Islam to a form of non-Islamic government that aimed at marginalizing Allah's religion and establish the hegemony of the West and Western values, what Sayyid Qutb called *jahili-*

---

[16] See Eric Hooglund, 'Letter from an Iranian village', *Journal of Palestine Studies*, 27(1), 1997; Mostafa Azkia, 'Modernization Theory in a Tribal- Peasant Society of Southern Iran', *Critique* 10(1), 1997; Anne-Sophie Vivier-Mureçan, *Afzâd: Ethnologie d'un village d'Iran*, Téhéran—Louvain: Institut Français de Recherche en Iran–Peeters, 2006. She shows how a village changed after the Islamic Revolution of 1979, the new elites, the administrative bodies and the new habits giving a new turn to the daily life in a remote Iranian village in Kerman province. Eric Hooglund describes how in the villages close to Shiraz the new change induced the shift of the culture from rural to urban ideals and attitudes.

[17] See examples of the rural youth in the town of Qom and their cultural outlook in Khosrokhavar and Nikpey, *Avoir vingt ans au pays des ayatollahs*.

yah. These ideologies promoted revolution in the name of Islam as the only way of combating Western imperialism. In Shiism, Shari'ati, was the leftist variant of this Islamic radicalism, which flourished in reaction to secular nationalisms such as Nasser's Pan-Arabism in Egypt or the Pahlavi regime's Persian nationalism in Iran. These ideologies were Islamic autocratic reactions to the secular ruling autocracies in the Muslim world. They had only contempt for the people as individuals and believed that Islam as a revolutionary principle would lead the world toward paradise, without any need for a secular principle. The blending of Islam and revolution had only one major political success, namely in Iran, where the Islamic Revolution of 1979 succeeded in toppling the Shah's autocratic regime, replacing it by an Islamic theocracy under the title of the Islamic Government (*velayat-e faqih*). In the 1990s and 2000s Iranian intellectuals put forward a new interpretation of Islam that rejected the tenets of Islamic radicalism and opposed autocracy in the name of an Islamic pluralism. The new liberal narrative on religion was a reaction to the authoritarian interpretation of Islam by the Islamic theocracy in Iran and the vivid expression of the disappointment towards the meagre achievements of the Islamic regime. It was also related to change in the international political system, most notably the discredit of communism and the crumbling of the Berlin Wall in 1989. The major motivation was to oppugn the cornerstone of the Islamic theocracy, *velayat-e faqih*, by disclosing the weakness of its Islamic credentials and by stressing the fact that Islam leaves the political and the social realm open to the believers' own choice, mainly occupying the realm of spirituality or for some people, the law (but not the politics). From the perspective of the new Islamic thinkers (also called 'religious intellectuals') among whom Abdolkarim Sorush, Mohammad Mojtahed Shabestari, Mohsen Kadivar, Yusefi Eshkavari, Mostafa Malekian and a few others played key roles, Islam is primarily not about governing society but about the legitimacy of the individual's spiritual life, Islamic rule applying more in the judicial realm than the political realm, and even then, being subject to change through the religious competence of the Islamic Jurists (*ijtihad*).[18] As to *velayat-e faqih*, after Ayatollah Montazeri, Mohsen Kadivar showed that it was based on 'weak' Hadith (the reported sayings of the Prophet), wherefore its credentials were subject to doubt (*za'if*), not confirmed by the long chain of Hadith literature (*qavi*). Therefore, he concludes, theocratic government cannot lay claim on any Islamic legitimacy and is nothing but a belated theorization, carried out in the name of a contested version of Islam. Bereft of any antiquity, this notion is devoid of any sacredness and can be put into question without breaking any Islamic precept. Akbar Ganji, another reformist in exile in the United States, believes that there are three ways of looking at *velayat-e faqih*.[19] The

---

[18] See for a synthetic summary of their works Mohsen Mottaqi 'Rowshanfekran-e eslah talab-e dini va jame'eh-ye madani' [The reformist religious intellectuals and the civil society], *Iran Nameh*, 19(4), 2001.

[19] Akbar Ganji, 'Talaqqi-ye fashisti az din va hokumat' [The fascist understanding of religion and government], *Tarh-e now*, 1999.

first is a monarchist one, granting the same privileges to the Islamic Leader as an absolutist king. The second is a fascist conception of it, giving totalitarian power to him. The third one is according to the democratic version, the Islamic governor being elected and subordinated to the sovereign will of the people. He rejects the two other views of *velayat-e faqih*, squaring the genuine Islamic government with democracy.

Mojtahed Shabestari attacks the entire construct of the Islamic theocracy by challenging the holistic picture of Islam on which *Velayat-e faqih* is based. In one of his major books,[20] he observes that a double crisis is shaking the ideology of the Islamic theocracy on Islam. The first crisis is due to the belief that Islam encompasses a political and economic system offering an answer relevant to all the times and all the problems; the second crisis is entailed by the conviction that the government has a duty to apply exclusively Islamic law (*shari'a*). According to him, these two ideas have emerged in relation to the historical circumstances pertaining to the Islamic revolution. The 'official version of religion', which is at the same time 'juridical Islam' (*eslam e feqahati*), is based on the historical conditions in which the conviction arose that religion had to dominate politics. In this version, the government, founded on divine legitimacy (*mashru'iyat-e elahi*), would enjoy the people's acceptance (*maqbuliyat e mardomi*).

This set of ideas, Mojtahed Shabestari writes, is based on a threefold principle. The first principle is that there is only one source of knowledge, namely religion. This in turn can be reduced to Islamic law (*feqh*). The second principle is a mythical version of the birth of religion and its evolution. All the deeds of the Prophet are to be applied as a universal norm to society, independent of the specific culture of his time, history, and the societal evolution since then. The third principle is the exclusive validity of one interpretation. There is an official Islam which excludes other understandings. This view of religion is the only self-proclaimed legitimate interpretation of Islam, and is embodied in *velayat-e faqih*. These three principles cannot be philosophically defended, and they lead to a stalemate. In Mojtahed Shabestari's view, Islam does not have all the answers to the social, economic, and political problems at all times in history. The second point is that no single hermeneutics of Islam exists as such, and there are different types of legitimate knowledge that are not religious. Islam is the quest for spirituality and it leaves the social and historical fields open to the autonomous understanding of mankind. In other words, the close connection between religion and politics is simply a usurped view and inexorably leads to the desecration of religion.

The 'new religious thinkers' opened the way to the contestation of Islamic theocracy from within the religious realm. After the Islamic Revolution, the major critical source against the regime had come from secular intellectuals who were branded as 'Western lackeys' or as being alien to the Iranian society

---

[20] Mohammad Shabestari, *Naqdi bar qara'at- e rasmi bar din* [A critique of official discourse on religion]. Tehran: Tarh-e now, 2000. See also Farhad Khosrokhavar, 'The New Intellectuals in Iran', *Social Compass*, 51(2), 2004, pp. 191–202.

and its religious culture. This time the denunciation came from the religious discourse itself, and it was impossible for the Islamic theocracy to denounce it as 'external' to the society and alien to its religious tenets.

In the meantime, secular intellectuals exerted a great albeit subterranean influence in Iran. Through their translations, teaching, and writing, they made available to the new generation of educated youth seminal notions like 'civil society'. Hoseyn Bashiriyeh is a case in point. He translated Jürgen Habermas, Barrington Moore, and Hobbes, as well as some major popularizers of Western political thought into Persian; he raised the issues of democratization process and totalitarianism, and above all, he instructed an entire generation of Iranian students in Tehran University. Through his publications he made available to the public the ideas of political pluralism and its legitimacy.[21] This concept was translated by some of the religious intellectuals into the notion of 'civil religious society'. Sorush stressed that a Muslim society in which people deeply believe in Islam does not need any formal supervision in this regard, and that a religious civil society made of Muslims can act in a democratic manner to resolve political problems. Contrary to the pre-revolutionary period, in which secular and Islamic intellectuals had strong suspicions towards each other, the new era has been marked by the 'Islamicization' of secular ideas, developed or elaborated upon by secular intellectuals. Other secular intellectuals like Aramesh Dustdar[22] and Javad Tabataba'i[23] exercised a significant influence on the new emerging student groups, in particular among the young clerics, by denouncing the 'religious turn of mind' of Iranians who cannot be deeply open to rationality, due to their unconscious religiosity. Criticizing this hidden underlying religious mentality of the Iranians, they invite them to become 'modern' by espousing Western rationality and by cutting off their ties to the Islamic Unconscious. This, in turn, opens up new vistas, making it possible to put into question the hegemony of religion over the people.

Dariush Shayegan, a French-writing Iranian intellectual, identifies the ills of the Iranian soul in the jump from a traditional, un-modern world to a postmodern one in which norms are relative, grand narratives do not exist, and the coherence of the former social order is gone. Without having passed through modernity, Iranians have been pushed to the postmodern stage, becoming thus 'schizophrenic': neither postmodern nor traditional, but combining these traits in an incoherent fashion, adopting features that lack homogeneity and predispose them to a dual system of thought that is devoid of cogency and breeds anguish and irrational attitudes. Iranian schizophrenia is most visible in the

---

[21] See for a tentative list of Bashiriyeh's publications: available:
http://en.wikipedia.org/wiki/Hossein_Bashiriyeh (accessed 4 September 2011).
[22] See Aramesh Dustdar, *Molahezat-e falsafi dar din, elm va fekr* [Philosophical considerations on religion, science and the thought], Vincennes: Khavaran, 2002.
[23] Javad Tabataba'i, *Zaval-e andisheh-ye siyasi dar Iran,* Tehran: Kavir, 1994.

Islamic Revolution in which a modern action (revolution) has been undertaken under the guise of tradition (Islam).[24]

Another author who opened up new perspectives was Dariush Ashuri. He began by taking a new look at language: in order to become modern, the major means of communication, namely language, should be able to express new concepts in a rationalized way, be they from the pure or social sciences. The Persian language should be enriched in a systematic, synthetic way, to let rational notions be expressed through its categories. In his book 'open language' (*zaban-e baz*)[25] as well as his dictionary of social sciences he proposed more or less systematic ways of coining Persian words for Western social science concepts. Ashuri believes that the Persian language as an instrument of rational thinking should be at the centre of Iranians' preoccupations.

Ashuri's indictment of Iranian intellectuals under the heading of the 'tragedy of our intellectual mind' or 'the tragedy of our intellectuals' (*terazhedi-ye rowshanfekri-ye ma*) identifies a major ingredient in the mind of the Iranian intelligentsia, namely the Nietzschean notion of resentment (*kin tuzi*).[26] Dumbfounded by the capacity of the West to master technology and to subdue the others, Iranian intellectuals reacted in variegated manners: some thought that one should become entirely Westernized, others rejected the West in the name of Islam or leftist ideologies, but the common denominator among them was the inability to distance themselves in a reflexive and critical manner from the West, being stricken by an ambivalent sentiment of awe and hatred towards the domineering West. The underlying hypothesis to this critic is that one should abandon this suicidal attitude and opt for a constructive and rational stand, based on a balanced view of the West and its aptitude to change the world by its technology and rationality. To tackle the problem of the language and our thought in a non-reactive manner would be preferable to the suicidal attitude of awe and rancour that characterizes most Iranian intellectuals.

Most secular Iranian intellectuals are critical and sometimes even contemptuous towards their own society and put into question religion, its worldview and theocracy. Their criticism has contributed to secularize the new generation of students in the universities where their overall influence, although less overarching than the religious reformists' impact, has continued to push towards a critical attitude towards Islamic theocracy. In sum, Iran is ruled by an Islamist theocracy but the dominant political culture within society is reformist thought, not fundamentalist or radical Islam. The utopia of political

---

[24] See Dariush Shayegan, *Le regard mutilé*, Paris: Albin Michel, 1989; *Qu'est-ce qu'une révolution religieuse?*, Paris: Albin Michel, 1991; *Les illusions de l'identité*, Paris: Editions du Félin, 1992.

[25] See Dariush Ashuri, *Zaban-e baz, pazhuheshi darbareh-ye zaban va moderniyat* [The open language, a research on language and modernity], Tehran: Nashr-e Markaz, 2008.

[26] See Dariush Ashuri, 'Terazhedi-ye rowshanfekri-ye ma', in *Parseh-ha va porsesh-ha* [Roaming and Questioning], Tehran: Agah, 2009.

Islam that impregnated Iranian public opinion in the first decade of the Islamic Republic is on the defensive and the major reformist ideas of a non-theocratic Islam that shuns politics are paramount. Islamic radicalism, embodied in the Iranian theocracy, legitimized its claim to rule in the name of martyrdom, abnegation towards the religious community, and anti-imperialism. These tenets have been marginalized by the religious reformists and the new secular thinkers who do not advocate a revolutionary society in its Islamic or secular version, but call for a society in which the rule of law will provide freedom to the citizens through a 'Protestant' narrative of Islam. This is the major change Iran has undergone in the last two decades. On the eve of the Islamic Revolution, most Iranian intellectuals were anti-democratically-minded. Many had Marxist or even communist leanings, and some of the most popular ones like Ali Shari'ati combined Shiism and revolutionary Western thought in order to build up anti-imperialist or even chiliastic ideas tinged with revolutionary ideals. The rupture in the intellectual landscape in Iran dates back to the second decade of the Islamic Republic that witnessed the breakdown of Utopian Islam and the dislocation of communist ideologies.

The Myth of the Gradual Change Within the Islamic Theocracy

The election of Mohammad Khatami as the president of the Islamic Republic in 1997 was the offspring of Islamic reformism. In its turn, it paved the way for the expansion of the ideas of Islamic reformism. This period gave legitimacy to the rule of law by identifying the 'civil society' (*jame'eh-ye madani*) with what Khatami called the 'golden age of the Prophet', i.e., his community in the town of Medina (*madinat al-nabi*) being ruled by democratic ideals after his exodus from Mecca. The stratagem of combining two different types of reality through the myth of the Islamic origins legitimized the notion of the civil society, making possible the demand for limited forms of political pluralism within the theocratic regime. During this period the ideal of the Islamic autocracy was replaced by that of Islamic pluralism. For the Islamic reformists the means to achieve it was the gradual change from an authoritarian regime to an open one through peaceful social movements, under the prevailing political system. This myth has been in part reinforced by the sincere and deep involvement of those who pushed towards reform and who, like Mohammad Khatami, in their overwhelming majority believed that the Islamic regime could peacefully open up to democracy without any major social and political upheaval. The myth of the gradual democratization of the Islamic theocracy made possible new social movements with a democratic content such as the Green Movement. At the same time it obscured the rigidity of the Islamic theocracy, which was too inflexible and autocratic to allow for any notable change. The new oligarchy in which the financial and political interests of the new military institution, the Revolutionary Guards or Pasdaran, were paramount did not accept accountability to the people as a sovereign body of citizens. Their view is that Islam and democracy are incompatible and the latter is an avatar of secularism that usurps the place of God and offers it to the people. Democracy, in this sense, is by definition an anti-Islamic, godless political system, utterly incompatible with Islam.[27] This anti-democratic ideological view coupled with the corporate economic interest of the ruling military elite makes gradual change very difficult, if not impossible. In fact, social movements inspired by democratic tenets began in the 1990s in Iran. The first one was the student movement that was crushed in 1999 under the Khatami presidency by the Basij, the former revolutionary organization that represses urban unrest.

The Iranian feminist movement is the second democratic one, and has spawned the 'Campaign for One Million Signatures'. It aims at promoting gender equality in Iran. The movement has been systematically quelled by the Basij militias under the aegis of the Ahmadinejad government since 2005. The founding members of the movement are young, between their twenties and at most forties, and their goal is to achieve legal and social gender equality. They face a deeply unequal gender situation due to the Islamic law which gives women a fraction of the rights of men within the family: divorce rights in general as man's privilege, guardianship of children as man's right after early childhood in case of divorce, man's approval being necessary to allow his wife to work or travel, man's share of heritage being twice that of his sister, women's testimony before the tribunal being valued half of men's. The Campaign intends to gather one million signatures from the citizens in their claim for legal equality. Many young men are among the sympathizers of the movement. They suffer in a different way from inequality: their inability to frequent young women in public, their frustration before a 'moral order' that imposes gender segregation as well as their rejection of a political order that denies them the capacity to be full-fledged citizens. In the name of God the Islamic theocracy robs its own youth of their aspiration towards individual autonomy and personal freedom in their daily lives.

The student movement of the 1990s, subdued by violence in 1999, is the first large-scale youth movement in Iran with a democratic content. The day of 9 July when the movement was crushed by the militia has become since then an anniversary that groups of students celebrate every year by taking to the streets and staging protests against repression. In the 1960s and 1970s the Iranian student movement was instilled with leftist or radical Islamic values. Democracy was regarded as the mere outgrowth of Western imperialism whose sole aim and intent was to dominate the Third World. The change came after the first decade of the Islamic Republic and the crisis of the utopian Islam in addition to the vanishing of the communist bloc. The new generations, less ideological and more concerned with personal freedoms that are constantly threatened by the theocracy, opted for the rule of law out of their own personal experience rather than out of any theoretical consideration. Contrary to many Muslim societies in which political Islam is regarded as a legitimate protest against the prevailing pro-Western autocratic regimes, in Iran

---

[27] See the complex debates on these topics in Shiite Iran as well as in the Sunni world in Farhad Khosrokhavar, *Inside Jihadism*, Boulder, CO: Paradigm Publishers, 2009.

the utopian side of Islamic radicalism showed its limits in the first two decades as well as its inability to implement the ideal of a just society. Weary of ideology and in quest for concrete personal autonomy, the youth turned towards a political system that would help them towards their aspirations to individual freedom and peace. The ideology of martyrdom that was the keystone of the Islamic radicalism in its Shiite version became less and less of an attraction, the notion of civil society replacing it in its potency to mobilize. The new society had broken away from the old ideological tenets glorifying abnegation and sacrifice on behalf of Islam and its community. A new type of nationalism, devoid of its anti-Islamic accretions burgeoned that asked for toleration and peaceful coexistence with the West rather than revolutionary intolerance and anti-imperialism. This attitude, nurtured by the new reformist ideology in its secular or religious form, was at the core of the so-called Green Movement that burst into the open during the presidential elections in June 2009.

The Green Movement: Its Political Failure and Moral Success

The Green Movement was not a premeditated social action. It was the indirect outcome of the presidential elections. Khatami's two terms from 1997 to 2005 culturally opened up Iran to the pluralist world without institutionalizing pluralism in Iran. On the contrary, the structure of the Islamic theocracy showed its inability to open up to new aspirations. The military, political, and economic elites who support the autocratic system rejected reform. It made extensive use of repression and intimidation, making good use of the large oil revenues and suppressing the movement toward reform. Through subsidies, pork barrel, and intimidation of the opponents, the regime built up a solid organization of networks tied to the Basij, the Pasdaran, and the Revolutionary Foundations, encompassing a few million people, financing their allegiance and directing their resentment and their gall towards the middle classes, stigmatized as anti-Islamic and pro-Western. A tradition of suspicion towards the modernized middle classes burgeoned in Iran from the nineteenth century onwards that fed the resentment of the lower classes. Governments used from time to time this feeling of hatred but it is the Islamic Government that has masterminded in a systematic way the opposition, feeding and fuelling it and making it one of the pillars of its own survival policy against the middle-class youth. The paradox is that by achieving middle-class status, many members of the anti-secular groups within the Basij and elsewhere joined the middle-class ideology, mainly through the medium of the university. The Islamic Revolution was the apogee of the implacable opposition between rancour-laden lower-class people (the "oppressed", *mostaz'afin*) and the Westernized middle classes who rapidly separated after the overthrow of the Shah and the establishment of the Islamic Republic. Ayatollah Khomeini used the social antipathy and mutual mistrust between the modernized middle classes and the urban underclass to repress the movements against his theocratic rule. The Islamic Republic made this distrust one of the pillars of its hegemony: the Basij became one of the milestones of its factionalist policies to dominate the urban areas. Almost every district in the cities is provided with a Basij grouping that supervises it and reports to their superior. In this fashion, in many districts in the urban areas the opposition to the theocratic government was crushed during the period of unrest (after the 2009 June elections), locally (in the residential areas) as well as in the main thoroughfares where the protest movement took place. The militias (Basij and other informal groupings subsidized by the government) have been instrumental in crushing the opposition movements since the establishment of the Islamic Republic. Still, many public demonstrations occurred in Iran after the elections, in spite of the rigid government supervision and intimidation.

The origin of the Green Movement is to be searched in the two major events that punctuated the election process. On 20 May 2009, the Guardian Council approved the Islamic legitimacy of four candidates, the incumbent President Mahmoud Ahmadinejad, Mir Hoseyn Musavi, Mehdi Karrubi and Mohsen Reza'i. They had all been major officeholders in the Islamic Republic. Musavi, prime minister from 1981 to 1989, had not been active since then. Their candidacies were approved by the Guardian Council, a body that exerts a strong political pressure by eliminating all those candidates who are suspected of not believing in *velayat-e faqih*. The four candidates were all beyond any suspicion as to their allegiance to the Islamic theocracy. To give lustre to the presidential elections and encourage people and especially the youth to take part in them, two major decisions were taken by the government: a series of TV debates and the slackening of the control in the cities to entice young people to pour out and give a semblance of ritual to the electoral process. Seven debates were organized during which the candidates attacked each other and which made the polarization possible. They attracted a huge attention and for the first time in the history of the Islamic Republic, candidates stood face-to-face, criticizing each other in a polemic way. Ahmadinejad, in spite of the inflation and the high level of unemployment, pretended to have changed the society for the better, curbed the rising prices, checked unemployment, and heightened the country's prestige and power at the international level. He became the paragon of an outright liar for the educated people, whereas his posturing about the dishonesty of his adversaries aroused the suspicion of many towards his record. However, many found him to be a redoubtable orator who could destabilize his adversaries, in spite of his poor record as a president in his first term of office. The debate revealed the rift that separated the reformist candidates (Musavi and Karrubi) from Ahmadinejad. The fourth candidate, former Pasdaran chief Mohsen Reza'i, gave a hard time to Ahmadinejad about the tampering of the labour statistics.

The illusion of freedom of speech and freedom to elect was total. The television debates enhanced the feeling among large fractions of the society that the elections would be honest this time; otherwise why organize lengthy debates between contending candidates on? This illusion was enhanced by another fact that played an even more crucial role in mobilizing the society, namely the freedom to organize debates on the street and to demonstrate for one's candidate, without any of the usual constraints that had characterized Iran during the last three decades. For a few weeks there was no surveillance nor monitoring by the morality brigades, the Basij, or any other repressive organ of the government to check the street demonstrations. During that time, many young people in the large cities stayed on the street until the early morning hours, around three or four o'clock. Tehran's streets for a few weeks became indistinguishable from those of Paris, London, or New York. What ensued on the streets was not only political discussions, but also intense socialization, hidden forms of flirtation, and contacts between young men and women. They chanted political slogans together, organized political meetings in concert, and formed long human chains from the south to the north of Tehran. They exchanged ideas but also invested subjectively in an election that was supposed to be free, as a reflection of the re-conquered freedom in the street. What differentiated this period from the others was first of all an effervescence of the glorious times of the Islamic Revolution. But whereas that period had been marked by the sadness of martyrdom and the Shiite culture of mourning and grief, this period was punctuated by a culture of joy that contrasted with the primal period of the revolution three decades before. The 'human chains' on the street constituted by men and women holding hands and chanting slogans for freedom and a new era in which their dreams could come true left deep imprints on the souls of many a young man and woman. The whole story denoted hope in a new kind of sincerity in the political system as its underlying condition. If unlimited street demonstrations and new forms of socialization, free of the stringent Islamic attitude, were allowed by the powers that be, this would be possible only under the condition of free and fair elections

The official result of the election caused a deep shock among the proponents of the movement. Not only was Ahmadinejad pronounced to be the winner, but he was supposed to have won by a landslide of more than 62 per cent of the vote in the first round of the election. Contrary to all predictions, Karrubi and Reza'i won a very tiny fraction of the votes (both less than 3 per cent), Musavi being credited with less than 34 per cent. The way the elections were conducted left a large room for rigging: lack of voting booths, in particular in the rural areas were members of the government supervised them and subsidies would have been denied to the reformist voters. The rural areas were supposedly in favour of Ahmadinejad, which contradicted the other presidential elections' results few years earlier as well.[28] Ahmadinejad's victory was announced the very same day by the Supreme Leader in a peremptory way, leaving no room for mounting a credible challenge of the results.

The first week after the announcement of the official results of the vote (13 June 2009) witnessed huge demonstrations in Tehran and some large cities almost every day. In Tehran, street demonstrations attained hundreds of thousands of people. Young people from all walks of life (but mostly stu-

---

[28] See Farhad Khosrokhavar and Marie Ladier-Fouladi, *The 2009 Presidential Election in Iran: Fair or Foul?*, EUI Working Papers, RSXAS 2012/29.

dents) took part in the manifestations and their peaceful slogans was: 'Where is my vote?'. Repression began immediately after. In spite of the hardening of the repression, demonstrations were held almost every day.

The second week, repression intensified and most of the organizers of the reformists' candidates were arrested. Internet and mobile phones replaced the organizers for some time but the lack of a direct leadership made the survival of the movement a real challenge. Musavi and Karrubi were surrounded and their ties with the external world were cut off. The Iranian diaspora in the West had massively participated to the vote. It helped set up Internet services alongside those inside Iran. The government cut off mobile phones and weakened the Internet band; communications became more and more difficult. In spite of the growing repression, imprisonment, torture and many deaths (more than 70), the movement lasted for many months, up to the anniversary of the Islamic Republic on 11 February 2010. Gradually, the movement subsided. But it resulted in the delegitimation of the regime. The slogans at the end were: 'Death to the Dictator', directly pointing to the Supreme Leader.

The Green Movement bore a fateful ambivalence from its inception. Its aim was to reform the Islamic theocracy from within, and its leaders, Musavi, Karrubi, and Khatami, belonged to the political elite of the Islamic Republic. When the regime began putting down the movement, its leaders could not break off their ties to the Islamic regime. Still, the myth that gave birth to the movement (smooth change from within the political system) made the movement possible as such (without this fiction the movement would have been repressed *in nuce*) but at the same time, limited its scope and made radical change impossible. What the Green Movement proved was the impossibility of opening up the Islamic theocracy. Since then, the nature of the reformist movement has radically changed and the regime has become more and more repressive and less and less legitimate in the eyes of a large section of the population.

The life of the Green Movement can be divided into three major periods. The first was the pre-election period stretching from the candidacy of Musavi and Karrubi to the day of the election. In this period, the fiction of a democratic transition gained momentum and the participation of a large part of the new urban generations in the movement made it the first peaceful social movement whose goal was democracy, contrary to the Islamic Revolution whose intent and purpose had been the consolidation of Islamic authoritarianism. The second period extended from the declaration of the election results to the end of the first week, during which massive demonstrations gradually changed into sporadic, small scale ones. The third period covered the next few months during which, devoid of organization and active leadership, the movement kept on going, massive state repression amputating its capacity for action. This period is at the same time witness to the loss of the legitimacy of the Islamic theocracy in the eyes of the large majority of the citizens.

The Green Movement was the first after the establishment of the Islamic Republic in which men and women rejected the segregation norms imposed by the Islamic theocracy. Young women not only mingled with men, but they became full-fledged social actors in their own right. Even in the street resistance against the militias, they defended themselves and the others, leaving many dead or wounded. This movement was the first democratic, gender-orientated, culturally innovative movement in post-revolutionary Iran: the old martyrdom motives gave way to new individualized themes like 'Where is my vote?'. Within this movement, the concrete individual, not a member of an idealized community ready for self-sacrifice, is at the centre stage. Through the massive participation of the youth the Green Movement underlined the new political culture in which respect for law and political pluralism were the major demand.

The movement showed many weaknesses, due in part to its improvised nature. One was the lack of participation, on a large scale, of the lower classes (the so-called 'oppressed', *mostaz'afin*). The reasons are lack of organization and the middle-class slogans of the leadership. On university campuses, students had the opportunity to organize on the basis of face-to-face relations or what remained of the student associations (such as the *Daftar-e tahkim-e vahdat*, Bureau for the Reinforcement of Unity, the reformist student association) after the repression of the student movement by Ahmadinejad. Outside the university, however, there was no organization at all. Young people in the working-class districts of Tehran and other large cities had no opportunity to take part in it. The Basij and other militias controlled the main districts in those quarters and massive demonstrations would not have escaped their notice. The ad hoc intermediary leadership of the movement made it vulnerable, after their arrest. No alternative leadership was envisaged and no connection could shape the movement and connect it to the outside world, except for the personal initiative of the demonstrators themselves. Nonetheless, the Green Movement put an end to the legitimacy not only of the Ahmadinejad government, but also to the Islamic theocracy embodied in the *velayat-e faqih*.

The Green Movement failed in implementing the democratic reforms within the regime and represented, in that sense, the end of the reformist movement in Iran. Many reasons can account for this failure. First of all, its leaders were all the elite of the Islamic Republic and therefore, any major rupture with the regime was rejected by them. In the first days after the official declaration of the election results (13 June 2009) millions of people poured into the major streets of Tehran. It could have been possible to peacefully occupy the key strategic places (like the TV or the parliament building). But the slogans were exclusively directed towards the elections and any reference to regime change through the slogans like 'Death to the Dictator' were banned by the leadership. This major weakness allowed the Islamic regime to progressively choke the movement and repress it step by step. The leadership refused to envisage the 'exit' from the Islamic Republic's system through peaceful demonstrations, following the models of the Colour Revolutions in Eastern Europe.

Another weakness of the movement was its inability to attract the workers and more generally, white-colour employees. Many workers associations and unions like *Sherkat-e Vahed*, the public transport in Tehran, or those of the textile industry, sugar production and car manufacturing were discontented by Ahmadinejad's policies and could have joined the movement but the leadership of the Green Movement did not actively take up their slogans and their demands. Contrary to the Jasmine Revolution in Tunisia, which succeeded in coalescing the trade union forces (the UGTT, Union Générale des Travailleurs Tunisiens) and the youth movement, the Green Movement remained essentially a youth movement, mainly supported by the students at its core.

Contrary to the Arab Spring movements in 2011, in which the lack of leadership played a key role in toppling the Tunisian and Egyptian regimes, in Iran, the clear-cut leadership made it impossible to choose the path of the rupture through a slogan akin to the Arab revolutions like 'The People want the fall of the Regime'. What made the Green Movement's predicament more dramatic was the Pasdaran's subservience to the Supreme Leader. The Pasdaran's leadership supported the union of Ahmadinejad and Ayatollah Khameneh'i and they did not show either the neutrality of the Tunisian army or the Egyptian army's willingness to preserve their own prerogatives at the price of the president's fall. The lower-level Pasdaran conscripts and the young members of the Basij could have been at least partially attracted towards the Green Movement, but the short lapse of time (the entire movement lasted only a few weeks) and the obedience of its leadership to the Islamic theocracy made it impossible to separate the military from the government.

The Green Movement and the Arab Spring

The Arab Spring revolutions succeeded where the Green Movement failed. After the Tunisian and Egyptian revolutions of 2011, a second Green Movement was initiated but the demonstrations of 14 February 2011 were crushed by the security forces. The second phase of the Green Movement did not last, due to the efficiency of the repression and the imprisoned leadership's inability to lead the movement. The major strength of the Tunisian and Egyptian revolutions lay in the fact that they were leaderless and the rank-and-file demonstrators were intent on overthrowing the regimes and not reforming them from within. The main slogan in those two revolutions was: 'The people want the fall of the regime' (*al shuab yuridu isqat al nizam*). These two major dimensions were missing in the Iranian Green Movement: the leadership (Musavi, Karrubi, and Khatami) were against the toppling of the Islamic Regime and they acted at the beginning of the movement as its promoter.

The partial success of the Arab Spring was in part inspired by the democratic mottoes of the Green Movement in Iran. But they innovated where the Green Movement remained imprisoned in the classical pattern of the social movements: a leadership that was unable to break off its ties with the Islamic theocracy, an army under the aegis of the Islamic theocracy, and a civil society under the yoke of the oil rentier economy.

Chapter 2

The Shah's Two Liberalizations: Re-Equilibration and Breakdown

H. E. Chehabi

> To give an accurate description of what has never occurred is not merely the proper occupation of the historian, but the inalienable privilege of any man of parts and culture.
>
> —Oscar Wilde[1]

In 2001, when, encouraged by a string of electoral victories by Iranian reformists, many hoped that the apparent liberalization of Iranian society and politics would lead to a democratization of Iran's political system, Mohammad-Reza Djalili cautioned that the obstacles to a transformation of the Islamist regime were structural, and that it was therefore an illusion to expect the reform movement to be the harbinger of a transition to democracy.[2] At the time, Djalili's scepticism raised many an optimist's eyebrow. Events, however, proved him right.

The fizzling out of the reform movement and the subsequent repression of the Green Movement were not the first instance in living memory that hopes for a peaceful transition to a democratic political system were dashed in Iran. Let us not forget that what later became the Islamic revolution started when beginning in 1977, Iran's ruler Mohammad Reza Shah stated his intention of liberalizing his regime. But unlike the more or less contemporary liberalizations in Southern Europe and Latin America, the liberalization failed and instead led to revolutionary change and ultimately another non-democratic regime. The object of social science being, in Max Weber's formulation, to

---

[1] Oscar Wilde, 'The Critic as Artist', in *The Artist as Critic: Critical Writings of Oscar Wilde*, Richard Ellmann (ed.), Chicago: The University of Chicago Press, 1982, p. 349.
[2] Mohammad-Reza Djalili, *Iran: l'illusion réformiste*, Paris: Presses de Sciences Po, 2001.

understand why events are so and not *otherwise*,[3] this chapter aims at complementing analyses of the revolution by explaining the failure of political reform in Iran under the Shah.[4] In so doing, it also hopes to add analytic depth to the study of the Shah era, which, oddly enough, is one of the less studied periods of modern Iranian history.[5]

Introduction

A regime crisis that finds its dénouement in the installation of a radically different regime is recognized to have been a revolution only after the fact. In the months preceding the successful overthrow of the old order, many actors work towards either peaceful and gradual reform or re-equilibration of the regime. Many theorists of revolution, like Charles Tilly, admit the relevance of politics to revolutionary change by locating revolutionary movements 'at one end of the spectrum of political activity'.[6] My purpose is therefore not to propose an alternative explanation of the revolution, but to explain why 'politics as usual' did not defuse the crisis of 1977–1979.

Throughout 1977–1978, while the Shah was intimating that he wanted to open up Iranian politics, the opposition also demanded free elections. In mid-1978 few people inside or outside Iran believed that the Shah's regime would crumble only a few months later, and with it the old social order: as late as October 1978 one of the leaders of the political opposition, Mehdi Bazargan, thought that in the event of parliamentary elections organized by the regime, the opposition would win at most twenty seats.[7] An analysis of the Shah's unsuccessful liberalization can throw new light on the revolution by complementing the study of the structural factors that favoured the revolution with an analysis of the political sphere that prevented a peaceful transition to democracy. More concretely, if the stated intentions of the Shah coincided with the demands of the opposition, why did the liberalization not succeed?

The Shah's initiatives of 1977–1978 were not his first attempt to liberalize his rule. Earlier, in 1960, he had also promised to liberalize the political system and to allow for more participation, but that episode ended with a harden-

---

[3] See his 'Objectivity in Social Science', in Max Weber, *The Methodology of the Social Sciences*, Edward A. Shils and Henry A. Finch (trans. and eds.), New York: The Free Press, 1949, p. 72. Emphasis in the original.
[4] For theoretically informed studies of the revolution see for instance Saïd Amir Arjomand, *The Turban for the Crown: The Islamic Revolution in Iran*, New York: Oxford University Press, 1988; and Charles Kurzman, *The Unthinkable Revolution in Iran*, Cambridge, MA: Harvard University Press, 2004.
[5] Cyrus Schayegh, '"Seeing Like a State": An Essay on the Historiography of Modern Iran', *International Journal of Middle East Studies* 42, 2010, pp. 7–61.
[6] Quoted in Michael S. Kimmel, *Revolution: A Sociological Interpretation*, Philadelphia: Temple University Press, 1990, p. 208.
[7] For details see H.E. Chehabi, *Iranian Politics and Religious Modernism: The Liberation Movement of Iran under the Shah and Khomeini*, Ithaca, NY: Cornell University Press, 1990, p. 241.

ing of the Shah's rule after 1963. The parallels between the two episodes are striking. The beginnings of both coincided internally with downturns in economic activities and externally with Democratic administrations in the United States succeeding Republican administrations that had enjoyed especially close relations with the Shah.[8] In both cases the Shah promised free elections, but they were not held, as the gap between the regime and the opposition proved too wide. In both instances the liberal Nationalists proved unable to take advantage of the political opening, which led to severe regime crises. Iran thus exemplifies Tocqueville's warning that 'there can be no doubt that the moment when political rights are granted to a people who have till then been deprived of them is a time of crisis, a crisis which is often necessary but always dangerous.'[9]

The liberalization of the 1960s ended with the re-equilibration of the Shah's regime and the departure of Ayatollah Khomeini into exile, while the second led to the disintegration of the Shah's regime and Khomeini's return to Iran. The parallels between the two failed liberalizations allow a comparative analysis, as a diachronic approach 'maximizes comparability', as Arend Lijphart put it.[10] For an analysis of these failures the literature on transitions to democracy can provide many useful insights. The breakdown of many Latin American democracies in the 1960s and early 1970s, and then in the mid-1970s, 1980s, and 1990s the restoration of democracies in Southern Europe, Latin America, East Asia, Eastern Europe, and a few countries in Africa have made the study of regime transitions one of the most analytically sophisticated subfields of political science.[11] By focusing on the political forces, choices,

---

[8] The impact of economic factors and US foreign policy in bringing about the two regime crises of 1960–63 and 1977–79 have been analysed so extensively that I will dispense with it, as my focus is the failure in both episodes to bring about a political settlement. On the economic background to both crises see Thomas Walton, 'Economic development and revolutionary upheavals in Iran', *Cambridge Journal of Economics* 4(3), 1980, pp. 271–92; on the role of the United States see Richard Cottam, *Iran and the United States: A Cold War Case Study*, Pittsburgh: University of Pittsburgh Press, 1988, pp. 110–88.

[9] Alexis de Tocqueville, *Democracy in America*, trans. George Lawrence, Garden City, NY: Anchor Books, 1969, p. 239.

[10] On the value of diachronic comparisons in political science see Arend Lijphart, 'Comparative Politics and the Comparative Method', *American Political Science Review* 65, 1971, p. 689.

[11] Juan J. Linz and Alfred Stepan (eds.), *The Breakdown of Democratic Regimes*, Baltimore: Johns Hopkins University Press, 1978; Leonardo Morlino, *Come cambiano i regimi politici: strumenti di analisi*, Milan: Franco Angeli, 1980; Guillermo O'Donnell, Philippe Schmitter, and Laurence Whitehead (eds.), *Transitions from Authoritarian Rule*, Baltimore: Johns Hopkins University Press, 1986; Larry Diamond, Juan Linz, and Seymour Martin Lipset (eds.), *Democracy in Developing Countries* (Boulder, CO: Lynne Rienner, 1988–89); and Samuel P. Huntington, *The Third Wave: Democratization in the Late Twentieth Century*, Norman and London: University of Oklahoma Press, 1991; Juan J. Linz and Alfred Stepan, *Problems of Democratic Transition and Consolidation: Southern Europe, South America and Post-Communist Eu-*

and dynamics involved in the two regime crises of 1960–1963 and the transition from the monarchy to the Islamic Republic in Iran, and by analysing them in terms and categories developed by that subfield for the passage from authoritarianism to democracy, we can both ask questions about the nature of Iranian politics that might elude us if we focused exclusively on explaining the success of the revolution, and refine our understanding of transitions in general.[12]

The appropriateness of the transition paradigm to the two episodes, especially to the period preceding the Iranian revolution, can be challenged on the grounds that all successful transitions in Southern Europe and Latin America were cases of *re*democratization, whereas Iran has never been a full-fledged democracy. It follows that the only appropriate analytic framework for any comparative endeavour would have to be the *longue durée*, as the sociohistorical factors favouring or impeding the movement toward democracy in Iran would have to be contrasted with long-term developments in other countries.[13] Such a project is indeed worthwhile, but does not obviate the need to study shorter episodes of regime transition and the opportunities for democratization that might arise in their course. There are three reasons for this.

First, while a discussion of long-term developments belongs to the sphere of *structure* and can illuminate the chances of democracy to take root in a country, the study of transitions is concerned with *conjuncture*: in moments of crisis what key actors do and when they do it can determine the course of events for years to come. I do not claim to answer the question whether democracy is viable in Iran, but instead seeks to understand why democracy was not established—however briefly—given that most actors in the regime crises of 1960–1963 and of 1977–1979 claimed it as their goal.

Second, while it is true that a hypothetical transition to democracy in Iran would not exactly be a re-democratization, Iranian politics have not always been equally authoritarian. The constitutional revolution of 1906–1911 put an end to the traditional monarchy, and the royal dictatorships of Reza Shah (1925–1941) and his son Mohammad Reza Shah (1953–1979) were in many ways modern dictatorships with traditional trappings; the two regimes were separated by twelve years of relative political pluralism in which the Shah reigned more than ruled.[14] Since neither autocrat ever abolished the liberal

---

rope, Baltimore: The Johns Hopkins University Press, 1996; and Lisa Anderson (ed.), *Transitions to Democracy*, New York: Columbia University Press, 1999.

[12] For a classification of regime transitions that includes violent revolution see Morlino, *Come cambiano i regimi politici*, pp. 86–107.

[13] As analysed for instance by Otto Hintze in 'The Preconditions of Representative Government in the Context of World History', in *The Historical Essays of Otto Hintze* (ed. with an Introduction by Felix Gilbert), New York: Oxford University Press, 1975, pp. 302–53; or by Barrington Moore, Jr., *Social Origins of Dictatorship and Democracy: Lord and Peasant in the Making of the Modern World*, Boston: Beacon Press, 1967.

[14] On this period see Fakhreddin Azimi, Iran: *The Crisis of Democracy 1941–1953*, New York: St. Martin's, 1989.

constitution of 1906–1907, that text remained a common point of reference for most politically articulate Iranians almost until the end of the monarchy. Democracy, or at least constitutional government, therefore, was an aspiration for significant sectors of Iranian society, which makes an argument for the historic inevitability of an Iranian *sonderweg* to theocracy an exercise in retrospective prediction. In this context it is significant that the fluctuations in Iran's long history of authoritarianism coincide quite closely with Huntington's five world-wide waves of regime changes, as the following table shows:[15]

TABLE 1: Iran's Regime Changes and the
Three Waves of Democratization

WAVES OF REGIME CHANGE	IRAN'S REGIME CHANGES
First Democratization 1828–26	Constitutional Period 1906–25
First Reverse 1922–44	Reza Shah's Rule 1926–41
Second Democratization 1958–62	Liberalization of 1960–63
Second Reverse 1958–75	Shah's Rule 1953–78
Third Democratization 1974–	Liberalization 1978–79

Third, to conclude that possibilities for democratization are so limited in Iran, given its authoritarian legacy and unfavourable socioeconomic preconditions, that the failure of liberalization and democratization is a foregone conclusion and need not be analysed, may become a self-fulfilling prophecy. As Huntington reminds us, a lack of significant experience with democratic rule 'is not a decisive impediment to democratization or no countries would be democratic.'[16]

Liberalizations occur when rulers come to the conclusion that the price of continued repression exceeds the cost of toleration.[17] Typically, fissures develop within the regime, leading some elements in the regime to seek an accommodation with parts of the opposition. Whether the liberalization can be sustained and lead to a genuine democratization depends on the ability of civil society to wrest more concessions from the regime and sustain the momentum of the reform.[18] At this point a few definitions are in order. Liberalization as defined here, entails 'a mix of policy and social changes, such as less censorship of the media, somewhat greater working room for the organization of

---

[15] Huntington, *The Third Wave*, p. 16.
[16] Ibid., p. 295.
[17] Robert Dahl, *Polyarchy*, New Haven: Yale University Press, 1971, chapter 1.
[18] See O'Donnell and Schmitter, *Transitions from Authoritarian Rule: Tentative Conclusions about Uncertain Democracies*, Baltimore: Johns Hopkins University Press, 1986.

autonomous working-class activities, the introduction of some legal safeguards for individuals such as *habeas corpus*, the releasing of most political prisoners, the return of exiles, perhaps measures for improving the distribution of income, and, most important, the toleration of opposition'. Democratization includes liberalization and in addition 'open contestation over the right to win control of the government, [which] in turn requires free elections, the results of which determine who governs'.[19]

The Shah liberalized his regime twice, with very different results. But political initiatives do not take place in a societal vacuum, and therefore this exploration of why the liberalizing episodes of 1960–1963 and 1977–1979 had different outcomes begins with the evolution of Iranian society in the intervening years.

The Evolution of Iranian Society

Between the early 1960s and the late 1970s Iranian society underwent tremendous changes.[20] For the purpose of assessing the chances of hypothetical transitions to democracy, three of these changes are of great import: new paradigms of Iranian politics, an increasing divergence between state policies and societal norms, and the resulting deepening of the cultural divide in Iran's dual society.

New Paradigms

Samuel Huntington has drawn attention to the importance of the external environment in influencing whether a society moves in a democratic or non-democratic direction.[21] While the direct actions of foreign states can contribute to regime change (as happened in Iran in 1941 and 1953), the external environment is also important in that it forces political actors to draw comparisons between their own country and foreign nations, and indicate preferences. In a country like Iran this is of great importance, for reasons that have to do with Iran's place in the international system as an old state whose political institutions were not a legacy of colonialism.

Given Iran's backwardness compared to Europe, the goal of the country's political elite since the nineteenth century was to catch up with the West. For Iran to join the company of the advanced nations of the world on an equal footing, to meet their 'standard of civilization',[22] it had to emulate Europe. The constitution of 1906 was modelled after the Belgian constitution of 1831,

---

[19] Linz and Stepan, *Problems of Democratic Transition*, p. 3.
[20] For a dated by still valid summary see Michael M.J. Fischer, 'Persian Society: Transformation and Strain', in Hossein Amirsadeghi (ed.), *Twentieth Century Iran*, London: Heinemann, 1977.
[21] Huntington, 'Will More Countries Become Democratic', *Political Science Quarterly* 99, 1984, pp. 205–07.
[22] Gerrit W. Gong, *The Standard of 'Civilization' in International Society*, Oxford: Clarendon Press, 1984.

and the various legal codes that were enacted sought to combine a Western-style legal order with aspects of the Islamic jurisprudence that had been the law of the land for centuries. In political life, Western models held sway after the rout of the traditionalists during the Constitutional Revolution.[23] Liberal Iranians wanted the Iranian polity to resemble Western democracies; the communists admired the Soviet Union. Although fascism made few explicit converts in what would later be called the Third World,[24] Iran's independence in the 1930s made it intellectually and emotionally possible for right-wing nationalists to sympathize with fascism and Nazism, quintessentially European phenomena, and to found parties in the 1940s.[25] As for the two Pahlavi Shahs, they, too, paid lip service to the Western-inspired constitution while violating it most of the time.

On the Iranian political scene of the early 1960s, the communists had been marginalized and the radical secular right was insignificant. Politics were dominated by the Shah, the Nationalists, and Ali Amini's circle. For the assessment of the chances for a transition to democracy, the important point is that most oppositionists still thought in terms of Western models. On the day in May 1961 when the Liberation Movement of Iran, then the most radical of Iran's constitutionalist opposition groups, was founded, Hasan Nazih, a leading member, said that his party wanted the Iranian governments to function like those of Sweden, Denmark, Britain, and Belgium.[26] The Third-World country Iranian Nationalists admired most was India. Clearly, the world's democracies provided the dominant paradigm for the Iranian opposition.

This changed after 1961, for a number of reasons. The first is generational. A new generation of Iranians blamed the inability of their elders to effect Iran's catching up with the West on their unquestioning acceptance of Western models. Jalal Al-e Ahmad's book *Gharbzadegi* exemplified this trend: it went so far as to praise the traditionalist opposition against the Constitutional Revolution for having resisted the imposition of Western models. Al-e Ahmad's book set the tone for oppositionist discourse in subsequent

---

[23] See Saïd Amir Arjomand, 'The Ulama's Traditionalist Opposition to Parliamentarism: 1907–1909', *Middle Eastern Studies* 17(2), 1981, pp. 174–90.

[24] See Juan J. Linz, 'Some Notes Toward a Comparative Study of Fascism in Sociological Historical Perspective', in *Fascism: A Reader's Guide*, Walter Laqueur (ed.), Berkeley: University of California Press, 1978, pp. 102–04.

[25] Iran is one of the few non-Western countries that had a self-consciously fascist, even Nazi, party in the 1940s. See Leonard Binder, *Iran: Political Development in a Changing Society*, Berkeley: University of California Press, 1964, pp. 216–19, who relates that at one point, in 1953, the court paid for the black shirts of Iranian Nazis who marched to place a wreath on Reza Shah's tomb on the day of his son's birthday. For a full study of Iran's Nazi party see Gholam-Reza Azizi, *Hezb-e Sosialist-e Melliye Kargaran-e Iran: Sumka*, Tehran, Markaz Asnad-e Enqelab-e Eslami, 2005.

[26] See Chehabi, *Iranian Politics*, p. 159.

years. His themes were amplified and given a religious twist by Ali Shari'ati, arguably the most influential Iranian intellectual in the 1970s.[27]

The second reason for this new critical attitude was the failure of the moderate opposition in 1960–1963 to wrest democratization from the Shah. The bloody repression by the Shah of the riots of June 1963 convinced many younger Nationalists that parliamentary methods were doomed in advance and that only armed struggle could topple the regime. The secular elements gradually coalesced with disgruntled members of the Communist Tudeh party to form the Marxist-Leninist Fada'iyan group, while the more religious activists soon founded the Mojahedin group.[28] Now even Mosaddeq's ouster in 1953 was imputed to his liberal ways and unwillingness to use more repression against his enemies. Beginning in the early 1970s the guerrilla groups mounted a more effective campaign against the Shah than their seniors in the National Front, the Liberation Movement of Iran, or the Tudeh— although in the end they were crushed too.

The third reason brings us back to the external environment. The decolonization of the 1950s and early 1960s and the rise of non-alignment as a new force in international politics provided new models for Iranians. Younger Iranians saw their country as a member of a Third World that had more in common with Asia, Africa, and Latin America than with Europe. Anti-imperialist struggles were much admired; Algeria, Cuba, and Vietnam replaced the European states as the new exemplars. Some, like Ali Shari'ati, went so far as to blame India's economic stagnation on its democratic politics.[29] Western democracy as a form of government also met with increasing scepticism because of the support many Western countries gave the Shah. Thus, while democracy-orientated discourse had dominated political debate in the early 1960s, this was no longer the case in the late 1970s.

At a different level, pro-regime intellectuals also began propagating a more critical view of the West.[30] In 1974 the Iranian sociologist and high UNESCO official Ehsan Naraqi, a nephew of Ayatollah Kashani and in his youth a Tudeh sympathizer, published a book titled 'The Alienation of the West', which he addressed to those Iranians who admired the West. Both the capitalist and the socialist West, he wrote, shared an unhealthy preoccupation with materialism. While not denying the West's achievements in science and

---

[27] See Brad Hanson, 'The 'Westoxication' of Iran: Depiction and Reactions of Behrangi, Al-e Ahmad, and Shariati', *International Journal of Middle East Studies* 15(1), 1983, pp. 1–23; and Mehrzad Boroujerdi, *Iranian Intellectuals and the West: The Tormented Triumph of Nativism*, Syracuse: Syracuse University Press, 1996.
[28] On the former see Maziar Behrooz, *Rebels with a Cause: The Failure of the Left in Iran*, New York: I.B. Tauris, 1999, and on the latter Ervand Abrahamian, *The Iranian Mojahedin*, New Haven: Yale University Press, 1989.
[29] Ali Shari'ati, *Ommat va emamat*, N.p.: LMI Reprint, 1977, pp. 161–69.
[30] See Boroujerdi, *Iranian Intellectuals and the West*, pp. 131–155; and Ali Gheissari, *Iranian Intellectuals in the Twentieth Century*, Austin: Texas University Press, 1997, pp. 92–97.

technology, he analysed such Western ills as drug abuse, suicide, environmental deterioration, energy over-consumption, and the erosion of family values, quoting copiously from Western social critics, and concluded that Iran did not need Western counter-culture, as its own culture was a counter-culture.[31] Three years later, the first publication of the regime-sponsored 'Iranian Centre for the Study of Cultures' was a book titled 'Asia facing the West', which analysed the West's nefarious effects on Asian civilizations, i.e. Islam/Iran, China, India, and Japan.[32]

By the mid-1970s, therefore, intellectuals of all persuasions affected a critical discourse regarding the West. Within the opposition, the new emphasis on anti-imperialism meant that when the Shah began liberalizing his regime in 1977, the heirs of the Nationalist movement were split: some wanted to resume where they had left off in 1963, others advocated a *guerre à outrance* against a regime they considered an American stooge. In terms of the types of transition, the veterans of the National Front and the LMI wanted to work toward a *reforma-ruptura pactada* (transplacement), while the younger people insisted on a *ruptura* (replacement). The latter's immediate aims coincided with those of Khomeini, the leader of the religious opposition. To understand the strength of this force compared to 1963, we have to analyse the unanticipated consequences of the Shah's policies, which from his point of view, came close to constituting perverse effects.[33]

Perverse Effects of Cultural Engineering

In spite of the Shah's sporadic attempts to portray himself as a Muslim ruler – he would visit the shrine in Mashhad and his government paid for the restoration of major religious edifices in Qom and elsewhere – his regime on the whole pushed back the role of religion in society. Traditional Iranian culture is characterized by a synthesis of Iranian and Islamic elements, and most people do not perceive a contradiction or tension between the two. Yet under the Shah certain elements of the non-Islamic component of the country's culture were increasingly stressed at the expense of the religious component. A significant segment of Iran's population, mostly in Tehran, did not object to secularization, even welcomed it, but as educational opportunities for more traditional Iranians expanded, and as the cities, the traditional centres of political activity in Iran, grew in size as a result of the rural exodus, more and more non-Westernized Iranians received a higher education and thus became more self-conscious of the cultural gap between them and the country's elite. As they prospered in the boom years of the 1960s and 1970s, they lost the

---

[31] Ehsan Naraqi, *Ghorbat-e gharb*, Tehran: Amir Kabir, 1974.
[32] Dariush Shayegan, *Asia dar barabar-e gharb*, Tehran: Amir Kabir, 1977.
[33] See Robert K. Merton, 'The Unanticipated Consequences of Purposive Social Action', *American Sociological Review* 1(6), 1936, pp. 894–904. For a good discussion of perverse effects as an extreme form of unanticipated consequences see Albert O. Hirschman, *The Rhetoric of Reaction*, Cambridge, MA: Harvard University Press, 1991, pp. 35–42.

deference with which lower-status Iranians had hitherto tended to regard higher-status Iranians, and became resentful. Economic growth also strengthened the clergy. Since the income of Iran's Shiite clergy derived mainly from the voluntary contributions of the faithful, among whom the bazaar merchants were the richest, the improving fortunes of the bazaar merchants led to greater financial resources for the clergy.[34] The Shah's relations with the bazaar, which had never been good,[35] reached their nadir in the mid-1970s when inflationary pressures induced the regime to humiliate and prosecute thousands of merchants in an anti-profiteering campaign.[36] The very strata of society that had financially benefited from economic growth drew closer than ever to the clergy.

Government policies thus had perverse effects on two grounds: they increasingly departed from expected norms, even mocking them at times, and at the same time they strengthened the social strata that objected most to these policies. At the same time many Westernized Iranians became tempted by an Islamic alternative, either out of a sense of cultural disorientation or as a means to signify opposition to the Shah. The secularizing policies of the Shah led to an increase in a self-conscious religiosity that regarded the state with suspicion, as even policies that had a rational basis, such as the introduction of day-light saving's time, were now interpreted as a deliberate attempt to interfere with people's religious duties.[37]

It is difficult to substantiate the claim that in the 1970s religious fervour grew in Iran, but we have some evidence for that contention. In 1975, for instance, 26 per cent of respondents in a poll expected the influence of religion to grow in the future, while only 9 per cent expected it to decline.[38] Students and teachers acquainted with academic life in this period report an increase in the activities and visibility of Muslim associations on the campuses. This was due to the influx of lower-middle-class students from more traditional backgrounds whose educational opportunities had improved, but whose personal value systems clashed with the dominant value system of the universities,[39] which was quite Westernized.[40] As Ahmad Ashraf and Ali Banuazizi

---

[34] For details see Ahmad Ashraf, 'Bazaar-Mosque Alliance: The Social Basis of Revolts and Revolutions', *Politics, Culture, and Society* 1, 1988, especially pp. 554–59.

[35] See Arang Keshavarzian, *Bazaar and State in Iran: The Politics of the Tehran Marketplace*, Cambridge: Cambridge University Press, 2007, especially pp. 128–46 and 228–69.

[36] For details see Nimah Mazaheri, 'State Repression in the Iranian Bazaar, 1975–1977: The Anti-Profiteering Campaign and an Impending Revolution', *Iranian Studies* 39(3), 2006), pp. 401–14.

[37] Siamak Movahedi, 'Cultural Preconceptions of Time: Can We Use Operational Time to Meddle in God's Time', *Comparative Studies in History and Society* 27(3), 1985, pp. 385-400.

[38] Abdolmohammad Kazemipur and Ali Rezaei, 'Religious Life Under Theocracy: the Case of Iran', *Journal for the Scientific Study of Religion* 42(3), 2003, p. 353.

[39] Farhang Mehr, president of Pahlavi University in Shiraz, confirms this; personal interview, 19 August 1992, Boston. Mehdi Zarghamee, who headed Iran's prestigious

have shown, it was precisely high-school and university students who were the most active elements in the 1978 demonstrations.[41]

Another indicator is publishing activity. As literacy rose, and as politically motivated censorship grew stricter,[42] the volume of religious publications grew both in absolute terms and as a percentage of total output. Between 1954 and 1963, an average of 56.7 religious books were published annually, representing 10 per cent of all published books. By 1974, the numbers had risen to 541 and 33.5 per cent respectively.[43]

Finally, we have some interesting figures about the names Iranians chose for their children. On the whole, secular Iranians are much more likely to choose Persian names for their children than Muslim/Arabic ones, and preference for Persian names has grown with Westernization. A recent study about the city of Hamadan shows, however, that while the percentage of Persian given names grew between 1963 and 1973, it declined between 1973 and 1979. Conversely, Muslim names declined in frequency between 1963 and 1973, and rose between 1973 and 1979. Incidentally, the trends have been reversed under the Islamic Republic, leading the author to conclude that 'since both the Pahlavi regime and the present Islamic regime were interested in manipulating cultural trends, our findings demonstrate that, at least when it comes to selecting names for their children, people seem to resist the official cultural propaganda.'[44]

These state policies did of course not affect everybody equally. Significant sectors of Iran's population did become more secular in outlook, and perhaps even their proportion in the population grew. But they remained a minority. The result was a deepening of the gap between the Westernized and the non-Westernized segments of Iran's dual society.

Iran's Dual Society

Until the end of the nineteenth century, urban Iranians, rich and poor, were united by a common culture. Most urban neighbourhoods were inhabited by people from all rungs of the economic ladder, and people of all stations of life participated in religious rituals, which mitigated the divisive effect of economic inequality. Beginning in the late nineteenth century, the Westerniza-

---

Aryamehr University in 1975–1979, relates that when he apprised the Shah of the situation, the Shah angrily dismissed his analysis and blamed everything on Marxist agitation; personal interview, 7 August 1992, Boston.

[40] Marvin Zonis, 'Higher Education and Social Change: Problems and Prospects', in *Iran Faces the Seventies*, Ehasan Yar-Shater (ed.), New York: Praeger, 1971, pp. 251–52.

[41] Ahmad Ashraf and Ali Banuazizi, 'The State, Classes and Modes of Mobilization in the Iranian Revolution', *State, Culture, and Society* 1, 1985, p. 26.

[42] *Encycopaedia Iranica*, s.v. 'Censorship'.

[43] Said Amir Arjomand, 'Shi'ite Islam and the Revolution in Iran', *Government and Opposition* 16, 1981, p. 311.

[44] Nader Habibi, 'Popularity of Islamic and Persian Names in Iran Before and After the Islamic Revolution', *International Journal of Middle East Studies* 24(), 1992, p. 260.

tion of increasing sectors of the Iranian elite, and later of the middle class, led to the appearance of a dual society. A minority of the population more and more abandoned traditional beliefs, behavioural patterns, and lifestyles, while the majority of Iranians remained faithful to their traditional way of life in which religious symbols played a key role.

In the early 1960s the societal dualism was still diffuse enough to allow both the Shah and the opposition to make appeals to both segments of the Iranian population, albeit on different grounds. The Shah presented himself as a modernizer to the elite and the middle class, and as traditional ruler to the masses. Likewise, the Nationalists drew support both from the Bazaar and from middle-class professionals. Cleavages in Iranian society were thus to some extent cross-cutting, a favourable precondition for democracy.[45]

After 1963 the situation changed and the gap between the two of segments of Iranian society widened. The traditional segment, increasingly urban as a result of the Shah's economic policies, witnessed with growing resentment the *nouveau-riche* excesses of the Westernized Iranian elite that benefited directly from the economic boom of the early 1970s, as Westernization and wealth now overlapped more and more. This widespread resentment made them receptive to Khomeini's populism:[46] 'resentment is a concomitant of that particular religious ethic of the disprivileged which . . . teaches that the unequal distribution of mundane goods is caused by the sinfulness and the illegality of the privileged, and that sooner or later God's wrath will overtake them', as Max Weber put it.[47] Since Khomeini articulated this resentment better than his rivals at the top of the Shiite hierarchy, his popularity grew, and this popularity in turn legitimized his explicitly non-democratic theory of the Islamic state. The 1906 constitution was a common reference of politically articulate Iranians no more.

The tension between the Westernized minority and the newly politicized traditional majority of the Iranian population had grave consequences for the regime transition of 1977–1979. Until 1963, regime figures and opposition leaders had shared a common background, and often socialized in spite of their political differences.[48] Had competitive politics been resumed after 1961, 'the severity of conflict [would have been] restrained by ties of friendship, family, interest, class, and ideology that pervaded the restricted group of

---

[45] See Dahl, *Polyarchy*, pp. 105–21.
[46] Ervand Abrahamian, *Khomeiniism*, Berkeley: California University Press, 1993, chapter 1.
[47] Max Weber, *Economy and Society*, Guenther Roth and Claus Wittich (eds.), Berkeley: University of California Press, 1978, p. 494.
[48] To give but two examples, the leader of the National Front in 1960–63, Allahyar Saleh, was the brother of Jahanshah Saleh, the pro-court rector of Tehran University. Mehdi Bazargan, the leader of the LMI, had been a *lycée* class-mate in France of Abdollah Riazi, who in the 1960s and 1970s was the speaker of the Iranian parliament, and who made the grave error to return to Iran after Bazargan had been named prime minister. Bazargan could not prevent his execution.

notables who dominated the political life of the country.' Mutual guarantees, another prerequisite for a successful transition to democracy, would have been easier to arrange, as 'tolerance and mutual security are more likely to develop among a small elite sharing similar perspectives than among a large and heterogeneous collection of leaders representing social strata with widely varying goals, interests, and outlooks.'[49] By contrast, mass politics in the context of the dual society of the 1970s was a particularly inauspicious starting point for a transition to democracy, for, to quote Robert Dahl again, 'if a country is divided into majority and minority subcultures, then members of the majority have less need to be conciliatory toward the minority.'[50] The experience of Algeria, where in 1992 open elections bade fair to lead to a total victory of the Front Islamique du Salut representing primarily the *arabisant* segment of the population, proves this point: the elections were aborted by a military establishment representing the more secular, often French-educated ruling segment of the post-independence years.

The confrontation between the Shah and Iranian society in the late 1970s did of course not pit the Westernized and the more traditional segments against each other, for the Shah met with a lot of opposition among modern Iranian as well. The anti-Shah coalition included both direct followers of Khomeini and secular allies of the Islamic movement. The cleavage in the opposition affected its responses to the liberalizing initiatives of the Shah in a decisive way.

Iran's transition from monarchy to Islamic Republic was decisively shaped by the charismatic personality of Ayatollah Khomeini. But the appearance of a charismatic leader, while in and of itself unpredictable, becomes more likely under certain conditions. Elaborating on Weber's notion that charismatic leaders are 'natural' leaders in moments of distress,[51] Robert Tucker and Erik H. Erikson suggest that societies become 'charisma-hungry' when three forms of distress appear: fear, anxiety, especially as experienced by persons in an 'identity-vacuum', and the 'existential dread' that people suffer when the rituals of their existence have broken down.[52] The above discussion of the state of both politics and society in Iran bears out this hypothesis. Iranian society in the mid-1970s was pervaded by fear, mostly of SAVAK, the secret police; the dual-society syndrome led to a widespread cultural malaise exacerbated by the intellectual output of ideologues such as Shari'ati; and government policies that seemed to attack, or at least question, much that most Iranians held sacred. Hence the appeal of Khomeini, who promised release from such an intolerable situation. But in 1978 it was not clear that the realization of this promise was incompatible with an orderly transition. Even inside Iran the

---

[49] Dahl, *Polyarchy*, pp. 36 and 37.
[50] Ibid., p. 116.
[51] Weber, *Economy and Society*, pp. 1111–12.
[52] Robert C. Tucker, 'The Theory of Charismatic Leadership', *Daedalus* 97(), 1968, p. 745.

word *enqelab*, revolution, was not used until after Khomeini's return, instead the word *nehzat* (movement) was used. While most street demonstrators demanded an 'Islamic Government,' it was not clear what *form* such a regime would take. Enough Islamists had argued for a compatibility of Islam and democracy that the replacement of one non-democratic regime by another one did not seem preordained.

Evolution of the Shah's Regime

The nature of a non-democratic regime is not unrelated to the chances for a liberalization to result in democratization. This leads us to analyse the evolving nature of the Shah's regime. We will successively look at its age at the onset of transition and its sultanization.

The Age of the Regime

The first difference between 1960 and 1977 was that in 1960 the Shah's regime was just seven years old. After the coup of 1953 the Shah had eschewed a militarization of his regime by dismissing its leader, General Fazlollah Zahedi, from the premiership in 1955, and then civilianizing his rule. To the politicians who had been active before 1953, the years of royal dictatorship could plausibly appear as an interlude, an 'authoritarian situation',[53] rather than an authoritarian *regime*. An 'authoritarian situation' means that power holders make no attempt to find new and permanent legitimacy formulas for their non-democratic rule, thereby implicitly admitting its exceptional nature. This, in turn, allows for a relatively smooth return to the status quo ante, as India's return to democratic governance after Indira Gandhi's 1975–1977 state of emergency exemplifies.

In 1960 Iran's opposition politicians were impatient to end their forced abstinence from politics and resume political life as it had existed before the 1953 coup. Their goal was a restoration of the pre-1953 regime. That regime having included the Shah, compromise with him was acceptable to the opposition.

Far less continuity with the pre-dictatorship days obtained in 1977. Some of Mosaddeq's ministers were still alive, but Mosaddeq himself was dead, and his companions were mostly septuagenarians whose very names were unknown to most of the population. After 1963, although the Shah still paid lip service to the constitution, the regime's legitimizing formulas increasingly acknowledged the autocratic nature of the Shah's rule and justified it in terms

---

[53] As defined by Juan Linz in his 'The Future of an Authoritarian Situation or the Institutionalization of an Authoritarian Regime: The Case of Brazil', in *Authoritarian Brazil: Origins, Policies, and Future*, Alfred Stepan (ed.), New Haven: Yale University Press, 1973, pp. 235–36.

of Iran's history and its developmental needs.[54] One can therefore speak of a different regime, especially after the establishment of a single party in 1975.

Exposure to periods of relative liberalism in one's formative years tends to favour democratic attitudes. In a survey carried out in 1960 among top regime and opposition leaders in Iran, it was found that democratic attitudes correlated very positively with having spent one's early twenties either before Reza Shah's dictatorship or after his fall, while more authoritarian attitudes were shown by men having spent those years under Reza Shah's dictatorship.[55] By 1977 the Shah had ruled Iran autocratically for over two decades, and his dictatorship was all many Iranians had ever known, especially the young militants who demonstrated in the streets of Iranian cities in 1978–1979. Iran's pre-authoritarian legacy had much less impact on the second transition than on the first.[56]

Increased Sultanization

From 1953 to 1960 the Shah's rule was authoritarian, in the sense that a limited pluralism still obtained in society. Parliament, although not freely elected, meant something, as did the office of prime minister. The Shah ruled in alliance with conservative elements in Iranian society. The regime made efforts to reconcile at least some elements in civil society: in the staged elections of 1954 both the leader of the influential Teachers Association, Mohammad Derakhshesh, and a nephew of the pro-court Ayatollah Behbehani had been awarded seats in parliament. Although an opposition press was not tolerated, not all the mass media were under direct government control.[57]

After 1963, the nature of the Shah's regime began to change. From 1964 to 1975 Iran officially had a two-party system, but the 'oppositional' Mardom party did not have an identity of its own and was led by men who also belonged to the regime. After 1964 the Shah increasingly discarded the 'men of the regime' who had been his allies, and surrounded himself first with technocrats, and then more and more with sycophants.[58] The press was also muz-

---

[54] The most elaborate formulations of the Shah's claim to legitimacy were written by non-Iranian academic scholars and published in the West at the very end of his rule. See Pio Filippani-Ronconi, 'The Tradition of Sacred Kingship in Iran', and George Lenczowski, 'Political Process and Institutions in Iran: The Second Pahlavi Kingship', in *Iran Under The Pahlavis*, George Lenczowski (ed.), Stanford: Hoover Institution Press, 1978, pp. 51–83 and 433–75, respectively.

[55] G. Hossein Razi, 'Democratic-Authoritarian Attitudes and Social Background in a Non-Western Society', *Comparative Politics* 13(), 1981, p. 64.

[56] For a discussion of the importance of pre-authoritarian legacies in determine the outcomes of transitions see O'Donnell and Schmitter, *Transitions from Authoritarian Rule: Tentative Conclusions*, pp. 21–23.

[57] For an interesting analysis of Iranian politics in the 1950s see Andrew F. Westwood, 'Politics of Distrust in Iran', *The Annals of The American Academy of Political and Social Science* 358 (March 1965).

[58] See Marvin Zonis, *The Political Elite of Iran*, Princeton: Princeton University Press, 1971, pp. 64–65, for an interesting episode symbolizing this shift.

zled: after 1963 about seventy publications that had generally supported the Shah without being controlled by the government were closed down. As his regime became more autocratic, it also became more corrupt, this corruption often involving family members and court cronies. Institutional decay was thus accompanied by ever-increasing corruption, which in turn was made possible by Iran's rising oil income. From being authoritarian in the decade 1953–1963, the Shah's regime became increasingly sultanistic after 1963.[59] There are many aspects to this sultanization, and each of them had implications for the liberalization of 1977, as compared to the liberalization of 1960.

The Role of the Shah

One basic fact about Iranian politics after 1953 was that for much of the Iranian opposition the Shah's authority was illegitimate, because of the outside interference to which he owed it. However, the institution of the monarchy was still legitimate enough for the Nationalists to work within the framework of the constitution and demand that the Shah reign but not rule. Given his perceived foreign connections, any compromise with the Shah was only possible if he accepted to reign within the limits assigned to him by the constitution.

The literature on transitions has emphasized the role of 'neutral' state institutions in successful transitions to democracy, for they can provide central foci of loyalty that transcend factional disputes. A constitutional monarch who is above politics can fill such a role, as King Juan Carlos of Spain demonstrated in the course of Spain's paradigmatic transition to democracy.[60] In Iran the Shah could probably have played such a role in 1960–1963, had he chosen to part with some of his powers. The moderate wing of the Nationalist opposition, essentially the National Front, never attacked the Shah openly and instead directed its criticisms at his prime ministers, thereby implicitly inviting the Shah to remain above the fray. The radical wing of the Nationalist opposition, essentially the Liberation Movement of Iran, did not keep up the pretence. Identifying the Shah personally as the source of autocracy, it explicitly invited him to assume his proper role as a constitutional monarch. As for Ayatollah Khomeini, even he addressed his remonstrances to Prime Minister Amir-Abbas Hoveyda as late as 1967, after having admonished the Shah in

---

[59] As defined in H.E. Chehabi and Juan J. Linz, 'A Theory of Sultanism 1: A Type of Nondemocratic Rule', in *Sultanistic Regimes*, H.E. Chehabi and Juan J. Linz (eds.), Baltimore: The Johns Hopkins University Press, 1998, pp. 7–23. For a full exploration of the last Shah's sultanism see Homa Katouzian, 'The Pahlavi Regime in Iran', in ibid., pp. 182–205.

[60] See Joel Podolny, 'The Role of the King in the Spanish Transition to Democracy', in *Politics, Society, and Democracy: The Case of Spain*, Richard Gunther (ed), Boulder, CO: Westview, 1992; and Charles Powell, *Juan Carlos: Spain's Self-Made Monarch*, London: St. Antony's/Macmillan, 1995.

1963 to better his ways.[61] On the government side, Prime Minister Ali Amini made it quite clear that he wanted to govern Iran rather than execute the Shah's orders. The Shah, however, could not accept any strong prime minister, and in 1962 he dismissed Amini.[62] The Shah's unwillingness to tolerate strong prime ministers cost him dearly in the long run, for, to quote Weber, 'a ruler needs a person who can take over responsibility for the acts of government, especially for failures and unpopular measures; this is still true of the Oriental caliph, sultan, and shah: They need the traditional figure of the Grand Vizier.' Weber goes on to say: 'In Persia, the attempt failed only a generation ago to abolish the position of the Grand Vizier in favor of bureaucratic ministries under the Shah's personal supervision, because this would have made him personally responsible for all troubles of the people and all administrative abuses; it also would have endangered, not only the ruler himself, but also his charismatic legitimacy. Therefore, the position of the Grand Vizier had to be restored so that it could protect the Shah and his charisma.'[63] Nasereddin Shah's monarchy, which Weber referred to, survived the constitutional revolution; Mohammad Reza Shah's did not survive the Islamic revolution.

After 1963 the Shah gradually dropped all pretence at reigning over a functioning democracy. The great wealth at his disposal after the oil price increases of the early 1970s fuelled the Shah's arrogance and self-righteousness, so that in a widely publicized interview he told Oriana Fallaci: 'I don't want that kind of democracy! . . . I don't know what to do with that kind of democracy' I don't want any part of it, it's all yours.'[64]

To legitimize his rule, the Shah tried to manipulate all symbols of legitimate authority: traditional (as monarch), legal-rational (by holding a plebiscite in January 1963 to approve his reforms), and charismatic (as leader of the White Revolution who would guide his people toward the 'Great Civilization').[65] But the very reforms the Shah set in motion after 1963 eroded the social bases of his traditional legitimacy, as the generally conservative landowners who had been his main allies before the agrarian reforms were eliminated as a powerful social class. Among the new professional middle class that became increasingly prominent in the 1960s and 1970s, the arbitrariness and corruption of his regime prevented its legitimation on legal-rational or charismatic grounds.

---

[61] See *Islam and Revolution: Writings and Declarations of Imam Khomeini* (trans. and annotated by Hamid Algar), Berkeley: Mizan Press, 1981, pp. 180, 189–94.

[62] In 1969 he admitted that Amini's tenure in office had been the worst period of American interference in Iran, when it tried to impose its type of regime on Iran. See his interview with *U.S. News and World Report*, January 27, 1969, p. 49. For an exhaustive treatment of this triangular relationship see Iraj Amini, *Bar bal-e bohran: zendegi-ye siyasi-ye Ali Amini*, Tehran, Nashr-e Mahi, 2009.

[63] Weber, *Economy and Society*, p. 1147.

[64] *The New Republic* 169 (1 December 1973), p. 18.

[65] The terms are used as defined by Max Weber in *Economy and Society*, pp. 215–16.

By 1978 the vast majority of Iranians opposed the Shah's rule, and given the experience of 1953 and 1963, the slogan that the 'Shah must reign but not rule' had lost its attraction: when the Shah finally stated in late 1978 that he accepted merely to reign, nobody believed him. The monarchy itself had become illegitimate in the eyes of most Iranians, for, in the words of Giuseppe di Lampedusa's Prince Salina, 'kings who personify an idea should not, cannot, fall below a certain level for generations; if they do . . . the idea suffers too.'[66] In 1978 the closest approximation to a neutral arbiter Iranians had was Khomeini, in the sense that he led a vast oppositional movement without *seeming* to identify himself with any one of its components.

Democratic Façade
Like his father, the Shah was heir to the constitutional revolution; in one of his books he had written that he would never institute a single party because that was what the communists and Hitler had done.[67] The Shah also had to assuage the conscience of his Western friends,[68] a factor that had not affected his father, during whose rule fascism had been a credible alternative to liberal democracy. As a result the Shah, like some Latin American dictators, regularly, went through the motions of holding elections.[69]

In 1960, the memory of the relatively honest elections to the 16th majles of 1950 was still alive. The elections of 1954 and 1956 had been rigged, but a number of relatively independent personalities had still been elected. The elections to the 20th majles of 1960 were rigged also, but the Shah, feigning neutrality, dissolved that chamber for that very reason and called for new elections in 1961.[70] This time Prime Minister Ali Amini dissolved the parliament that resulted, arguing that better electoral laws were needed before Iran could have honest elections. Between 1954 and 1961, therefore, the hypocrisy was not total, and with some goodwill on both sides relatively honest elections could have been held.

Beginning with the elections to the 21st majles in 1964, however, elections became a complete farce. The results no longer had to be rigged, since the winning candidates were designated in advance. In the elections of 1964, 80 percent of the deputies entered parliament for the first time. When they began behaving like members of parliament, the secretary general of the ruling Iran

---

[66] Giuseppe di Lampedusa, *The Leopard*, trans. Archibald Colquhoun, New York: Pantheon, 1960, p. 23.
[67] His Imperial Majesty Mohammed Reza Shah Pahlevi, Shahanshah of Iran, *Mission for My Country*, London: Hutchinson, 1960, p. 173.
[68] At the time the fictional character of the three legal parties was not apparent to everybody outside Iran. See for example Wolfgang Ule, 'Entwicklung und gegenwertiges Parteiwesen im Iran', *Vierteljahresberichte* 31, 1968.
[69] On the functions of these electoral exercises see A.-H. Banisadr, A. Ghazanfarpour, S. Ghazanfarpour, and P. Vieille, 'Les elections et leurs fonctions en Iran', *Revue Française de Science Politique* 27, 1977, pp. 34–63.
[70] For details see Andrew F. Westwood, 'Elections and Politics in Iran', *The Middle East Journal* 15(2), 1961, pp. 153–64.

Novin party, Manuchehr Kalali, reminded them that they had not been elected by the people, and should therefore stop acting as if they represented a constituency.[71]

The composition of the 1964–1979 parliaments compounded its increasing subservience. The proportion of landowners had held steady at 40 per cent between 1925 and 1961; in 1964 it fell to 23 per cent, and in the last majles of the monarchy it had reached 10 per cent.[72] While this reflects the Shah's attempt to change the social bases of his regime by replacing conservative landowners with middle class technocrats, it also meant that deputies were less independent, and less likely to challenge the government.

This type of pseudo-democracy is a very unfavourable starting point for democratization, as the prolonged and regular cynical manipulation of democratic procedures, practices, and symbols erodes their appeal among the citizenry. In a hypothetical transition to democracy, 'free elections' no longer constitute a clear and universally accepted break with the past, because the old regime maintains that elections have been free all along, and the losing parties of any really free election might contend that they lost only because the new elections were as farcical as previous ones.

As to the two official parties, they never acquired any autonomous status in the regime, and failed to provide a link with civil society. It is possible for regime-sponsored opposition parties to develop some life of their own and become authentic opposition parties in the course of a liberalization. The Brazilian MDB is an example of that,[73] but, unlike the Mardom Party in Iran, it had been cobbled together on the basis of pre-existing groups in civil society. Iran's parties, even the government party, resembled much more the so-called 'bloc parties' of Communist Eastern Europe.

In Iran the Shah reaffirmed his belief in a two-party system when he granted an audience to Mardom Party members on September 1, 1973.[74] Consequently, in 1974 the new secretary-general of the Mardom Party, Naser Ameri, showed considerable initiative during a by-election campaign in the north of the country. His attacks on the government of Amir-Abbas Hoveida met with a degree of popular enthusiasm that frightened the regime. After a vigorous campaign on both sides, the government candidate was declared the winner of the election. Ameri resigned and died in a car accident soon after. As a direct consequence of the spirited campaign waged by Ameri, the Shah, in a move that caught everyone by surprise, announced in early 1975 that the existing parties had not fulfilled their purpose, for which reason he ordered the

---

[71] Interview with Manuchehr Kalali in the *Harvard Iranian Oral History Project*, transcript of tape 2, pp. 16–18.

[72] *Encyclopaedia Iranica*, s.v. 'Class System VI: Classes in the Pahlavi Period'.

[73] See Bolivar Lamounier, 'Authoritarian Brazil Revisited: The Impact of Elections on the Abertura', in *Democratizing Brazil: Problems of Transition and Consolidation*, Alfred Stepan (ed.), New York: Oxford University Press, 1989.

[74] See Shaul Bakhash, 'Party politics', *Keyhan International*, 2 September 1973.

establishment of a new single party, the Rastakhiz, or Resurgence party.[75] Although the initial party program was frankly totalitarian,[76] the regime justified the creation of the single party in democratic terms, promising not to intervene in the parliamentary elections of June 1975, in which the electorate had the choice between different candidates all representing the same party programme. Unsurprisingly, a poll conducted by the Rastakhiz party among the youth indicated that only 13 per cent believed that people had a real and valid reason to participate in the elections.[77] A policy designed to mobilize the population in favour of the regime had the opposite effect: since party-membership was obligatory, one could no longer remain apolitical, and many Iranians became passive opponents of the regime. Even though the Shah soon ordered the Rastakhiz party to constitute two competing wings (each under a cabinet member), a Brazilian-style *abertura* was now ruled out, given that the Rastakhiz party was accorded a monopoly of political life. During the liberalization of 1977, the regime maintained the monopoly of the party in the early period, when moderates still dominated the oppositional movement. By the time the regime indicated that it would accept other parties, the moderates had been marginalized by the hardliners under Khomeini, who refused to work within the system.

By 1978 the Iranian state's very capacity to organize free elections was doubted. Even though the moderate opposition would probably have liked to participate in elections (knowing that it would not be allowed to win them), Khomeini made it quite clear that he opposed any electoral exercise staged by the Shah's government. This made the holding of 'transitional elections' in the course of a *reforma*, or 'transformation', to use Linz's and Huntington's terms, respectively, very unlikely. Any free elections would have to be carried out by the new regime, after a *ruptura*, or 'replacement'.[78]

The Fusion of Regime and State and the Disappearance of Semi-Oppositions

Robert Fishman has drawn attention to the different implications of regime-initiated, as opposed to state-initiated transitions. If the impetus for change comes from within the regime, as it did in Spain, the state structures can remain intact, and the change-oriented elements of the regime can partici-

---

[75] There is a certain parallel here with King Carol of Romania's 'Front for National Resurrection' of 1938, but the immediate inspiration for the name seems to have come from the Arab Ba'th party.
[76] See Mehdi Mozaffari, *L'Iran*, Paris: Librairie générale de droit et de jurisprudence R. Pichon et R. Durand-Auzias, 1978, for a detailed discussion of the party program. See also Robert Graham, *Iran: The Illusion of Power*, New York: St. Martin's Press, 1980, pp. 136–38.
[77] Hassan Mohammadi-Nejad, 'The Iranian Parliamentary Elections of 1975', *International Journal of Middle East Studies* 8(), 1977, p. 109.
[78] Huntington, *The Third Wave*, p. 114.

pate in shaping the post-transition polity. More continuity and stability are the result.[79]

Typically, 'semi-oppositions' play a crucial part in such transitions.[80] Semi-oppositions are specific to authoritarian regimes, and Juan Linz has defined them as 'those groups that are not dominant or represented in the governing group but, that are willing to participate in power without fundamentally challenging the system.' In Iran Ali Amini and his circle personified one subtype of this semi-opposition in the early 1960s, i.e., 'dissidents within the elite favouring long-run policies and institutional alternatives but accepting the top leadership—perhaps somewhat conditionally and temporarily—and willing to hold office.'[81]

In 1960–1963 the presence of Ali Amini on the political scene, occupying the political space between the Nationalists and the Shah, made a regime-initiated transition plausible. But Amini failed due to the combined efforts of the Shah and the Nationalist opposition. In 1977 the situation was very different: by then the personalization of the Shah's power had gone so far that there no longer was any respectable semi-opposition in Iran.

The second consequence of the increased personalism of the Shah's later years was that the distinction between regime and state became increasingly blurred.[82] By 1977, therefore, a regime-initiated transition had become more difficult to enact because no semi-opposition could act as a bridge between the regime and the opposition,[83] and because even within the narrow circle of power of his regime the Shah had not allowed any independent personalities to emerge, men who might have provided imaginative leadership in the Shah's stead.[84]

Alternatively, a state-initiated transition, in the form, for instance, of an army coup à la Portugal, was unlikely because state institutions, and in particular the army, lacked the autonomy to act on their own. As the state disintegrated in the last months of the Shah's regime, popular mobilization reached

---

[79] Robert Fishman, 'Rethinking State and Regime: Southern Europe's Transition to Democracy', *World Politics* 42(), April 1990, pp. .

[80] On the parts played by semi-oppositions in the Spanish and Portuguese transitions see Nancy Bermeo, 'Redemocratization and Transition Elections', *Comparative Politics* 19(), 1987, pp. 224–28.

[81] Juan J. Linz, 'Opposition to and under an Authoritarian Regime: The Case of Spain', *Regimes and Oppositions*, Robert Dahl (ed.), New Haven: Yale University Press, 1973. Quotes are from pp. 191 and 193–94.

[82] On this point see Khosrow Fatemi, 'Leadership by Distrust: The Shah's *Modus Operandi*,' *The Middle East Journal* 36(1), 1982, pp. 48–61.

[83] Amini was still around and offered his services, but the Shah distrusted him until the end.

[84] On the importance of imaginative leadership in moments of transition see Juan J. Linz, 'Innovative Leadership in the Transition to Democracy and a New Democracy: The Case of Spain', in *Innovative Leaders in International Politics*, Gabriel Sheffer (ed.), Albany, NY: State University of New York Press, 1993. In Iran the term *qaht al-rejal* (dearth of statesmen) came to denote the situation.

revolutionary proportions, and the transition became in effect society-led. And as Alfred Stepan has argued, 'the most likely outcome of sharp crises of authoritarian regimes stemming from diffuse pressures and forces in society is either a newly constituted successor authoritarian government, or a caretaker military junta.'[85] The second scenario was ruled out because of the insufficient state autonomy, and the first was indeed what happened.

To sum up, the delegitimation of the Shah's personal role, of the state apparatus he headed, and of the procedures of liberal democracy were additional factors favouring the emergence of a political force totally unrelated to the existing regime, a force that would be embodied by Ayatollah Khomeini's charismatic leadership. As G. K. Chesterton so aptly put it, 'men trust a great man because they do not trust themselves. And hence the worship of great men always appears in times of weakness and cowardice. We never hear of great men until the time when all other men are small.'[86]

The Islamic Revolution as Failed Liberalization

When the Shah put an end to torture in Iranian prisons, released some political prisoners, relaxed censorship, and let it be known that henceforth he would grant greater civil liberties to his subjects, Iranians, unaware as they were of the Shah's terminal illness and hence his desire to bequeath a stable system to his son, imputed the liberalization of Iran's politics to President Carter's human rights campaign. The assumption that the Shah would not dare to clamp down as long as Carter was in office, encouraged the opposition to raise it head.

The first initiatives of the opposition were quite congruent with the experiences of transitions elsewhere. The writer and essayist Ali-Asghar Hajj-Seyyed-Javadi typified the 'exemplary individuals, who begin testing the boundaries of behaviour initially imposed by the incumbent regime'[87] when he wrote a 200-page letter outlining the ills of the system. Subsequently civil society revived, as professional associations showed new initiative and democratically elected their leaderships, who were often associated with the opposition. All this took place in 1977. At this point, the clergy had not joined the fray, and from his exile in Najaf Khomeini exhorted them to become active too:

> A new opportunity has appeared in Iran today ... Now, writers belonging to political parties criticize [the regime]. They write letters and sign petitions. You should write letters too ... This is an opportunity that should not be lost.[88]

---

[85] Stepan, 'Paths toward Redemocratization', pp. 78–79.
[86] G.K. Chesterton, *Heretics*, New York: Dodd, Mead & Co, 1923, p. 269.
[87] O'Donnell and Schmitter, *Transitions from Authoritarian Rule: Tentative Conclusions*, p. 49.
[88] Quoted in *Shahidi digar as rowhaniyat*, Najaf: n.p., 1978, pp. 56–57.

In 1977, the revival of civil society, a concomitant of liberalization, touched mainly the modern segment of society. Unnoticed by most of the Westernized Iranians who made up the memberships of the professional associations, unnoticed also by the Shah's security apparatus that had concentrated its vigilance on leftist groups, a vast associational network based on religious activities had sprung up in the traditional segment of Iranian society. In 1974, there were 12,300 religious associations in Tehran alone.[89] Most of the membership of these associations was made up of recent migrants to Tehran who were negatively affected by the deflationary measures announced in 1977 to cool down the overheated Iranian economy. In the liberalizing climate of 1977–1978 they became politicized and channelled their energies into anti-regime activities. The traditional *Ashura* celebrations thus gained a political significance whose emotional intensity the secular opposition could not match.[90] Therefore, civil society's mobilization was not coordinated by the secular opposition that had begun testing the limits of the Shah's liberalization in 1977, but by Khomeini's followers. After January 1978, when an article insulting Khomeini was published in the Iranian press, the religious opposition became a mass movement. The secular, liberal opposition, frustrated by the frequent reversals and incidents of repression that tend to accompany liberalizations, allied itself with the mass movement so as to escape irrelevance.[91]

The dualism of Iranian society meant that the secular elements based in the professional associations could not control the mass movement: the popular sector did not trust the middle-class professionals enough to be led by them, their tactical alliance notwithstanding. This in turn meant that their capacity to negotiate with the regime, and demand further concessions in return for foregoing further mass mobilization, was seriously impaired.[92] More generally, the whole strategy of reform 'with the help of the perspective of revolution', possible in 1961, was not credible, since a successful implementation of this strategy depends on the revolutionaries being neither too strong nor too weak.[93] Pacts, in which moderates on both sides settle on a peaceful transition that marginalizes hardliners, became impossible, and with them any realistic hope for a negotiated settlement.

---

[89] For details see Amir Arjomand, 'Shi'ite Islam and the Revolution in Iran', p. 312.

[90] See Farhad Kazemi, *Poverty and Revolution in Iran: The Migrant Poor, Urban Marginality and Politics*, New York: New York University Press, 1980, especially chapters 5 and 6.

[91] For details on the progress of the oppositional movement see Abrahamian, *Iran: Between Two Revolutions*, chapter 11.

[92] This tactic is key to many successful transitions. See O'Donnell and Schmitter, *Transitions from Authoritarian Rule: Tentative Conclusions*, p. 41.

[93] A.O. Hirschman, 'Models of Reformmongering', in *Journeys Toward Progress: Studies of Economic Policy-Making in Latin America*, New York: The Twentieth Century Fund, 1963, p. 284.

Another factor that contributed to the impasse was the Shah regime's tendency to make concessions too late. Timing is crucial in transitions, as Juan Linz has shown; *delayed* actions, in particular, are likely to be *belated* actions in that they are taken too late to achieve their purpose.[94] Iranian politics in the second half of 1978 exemplifies this.

In 1977, when the moderates still dominated the opposition, the regime insisted that political activity be carried out within the Rastakhiz party. In July 1978 Bazargan accepted the principle of an electoral dénouement of the crisis by stating that 'if the Shah is ready to implement all provisions of the Constitution, then we are prepared to accept the monarchy and participate in the elections,'[95] but the Shah would have nothing of it. In October 1978 the leaders of the political opposition, Bazargan for the LMI and Karim Sanjabi for the National Front, went to Paris to try to induce Khomeini to agree to a negotiated settlement, perhaps involving elections, but Khomeini turned down their request, arguing that the Shah's regime did not have enough legitimacy to hold elections, and that an election campaign would dissipate the energies of the movement.[96] Given the Shah's and Khomeini's intransigence, the moderate opposition leaders publicly committed themselves to support Khomeini's call for an end to the monarchy. And so it happened that when in November 1978 the Shah finally conceded that opposition parties would be allowed to contest the elections, the moderates were in no position to accept such a deal.

In December 1978 anti-Shah demonstrations of unprecedented proportions left no doubt that a 'coalition government' consisting of oppositional politicians and pro-Shah figures was out of the question. The alternative now was between a bloody repression, which would almost certainly have led to civil war, and the departure of the Shah and his replacement by a revolutionary government. A military coup was unlikely, for two reasons. First, the organizational structure of the armed forces under the Shah's increased sultanization impeded unity of purpose among the top commanders—in fact, many officers started negotiating with the revolutionaries on an individual basis. Second, defections among the rank and file reached proportions that put the reliability of the troops in serious doubt.[97] In this situation, the question was whether the revolutionaries would seize power (as had happened twenty years earlier in Cuba), or receive the reins of power from their predecessors (as in Czechoslovakia in 1989), thereby avoiding the bloodshed of a showdown.

---

[94] Juan J. Linz, 'Time and Regime Change', in Juan J. Linz, *Robert Michels, Political Sociology, and the Future of Democracy*, H. E. Chehabi (ed.), New Brunswick: Transaction Publishers, 2006, pp. 85–87.
[95] *Asnad-e Laneh-ye Jasusan* [Documents of the Spies' Nest], vol. 24, p. 16.
[96] For details see Chehabi, *Iranian Politics*, pp. 242–46.
[97] On the mood among the military in the last months of the revolution see the memoirs of the last joint chief of staff, General Qarabaghi. See *E'terafat-e zheneral*, Tehran: Ney, 1986.

The prospects for a negotiated denouement of the crisis seemed to brighten when the Shah succeeded in persuading one of the moderate opposition leaders, Shapur Bakhtiar, to accept the position of prime minister and soon thereafter left the country in January 1979. Since Bakhtiar lacked a strong independent social base, the revolutionaries interpreted his nomination not as a victory, as he had hoped, but rather as a defection to the Shah's side on his part. Given his ties of friendship with the political leadership in Tehran, however, negotiations continued. It is indicative of the weariness of the liberals within the regime (due to the fusion of regime and state, as discussed above) and of the general disarray that befell it after the Shah's departure, that American officials partook in the negotiations, playing the role of surrogate regime liberals. But now the object of these negotiations could only be to arrange a *machtübergabe*, or transfer of power.[98] By early February 1979 it was agreed that Bakhtiar would go to Paris, present his resignation to Khomeini, and be reinstalled by him as prime minister, taking more oppositionists into his cabinet. This plan was sabotaged by opposition hardliners in Tehran,[99] much to the regret of political moderates like Bazargan, who wrote later that 'if this path had been taken, God knows how much destruction and bloodshed could have been avoided.'[100]

Bakhtiar could not prevent the return to Iran of Khomeini, who named the liberal Islamist Mehdi Bazargan prime minister on 4 February 1979. Iran now entered a brief period of 'dual power', to use Trotsky's term, and in these days of mass mobilization the state rapidly disintegrated, as entire ministries went over to the revolutionaries and declared their allegiance to the Bazargan government. On 9 February mobs stormed barracks and armed themselves, and two days later the army declared its neutrality. Bakhtiar went first into hiding and later into exile, while Bazargan put together a provisional government consisting of moderate Nationalists. The new regime thus came into place through a process of *machtergreifung*, seizure of power.

The nine months from February to November 1979, when the Provisional Government resigned in the wake of the seizure of the American embassy, were a period of liberal government in Iran. However, since no free elections took place during this period, it must be considered a liberal transition temporarily brought about by the power vacuum created by the Shah's departure, rather than a democratic interlude separating two non-democratic regimes. The cause of democracy was not completely lost in 1979, for the men who ran the Iranian government until November belonged to the liberal and democ-

---

[98] The terms *machtübergabe* and *machtergreifung* are taken from M. Rainer Lepsius, 'Machtübernahme und Machtübergabe: Zur Strategie des Regimewechsels', in *Sozialtheorie und soziale Praxis: Eduard Baumgarten zum 70. Geburtstag*, Hans Albert (ed.), Meisenheim am Glan: Anton Hain, 1971, pp. 158–73.
[99] For a good, if somewhat tendentious, account of these last minute negotiations see Ibrahim Yazdi, *Akharin talashha dar akharin ruzha*, Tehran: Zafar, 1984.
[100] Mehdi Bazargan, *Enqelab-e Iran dar do harekat*, Tehran: Naraqi, 1984, p. 74.

ratic wing of the anti-Shah opposition. The 'confining conditions'[101] they faced, however, were such that an inauguration of democracy was extremely difficult. But that is another story.[102]

Conclusion

Our discussion of the transition of 1977–1979 compared to the crisis of 1960–1963 has shown that the prospects for democratization in 1978 were far less favourable than in the earlier period. To use metaphors popularized by the transition literature, in both episodes Iranian leaders lacked *virtù*, but in 1977–1979 *fortuna* had turned against them as well in the form of increased social tensions, increased mass-mobilization, and the emergence of a charismatic leader championing a non-democratic form of government.

Whether democracy would have survived in Iran if the Shah had been serious about democratization in 1960–1963 is a hypothetical, and therefore unanswerable, question. What I have tried to show is *how* the failure of democratization in the early 1960s, and the subsequent changes both inside the regime and in society at large, made a transition to democracy *even more* difficult to effect in 1977–1979. Let us hope that just as the uprising of 1963 was a dress-rehearsal for the revolution of 1978/79, the Green Movement of the summer of 2009 will one day be seen as the precursor of a genuine democratization in Iran.[103]

---

[101] As used and analysed by Otto Kirchheimer, 'Confining Conditions and Revolutionary Breakthroughs', *The American Political Science Review* 59(4), 1965, pp. 964–74.
[102] Which I have told in 'The provisional government and the transition from monarchy to Islamic Republic in Iran', in *Between States: Interim Governments and Democratic Transitions*, Yossi Shain and Juan J. Linz (eds.), Cambridge: Cambridge University Press, 1995, pp. 127–43 and 278–81.
[103] On the Green Movement see Nader Hashemi and Danny Postel (eds.), *The People Reloaded: The Green Movement and the Struggle for Iran's Future*, Brooklyn, NY: Melville House, 2010; and Farhad Khosrokhavar's chapter in this volume

Chapter 3

The End of a Beautiful Friendship?
Mahmoud Ahmadinejad and the Principalists

Walter Posch

Until the 'political tsunami' of 2011 when the Arab youth stood up to their sclerotic security-minded autocrats, the Islamic Republic of Iran could legitimately claim to have a political system that, whilst far from perfect, was more representative than that of any Middle Eastern country, perhaps with the exception of Israel. The comparison was even more favourable if one compared the Islamic Republic of the late 1990s with the post-Soviet autocracies in Central Asia. Indeed the Islamic Republic held elections even during the long Iran-Iraq war and had no political role for the military as has been the case in important countries like Turkey, Pakistan, and Algeria. To this one has to add a vibrant press and lively intellectual debates. These and other positive trends were taken as proof of an 'Iranian democracy' coexisting with authoritarianism as enshrined in the principle of the 'Rule of the Jurisprudent' or *velayat-e faqih*. Hopes for a breakthrough of democratic tendencies peaked during the two presidencies of reformist president Seyyed Mohammad Khatami. It was at this point that Mohammad-Reza Djalili poured cold water on the heated expectations of those who saw in Khatami the politician who would introduce real democratic change to Iran (apparently people failed to differentiate the two sides of Khatami's persona: Khatami the political philosopher and Khatami the politician who belongs to a political faction). Djalili's scepticism was substantiated in 2005 with the election of Mahmoud Ahmadinejad and even more so in 2009 with his contested re-election.[1]

In this chapter I would like to examine the internal developments that led to the anti-reformist rollback which climaxed in the 2009 presidential elections. This said, I will not deal *in extenso* with the conduct of the elections nor in detail with the Green Movement,[2] rather I would like to refer to these elec-

---

[1] Mohammad-Reza Djalili, *Iran: l'illusion réformiste*, Paris: Presses de Sciences-Po, 2001.
[2] See the contribution of Farhad Khosrokhavar in this volume.

tions in order to examine the Iranian factional dynamics that led to the crisis of 2009 and that continue to reverberate. The emergence of the new 'principalist' faction during this period is worth considering, for, while we have excellent studies of political factionalism in Iran,[3] the 'principalist' faction is still an understudied topic. Needless to say, any reflection on the Islamic Republic has to start with the Islamic ideology.

Ideological Roots of Iranian Factionalism

The late Imam Khomeini bequeathed an ideology to his followers that contained Islamist, modernist, traditional, and Third-Worldist elements. He was more a political pragmatist and practitioner than a political theorist; hence his work lacks the clarity and intellectual stringency of other political Shiite thinkers. Even so, Khomeini's work on 'Islamic governance' includes some clues as to how he would like to see the perfect Islamic state emerge.[4] Of course, the core principle aims at keeping (or making) Iranian society more Islamic by 'ordering the good and interdicting evil' (*al-amr bi'l-ma'ruf wa'l-nahy 'an al-munkar*). Other elements include a combination of revolutionary political Islam claiming to play a global role and pure, originally left-wing Third-Worldish elements. In this, Khomeini was the last in a long line of Iranian political thinkers, both clerical and non-clerical, including controversial figures such as Mojtaba Navvab Safavi, Jalal Al-e Ahmad, Ne'matollah Salehi Najafabadi, Ali Shari'ati, and many others.[5] Hostility to the United States and Israel and fear of the 'cultural onslaught of the West' or 'Westoxication' are considered to be core principles and, thus, they are non-negotiable. The main element of Khomeini's ideology is, of course, the doctrine of the 'Rule of the Jurisprudent' (*velayat-e faqih*) which originally ensured him oversight of the political process and over the ensuing years has developed into an elaborate bureaucratic apparatus, namely the bureau of the Revolutionary Leader (*Beyt-e Rahbar-e Enqelab-e Eslami*). To this one has to add a good dose of Iranian populism and the legacy of the long war with Iraq, which

---

[3] See Abdolkarim Lahiji: *Peluralizm-e siyasi dar Jomhuri-ye Eslami-ye Iran* [Political Pluralism in the Islamic Republic of Iran], Paris: Khavaran, 2000; Sa'id Barzin, *Jenahbandi-ye siyasi dar Iran. Az daheh-ye 1360 ta dowreh-ye Dovvom-e Khordad 1376* [Political Factionalism in Iran. From the 1980s to the era of the Second Khordad 1376/1997], Tehran: Nashr-e Markaz, 1998; Wilfried Buchta, *Who Rules Iran? The Structure of Power in the Islamic Republic*, Washington DC: WINEP, 2000; Mehdi Moslem, *Factional Politics in Post-Khomeini Iran*, Syracuse: Syracuse University Press, 2002.
[4] On the 'Islamic Governance' according to Khomeini see his text edited by Hamid Algar, *Islam and Revolution. Writings and Declarations of Imam Khomeini (1941–1980)*, Berkeley: Mizan Press, 1981, pp. 55–126.
[5] For Khomeini's ideological forerunners see Hamid Dabashi, *Theology of Discontent. The Ideological Foundation of the Islamic Revolution in Iran* (2nd enlarged edition), New Brunswick: Transaction Publishers, 2008, pp. 491–501.

is interpreted in almost chiliastic rather than nationalist terms.[6] This is important because the war veterans and their families are an important political constituency and they dominate the Iranian bureaucracy, especially the security apparatuses. As a matter of fact, all Iranian political factions have to adhere to these principles and publicly pay homage to the late Imam Khomeini and his legacy as well as to the sacrifice made by the 'martyrs' of the war. In this way, the Islamic Ideology is indeed a straightjacket excluding all those ideological debates and discourses deemed hostile, including those originating from secularists of all trends and tendencies as well as those put forward by Sunni Muslims and non-Khomeinist Shiite Islamists like the People's Mojahedin Organization.

Beyond this point, political debate among political factions in Iran is surprisingly free and lively because Khomeinism has in practice provided room for factionalism. There are three reasons for this. First, pre-revolutionary Islamic organizations and their respective ideological discourses were incorporated into 'Khomeinism' (for instance the traditions of the *Feda'iyan-e Eslam*, the *Hojjatiyeh*, or the Liberation Movement). Second, the idea of *maslahat* allows a pragmatic debate on the implementation of Islamic principles; in this sense *maslahat* justifies the existence of several opinions on a given topic.[7] Finally, the fact that Khomeini has changed his views on certain political issues several times forced his followers to consult *feqh*, the works of other Islamic scholars, and the Iranian constitution.[8]

For all these reasons the implementation of various polices was accompanied by debate, forcing policy makers to discuss matters and ultimately to compromise. Factions developed along ideological lines reminiscent of the political spectre elsewhere, and the heated debate among them was often taken as proof of Iranian democracy, although of course, it has to be read as pluralism within one ideological system. Depending on their position towards the economy, and their domestic and foreign policies, one may draw the following sketch of ideological factions in Iran during the period preceding the end of Khatami's first term:[9]

> Ideological Factions within the power apparatus and representation in the Parliament:

---

[6] See Saskia Gieling, *Religion and War in Revolutionary Iran*, London: I.B. Tauris, 1999.
[7] On *maslahat* see Asghar Schirazi, *The Constitution of Iran. Politics and the State in the Islamic Republic*, London: IB Tauris, 1999, pp. 237–45.
[8] This is the argument of Mehdi Moslem, *Factional Politics*, p. 4; see also the 'Acknowlegements', in Daniel Brumberg, *Reinventing Khomeini. The Struggle of Reform in Iran*, Chicago: The University of Chicago Press, 2001.
[9] The following after Barzin, *Jenah-bandi-ye siyasi*, p. 95; and Buchta, *Who Rules Iran*, pp. 14 and 81.

Traditional Right, (Conservatives, Traditionalists) centred around the *Mo'talefeh* organization and its aligned (*hamsu*) groups, like the *Association of Combatant Clerics*
Modernist or *Moderate Right*, centred around the *Kargozaran-e Sazandegi*,
Islamic left, comprising a variety of groups and parties, the main ones being the *Hezb-e Mosharekat-e Iran-e Eslami, Sazeman-e Mojahedin-e Enqelab-e Eslami*, and the clerical organization *Majma'-e Ruhaniyan-e Mobarez*
Hezbollah, also *New Radical Islamic left* and later *New Radical Islamic Right*; now *Neo-Fundamentalists*, their main organizations: *Ansar-e Hezbollah*, Society for the defence of revolutionary values;

Tolerated Factions, no presence in the power apparatus or in the parliament, but important because they occasionally contribute to the political debate and/or can provide manpower with regards to voter mobilization:
Nationalists, including liberals, main organization is the *Nehzat-e Azadi* (Liberation Movement) (Mosaddeq-Tradition)
Student organizations; main organization is *Tahkim-e Vahdat*
Intellectuals, around the newspapers *Kiyan* and *Iran-e Farda*

This classification is on the whole still valid, but factions have re-aligned. With Khatami's electoral success the reformists' 'Second of Khordad Front' came to comprise the moderate right and the Islamic left, including prominent individuals from Hezbollah. This Front garnered support from all tolerated factions and finally coalesced into the 'Green Movement' or 'Green Struggle' with the 2009 elections. As a countermove, the Traditional Right united with Hezbollah and created the new 'principalist' block (see below). Thus, the alignment of factions into the left-leaning 'reformist' block and the right-wing 'principalist' block has become a constant feature of Iranian politics since the Khatami presidency. However, the importance of factions has not ceased. Factions are, and remain, the main outlet for the political process and political organization as will be shown presently.

The Importance of Political Factions

In this chapter I use the term '(political) faction' for the Persian *jenah*, literally 'wing,'[10] which is by far the most widely used term, others being *teyf*, 'spectrum', *jarayan* 'current', and *harakat* 'movement', but also *ordugah* '(military) camp'. We have to sharply distinguish this use of 'faction' from

---

[10] Following the definition of 'faction' (*jenah*) by Barzin in *Jenah-bandi-ye Siyasi*, passim.

the 'parliamentary faction' (*fraksyun,* from German *Fraktion*), which will be discussed in its proper context.

A political faction (*jenah*) shall be defined less by its size and more by its degree of visibility to the public and level of transparency. Hence, Iranian factions are situated halfway between 'circles' (*mahfel, dowreh*), which are centred around an influential personality and which are sometimes extremely short lived, and full-fledged political parties, which are registered with the interior ministry and hold public party congresses. This is not the case with factions. Factions are not registered, not mentioned in the constitution, have no juridical persona, and may even lack an official name. And yet, they are certainly more important than parties, and as such, they form a core element of Iran's political reality. Factions are definitely larger and more stable than mere circles, but they are much less transparent than parties. Factions consist of a leading or a steering element composed of a small circle of influential personalities forming a *noyau dur* or the centre of gravity of the faction. Factions also usually draw adherents from multiple networks, interest groups, and parties (on this see below). In this sense, a faction is a loosely knit organizational unit. Members of the faction share the same political views, and in most cases, the same sociological and often the same professional background. Factions have strong political identities and, thus, they are sharply and easily delimitated from other factions, although in individual cases criss-crossing of factional limitations may well occur (such as the arch-Hezbollahi Ali Akbar Mohtashamipur and the Conservative Ali Akbar Nateq Nuri supporting the reformists in 2009). In other cases, especially in the case of factions whose members trace their cohesion back to the Iran-Iraq war, there is a strong friend-foe and insider-outsider mentality (*khodi va gheyr-e khodi*).[11]

All factions are well represented in the bureaucracy. In fact, getting hold of elements of the state apparatus and, thereby, gaining access to its financial resources, is one of the faction's most important functions. It is primarily their dominant role in the bureaucracy that enables factions to exert influence and provide patronage (*parti-bazi*). In this sense, members of the political factions have replaced the pre-revolutionary upper class, which previously could grant patronage.[12] In general, it is quite possible to identify the influence of political factions in certain institutions like research institutes, departments of ministries, but also newspapers and, most importantly, internet sites and blogs, through which the factions try to convince the public of their own positions.

Needless to say, due to the interwoven nature of factions and institutions, competition among factions is difficult to distinguish from inter-institutional

---

[11] Navid Kermani, 'The Fear of the Guardians. 24 Army Officers Write a Letter to President Khatami', in *The Twelver Shia in Modern Times, Religious Culture and Political History*, Werner Ende and Rainer Brunner (eds), Leiden: Brill, 2001, pp. 354–64.

[12] For this term and general on protection in the Iranian society see William O. Beeman, *Language, Status and Power in Iran*, Bloomington: Indiana University Press, 1986, pp. 48–50 and passim.

competition or bureaucratic infighting, similar to that in other political systems. Networks belonging to a faction may also span several institutions, as in the case of the network of former deputy intelligence minister Mostafa Purmohammadi.[13] But factions may also include important members who do not hold any official position, but for several reasons wield considerable influence (like Ali Akbar Hashemi Rafsanjani within the moderate Conservatives). The support of these holders of 'informal power" is important in the case of decisions that require popular support. Since the public lies outside the official lines of communication, only the factions can provide the necessary information to garner the needed support for such decisions.

Factions also differ in their degree of visibility. Some factions have successfully hidden their existence from the public eye and, while not actually acting clandestinely, are perceived to be nothing more than some radical fringe elements, despite their real importance within the factional system. This applies to the Hezbollah faction, including the semi-clandestine organization *Ansar-e Hezbollah* as well as the circles from which president Ahmadinejad hails: hence the analysts' surprise at his election. But this is rather rare and has changed with the Ahmadinejad presidency anyway. In general, at least some members of the factions, as well as media and clerical figures that are aligned with them or are supportive of their positions, are known to the public.

Competition among factions is fierce and aims to alter the political conduct of the ruling faction, or to acquire political and bureaucratic positions held by opponents, or both. Violence can also occasionally occur. For example, this was the case in the 1990s when Khatami's liberal positions were challenged with the help of the so-called 'chain murders' (*qatlha-ye zanjireh'i*) and an open threat of a coup from the Iranian Revolutionary Guard Corps (IRGC) generals, all of whom belonged to competing political factions. Needless to say, violence is not the preferred way to regulate competition. Mediation by the Supreme Leader's office is another possibility. The Supreme Leader's representatives are present at all layers of the bureaucracy, which keeps his own apparatus up-to-date on internal political debates. This allows the leadership to intervene as a mediator in a timely manner in order to prevent institutional stalemate. Owing to the nature of the Iranian factional system such mediation also includes mediation between the factions. This is also necessary because the system and the representation of the political factions are evenly balanced; therefore, it is almost impossible to ameliorate one faction's position in the bureaucracy. There are only two exceptions to this rule: the presidency and the parliament. If victorious, the winning faction can use its power via the presidency or the parliament to curtail the influence of competing factions and to position its members throughout the bureaucracy. A widely held view has it that the Iranian system hindered President Khatami from doing precisely this and, thus, prevented him from staffing all bureaucratic positions with his followers. This sounds plausible given the fierce resistance against him personally and against the Islamic left and the reformists

---

[13] See below.

in general. However, the fact that his opponents had to rely on violence can be read as proof to the contrary. In any case, elections are the primary means to compete and to measure the popularity of one's own positions within the population. This is where the political parties enter the mix.

Parties and Elections

Political parties are not the primary player in Iranian politics and in the vast majority of cases parties belong to one of the political factions. Political parties in Iran are notoriously weak and very few of them maintain a strong party structure throughout the country. Thus, there is nothing akin to a European *Volkspartei* (mass party); this role if at all, would be played by the faction – if Iranian factions were more transparent and registered with the interior ministry.

Weakness of Political Parties

The weakness of Iranian political parties is only partially due to the system's unwillingness to allow their emergence; historic reasons play a role as well. Modern Iran simply has no history of multiparty democracy worthy of such a name. The moderate centre could only choose between pro-regime parties—and towards the end a totalitarian pro-regime mass party, the *Rastakhiz*[14] —and parties of the radical opposition like the Communists, certain Marxist and Islamist sects, or separatist parties. In other words, there was never real democratic competition between democratic forces (like centre-left and centre-right) within the same political system because opposition was always tantamount to opposition to the system as a whole. Hence, the existence of lively competition in the Islamic Republic within the same system indeed represents progress from a democratic perspective. Apart from the lack of historic precedent, Khomeini's followers had a negative experience with their own party, the Islamic Republican Party (IRP). The IRP was intended to become the main political party for Khomeini's followers, but it failed to reconcile their divergent positions and views, notably on the economy, and it finally broke apart roughly along the lines of today's political factions.[15] Needless to say, once his own party was unable to become the main tool for political influence, Khomeini's willingness to allow the existence of other parties, especially those which were better organized, rapidly declined. This included non-Islamist parties like the communist Tudeh, other Islamist parties, and ethnically based parties. Only towards the end of Rafsanjani's second term was a new debate on political parties in Iran conducted. This debate had the relationship between political parties and the *velayat-e faqih* at its centre. However, it

---

[14] Jean-Pierre Digard, Bernard Hourcade, Yann Richard, *L'Iran Au XXe Siècle*, Paris: Fayard, 1996, pp. 138f.

[15] On the Islamic Republican Party see Yann Richard, *Geschichte der Schia in Iran. Grundlagen einer Religion*, Berlin: Wagenbach, 1989, pp. 151–57; on its dissolution see Schirazi, *Constitution*, pp. 128f.; Digard et.al., *L'Iran Au XXe Siècle*, p. 201.

ended inconclusively because many important figures doubted the value and usefulness of political parties for an Islamic system like Iran's.[16] The result was a hybrid situation straddling the spectrum between an open party arrangement and a fully authoritarian system. On the one hand, a law was promulgated regulating the creation of political parties, but this did not amount to the opening of the political sphere,[17] ideological control dominated, as illustrated by requirements such as mandating that all parties add 'of Islamic Iran' to their name in order to make clear there would be no secularist 'deviation'. On the other hand, even those who were the most outspoken against political parties *per se*, like the once almighty conservative *Mo'talefeh* 'Confederation' and its aligned organizations (*hamsu*) or the ultra-*Hezbollahi*s surrounding former intelligence minister Mohammad Reyshahri, registered as political parties. In itself, this has been a positive step towards more transparency.

Faction and Party

In spite of their structural weaknesses, political parties are important supporting elements for the factions. As might be expected, parties contribute manpower for campaigning. This is important in a country which lacks many structures for social mobilization apart from religious societies (*hey'at*). Hence, parties help promote the political views, positions and candidates of the factions to the public. Parties also enable local elites throughout the country to connect with the leading circles of the factions, which in turn allows the factions to discover political talent in a timely manner. However, even if parties are created on behalf of the factions, they quickly develop an independent identity that grows stronger from one electoral campaign to the next. For instance, the reformist camp has been a loose coalition of diverse political forces dominated by political parties from the Islamic left and the modernist right. This coalition held together through Khatami's two presidential mandates and is still maintaining cohesion in Ahmadinejad's second term. As a result, a new common 'reformist' identity developed. Had Mir Hoseyn Musavi won the presidential election of 2009, one could legitimately speculate whether the now strengthened reformist identity would have superseded its adherents' former individual political identities, thereby giving way to the development of a mass party. However, several parties were singled out and persecuted separately and, consequently, their particular identities were strengthened, as exemplified by the *Mojahedin-e Enqelab-e Eslami* and the *Mosharekat* par-

---

[16] On the suppression of political parties under Khomeini and on the new debate see Schirazi, *Constitution*, pp. 124–35; see also Sa'id Hajjariyan, 'Jaygah-e ahzab dar nezam-e Jomhuri-ye Eslami' [The place of political parties in the System of the Islamic Republic], and 'Nezam-e hezbi, mokammel-e nezam-e parlemani' [The Party system as a completion to the parliamentary system] in idem, *Jomhuriyat: Afsunzadayi az Qodrat*, Tehran: Tarh-e Now, 1379/2000, pp. 182–84 and 223–32, respectively, and Mohammad Quchani, *Naziabadiha* [The People from Naziabad], Tehran: Sara'i, 1383/2004, pp. 89–92.
[17] Lahiji, *Peluralizm*, pp. 83–103.

ties, both of which suffered terribly during the 2009 crackdown and most of whose members are now in exile. Other parties, like Reyshahri's 'Society for the Defence of Revolutionary and Islamic Values' and Mehdi Karrubi's *E'temad- e Melli* (National Trust) are, in principle, parties that revolve around their front men and, as a result, these parties share their political fate with their leaders' personal political standing. Although Iran's system of political parties is underdeveloped and politics as well as policy are still conducted informally within the factions, the trend towards a stronger role for political parties has only accelerated.

We have already mentioned the role of the elections in general and the crackdown after the 2009 in sharpening party identity. To this one has to add two more facts. First, President Ahmadinejad brought elements onto the political stage that had previously eluded public attention; he even created platforms like *Khedmat* and *Abadgaran* in order to have an outlet for gathering support.[18] But, with more and more people from his camp becoming known to the public, the most important feature of political factions in general and of his radical *Hezbollahi* faction in particular, namely its semi-clandestine nature, vanished. Hence, during the two Ahmadinejad presidencies hitherto unknown networks and relationships of powerful backdoor-men and influential schemers have been exposed to the Iranian public – and many of them have been harshly criticized. Secondly, his policies clearly sharpened political identities within the political right. Originally, the creation of the 'principalist" (*osulgara*) faction was intended to overcome the cleavage between the conservative and radical (*Hezbollah*) right wings. This should have allowed for a stable 2/3 majority for the new faction of the united right in both the parliament and for the presidency.

The Faction in Parliament (fraksyun)

Finally, a comment on the difference between 'faction', 'party', and 'parliamentary faction or *fraksyun*', a German term (*Fraktion*) borrowed from German parliamentary usage. Candidates hailing from a certain faction would be supported by electoral platforms and/or political parties belonging to a certain faction or, as in the case of the reformists, two political factions would join forces and coordinate work with the parties and other aligned networks. Candidates may also run on their own, i.e., without support of any particular political party, but they would not be independents nor wild-card politicians in the strict sense of the word, because after all, they too would depend upon the support of a faction, and once elected to parliament, they would join one of the parliamentary factions (*fraksyun*). In this sense, the parliamentary faction and the presidency are positions for those members of political factions who pass the political popularity test, namely elections. In other words, the *fraksyun* in parliament brings politicians back to their proper factional roots,

---

[18] www.khedmat.ir; Sadegh Zibakalam, *Abadgaran: A Preliminary Study of the New Generation of Hard-Line Conservatives in Iran*, September 2004; the Abadgaran's website is inaccessible.

thereby devaluating the role of political parties once more. Two examples shall clarify this point. The first example refers to the reformists; the second to the principalists.

We have already described the reformists as a coalition of various groups, parties, and networks that span two factions, the moderate right and the Islamic left. Once elected to parliament, the reformists would join a faction with the revolutionary name of *Khatt-e Emam*, i.e., the 'Line of the Imam' (Khomeini). There is hardly any better name than *Khatt-e Emam*, which was the self-description of the students who took the US diplomats hostage in 1979, thus serving as a salutary recognition of the reformist camp's ideological roots. The question arises whether a reformist platform under the revolutionary name of 'Line of the Imam' would stand a chance with the liberal part of its constituency at elections. The magnitude of the cleavage between the faction and the *fraksyun* on one hand, and the followers of the spontaneous Green Movement on the other, can be seen in the *fraksyun*'s reaction in the aftermath of the 2009 crackdown. The *fraksyun* tried to tread a careful line between openly endorsing the movement and distancing itself from both the protesting masses and their leading candidates. In other words, the reformists want to have it both ways: liberal towards the broader public and revolutionary towards the system as a whole.

The 2008 parliamentary elections provide a second example of how much more important the parliamentary *fraksyun* is than the political party. These elections were conducted as a great test run for the newly created 'principalist' (*osulgara*) faction, which sponsored two electoral platforms, 'The United Front of Principalist Forces' (pro-Ahmadinejad conservatives and Hezbollahis) and the 'Broad Coalition of Principalists' (anti-Ahmadinejad conservatives, some Hezbollahis and modernist right). The 'Broad Coalition' was created for the express purpose of garnering votes from sympathizers within the reformist camp, whose candidates were blocked. Given the existence of two different principalist electoral platforms, voters could expect them to join different factions once candidates were elected to parliament. However, after the elections both platforms were quickly disbanded and the elected Majles members joined the faction (*fraksyun*) 'Revolution' (*Enqelab*), which includes both trends.

Hence, taking both examples into consideration, the following model emerges: for a faction to obtain either the presidency or the greatest possible number of seats in parliament, it must work with political parties or electoral platforms. Here the faction would embrace more liberal language for electoral purposes before finding itself represented again in the parliamentary 'fraction', which is in some ways a mirror of the factional reality. Even so, no one can avoid the test of elections.

Elections

Elections are perhaps the best and most important democratic element in the Iranian body politic. There are four kinds of elections in Iran: to the Assembly of Leadership Experts, to the city councils, to parliament, and for the presidency. In this chapter only the latter two are considered. Parliamentary and presidential elections are enshrined in Articles 58 and 114, respectively, of the Iranian constitution. The basis for elections, namely popular sovereignty, can be deduced from the Iranian constitution. According to Article 55, Iranian citizens have a 'divine right of sovereignty' because God 'has made man master of his social destiny' and, therefore, entitled the people to exercise this divine right,[19] hence popular sovereignty is justified theologically, not democratically. As a result, elections are widely regarded as a divine right and anecdotal evidence indicates that this view is extremely strong within the lower-middle classes in Iran. But, elections are both a right and a duty, and most importantly, they are the single key element that can judge the legitimacy of the system. Hence, the system does its best to ensure a high voter turnout, which becomes an informal referendum of sorts on the system's popularity and the authorities regard the notoriously low voter turnout as quite an embarrassment.[20]

Needless to say, elections are the most effective way to defuse intra-elite struggles, whilst simultaneously allowing the participation of the public and maintaining control over the political process. Thus, elections allow the factions to measure the standing of their ideas amongst the wider public. As Güneş Murat Tezcür has shown, despite undeniably positive developments such as the maturation of the political system in Iran, elections in the Islamic Republic of Iran are still very much in the tradition of pre-revolutionary electoral processes.[21] To make a long story short, elections in Iran fall far short of the globally accepted OSCE standards and the electoral system has often been criticized for its non-transparent nature.

Pre-selection of candidates takes place on two levels. First, informally within the factions and second, formally via the Council of Guardians, an institution that is heavily biased against the Islamic left and, thus, facilitates the candidature of conservative and right-wing candidates. Rigging occurs regularly, although it is not necessarily the factor determining the outcome of the race. In the end, elections allow for real political emotions and passions which sometimes get out of control, as one could see with the 2009 electoral unrest.

Before the Storm: Build-up of the Anti-Reform Coalition

The tenth presidential elections in 2009 can best be understood as a final step in a great rollback against the reformists. This rollback comes after the Iranian

---

[19] For an English translation of the Iranian constitution see
<http://www.servat.unibe.ch/icl/ir00000_.html>;
see also Silvia Tellenbach, *Untersuchungen zur Verfassung der Islamischen Republik Iran vom 15. November 1979*, Berlin: Klaus Schwarz Verlag, 1985, pp. 76f. (German text) and 205–08 commentary.
[20] Schirazi, *Constitution*, pp 103-06.
[21] Güneş Murat Tezcür, 'Intra-Elite Struggles in Iranian Elections', in *Political Participation in the Middle East*, Ellen Lust-Okar and Sloua Zerhouni (eds), Boulder, CO: Lynne Rienner, 2008, pp. 51–74.

public has been widely disillusioned with the reformists' performance both politically and economically. It also comes under dire economic circumstances which necessitate painful economic reforms and finally, it coincides with a generational change in the political elites. The younger generation of Iranian politicians belongs entirely to the '1360s-generation', that is the generation of those who fought in the Iran-Iraq War (1980–88) and, thus, have a military background of sorts, be it Army (*artesh*), IRGC (*sepah*) or Mobilization Force (*Basij*).[22] Politically, most of them belong to the *Hezbollah* faction and refer directly to the *Feda'iyan-e Eslam* tradition.[23] Their rise has been misinterpreted as a 'military' (read revolutionary Guards) 'takeover of Iran'. Yet one cannot deny the fact that a securitization of the regime is ongoing with former administrators and intelligence – not military – operatives playing a crucial role in it. Finally, we have to underscore the importance of longstanding feuds in which personal and political motives are conflated. This aspect is important because Iranians are aware of these feuds and take knowledge about them for granted; hence they are part of their frame of reference.

Towards the Backlash: Motivation and First Attempts

The events leading up to the 2009 climax cannot be understood without considering the shockwave that the Khatami's two presidential terms sent through the political establishment. For once the radical Islamic left, which Khameneh'i and Rafsanjani so successfully sidelined in the late 1980s, made a triumphant comeback with a set of new, democratic ideas,[24] rendering them more attractive and almost unbeatable at elections. Even worse, they joined

---

[22] The world view and ideals of the volunteers of the war have been analysed by Farhad Khosrokhavar, *L'Utopie sacrifiée. Sociologie de la révolution iranienne*, Paris: Presses de Sciences Po, 1993 and idem *L'Islamisme et la mort, Le martyr révolutionnaire en Iran*, Paris: L'Harmattan, 1995; on the importance of this generation for Iran's domestic politics see Farideh Farhi, 'The Antinomies of Iran's War Generation', in *Iran, Iraq, and the Legacies of the War*, Lawrence B. Potter and Gary G. Sick (eds), New York: Palgrave Macmillan, 2004, pp. 101–20.
[23] The *Feda'iyan-e Eslam* were one of the most important Islamist organizations of Iran, active in the 1940s and 1950s. They have often been reduced to their role as rightist hit-men and terrorists. This is certainly true, however they played a crucial albeit violent role in Iranian politics. Publications on the Feda'iyan have mushroomed inside Iran in the last years. Works of reference are Davud Amini, *Jam'iyat-e Feda'iyan-e Eslam va naqsh-e an dar tahavollat-e siyasi ejtema'i-ye Iran* [The Society of the Islamic Feda'iyan and their role in Iranian Politics and Society], Tehran: Entesharat-e Markaz-e Asnad-e Enqelab-e Eslami, 1381/2002; and Sohrab Behdad, 'Utopia of Assassins: Navvab Safavi and the Fada'ian-e Eslam in Prerevolutionary Iran', in *Iran. Between Tradition and Modernity*, Ramin Jahanbegloo (ed.), Boulder, CO: Lexington Books, 2004, pp. 71–94.
[24] With the notable exception of Brumberg, *Reinventing Khomeini*, almost no in-depth analysis detailing the reasons for the de-radicalization of Iran's Islamic left exists. Alternatively one may compare this development with the experience of idealistic communists in Czechoslovakia between 1945 and 1968; see the role of Ludvik Jahn, the protagonist of Milan Kundera's 1967 novel *Žert* (The Joke).

forces with Ayatollah Rafsanjani and his supporters on the moderate or modernist right, which was—and still is—well entrenched in the bureaucracy. With the enormously popular President Khatami at the helm and backed by a solid 2/3 majority in the 1997 presidential elections and subsequent reformist victories in local and then parliamentary elections, the reformists felt quite assured. History undoubtedly appeared to be on their side. The demise of the once powerful *Mo'talefeh* and its aligned clerical organizations like the 'Society of Fighting Clergy' (*Jame'eh-ye Ruhaniyat-e Mobarez*) confirmed the impression of an absolute reformist victory and its longevity. Structurally speaking, they would have been able to unsettle the balance of power within the political factions. Again, as seen from a purely structuralist and factional perspective, the system had to counterbalance.

The repercussions of a perpetuated Islamic left plus moderate right electoral union under a reformist banner (the so called 'Second of Khordad Front' and the popular name 'Eslah-talaban' reformists) were tremendous. They strengthened both factions to the detriment of all others, notably the traditional conservatives and the *Hezbollah* groups. In the long run, this meant that the reformists would further boost their position and increasingly acquire many more key positions in the bureaucracy and the state apparatus. In a candid interview given in 2010, former deputy intelligence minister Mostafa Purmohammadi confirms the political right's fear of the 'Second Khordad' movement's stable majority which could result in permanently sidelining the political right and their eventual exclusion from the political process. After all, the reformists not only dominated government and the parliament, but also the media.[25] Purmohammadi admitted to another aspect: since many of the supporters of Khatami, like Sa'id Hajjarian belonged to the intelligence community themselves, they did not trust Purmohammadi and his kindred spirits who were 'of *hezbollahi* and *arzeshi*-revolutionary conviction' and did their best to purge them from the 'IRGC, the ministry of intelligence and revolutionary foundations' where they were well entrenched. So, the motives were both ideological-factional and institutional.[26]

Towards the end of the first Khatami presidency, the anti-reformist camp was certainly in disarray. The *Mo'talefeh*, although still a pillar of the conservatives' influence with many of its members well entrenched in high positions, had been weakened and was forced to reconstitute itself as a political party under the same name for its traditionalist constituency,[27] and as a party

---

[25] See 'Purmohammadi: Beh Musavi goftam: 'alayem-e khatar mibinam' [I told Musavi: I see signs of danger], *Tabnak*, 8 Esfand 1388/27 February 2010.
[26] Personal animus played a role too: Purmohammadi complained that the reformists would incorrectly connect him to the 'chain murder affair'. Ibid.
[27] On this painful process see Mohammad Quchani, 'Hey'ati keh hezb shod' [The society that became a Party], in *Pedar-kh^{v}andeh va rastha-ye javan, Oful-e eslah-talaban va zohur-e osulgarayan* [The Godfather (i.e.,Rafsanjani) and the New Right: the demise of the Reformists and the rise of the Principalists], Tehran: Sara'i, 1385/2006, pp. 157–62.

under the name *Jam'iyat-e Isargaran-e Iran-e Eslami* for the younger generation of conservatives.[28] A similar development already affected some of the more radical groups in the neo-fundamentalist faction. For example, former intelligence czar Reyshahri created a political party called 'Society for the Defence of Revolutionary Values' (*Jam'iyat-e Defa' as Arzesh-ha-ye Enqelab-e Eslami, Arzesh*) that remained on the radical left of the Islamist spectrum. Given Reyshahri's background, he was most likely to draw personnel from the intelligence community. Although Reyshahri's party failed miserably in the 1995 parliamentary elections, the party was echoing the demands of a political current within what later came to be dubbed the neo-fundamentalists. And, in spite of the relative failure at the ballot box, Reyshahri's party must have had a significant following amongst members of the younger radical generation who collectively called themselves the 'value-oriented groups' (*goruhha-ye arzeshi*). As *arzeshiha* these young people have gained a political identity of their own.[29]

Other groups referred explicitly to the *Feda'iyan-e Eslam* tradition and the long Iran-Iraq war. One of them was *Ansar-e Hezbollah*, which initially consisted of war veterans. The Iranian public soon learnt about the existence of an extensive network of vigilantes with excellent access to high members of the clergy and the security apparatus,[30] as the aforementioned groups did not eschew the use of force to correct 'wrongs' in the society in their attempt to remedy 'false', namely reformist, policies.

It is most likely that the odious 'chain murder affair' originated from these circles. Although much has been published on the topic, it is far too early to make a final historic assessment of this affair.[31] As viewed through the factional lens, we understand the affair as the last round in which some individuals within the traditional conservative faction mustered the support of the Hezbollah hit-men to promote their common interests, namely disrupting Khatami's policy of cautious liberalization. Another, similarly dramatic, intervention occurred after the student-driven unrest in 1999 when twenty-four

---

[28] Seyyed Ammar Kalantari, 'Mardi qadd-bolandtar az jenah-e rast, baz-kh^{v}ani-ye zohur-e Ahmadinejad' [A man taller than the right wing? A Review of the appearance of Ahmadinejad], *Ayandeh,* 19 Farvardin 1388/8 April 2009; see their website at <http://www.isargaran.com/>.

[29] < http://www.arzeshiha.ir/ >.

[30] This is not the place to detail the shadow empire of Iran's vigilantes. The standard study is Michael Rubin, *Into the Shadows: Radical Vigilantes in Khatami's Iran,* Washington, DC: WINEP, 2001. I have utilized and slightly updated his main arguments in Walter Posch, 'Islam und Religion in Iran oder Schiismus als Politik', in *Islam, Islamismus und islamischer Extremismus: Eine Einführung,* Walter Feichtinger and Sybille Wentker (eds), Vienna-Cologne-Weimar: Böhlau, 2008, pp. 108–21.

[31] The so-called 'chain murders' were conducted in the 1990s against Tehrani liberals, Kurdish ulema and Christian priests; for a good Iranian source see Emadeddin Baqi, *Terazhedi-ye demokrasi dar Iran. Bazkh^{v}ani-ye qatlha-ye zanjireh'i* [The Tragedy of Democracy in Iran: the chain murders reconsidered], Tehran: Nashr-e Ney, 2 vols., 1379/2000.

IRGC officers threatened Khatami with an intervention in politics.[32] Both interventions were of only limited success. They certainly had their impact on Khatami personally and on the standing of the reformist government. However, they did nothing to change political realities; on the contrary, Khatami strengthened his grip on the intelligence ministry when he sacked minister Qorban Ali Dorri Najafabadi.[33] In the end, in spite of all its faults and weaknesses, terror and threats could not stop the political process. Hence, if right-wing conservatives and populist *Hezbollahi*s wanted to prevail over the reformists, they had to fight them politically. And to accomplish this, a new platform and fresh ideas were needed.

Towards a New Framework

Previous attempts to create a new framework for the *Hezbollahi*s failed under Reyshahri, obviously due to his still very left-leaning position concerning the economy.[34] Yet such a platform was direly needed. An inclusive platform should have offered a political home for all discontented forces including the conservatives, the *arzeshi*s and *Hezbollahi*s, and their aligned pressure groups and some high-brass IRGC officers. Former intelligence minister Purmohammadi laid the organizational foundations for such an alliance.[35] After leaving the ministry, Purmohammadi met periodically with discontented conservative politicians, like Larijani and Nateq Nuri. Their task was to cobble together a strong alliance between conservatives and *Hezbollahi*s, similar to the reformist alliance. This was not an easy endeavour because the *Hezbollahi*s and the conservatives hail from different social strata and the relationship between both groups has been strained at times. It is important to understand that in contrast to the conservatives or the traditional right, the *Hezbollah* camp never held prominent high positions in the Iranian power apparatus, hence the reference to 'fringe' and 'radical' groups. The traditional right would eagerly use their services to intimidate the Islamic liberals, but otherwise was very content to see the *Hezbollah* remain on the extremist fringe of the political spectrum while the traditional right occupied the centre. However, with the formation of a new alliance, this relationship changed because the formerly opposing camps were now up to forming a common faction based on equality. Even more, within the newly formed right camp the 'angry young men',[36] as they have been called, were on the rise, that is, to the detriment of the traditional conservatives.

---

[32] Cf. Kermani, 'The Fear of the Guardians'.
[33] Barbara Slavin, *Bitter Friends and Bosom Enemies. Iran, the US and the Twisted Path to Confrontation*, New York: St Martin's Press, 2007, pp. 104f.
[34] See Mohammad Quchani, 'Bonyadgarayan ba modernha amadan', in *Pedarkh^{v}andeh va rastha-ye javan*, pp. 168–78.
[35] The following is based on 'Purmohammadi'.
[36] Mohammad Quchani, 'Farzandan-e khashm' [Angry young men], in *Pedar kh^{v}andeh va chapha-ye javan. Mobarezeh bara-ye naqd-e qodrat Dey 78-Khordad 79* [The God-

In order to roll back the reformists, they had to challenge them on several levels, the ballot box being just one of them. They also had to confront the reformists on the factional and institutional levels and most importantly, they had to drive a wedge between reformists hailing from the Islamic left and those close to Rafsanjani, whom the *Hezbollahi*s thoroughly hated (see below). The traditional conservatives of the *Mo'talefeh* at times also criticized Rafsanjani because they found certain aspects of his economic liberalization worrisome. But, most importantly, they could not forgive him for having forged an alliance with the left. However, both groups were united in their critique against President Seyyed Mohammad Khatami who had already been forced to step down as minister for culture, higher education and Islamic guidance in an earlier government, allegedly for being too liberal. When he became president, his policies were either criticized for being too intellectual, and hence out of tune with the needs of the people, misguided, or even a deviation from the path of the revolution. In the end, Khatami must have lost the support of key figures at the top of the political hierarchy, as indicated by remarks of politicians like Ali Akbar Velayati, who accused him of being an Iranian Gorbachev.[37] Without a doubt, many in the power apparatus resented his general liberalization policy and intellectual talk of human rights, democracy, and transparency. However, it was likely the economy that counted most. Purmohammadi voiced the political right's widespread discontent with the reformists when he said that the reformist camp lacked 'any plan or programme to address questions regarding the development of the country' and that the reformists would rather indulge in propagandistic language instead of offering clear and sound proposals.[38]

Indeed, rising public discontent over the social situation made the opportunity to roll back the reformists a real one. But, elections were still essential and before an electoral victory could be envisioned, re-structuring the political right was necessary. The first step in this restructuring consisted of creating a proper platform. The original plan to create a political party was quickly abandoned, thus a 'Coordination Council of the Forces of the Revolution' (*Shura-ye hamahangi-ye Niruha-ye Enqelab*) was created, initiated by Purmohammadi. This council would soon become the main framework for conservatives and the *Hezbollahi* forces. The 'Coordination Council' was operational in 1999 and prepared for the city council elections, for which purpose Purmohammadi travelled throughout the country in order to garner support. The Tehran group of the Council was organized by another former administrator with close ties to the intelligence community, Mahmoud Ahmadinejad, who was at the same time the executive secretary of the 'Coordination Coun-

---

father (i.e., Rafsanjani) and the young Left. Struggle for Political Hegemony December 1999 to May 2000], Tehran: Nashr-e Ney, 1379/2001, pp. 64–71.
[37] Hajjarian, 'Ankeh fekrash gereh az kar-e jahan begoshayid' [So that his thoughts might overcome the problems of the world], in *Jomhuriyat*, pp. 545–53.
[38] 'Purmohammadi'.

cil'.³⁹ His group, the *E'telaf-e Abadgaran-e Iran-e Eslami,* had already developed its own individual political identity and had declined to join forces with Reyshahri in the mid-1990s. The fact that they had been invited by Reyshahri proves their affiliation with the *Hezbollahi*s rather than with the traditional conservative faction.⁴⁰ As a result, it enjoyed greater autonomy, but Purmohammadi insists that it was basically the Coordination Council's group in Tehran. After their electoral success in the city council elections the Tehran group kept its name and assumed its own identity, thus obfuscating its relationship with the Coordination Council. The 2003 city council elections of Tehran were Ahmadinejad's great chance. Back then the public was already frustrated with the reformist governments' performance and voters abstained from the election in great numbers. Under these circumstances Ahmadinejad, who successfully mobilized the maximum support from right-wing forces, obtained a victory. Very much to the surprise of everybody, including the Supreme Leader who travelled to Sistan and Baluchistan instead of casting his ballot for the City Council elections in Tehran,⁴¹ lest he live through another reformist victory.

Principalists **(osulgarayan)**: *The New Right*

The city council elections of 2003 had three main results. First, they marked the real beginning of Ahmadinejad's political career because from now on, he would have the resources of the Tehran city council at his disposal, including the mass daily newspaper *Hamshahri*. And, it would also allow his supporters to accrue administrative experience outside the intelligence apparatus. Second, they signified the integration process of the more radical *Hezbollahi* groups and, thus, diminished their reliance on violence. And third, by the time of the elections the two factions—*Hezbollah* and Traditional Conservatives—had joined forces and developed towards a new concept while maintaining their distinct identities. This also meant that the *Hezbollahi*s now became equal partners of the conservatives, which in itself was a dramatic change in their relationship.

In order to unify all divergent trends in both factions the name 'principalist' (*osulgara*), which had previously been promoted by Meh-di Nasiri, a former editor of *Keyhan* and later *Sobh* newspapers, was adopted,⁴² which is the reason why the continued existence of the 'Coordination Council' is often overlooked. As the new principalist entity earnestly attempted to become a serious power, it had to avoid the risk of disintegrating along factional lines. This had happened with the Islamic Republican Party, as well as Reyshahri's stillborn attempt to unify the *Hezbollah* and *arzeshi* forces. In both cases divergent views on the economy had led to the disintegration. Hence, a new discourse had to be formulated.

---

³⁹ Kalantari, 'Mardi qadd bolandtar'.
⁴⁰ Quchani, 'Bonyadgarayan', p. 171.
⁴¹ Kalantari, 'Mardi qadd bolandtar'.
⁴² Moslem, *Factional Politics*, p. 136.

In contrast to the bazaari-minded conservatives, much of the *Hezbollah*'s social populist attitudes and language against the 'rich' were maintained, implicitly accusing the 'rich' for having practically 'stolen' their wealth from the disfavoured layers of the society, the *mostaz'afin*. But only so long as they would utilize this language in order to channel their social frustration against those like Rafsanjani. Beyond that the *Hezbollahi*s had to abandon whatever was reminiscent of class struggle in their political language, which eased, to a certain degree, the socially based conflict of interest between the two factions, forming one.

The broad outlines of economic reform have been a consensual decision on behalf of the whole system. Obviously, economic modernization meant privatization and liberalization. However, there was a general fear of the interdependent nature of economic and political liberalization, something the reformists wanted to embrace. Another problem was the conservatives' bazaari constituency's fear of both too much liberalization and too much state intervention. As such, the bazaari constituency pushed for a middle-of-the-road approach. Ahmad Tavakkoli, a renowned Iranian economist and politician from the fundamentalist camp, formulated a compromise position which would allow for both privatization and economic activity on behalf of private individuals, but only if sanctioned by the state.[43] This solution was warmly received by the IRGC which has not hesitated to increase its stake in the Iranian economy over the last few years. In the end, perhaps without knowing it, Tavakkoli's economic-ideological 'solution' was nothing but a mirror image of Iran's political system: economic activity is allowed as long as the factions whose members are well placed throughout the government administration can properly benefit from it. And, for this the system had to be purged of reformists and the most prominent positions had to be filled with the 'right' people, be they *Hezbollahi*s, who previously had never been in such key positions, or conservatives who had lost or where about to lose their positions. Once power and control ended up in the hands of the right people, they would eschew economic adventures and tacitly adopt a sounder economic policy, such as cutting subsidies. Therefore Ahmadinejad even cites 'imperialist' institutions like the World Bank and the International Monetary Fund for lauding Iran's measures to cut subsidies.[44] Thus, the year 1390/2011 marks the final breakthrough for economic rationalism properly couched in revolutionary Khomeinist language: the 'Year of the Economic Jihad'. Clearly, the invisible hand of the market also prevails in the Islamic Republic, or more importantly, in the Supreme Leader's office.

---

[43] Mohammad Quchani, 'Az Sosyalizm takhayyoli ta mohafezehkari-ye enqelabi' [From illusionary socialism to revolutionary conservativism], *Pedar Kh^{v}andeh, va rast-ha-ye javan, Oful-e Eslah-talaban va zohur-e osul-garayan* [The Godfather and the New Right: the demise of the Reformists and the rise of the Fundamentalists], Tehran: Sara'i, 1385/2006, pp. 196–99.

[44] 'Ahmadinejad Calls Iran new Economic Power', *Fars*, 16 May 2011.

Divergent views on the economy could have seriously harmed the new-found unity. But economic policy is not the sole motivation for the *osulgarayan*. The next common feature for both factions was and is their unwavering support for a most rigid reading of the 'absolute' powers of the Supreme Leader (*Velayat-e faqih-e motlaq*). This too was a genuine *Hezbollahi* contribution to the political debate because the traditional conservatives – quite traditionally – would rather stick with the plurality of the *marja*'s who are the most high-ranking ayatollahs. It was also one of the most contested topics to fight over between authors from the Islamic left like Hajjarian and their right-wing contenders.[45] For the conservatives and the more realistic elements among the *Hezbollahi*s, this meant essentially a strengthening of the role of the Supreme Leader's office. For some minority groups, however, fidelity to the Supreme Leader became their very *raison d'être*, sometimes with almost sectarian connotations.[46] These circles were then responsible for much of the violence that occurred in the 2009 electoral unrests.

Another common denominator fusing the two factions together was the fear of the 'cultural onslaught of the West', a moniker coined by Khomeini himself. Instead, honouring the martyrs of the war and attention to Islamic attire in the public space were promoted. It also included two more aspects: the attempt to further Islamicize Iranian universities and the concept of 'soft war'.

Finally, another problem had to be tackled, that of generational change. This was less an issue for the *Hezbollahi*s than it was for the traditional conservatives. Here younger politicians like Gholam-Hoseyn Haddad Adel and

---

[45] See for instance Sa'id Hajjarian, 'Velayat-e faqih-e motlaq va qanun-e asasi' [The absolute rule of the Jurisprudent and the Constitution], in idem, *Jomhuriyat*, pp. 256–78.

[46] Sectarianism and religious hysteria appear to have become a serious phenomenon, especially with the lower classes in Iran. See Anahita Grisoni, 'La survie paradoxale des festivités d'Ashura sous la présidence de Mahmoud Ahmadinejad : Entre contrôle et clientélisme, parmi public et privé', in *L'Iran sous la présidence de Mahmoud Ahmadinejad: Bilan et Perspectives*, Djamshid Assadi (ed.), Paris: L'Harmattan, 2009, pp. 113–28; Mahmoud Sadri and Ahmad Sadri, 'Three Facets of dissent. Cognitive, expressive and traditionalist discourses of discontent in contemporary Iran', in *Iran in the 21st Century: Politics, Economics, & Conflict*, in Homa Katouzian and Hossein Shahidi (eds), London: Routledge, 2008, pp. 63–85. According to one chiliastic belief (not recorded in Sadri and Sadri), a certain 'Seyyed-e Khorasani' with the name of 'Ali' will appear as a forerunner for the messiah (*mahdi*). From the 1990s onwards some in Iran identified the figure of Seyyed Khorasani with Supreme Leader Seyyed Ali Khameneh'i, who originates from Khorasan province. Mainstream clerics including the Supreme Leader himself have time and again refuted any allegations of this kind. Even so in the aftermath of the 2009 crackdown some eccentric circles managed to produce a DVD where not only the Supreme Leader was identified with the Seyyed-e Khorasani but also Lebanon's Nasrallah and Iran's Ahmadinejad were added. Mehdi Karrubi's *Saham News*, put this programme on the internet. Available: http://www.youtube.com/watch?v=-IgMiXzDvtQ&NR=1 (accessed 20 September 2011).

Ali Ardashir Larijani successfully convinced older politicians to step aside allowing new dynamic cadres to compete for seats in the 2004 parliamentary elections. The elder generation, however, was still important since they held the majority in the Council of Guardians which enabled them to ban as many candidates from the Islamic left as they liked. By that date, the principalists were consolidated; the breakthrough came with the 2005 presidential elections, a further consolidation with the 2008 parliamentary elections—but here the first fissures occurred while the rollback against the reformists climaxed in the 2009 presidential elections, ultimately throwing the country into a crisis of legitimacy.

Principal Powers and Weaknesses

The 2004 parliamentary elections were a showcase example of careful canvassing of votes, good organizational skills, and realistic expectations of what the people wanted. The older generation stepped down opening the way for a new generation of politicians whose youngish members used a more modern and moderate language.[47] But, of course, this was underpinned by blocking as many reformist candidates as possible. Thus, in his last year, Khatami faced a hostile parliament. But, the breakthrough for the principalists came with the 2005 presidential elections.

The Principalist Breakthrough

There are two main lessons to be taken from the 2005 elections. First, Ahmadinejad established himself as the paramount politician within the political right, sidelining competitors like Ali Larijani and the former head of the police Mohammad Baqer Qalibaf. There were certainly many contributing factors that counted towards his victory, including his position as the mayor of Tehran which allowed him to make himself known to a wider public audience. However, until now, nothing concrete about the internal reasoning within the principalists is known. Many take allegations that the Supreme Leader himself weighed in in favour of Ahmadinejad and against Qalibaf and Larijani at face value. My own hypothesis is that Ahmadinejad was

a) able to secure a *nihil obstat* on behalf of the Supreme Leader's office (as many others have done) or even active support on behalf of some of the heavyweight administrators therein;

b) he was better entrenched within the *Hezbollah* faction than both of the other right-wing candidates, which was important given the high percentage of *Hezbollahi*s within the *basiji* units, one of the few institutions present nationwide;

c) he became the focal point and only hope for many other groups in and outside the *Hezbollah* faction *sensu strictu*; such as the eccentric Ayatollah

---

[47] Farhad Khosrokhavar, 'The New Conservatives Take a Turn', *Middle East Report* 233, Winter 2004, pp. 24–27.

Mohammad Taqi Mesbah Yazdi's network and some almost sectarian fringe groups; and finally

d) he was able to accumulate the vote of the war veterans and their families, a core constituency, more effectively than any other candidate.

Secondly, the regime was fully aware of the social tensions inside the country and a tendency must have existed to defuse these tensions within the population as well as to divert the anger of the *Hezbollahi*s over what they perceived to be the spread of liberalism in Iran, by scapegoating one of the founding fathers of the Islamic Republic: Ayatollah Ali Akbar Hashemi Bahramani Rafsanjani. Needless to say, we do not know whether such a decision was made formally or whether it just 'happened' in the course of political praxis.

Without a doubt, Rafsanjani's third candidacy for president annoyed those who wanted to see him become less active in politics, or to retire altogether. Thus, he should have left politics and made room for younger blood, such as the Larijani brothers, especially Ali Ardashir Larijani, who himself ran for the presidency in 2005.[48] Rafsanjani's candidacy was a grave mistake from several points of view: First, it was a clear violation of the spirit of the constitution, if not the letter of the law, because limiting the tenure of the president was a wise decision in a region full of lifelong presidents; secondly, from a domestic-policy point of view, it was an irresponsible gamble because the potential damage inflicted upon Rafsanjani's persona by an electoral loss would outweigh the advantage of him being elected president and presiding over a largely hostile parliament. By 2005 the frustration over the social situation had further increased and the wealth possessed by Rafsanjani and his extended family became the symbol for all social injustice in the Islamic Republic, even leading to quips and disruptions of relations amongst the reformists themselves.[49] The *Hezbollahi*s, who had their own argument against Rafsanjani, did their best to fan popular discontent. Their resistance against political moderation and economic liberalization predated the reformist victories. By the early 1990s, some of the *Hezbollahi*s were already accusing Rafsanjani of promoting corruption by liberalizing the economy and betraying the revolution through his conduct of a relatively moderate foreign policy.[50] The 2005 victory of Ahmadinejad was therefore the first real triumph for the *Hezbollah*, which by that date had shown that they enjoyed key political support in the power apparatus and were able and willing to challenge even the most powerful politicians. Rafsanjani never really recovered from this blow in spite of the fact that he continued to play an important role as secretary of the Expediency Council. His opposition to Ahmadinejad and his continued support for the reformists led to his humiliation in the summer of 2009 and his ultimate loss

---

[48] For the Larijanis' as a new 'power-house' in the Iranian body politic see Mohammad Quchani, 'Baradaran-e Larijani' [The Larijani brothers] in idem, *Pedar Kh^{y}andeh va chapha-ye javan* [The Godfather and the new Left],Tehran: Nashr-e Ney, pp. 42–47.
[49] Barbara Slavin, *Bitter Friends*, p. 114.
[50] Mehdi Moslem, *Factional Politics*, pp. 137–138.

of his position as speaker of the Assembly of Leadership Experts. These political failures were the result of an old struggle which lasted for more than two decades, but the ultimate event leading to Rafsanjani's downfall was the outcome of the 2005 presidential election which allowed the younger generation to wrest power from the old guard.

The principalist victory of 2005 was a seminal moment because it gravely weakened Rafsanjani and allowed a part of the *Hezbollahi*s to ascend to high positions in the administration and bureaucracy for the first time. These *Hezbollahi* newcomers replaced experienced old hands, many of whom were deemed to be too close to the reformists. The principalists secured a victory in the 2008 parliamentary elections using, as expected, tried and true methods with only minor adjustments.[51] First, most of the reformist candidates were blocked. Second, a new fundamentalist platform settled on by the younger generation of conservatives, namely Larijani and Reza'i, was set up in order to attract votes from those who otherwise would have supported the reformists. Finally, once elected, both lists would reunite into one faction ensuring an absolute principalist majority. But, one thing had changed between the two elections: in 2005 the octogenarian conservatives of the Council of Guardians tended to block reformist candidates on their own initiative; in 2008 and in 2009, on the other hand, these conservatives were left no choice other than blocking reformist candidates. In other words, the relationship between the two right-wing factions has shifted. Thus, a final defeat for the reformists should have been guaranteed in the 2009 presidential elections. The principalists clearly hoped that the reformist camp would weaken itself, perhaps splitting along internal rifts between those hailing from the Islamic left (*Mojahedin-e Enqelab-e Eslami, Mosharekat*) and the *Kargozaran* and other former Rafsanjani followers, and that the Islamic left would split between followers of former President Khatami and the National Trust Party of Mehdi Karrubi. If that scenario had materialized, the principalists could have indeed harboured realistic hopes that their candidate would make the race. The candidacy of Ahmadinejad as the only plausible candidate for the principalist faction made sense for the following reasons: First, he would have competed in the election with or without the backing of the principalists. Second, he was more popular with the masses than most of the other principalist candidates. Third, a decision made by the principalists to deny Ahmadinejad their support would have been tantamount to admitting to having made a mistake when supporting him in the previous elections. Finally, it would have deepened existing fissures and ultimately led to the premature demise of the newly created principalist faction.

---

[51] For a different interpretation of the 2008 parliamentary elections see Kaveh-Cyrus Sanandaji, 'The Eighth Majles Elections in the Islamic Republic of Iran: A Division in Conservative Ranks and the Politics of Moderation', *Iranian Studies*, 42, 2009, pp. 621–48. The problem is the term 'conservative' (*mohafezehkar*), for what the author seems to mean is 'right' (*rast*).

Even so, the reformists would not have stood a chance if it had not been for Seyyed Mohammad Khatami, who in a timely manner made the necessary moves to prevent the reformist coalition from unravelling, while simultaneously correctly estimating a potential reformist candidate's prospects for success.[52] First, Khatami pronounced his own candidature, despite knowing of extremist groups among the *Hezbollah* that would not shy away from using violence if he were elected. Khatami's candidature injected a necessary jolt of enthusiasm into his main organizational base, the *Mosharekat* party. He then retreated and handed his candidacy over to Mir Hoseyn Musavi. This was just another blow against one of the main obstacles hindering fair elections: the Council of Guardians' practice of banning candidates. The Supreme Leader himself rectified the decision to ban Musavi, who after all had been Imam Khomeini's prime minister when he, Khameneh'i, was president in the 1980s. And finally, Khatami was crucial in brokering successful negotiations with the modernist conservatives, thereby completing the old reformist faction. Mehdi Karrubi's decision to campaign supported by the National Trust Party, was reduced to a mere nuisance when it became clear that the powerful and highly efficient women's organizations would support Musavi—thanks to his wife Zahra Rahnavard, who had been active in the women's scene for years. Thus, the reformists were far from a spent force and had to be taken seriously.

The particulars of the conduct of the elections and their immediate aftermath have been dealt with in great detail elsewhere.[53] From a factional point of view, the following observation is important. Musavi, who never belonged to the reformists in the strict sense of the word, but was very well known for his radical leftist and revolutionary attitudes, was the first to claim victory. The important point is not whether indeed he did win or not, but that he had a sufficient number of confidants in the ministry of interior who fed the necessary information to him; after all, this ministry was created under his prime ministership in the year 1984.[54] The countermove came hours later when the final results were proclaimed. By that time it had become clear that members of the united principalist faction were already dominating the intelligence and

---

[52] Developments concerning the run-up to the 2009 presidential elections see Walter Posch, *Prospects for Iran's 2009 Presidential Elections*, Washington DC: Middle East Institute Policy Brief 24, June 2009, available:
http://www.mei.edu/Portals/0/Publications/Posch2.pdf (accessed 20 September 2011).
[53] For an excellent overview see Bernard Hourcade, 'Iran: la difficile marche vers la démocratie', *Differences*, 273, 2010 pp. 21–23; Michel Makinsky, 'L'Iran un an après les présidentielles du 12 juin 2009: une crise de régime … et plus?' *Cahiers de l'Orient*, 99, 2010, pp. 23–72; Walter Posch, *A Last Chance for Iran's Reformists? The 'Green Struggle' Reconsidered* (Working Paper based on a presentation delivered on 17 March 2010 at the European Parliament), SWP Berlin, May 2010.
[54] Back then Musavi had warmly supported Mohammad Mohammadi-Reyshahri's candicacy as first minister of intelligence. On the creation of this ministry see Mohammad Mohammadi-Reyshari, *Khaterehha, Jeld-e sevvom, Ta'sis-e Vazarat-e Ettela'at* [Memoirs, Vol. III, the Creation of the Intelligence Ministry], Tehran: Markaz-e Asnad-e Enqelab-e Eslami, 1388/2009, p. 41.

interior ministries. This said, nothing indicates to us that the tug of war within the political factions inside the intelligence community had abated.

The Rise and the Unlikely Fall of Ahmadinejad

In the beginning of his political career, Ahmadinejad was fully aware that he did not command the most powerful faction within the *Hezbollah,* let alone within the whole political right organized in the principalist faction.[55] True, he had forged a close alliance with the *Jam'iyat-e Isargaran-e Enqelab-e Eslami* (Society of the Self-Sacrificers for the Islamic Revolution) an important political party headed by Gholam-Hoseyn Haddad-Adel, and his election was warmly welcomed by *Ansar-e Hezbollah* and others.[56] However, his relations with the traditional clergy were very weak and mostly limited to the followers of Ayatollah Mesbah Yazdi.[57] Other experts were also hard to come by, something which explains his temporary reliance on crackpot semi-intellectuals like Mohammad-Ali Ramin who became Iran's foremost 'expert' on the Holocaust and Germany, and who appears to have been behind the odious Holocaust conference and much of the anti-Semitic smear campaign in Iran. Furthermore, Ahmadinejad was in a disadvantaged position and relied primarily on old brothers-in-arms from the long war.

As president, Ahmadinejad made a loud entry into politics both domestically and on the international scene. Much of what he said, and more importantly how he said it, derived from his inexperience with the international political and diplomatic scene, inferior preparations conducted by less than excellent advisors, and highflying, almost naïve, idealism. Even so, Ahmadinejad 'functioned' in some crucial ways. For example, at least for a few years he was popular within the lower classes and the war veterans, which made it easier to cut subsidies, an economic necessity that all previous governments had failed to implement. In the foreign policy realm his Third-Worldism did not harm, but rather contributed to Brazil's willingness, together with Turkey, to support the Iranian position on the nuclear issue in 2010. And, given the fact that the broad outline of Iran's nuclear policy had been decided consensually elsewhere anyway, Ahmadinejad's radicalism could have proved helpful in preventing or convincing radical *Hezbollahi*s to stay calm in case a negotiated solution with the international community could have been found. In the cultural field, notably in the field of public morality, he was flexible enough to loosen and tighten control over the liberal segments of the society in such a

---

[55] For Ahmadinejad's biography see Janet Kursawe, 'Mahmoud Ahmadinejad', *Der Orient,* 3, 2005 pp. 345–58; Kasra Naji, *Ahmadinejad: The Secret History of Iran's Radical Leader,* Berkeley: University of California Press, 2008.
[56] Posch, 'Islam und Revolution oder Schiismus als Politik', p. 116.
[57] There is a longstanding allegation according to which Mesbah Yazdi is the spiritual guide of Ahmadinejad. This is not true: first, Mesbah Yazdi is not a *marja',* second, like most *Hezbollahi*s and most officers working in the administration and the security apparatus, the president too emulates Iran's Supreme Leader Ali Khameneh'i as *marja';* and finally, Mesbah Yazdi has distanced himself from Ahmadinejad.

way as to alleviate lower-class and *Hezbollah* grievances without driving the liberals too quickly into despair. In a strange way, perhaps because he knew about his own weaknesses, he and his relative (their children are married) and chief advisor Esfandiar Rahim Masha'i, who heads the presidential office, embraced a set of nationalist positions that previously had been almost exclusively promoted by the secularist nationalists. These stances included making positive remarks about former prime minister Mohammad Mosaddeq when meeting Iranians in the West, retrieving ancient Persian artefacts from European museums and displaying them for a while in Iran, and aggressively embracing Iranian expatriates. These policies smack of 'reformism' in the sense that Ahmadinejad, like the reformist faction before him, wooed support from non-Islamist circles. If properly integrated into the official discourse of the regime, it could have supported the system as a whole.

However, either policy could have been successful only if it had been underpinned by careful back channelling to all relevant circles within the *osulgara* faction. Ahmadinejad did the opposite when he made it clear that he was willing to exert full presidential powers and that he would refuse to accept power-sharing agreements of any kind. The first politicians to be affected by this were the traditional conservatives who had hoped to obtain ministerial seats, as had been the case during the Rafsanjani era. Ahmadinejad did not stop there, and a subsequent sacking spree targeting important politicians from within and outside his government puzzled observers. In 2005, he sacked nuclear negotiator Hasan Ruhani and replaced him with Larijani who, in turn, was demoted in 2007. In 2008, he fired Interior Minister Purmohammadi. Prior to the elections in 2009 he went after the first incumbent of the intelligence ministry, Mohammad Mohammadi Reyshahri, who at that point headed the politically unimportant department of hajj affairs. After the elections he replaced Gholam-Hoseyn Mohseni Ezhe'i as minister of intelligence and in late 2010 he replaced Manuchehr Mottaki with Ali Akbar Salehi, a reformist whom he himself had relieved of his position as ambassador in 2005. There are very few in-depth analyses of these replacements, but they seem too systematic to be overlooked.[58] About half of those mentioned were heavyweights in the Iranian intelligence apparatus (Reyshahri, Purmohammadi, Mohseni Ezhe'i) with clear affiliations with the *arzeshi* and *Hezbollah* groups, the others belonged to the traditional conservatives. But all of them have had direct access to the Supreme Leader, whether on a personal or on an institutional basis. In other words, they could have acted as potential counterweights to the groups Ahmadinejad favours and the policies he advocates.

From a strictly personal point of view, sidelining potential competitors certainly made sense. However, for this political manoeuvre to be successful it had to be undertaken with much tact and grace and it had to avoid annoying

---

[58] Walter Posch, 'Only Personal? The Larijani Crisis Revisited', *Policy Brief* 3, Durham University November 2007; and idem, 'Foreign Minister Mottaki Dismissed and Salehi Installed, New Trends in Iranian Diplomacy before Istanbul Nuclear Talks', *SWP Comment* 2, Berlin, January 2011.

the networks supporting the politicians that were slated to be sidelined. However, this necessary tact is neither *Hezbollahi* style, nor is it Ahmadinejad's. As a result, Ahmadinejad successfully annoyed every important political group associated with political power in Iran. To make matters worse, his reliance on Masha'i, who started to play an increasingly important role and who quickly became the *enfant terrible* of the Islamic Republic's political elite, estranged Ahmadinejad from many of his supporters. Even worse, since Masha'i and Ahmadinejad did not hesitate to expound their own theological knowledge and comment about spiritual matters, they made many enemies within the clerical hierarchy.

Just how big the rift had already become could be seen during the elections of 2009 and their aftermath. During this period of tumult, Ahmadinejad stood strangely aloof from the political process while all those forces that supported him fought the reformists. The actions of Ahmadinejad's supporters contrasted sharply with his absence from the public and his lack of leadership. As president re-elect, he clearly failed the test of mastering a major domestic crisis because he was not able to provide a political framework to accompany and ultimately replace the crackdown. He was also unable to restore calm on the streets or to prevent any of the human rights violations that took place during these turbulent days. He simply was not in charge. As a result, Ahmadinejad and his followers did not play a central role in formulating the three key domestic policies that were tested during those days:

a) He had no say, let alone did he play any direct role, in the humiliation of Rafsanjani, by which an important chapter in the Islamic Republic's history was closed—here the pressure came from certain *Hezbollahi*s;

b) He was not involved in developing either the strategy or tactics for 'combating the soft war', which is a set of policies combining cyber warfare with pressure on dissidents (including clerics and human rights activists) into an ideological framework that takes modern theories on democratization as a point of departure and turns them on their head. This initiative was very much an IRGC and Basiji affair;

c) He was not involved in containing the crackdown and preventing it from spiralling out of control, nor did he play any role at all in forging a potential reconciliation with the reformist camp. This initiative came from the Supreme Leader who largely delegated this task to the Larijani brothers.

In retrospect, 2009 was a pyrrhic victory for Ahmadinejad, who won the presidency but began to lose power. He himself did not see it this way. In spite of having been 'out of command' during what has been the Islamic Republic's most dramatic domestic crisis, and despite being indebted to almost everyone within the political right for his re-election, Ahmadinejad remained obstinate against sharing power with anyone, even in those cases where he, as president, would act on behalf of the nation and the regime. This was especially the case on the nuclear issue, which is viewed as a prelude to a normalization of US-Iranian relations. It is a moot point whether Ahmadinejad had already talked about amelioration of relations or whether Masha'i had indeed sent out feelers to the United States via some intermediates, as rumours indicate. What is important is the conviction that Ahmadinejad and his confidants insisted on being the only ones to benefit from a changed situation. Hence, a countermove had to be expected.

To sum up, there are three main reasons why Ahmadinejad and Masha'i were attacked: their promotion of an 'Iranian school of Islam'; their unwillingness to consider those who ultimately brought them to power and to satisfy their interests; and their attempt to strengthen control over the intelligence apparatus and the economy.

It was this last point that prompted the regime to act, because success in this field would have changed Ahmadinejad's domestic policy from a mere nuisance to a real threat to vested interests. Therefore, the regime counteracted at the proper moment, namely after the subsidies reform was put in place. The time to act came when the president wanted to replace—once again—one of his ministers. This time intelligence minister Hojjat al-Eslam Heydar Moslehi was the one targeted for dismissal. However, on this occasion a pre-emptive reaction came directly from the Supreme Leader's office. On 20 April 2011 Grand Ayatollah Khameneh'i issued a *hokm-e hokumati*, a leadership order overruling his president's decision publicly.[59] From that date onwards a barrage of revelations and attacks in the right-wing press was unleashed on Masha'i, whom Ahmadinejad had hoped to install as a successor. This time Ahmadinejad could not shrug off the attacks as he usually would have done. He also would not abandon Masha'i, whose position became increasingly untenable, while at the same time a witch-hunt of sorts was conducted against his followers and his family. Economic misconduct, administrative incompetence, and cultural laxity which had been graciously overlooked in previous years now became grave political problems, literally destroying the political careers of those who had weighed in their luck with Ahmadinejad.

However, President Ahmadinejad took even this especially dramatic development to be just another engagement in an uphill political battle that he has been fighting since his career began. After a dramatic retreat lasting a few days, President Ahmadinejad regrouped and continued his plan to reshape the government when on 15 May 2011 he accepted the resignation of the ministers of welfare, economy, and mines and industries in order to reduce the number of ministries as proscribed in the five-year plan 2010–2015.[60] In other words, Ahmadinejad proved through this manoeuvre that he is still in charge and that he thinks of himself as having enough support within the system to

---

[59] 'Nameh-ye rahbar-e mo'azzam-e enqelab beh Hojjatoleslam Moslehi + matn' [Letter of the Supreme Leader of the Revolution to Hojjatoleslam Moslehi + facsimile], *www.598.ir;* 31 Farvardin 1390/20 April 2011; a good overview on the narrative of events is 'Dastan-e raft va amad-e Moslehi cheh bud?' [What is the story about the leaving and coming of Moslehi?], *Shaffaf* 29 Farvardin 1390/19 April 2011.
[60] Borzou Dargahi and Ramin Mostaghim, 'Ahmadinejad Fires 3 Cabinet Ministers', *Los Angeles Times*, 16 May 2011; 'Iranian Parliament Approves Merger of five Ministries,' *Radio Zamaneh,* 29. Juni 2011.

continue. The beautiful friendship between his followers and the principalists must have ended by that moment. Hence, one may view him as a politician who looks beyond the ideological and structural confines of the principalist faction, as Seyyed Ammar Kalantari has observed already in 2009.[61]

Conclusion: A Victory Worse than Pyrrhus's

In sum, the political scheming and manoeuvring of the last few years, which climaxed with the 2009 elections, turned out to be a major disaster. This said, the elections were a success in the sense that voter mobilization worked even with the large Iranian expatriate community, whose members explicitly endorsed the political system of the Islamic Republic by casting their votes at Iranian embassies and consulates abroad. Needless to say, only someone like Khatami could have generated such a success. However, the necessity of embracing Iran's vast expatriate community in order to benefit from their skills, which are necessary for developing the country, and in order to benefit from their contacts, which is crucial to promoting the standing of the Islamic Republic on the international stage, was understood and embraced by Ahmadinejad too. He also embraced other policies such as his attempts to cautiously approach the United States, which can be seen by the energy and political credit he had put into the nuclear negotiations. Indeed, apart from the American president, it is Ahmadinejad who needed, almost desperately, a success on the nuclear front in order to strengthen his domestic position. What Ahmadinejad and his kindred spirits have gravely underestimated were the following three facts:

First, in spite of their scoring points in the power game every day, they could not change the basic arithmetic of the power distribution among the principalists, namely that their group was one of the weakest; secondly, they had an inadequate grasp of their own expertise and political capabilities, which led to the appointment of problematic figures and resulted in misguided policies. This is especially true with regards to the Holocaust conference; in sum, this led to the third fact, which is that neither the domestic nor the international public understood how traces of de-radicalized, constructive and reasonable policies could be commensurate with the public image of Ahmadinejad. In other words, the public image of the president totally obscured Iranian goodwill, hence a positive spiral of goodwill begetting goodwill could never come into being.

As a result, Ahmadinejad and his followers could only continue to fight an uphill battle against the power apparatus. Their rage against the political machine made them blind to compromise and led to permanent tensions and frictions and ultimately may lead to their downfall— without harming the functioning of the state apparatus. The confirmation of Moslehi's position issued

---

[61] Kalantari, 'Mardi qadd bolandtar'.

by the Supreme Leader was a simple, but significant, assertion of authority and influence that curtailed the powers of the president.[62]

For the principalist faction, checking the power of Ahmadinejad is just half of the story. Ahmadinejad played a crucial role in changing the tide against the reformists and for at least a few years he commanded real popularity among important Islamist constituencies. It is by no means clear whether a similar figure will be at their disposal in the next elections. All of the potential candidates who come to mind— Ali Larijani, Mohsen Reza'i, and Mohammad Baqer Qalibaf—have already lost the presidential elections of 2005. But, even worse, the future of the principalist faction as it is now known is in jeopardy, since no potential candidate is known who would be entrenched in both *Hezbollahi* and conservative factions. As such, the idea of creating a viable anti-reformist platform, appealing enough to attract voters from all walks of life to challenge the reformists at the ballot box, went nowhere – not to mention the fact we have already mentioned, namely that Ahmadinejad has looked beyond the ideological and sociological limits of the principalists for years. It would seem that the 'God given' electoral triumph of 2009 was actually a victory worse than Pyrrhus's.

---

[62] 'Ahmadinejad: Ekhtiyarat-e man dar dowlat salb shodeh ast' [My competences in the government have been curtailed], *Saham*, 27 April 2011.

Chapter 4

'Human Rights' by Any Other Name: Iranian Activism in an Authoritarian State

Arzoo Osanloo

> *'What's in a name? that which we call a rose*
> *By any other name would smell as sweet.'*
> Act II. Scene II, Romeo and Juliet
> —William Shakespeare

In February 2006 then-Secretary of State, Condoleezza Rice, declared that the United States would financially support regime change activities in Iran in hopes of helping to bring about a 'velvet revolution'. Since that time, Iranian activists for reform have fallen under new kinds of governmental scrutiny and surveillance. Their activities, some begun even before the US announcement, are viewed by some Iranian government officials as threats to national security, falling conveniently under an expansive definition of 're-gime change'. Iranian activists, meanwhile, continue advocating for change under these new conditions, at increasingly great personal risk. Many take the position that their advocacy is based squarely on Iranian laws and the principles embedded in the *shari'a* (Islamic guidelines) and that they are simply calling for enforcement of the existing legal codes. Even so, such activists are under suspicion for having a political allegiance to the United States and its regime-change policies. Despite a new US administration, domestic rights groups and individual activists continue to be targeted for their local activities.

The rise in governmental crack-downs on activists since the contested June 2009 presidential elections has further dampened hopes for reform, but activities continue in different forms. This essay focuses on the activities of reformers and activists with attention to a new politics of 'rights talk' (including women's rights, human rights, and children's rights) that is attendant to the increasingly sensitive nature of any kind of rights-based advocacy. By exploring changes in domestic reform activities by non-state actors, this essay suggests that activism continues in innovative forms as part of a dialogical response to the new constraints. This essay considers some specific forms of advocacy, including individualized activism and less organized and informal networking activities to gauge some of the possibilities for legal and social reform in Iran.

Human Rights Politics and International Accountability

International human rights accountability focuses on practices engendered by law, diplomatic and non-state engagement, and venues for making claims. The broad continuum of human rights accountability ranges from engagement, at one end of the spectrum, to punishment and potentially military ('humanitarian') intervention, at the other. Thus, in the context of international law, human rights intervention or engagement invites the suspension of the paramount right of sovereignty. At its foundation, the system emerges through the geo-political order of a world of nation-states. Human rights conventions are laws between nation-states, and importantly, the international human rights system is one that simultaneously questions the sovereign authority of the state, while also authorizing and strengthening it. This world system presents a problematic for the underlying philosophical basis for human rights. That is, human rights exist, especially in a post-World War II context, in order to protect the rights of humans that the state in which they are living has violated. Philosophically, human rights precede the state and inhere in every human simply by virtue of his or her humanity. Natural rights theories suggest that human rights are not granted, per se, but exist for humans solely on the condition of their humanity. Yet we have a problem, one that many have pointed out before: in the nation-state system, we depend on the nation-states to define 'humanity' through their juridical institutions. By defining who counts as human, the institutions of the nation-state determine just who may avail themselves of its protections and who may not.[1] Juridical institutions also determine the meaning and practices of internal human rights because of the weak and politically inspired international oversight system and because positive laws on human rights are created and put into practice in a system in which nation-state sovereignty is supreme and the principle of non-intervention is paramount.

This principle was codified in the Charter of the United Nations in 1945 where, for the first time, there was a definition of the rules of intervention in the internal practices of sovereign states in times of peace. Its codified principles—nterventions based on violations of human rights by states against their own citizens and residents—were based on the recognition of the inherent and inalienable dignity of individuals. Still, international laws, including human rights laws, guide the relations between nation-states and generally do not bestow rights upon individuals, although some exceptions do exist. One finds

---

[1] This issue was most poignantly expressed in Hannah Arendt's 'The Decline of the Nation-State and the End of the Rights of Man', in *The Origins of Totalitarianism*, New York: Harcourt, [1951] 1973, pp. 267–304.

the origins of this valuing of humanity in religious traditions, in natural and positive laws. An inherent quality, humanity, is independent of state recognition—or at least should be.

Some criticize the operation of the international system and consider it regrettable that human rights exist only through the legal recognition of individuals by a state. Even if we say that individuals theoretically or spiritually possess an inherent dignity, the extent to which human rights can be realized usually depends on nation-states because institutions of the state define humanity through their juridical categories, whether that is citizen, resident, or the naming of select protected classes – thus leaving out others. Philosopher Giorgio Agamben explores these challenges in the context of Western democracies and the state's recognition of humanity at the moment when elected officials declare a state of emergency and thus suspend democratic rights of peoples.[2] In the past decade, Iran's experiment in Islamico-civil governance has laid bare the battle for a democratic republic through struggles around the role of unelected segments of the government, such as the Council of Guardians and the Guardianship of the Jurist, *velayat-e faqih*. The shift away from republican processes was further evidenced in the 2009 claims of righteous victory by incumbent president, Mahmoud Ahmadinejad, who, at the time, had the support of Iran's Supreme Leader, Ayatollah Ali Khameneh'i. With the demise of the state's more republican and thus representative elements, the move towards authoritarianism has emerged and has been documented in numerous state actions especially in response to rights activism in the post-election era. Since the June 2009 elections, new challenges have emerged for possibilities of engagement at the level of international human rights. In this context, I would like to examine the role of the sovereign in defining women's and human rights because it is the sovereign that defines who is a legal person and therefore covered, at least minimally, by the laws of the state. In other words, what happens when the state does not recognize a human as such? That is, when is an individual denied minimal protections because the state does not recognize his or her humanity? One key point here is that states, through their laws, define who receives the rights associated with being human. Thus the rights and responsibilities that accompany humanity cannot escape the institutions of the state, particularly the juridical.

The challenge that emerges for putting human rights ideals into practice is that despite the aims to produce a world system in which a supranational authority can intervene in matters of domestic human rights violations, the principle of sovereignty provides that human rights largely depend on states, especially state recognition of the humanity of the individuals inside their borders. Armed with an increasingly well-defined and legally-binding body of human rights enforcement instruments, the international community stands firm against the mistreatment of individuals inside non-compliant, authoritarian, and even failed states. Since Nuremberg enforcement has rested increas-

---

[2] Giorgio Agamben, *Means Without End: Notes on Politics*, Minnesota: University of Minnesota Press, 2000.

ingly on the rule of law. The international judicial bodies developed to enforce binding human rights laws, such as genocide or crimes against humanity, are designed for the most egregious of crimes and, under the principle of complementarity, operate only as a last resort when the states themselves have proven unable or unwilling to investigate and punish such crimes. In the context of international law and the further development of the rule of law with regard to humanitarian intervention, the international community and state judiciaries rely heavily on domestic human rights practitioners to reveal violations, exhaust domestic remedies, and produce evidence. In the context of non-compliant states, however, such human rights activists are often the first victims of state vigilance of its sovereignty and the politicization of human rights activism that ensues. In the increasingly authoritarian context of post-2009 Iran, the question of how activists do the important work of recognizing and protecting the humanity of individuals living inside the country's borders emerges.

Despite its violent crackdowns on civilian protesters in the aftermath of the 2009 elections, the Iranian government attempted to gain a seat on the United Nations Human Rights Council. While sitting on the Council would have required the Iranian government to submit to systematic evaluations of its human rights record through the Council's Universal Periodical Review process, numerous activists and state parties fought to oppose Iran's admission into the Council, citing its disturbing human rights record. Indeed, in early 2011, the Council voted to appoint a Special Rapporteur to study human rights violations committed by Iran. To date, Iran has not permitted the Special Rapporteur, Ahmed Shaheed, to enter the country for on-site investigations, but using evidence gathered from sources outside of Iran, he issued an interim report in September 2011.[3] In it, he outlined the 'pattern of systematic violation' of Iranians' rights but continues to appeal to the Iranian government for access inside the country. Meanwhile in Iran, state forces have reframed, reversed, and in some cases even criminalized what it means to engage in human rights activities by Iranian activists inside the country.

Iran and (Re-)Politicization of Human Rights since 2009

In my book, *The Politics of Women's Rights in Iran*, I argued that in the immediate post-1979 revolutionary era, rights talk emerged as a distinct problem associated with Western individualism, but then that the republicanization of the state's organizations and apparatuses unexpectedly allowed a measure of renewed rights talk for some, one that was now in conformity with, *shari'a* (Islamic principles).[4] While the state formation that allowed the renewal of

---

[3] UN General Assembly, A/66/374, 'Report of the Special Rapporteur on the situation of human rights in the Islamic Republic of Iran', September 23, 2011,http://www.un.org/ga/search/view_doc.asp?symbol=A%2F66%2F374&Submit=Search&Lang=E.

[4] Arzoo Osanloo, *The Politics of Women's Rights in Iran*, Princeton, NJ: Princeton University Press, 2009.

rights talk was a part of a broader experiment in Islamic republicanism, it, too, was part of a greater compromise on the part of revolutionary actors who covered the spectrum of political parties and opinions, including secular, nationalist, and religious. Then the fight was against a monarchy; the victors, who formed a transitional government, struggled to reach a compromise with the leading figure of the revolution, Ayatollah Ruhollah Khomeini and his supporters. Since that time, an internal struggle has persisted between different powerful factions. The struggle is not just about leadership authority, but the meaning of the revolution, who owns Khomeini's legacy, and in particular, the nature of governance in an Islamic republic.

Since the reform period defined through the presidency of Mohammad Khatami (1997–2005), the renewed rights talk has come to be associated with the aim of strengthening civil institutions, thus making state actors more accountable. Khatami's attention to the republicanization of the state also came to be associated with an active and participatory *feqh* (jurisprudence) that would not be solely under the purview of the ulema (scholars of Islam). This dynamic jurisprudence (*feqh-e puya*) allowed for greater latitude in analyzing, debating, and even producing guidelines for Shiite Muslims in Iran. The problem was that this also allowed for the questioning of the authority and legitimacy of the leadership, particularly the role of the Supreme Leader. If the people themselves could be called upon and relied upon to propagate laws and serve the state in conformity with Islamic principles, then what role would that leave the ulema, particularly the country's Supreme Leader?

Hardliners, members of the ulema, and laypersons in leadership positions who did not believe they could rely on self-taught non-ulema to lead the country onto the righteous path, took issue with the development of the civil structures that left ultimate authority in the hands of the voters. Alongside of this, the renewed discourses of rights talk, what I have elsewhere referred to as *Islamico-civil* rights talk (2006),[5] has come to be seen as a challenge to the project of creating a Islamic state (*hokumat-e eslami*) in what was ostensibly seen by the strict-constructionists (*osulgaran*) as Khomeini's vision for post-revolutionary Iran. Rights talk even with the overall cast of Islamic legitimacy is again increasingly viewed by these groups as Western-imposed, concerned with individualism, and foreign to the project of Islamic state formation. Indeed it was the proliferation of rights activism in the post-2009 elections that led to massive arrests by government forces. The indictments that charged some of the leaders of the protests with *moharebeh* (acting as enemy of God and state), charges that amounted to treason and carried with them the death penalty, presented rights activism as evidence for such 'crimes' having been committed. In the post-election era, moreover, human rights training in law schools and in the non-governmental sector has been pared down and revised to engage primarily with Islamic principles. A number of activists have been

---

[5] Arzoo Osanloo, 'Islamico-civil "rights talk": women, subjectivity, and law in Iranian family court', *American Ethnologist* 33(2), 2006, pp. 191–209.

arrested, jailed, and/or banned from practice, while others have been forced to flee the country.

This discussion aims to show the importance of states, which of course are not monolithic entities but have the power, through their juridical institutions, to define who is a legal person and can therefore avail themselves of the juridical institutions' protections. Such practices have, of course, engendered massive critiques of the Islamic Republic. But as with any other state eschewing international accountability for human rights, the Islamic Republic is simultaneously redefining the parameters of humanity. Thus, in human rights practice, the simple naming of an act, the speech act of measuring a state action through the domain of international human rights law, has itself emerged as a dangerous practice. The question thus emerges, how do activists 'practise' human rights in such a context?

Anthropologist Alexei Yurchak studied the fall of the Soviet Union and published his findings in a book entitled, *Everything Was Forever Until It Was No More*.[6] In it, he offered an understanding of the suddenness of the demise of the Soviet Union. In a context where the state controls everything and everything appears to be politicized, Yurchak argued that the cracks in the authoritarian state's armour were to be found in the seemingly ordinary or apolitical. Yurchak found that the ordinary acts of everyday people laid the foundations for the demise of the Soviet Union because as the authoritarian state controlled all that appeared political, including the body of the human, those spaces that were seen to be apolitical—not anti-political—offered important clues for investigating the fall of the world's second greatest superpower.

Yurchak's work resonates with research on the increasingly authoritarian nature of the Iranian state as well as my own research. In large part, my research has focused on the status of women in Iran. Through this research, I have argued that because the discriminatory laws of the state delegate greater control and ownership over family matters to males, they require women to become literally legal actors in marriage dissolution, custody, and other family law issues. As a result, women have become increasingly savvy legal actors who have not only learned how to make use of their none-too-explicit rights, but have, through sheer necessity, paved the paths for reform.[7] Through their engagements with the state's diverse legal institutions, including courts and bureaucratic agencies, women are forcing the state to recognize their humanity. This is why commentators on Iran frequently argue that women and women's rights activists are the vanguard of reform. Today rights activists are increasingly thwarted in their work, but activism continues in different forms, and without understanding the deeper political and ideological logics underlying the current repression in Iran, it is hard to identify advocacy when we see it.

---

[6] Alexei Yurchak, *Everything Was Forever, Until It Was No More: The Last Soviet Generation*, Princeton, NJ: Princeton University Press, 2006.
[7] Osanloo, *The Politics of Women's Rights in Iran*.

It may seem unremarkable to see in Iran certain forms of activism that resonate with activism in Western nations-states with strong civil societies. In the context of the struggle for power in Iran, actions by civil society actors, including lawyers or social workers, may at first appear unremarkable, but given the legal and political constraints through which such agents are advocating, some further consideration may be warranted. Under what ideological logic does this activism succeed or fail? Studying these 'unremarkable' sites, then—in their ordinary and rather mundane settings—may shed light on new possibilities and avenues of activism that are on-going in Iran today. Thus with the repoliticization of rights talk, and of women's and human rights in particular, I am increasingly interested in certain, perhaps unremarkable places or practices that do not *name* human rights as their object of concern, but at the same time broaden and deepen the terrain of what it means to be human.

Humanity and Bare Life in the Realm of the Political

One of the most important critics of human rights has been Hannah Arendt, who noted the internal contradictions within human rights because while they are supposed to be protections against state actors, it is, nonetheless states whose recognition of an individual permits or allows those protections to apply.[8] Building on that theory, Giorgio Agamben has added a critique of human rights by looking at what it means to be human in the contemporary global system.[9] Arguing that today those who are reduced by the state to a bare life, that is, stripped of any political identity—such as citizen, resident, even refugee—have no recognition of their personhood, and thus no state protection. Agamben makes a distinction between political life (*zöe*) and bare life (*bios*). Citing earlier philosophers who argued that this distinction mattered because when the sovereign entity, whether it is the government in a modern state or the king in a pre-modern context, denied a political identity to a person, it reduced the person to bare life, a life that could be killed with impunity. Theoretically, after World War II and the further entrenchment of a transnational rule of law, heads of state can no longer kill with impunity or leave their own people to languish in inhumane conditions. Instead, with international laws, especially human rights laws aimed at protecting individuals as opposed to states, heads of state can be held accountable—they are no longer above the law, so to speak.

Agamben provides a critique of this modern nation-state system arguing that the sovereign of the modern state makes the laws and can also stand above them. Through such state actions as suspending the laws in a state of emergency, he can kill with impunity as in pre-modern times, or treat individuals with aggressive tactics in the name of securing the state. In many cases still today, individuals are denied political personhood by states and thus

---

[8] See note 1.
[9] Giorgio Agamben, *Home Sacer: Sovereign Power and Bare Life*, Stanford, CA: Stanford University Press, 1998.

reduced to bare life. In such cases, these individuals who are reduced to bare life are at the mercy of the state. While the state may not be as readily able to kill as in pre-modern times, the state's unwillingness to recognize the political identity of some individuals living within its borders is tantamount to their having no humanity because it is state forces that ultimately determine personhood through juridical recognition, which includes minimal legal protections. Where individuals have no recognition by state officials, they stand outside of any legal protections. Agamben also refers to this as abandonment. Unlike the classical theorists which he invokes, Agamben argues that even the so-called bare life, the life which has no claim to political protection, is part and parcel of the state's sovereign powers because the state has the right to name and include or completely ban or abandon individuals. Thus, according to Agamben, even that which we call the bare life, which the state can seemingly dispose of with impunity, is so defined by politics.

Such individuals who have no political recognition are relegated to what anthropologist João Biehl has called 'zones of social abandonment'. For Biehl, working in the urban slums of Porto Alegre, Brazil, '[T]these zones are symbiotic with changing households and public services – they absorb those individuals who have no ties or resources left to sustain themselves' and they are places where living beings go 'when they are no longer considered people.'[10]

The notion of bare life is an important point of departure for this essay in which I seek to show how groups manage to take notice of those whose personhood, and thus legal interpolation into the state's protective fold, is missing. In this essay, I take note of how some activists and groups work with individuals whose humanity has been reduced to bare life and who have no legal and social protections. These groups and individuals then work shrewdly through the politicized state system, careful of the pitfalls of human rights discourses, in serving the ultimate goal of gaining some modicum of political recognition for those who, in the eyes of the state, do not exist. This work allows these previously bare lives to gain some political existence to then make claims and seek protections through law and social services. In what follows, I introduce the work of several groups and individuals who have committed themselves to the recognition of those persons whose personhood has disappeared through the sovereign's neglect or failure to acknowledge their existence, thus giving them a political life.

Defending the 'Defenceless'

In his personal weblog, Mohammad Mostafa'i described his work as defending the defenceless (*defa' az bi-defa'*). Mostafa'i is a renowned criminal defence attorney who has often taken up the most difficult cases, the most egregious crimes, with defendants who faced Iran's harsh retributive penal justice

---

[10] João Biehl, *Vita: Life in a Zone of Social Abandonment*, Berkeley, CA: University of California Press, 2005, p. 2.

system. While easily among the best known, Mostafaʻi was hardly alone in seeking to protect criminal defendants, particularly those under the age of eighteen.

Iran has a complex criminal justice system which integrates elements of the pre-revolutionary penal code with a post-revolutionary overhaul of its codes of criminal punishment and procedure, harkening back to what its lawmakers claimed was a penal code in conformity with Islamic principles. In doing so, the penal codes codified physical retributive punishment (*lex talionis*) as part of the sanctioning process and gave significant voice to victims' families or next of kin (*owlia-ye dam*) by privatizing murder as primarily a tort. In such cases, next of kin are authorized to demand in-kind punishment (*qesas*) including what amounts to the death penalty for murder cases. In such cases, thus, the victims' families are plaintiffs in criminal proceedings as opposed to simply witnesses for the prosecution. Until 1991, the state was not a decision-maker in the sanctioning process in murder cases. Iran's parliament then revised the sanctioning laws allowing for a prosecution for murder on the theory that in addition to the private harm to victims' families, a murder has also created a social harm for which the prosecutor, as the representative of the public, can also seek damages. Importantly, however, the state prosecutor can only seek up to a fifteen-year prison sentence, but not death. Thus in murder cases in Iran, there are always at least two plaintiffs, the prosecutor and the victim's family. But it is only the victims' families that can make a demand for death.

Only a few years after Iran revised its penal codes, on July 13, 1994, its parliament also ratified the United Nations' Convention on the Rights of the Child (CRC), which was approved by the governmental body that vets all laws for their conformity with Islamic principles, the Council of Guardians.[11] In tandem with the country's ratification of this convention, the Islamic Republic licensed the creation and operation of organizations to support underage defendants in death penalty cases. In some cases, such organizations might send social workers to speak to members of victims' families to attempt to negotiate their forbearance (*gozasht*)—forgoing their right to exact in-kind punishment. Defence attorneys and even government agencies have also come on board to form a sort of 'cottage industry' of groups and individuals working against the death penalty through the logic of Islamic principles of forgiveness (*bakhshesh*) and the international human rights doctrines. In the increasingly politicized context in which hardliners gain support by aligning their political opponents with Western human rights defenders, many activists have taken a different tack, one which aims to highlight the Islamic nature of the forbearance and move away from a discourse of rights towards one of

---

[11] Upon ratification, Iran took a general reservation stating that it 'reserves the right not to apply any provisions or articles of the Convention that are incompatible with Islamic Laws and the international legislation in effect'. 'Iran, Reservation', Convention on the Rights of the Child, accessed 11May 2011, http://treaties.un.org/doc/db/survey/Rightsofthechild.pdf.

humanity. As one attorney told me in November 2007, 'we cannot explicitly talk about ending the death penalty. This is why the CRC has proven useful. We start with juvenile defendants and can refer to Iran's own normative legal structure and its ratification of the CRC as a part of this.'[12]

In a 2010 interview, Mostafaʻi, like the other attorney, explained that he is against the death penalty for anyone, 'but it is hard to change the law without changing the way people think.' Mostafaʻi's advocacy, thus, addresses the existing laws in Iran. Mostafaʻi laid out his legal case in a letter he sent to the head of Iran's judiciary, Ayatollah Sadeq Larijani, asking for a stay of his client's execution:

> Finally, one important issue that has been neglected by all the judges who have tried similar cases is the fact that in 1993 the Majles debated the Convention on the Rights of the Child durin[g] an open session. The honourable members of the Majles ratified the convention by a majority and sent the bill to the honourable [Council of Guardians] for approval. The honourable members of the [Council of Guardians] also conditionally ratified the convention. The single amendment attached by the Islamic Republic of Iran to the aforementioned convention states that 'the Convention for the Rights of the Child, including its introduction and its 54 articles, is ratified and binding by the Islamic Republic of Iran if the content of each and every article is not in contravention with the national laws or the religious regulations. If they are in contravention, they will not be considered binding.' In their opinion #5760, the honourable members of the [Council of Guardians] listed the articles that were in contravention with the religious laws. The list is as follows: 'Articles 12 (1), 13 (1, 3), 14 (1, 3), 15 (2), 16 (1), and 29 (1-d) are in contravention with known Islamic norms.' Therefore, with the exclusion of the aforementioned articles, the rest of the articles of the Convention are not in contravention of Sharia law and shall be enforced by all officers of the courts, based on Article 9 of the civil law that states, 'All international treaties that, in accordance with the Iranian constitution, are articles of law.' Article 37(a) of the Convention of the Rights of the Child states that '[n]either capital punishment nor life imprisonment without possibility of release shall be imposed for offences committed by persons below eighteen years of age'. Therefore, death sentences issued to young offenders culpable of murder are in strict contradiction with the law.[13]

Although Mostafaʻi makes the case for changes to the law, as, insofar as the laws stand and victims' families are the final arbiters of life, activists and

---

[12] Personal interview, name withheld for confidentiality, November 2007.

[13] Letter to the head of Iran's judiciary for a stay of execution, 14, Mehr, 1388 (6 October 2009), *Mohammad Mostafaei Blog*, accessed May 14, 2011, http://www.modafe.com/NewsDetail.aspx?Id=197. The blog was initially found at www.mohegh.blogfa.com, but has since been changed to http://www.modafe.com/. All entries can be accessed in the archives based on the Persian calendar date (month/year). English translations of Persian entries are made by the weblog owner and not this author.

lawyers like Mostafa'i appeal to the humanity of the defendants, their youth, their often beleaguered lives, and the compassion of the victims' families – their capacity for mercy in the face of their own tragic losses.

The laws allow for privately negotiated settlements in which the victims' families sometimes receive compensation (*diyeh*) in exchange for their forbearance.[14] During my visits to Mostafa'i's office in both 2009 and 2010, it was frequently abuzz with telephone calls from victims' families or his defendants' families trying to negotiate such settlements. The negotiations and discussions with victims' families by lawyers, social workers, even state agents often involved the language of humanity, either by encouraging the humanity of the potential forgiver or the defendant's. This was especially the case with juveniles. 'You gain nothing by killing another human, but if you forgo this right of retribution, you show your humanity', was how one social worker described to me her attempts at convincing victims' families to forgo a retributive death sentence. Her words closely followed on the Koranic verse 5:45:

> And We prescribed for them therein: The life for the life, and the eye for the eye, and the nose for the nose, and the ear for the ear, and the tooth for the tooth, and for wounds retaliation. But whoso forgoeth it (in the way of charity) it shall be expiation for him. Whoso judgeth not by that which Allah hath revealed: such are wrong-doers.[15]

In some communities, family and neighbours come together to talk to victims' families and they, along with members of the ulema, recite and discuss the verse and the virtues of forgiving over revenge. When I asked whether they use the Koran in their advocacy work, several lawyers I interviewed said they did not need to. One attorney added that he endorsed the use of any tool or discourse available (because he was adamantly against the death penalty) and that 'the victims' families to whom they (the lawyers) are talking are already aware of the greater virtue in forgiveness.'[16]

Mostafa'i saved many lives through his advocacy, but was deeply troubled when victims' families went through with the process. After witnessing the unfair and tragic execution of one of his juvenile defendants, Behnud Shoja'i, who killed another boy when he was only seventeen, and under age, according

---

[14] In such cases, there is actually a slight shift in the pleading. In the Iranian penal code, technically, there is no compensation for intentional murder, akin to murder in the first degree in US penal codes. In such cases, the victims' families may either seek punishment in-kind, *qesas*, or forgo *qesas* entirely. When the victim's family does accept compensation in exchange for forbearance, the crime is technically plead down to an unintentional homicide, similar to murder in the second degree, for which compensatory punishments exist.

[15] *Holy Qur'an*, trans. Muhammad M. Pickthall (Tahrike Tarsile Qur'an; 1st edition, 2001), 5:45. Pickthall's and others' translations of this verse are similar. Pickthall's translation can be accessed online as well, see,
http://www.islam101.com/quran/QTP/QTP005.htm, accessed May 11, 2011.

[16] Personal interview, name withheld to protect confidentiality, November 2008.

to the CRC, to receive death as a punishment, Mostafa'i wrote on his blog: 'Today, [Behnud] is not among his friends in prison anymore. They feel his absence. I did everything I could, but it was not effective. I still believe that he did not deserve to die. He shouldn't have been executed. But he was executed. Executed.'[17] Most troubling to Mostafa'i was the fact that the family of the victims had initially agreed to forgive, then suddenly, at the gallows, retracted.

After Shoja'i's execution, Mostafa'i intensified his strategy of negotiating with victims' families for their forbearance. Mostafa'i opened a bank account and publicized it on his personal blog:

> In order to obtain consent from a victim's family, there is a need for money to be paid to the family at the time of their forgiveness. I was forced to open an account that would help save lives of offenders who were minors at the time of their crime. I say I was 'forced', because I just could not find any other organization or group that I could trust with this matter.
>
> Please transfer your donation to the following account number: 0205327104006 at Bank Melli Iran, branch of Jamal al-Din Asadabady Square. Please tell others about this. If you live out of Iran, you could collect the blood money as a group and transfer the sum into the account using money-transferring processes.
>
> If we raise around approximately $200,000, we can save three or four lives of teenagers.
>
> I sincerely thank you for putting your confidence in me. I will publish the amounts collected and payments paid to the victims' families at the end of each month on my personal blog. www.mohegh.blogfa.com.[18]

With his work negotiating for the lives of his defendants, Mostafa'i was able to save the lives of over fifty defendants by parleying financial settlements with victims' families.[19] The work of lawyers and activists like Mostafa'i makes use of the available domestic and international resources, legal processes, and transnational activism, to bring awareness of the plight of their clients and recognition to their humanity. Their actions challenge authorities on their own terms, that is, in terms of the state's own penal codes. Advocacy can also challenge the authority when lawyers and activists such as Mostafa'i expose the contradictions and inconsistencies of the state's own policies. The work of advocates highlights the policies of the Islamic Republic and transgressions of its own laws as well as the international laws to which it has, by ratification, promised to adhere. Mostafa'i's advocacy has gained him, and

---

[17] 'Behnoud Shojaee Was Hanged in front My Eyes', *Mohammad Mostafaei Blog*, 20 Mehr 1388 (12 October 2009), accessed May 14, 2011, http://www.modafe.com/NewsDetail.aspx?Id=213, accessed 14 May 2011.

[18] 'A Call for Saving Children's Lives on Death Row', *Mohammad Mostafaei Blog*, 29 Mehr 1388 (21 October2009), accessed May 14, 2011. http://www.modafe.com/Default.aspx?Year=1388&Month=07.

[19] Personal interview July 2010.

others like him, international fame and authority, and at the same time, the ire of state officials. In the summer of 2010, Mostafa'i was called in by Iranian authorities for questioning of his activities, ostensibly with regard to the above-mentioned bank account calling for donations. In the summer of 2010, Mostafa'i had been advocating internationally on behalf of his juvenile and other defendants, including Sakineh Mohammadi-Ashtiani, who had been handed a sentence of death by stoning for alleged adultery.[20] Mostafa'i went to the international press to condemn both the sentence by stoning as well as the process by which she was being held, and potentially executed. Finally, Mostafa'i went into hiding, whereupon the authorities took his wife and brother-in-law into custody for several weeks. In the meantime, Mostafa'i fled the country to seek asylum in Norway. His international advocacy on behalf of Iranians continues, now from exile. In the fall of 2010, Mostafa'i was convicted *in absentia* of spreading propaganda against the state, and sentenced to six years in prison.

During an interview on anti-death penalty advocacy, a social worker who attempts to negotiate settlements between victims' families, who are plaintiffs in murder cases, and defendants, explained the logic behind her work, 'Changing the law can change the culture, but educating the people can change their culture and in turn lead to changing the law, as well. While others work on reforming the laws, we work on changing the culture.'[21]

Through their advocacy, Mostafa'i and other advocates lay bare the naked humanity of defendants, revealing that this naked life, Agamben's 'bios', is actually defined by the juridical field and is assigned through law. Agamben reminds us that the division between naked and political life is defined by actions of the sovereign, revealing, thus, that all life is politically-assigned and thus can be re-assigned. Mostafa'i's advocacy, especially on behalf of underage juvenile defenders, whom he calls 'the defenceless', re-signifies their humanness and brings the life of these youth back into the fold of humanity, even though it may sometimes come at the cost of their own political life through legal banishment: prison or exile.

Shining a Light on the 'Invisible': House of Sun

Khaneh Khorshid (House of Sun) is Iran's first women's harm-reduction drop-in centre (DIC) for addict women, often abandoned by their families and

---

[20] Later the Iranian government suspended the stoning sentence (earlier the Iranian government claimed to have stopped carrying out stoning altogether as a form of punishment), but now a death sentence hung over Mohammadi-Ashtiani. Conflicting reports stated that the form of execution, the stoning, was 'converted' to a hanging. Other reports indicated that now Mohammadi-Ashtiani had 'confessed' to having killed her husband, a crime which carries the death penalty. Mostafa'i argued that the crime of adultery does not have 'hanging' as a punishment, while the state cannot execute for murder: it is the victim's family that makes that decision and thus a new legal process would be required.

[21] Personal interview, November 2007. Name withheld to protect confidentiality.

left with nowhere to go. I first learned about Khaneh Khorshid from a lawyer who told me about the active networks in Tehran civil society that seek the help those whom society seemed to have left behind, who lived in the shadows, seemingly invisible to the mainstream or did not exist at all. As a harm-reduction drop-in centre, Khaneh Khorshid provides MMT (Methadone Maintenance Treatment) to more than 100 women addicted to crack, heroin, and other lethal drugs per day. The centre also provides social services for these women and their families free of charge. Such services include psychological counselling, social work, medical, dental, psychiatric, gynaecological, and educational services.[22] Most of the women who drop in to the centre (eighty per cent) are between 20 to 49 years of age and over half are nearly illiterate. Unfortunately these women were either never given the chance for formal education or were forced to drop out of school at an early age.[23]

In an autumn 2008 interview, its founder and director, a social worker, Leyla Arshad, explained to me that she and her co-founder and assistant director, Sorur Monshizadeh actively work to make contacts with service providers, including doctors, dentists, lawyers, and social workers, and convince them to offer their services pro bono. Arshad explained that while the ministry of health provides some financial support, most of Khaneh Khorshid's funding comes from private donations, both monetary and in-kind services and active fund-raising by the directors and staff. Khaneh Khorshid must pay for rent and supplies, including medical, such as the methadone and syringes. When she tried to speak with the city's leaders about raising municipal funds to support the women who drop in at Khaneh Khorshid – homeless, addicts, prostitutes, and persons infected with HIV/AIDS –, they responded dismissively stating, 'We do not have such persons in Tehran. They do not exist.' Arshad told government officials that while they might not want to believe that such persons exist, they very much do. She explained further that city officials' recognition of their existence is very important because if nothing is done to address the societal problems that produce these women, there may come a time when troubles such as these find their way into their own posh and upscale neighbourhoods in Northern Tehran. She told me, 'It is only by recognizing that these people exist, that they are living among us and are part of our community that we begin to realize we have a responsibility to help them.' Then she added, 'These women have nowhere else to go.' Finally, with a dimpled smile, Arshad ended the story by relating that not only had she convinced her audience of the reality of these women's lives, but now, the very same people who once disavowed their existence, were actively fund-raising for Khaneh Khorshid.

---

[22] Khaneh Khorshid, accessed 11 May 2011, http://www.khanehkhorshid.ir.
[23] Ibid

In 2008, the renowned Iranian filmmaker, Rakhshan Bani-E'temad, directed a documentary about Khaneh Khorshid,[24] which reveals the humanity of lives in this, to use Biehl's words, 'zone of social abandonment'. About halfway into the film, in a group-counselling scene where the women are asked to discuss their feelings, they only come up with negative feelings: 'depression', 'hate', 'violence', 'loneliness'. The counselor then tries to get the women to express the emotions or experiences behind such negative feelings: 'Look, I want to know why we call a feeling such as hate a bad feeling. What happens that we attribute to hatred a negative feeling?' Then one woman responds: "When my children's father was alive, he would harm us when he was angry, beat us every other minute, right now my body is fifty-five percent burned, he poured boiling water on me, I put up with him when he had five wives. We grew up with a step-father that beat us, lived through hardships. These were angry things we have seen in our lives. Even right now, we live in a place where, pardon my language, there are no signs of humanity. I mean if your rent is late one day, they'll come and beat you like an animal, throw out your belongings."

Indeed, many of the women who come daily to the DIC are attempting to find respite from their families and, in a sense, recognition of their humanity. About three-fourths of the women live with at least one other addict and over half became addicts from an addict spouse. Their spouses encourage their wives' addictions so that the women can provide their husbands with narcotics, starting with opium, and then moving on to heroin, crack and other serious drugs. To pay for their addictions, the women are often pushed, sometimes violently, into selling their bodies, other their only assets. As day draws to an end at Khaneh Khorshid, the long hallway near the exit fills with women gathering to leave because the DIC is only open during business hours. Polite exchanges do not drown out the reluctant groans of those weary of going home to a night of uncertainty and possible danger.

In addition to treating the women for their addictions, mental and physical harms related to them, or other abusive elements in their lives, Khaneh Khorshid provides the women with educational and career training opportunities, alternative life-style choices, on-going life and psychological counselling, as well as an active social life to lure them away from their previous practices and help them stay away for good. Religious ceremonies and birthday parties are often held at the centre, as are celebrations when someone finds employment. During one visit in the summer of 2010, I met an animated young woman, Shadi.[25] Tall and lanky, her jet-black hair and ivory skin were accented by bright pink lipstick. Off drugs and having been clean for three months, Leyla and Sorur had helped train Shadi in bookkeeping. They connected her with a government agency for an interview in a secretarial post. She had given Leyla's and Sorur's names as references. While the women awaited the call for

---

[24] Angels of the House of Sun, *Khaneh Khorsheed*, DVD, directed by Rakhshan Bani E'temad (Tehran, Iran: *Hayat Khalvat*, 2008).
[25] Names of all clientele have been changed to protect their privacy.

their recommendation, Shadi stopped in to tell them how well the interview had gone. The job, if she got it, she buzzed joyfully, would provide her with an income and thus independence from her addict husband. The two women praised her efforts and applauded her tenacity, especially amidst such difficult challenges.

Other times, social workers at Khaneh Khorshid conduct marriage counselling for the women, especially since most were forced into addiction through addict husbands. Social workers also talked to some women about the possibility of dissolving marriages to addict husbands, especially when they were the sources of their addictions. On another visit, I met one such woman who had just returned from Tehran's municipal family court. She was in the process of determining the necessary filings she would need and asked the supervisor on duty if Khaneh Khorshid could give her a loan for the filing fee. Instead, one of the social workers called the court to see if she could get a hardship waiver from filing the fee.

Khaneh Khorshid also employs social worker interns, often college students or recent graduates and provides training to treat addict women. This experience has had an effect both on the interns and Khaneh Khorshid's clientele. The interns, often coming from Tehran's more affluent areas, would otherwise have scarce contact with the marginalized women of the city and have little understanding of their plights. The social workers serve as role models for the clientele, modelling behaviour of caring, compassion, and self-assurance, and often a degree of independence. Perhaps even more significant, former clientele who have moved on to live productive lives will often return as volunteers, simultaneously modelling for and counselling the clientele at Khaneh Khorshid.

The work of Khaneh Khorshid serves as one example of the way in which local activists work through the political constraints of human rights work and seek to expose the plight of their clientele by seemingly simple acts of recognition—not of their human rights, specifically, but of their humanity. Indeed today the numbers of harm-reduction DICs have gone up throughout in the city. Khaneh Khorshid remains among the most active. Its social workers see some 100 women and children per day,[26] and have successfully treated over 600 women since opening their doors in 2007.[27] The way in which Khaneh Khorshid and its leaders operate to make the seemingly invisible citizens visible is a way of making others see and recognize the humanity of such women and their human rights, without calling it such.

Conclusion

What does any of this matter in a context where people are consistently being denied their human rights? This essay has considered how social practices can

---

[26] Personal interview, September 2009.
[27] Khaneh Khorshid, accessed 11May 2011, http://www.khanehkhorshid.ir.

change perceptions, and in changing perceptions, there may come a time when the laws change to recognize the humanity of those living on the margins of society. Studying the so-called ordinary acts of social workers, lawyers and other individuals gives us a sense of what is going on inside the country and how human rights issues can be initiated and addressed in a context where human rights activism can be unpersuasive to state actors and dangerous to activists.

The examples above aim to recognize and show some of the impact of the humanitarian work being done in a context in which the defining and naming of activism as 'human rights' is an unproductive discourse that has been politicized to such a point that it is of little use to actors seeking material changes on the ground . Instead, through seemingly unremarkable practices of social work or lawyering, individuals produce remarkable results by bringing bare lives, those unacknowledged by the state, back into the fold of political life. By working with strategic state agencies and officials, such actors force the state to recognize and indeed protect the lives of some whom its laws had removed from the juridical field of legal personhood. Moreover, these seemingly mundane practices take place in the highly politicized context where making claims on the state in terms of human rights can be counterproductive. Studying such practices that specifically avoid the language of rights and rights-based discursive strategies can enrich and deepen the context for understanding how rights claims come to be politicized. It may also be useful in understanding how risky it is to make rights claims in some contexts, while in others, it is valid to do so. When conflicts over rights claims are placed in temporal and spatial contexts, they highlight the complexities of wider struggles. In Iran, the contest over rights activism is waged in part through challenges to sovereignty and the possibility of intervention, both internally and externally.

Chapter 5

Inter-Confessional Relations in Iran: Conflicts and Transfers in the Aftermath of 9/11

Stéphane A. Dudoignon

Among the numerous contributions by Mohammad-Reza Djalili to our understanding of the Islamic Republic of Iran, one must mention his assessment of the resonance of ideology in the most varied domains of the country's life, including its foreign policy, despite the difficulty to isolate the 'Islamic variable' among the protagonists' often complex motivations.[1] Unlike many historical studies on modern and contemporary Iran centred on reform and modernization, Djalili's work also pays attention to the weight of the majority which, in Iran's recent history, has almost always sided with reaction: such was the case even during the Khatami presidency, when the conservative parliament and judicial apparatus were constantly undermining the executive power's liberal initiatives in the field of culture.[2] A modest homage to this illustrious predecessor's contribution, the present study seeks to deal with some of the 'villains' of progressive historiography, with some of those who during the past thirty years, not content with siding from time to time with the most conservative forces of the Islamic Republic, have also managed to overbid them in their own discourses and practices. Through a brief overview of confessional relations in Iran in the 2000s, we shall tackle briefly the world vision and strategies developed by the religious and political leaders of the most significant confessional minority of Iran, in demographical

---

[1] E.g., Mohammad-Reza Djalili, *Diplomatie islamique: stratégie internationale du khomeynisme*, Paris: Presses Universitaires de France, 1992, pp. 43f.
[2] Mohammad-Reza Djalili, *Iran: l'illusion réformiste*, Paris: Presses de Sciences Po, 2001, pp. 95–97.

terms and symbolic value: the Sunni populations located principally in the country's western and eastern peripheries.[3]

The reactionary nature of the neo-traditionalist and neo-fundamentalist movements that have developed since various dates among these populations probably explains in part the relatively low level (if compared with neighbouring countries) of inter-confessional confrontation and violence between Iran's Shiite majority and Sunni minority during the last thirty years. Other, more decisive factors have of course played a part in the relative rarity and modest dimensions of ethno-confessional pogroms in Iran's contemporary history, beginning with the role played by the Islamic Republic itself in coercion against confessional minorities, and with the latter's often modest numbers. (Besides, several of these minorities have opted for rapid or gradual emigration from Iran in the course of the nineteenth and twentieth centuries.) Another, even more significant reason why conflicts have been limited in the course of the past two centuries is the geographical isolation of many of these communities. More recently, however, mass migrations from the rural areas have led to unprecedented spatial confrontations with the confessional majority. If modern inter-confessional violence has long remained quantitatively limited (concentrated on the adherents of the Baha'i Faith and, since 1979, on Iranian Christian preachers and converts), by contrast one can only be struck by the symbolic significance and by the proportions taken since the early 1990s— i.e., since the aftermath of the war with Iraq and of Khomeini's death—by intra-Muslim tension between Iran's Shiite majority and Sunni minority. A tension accentuated by the sharp qualitative turn taken by state violence in the mid-2000s, since which the Islamic Republic seems to have opted for campaigns of assassination against a wide range of alternative voices.[4] The eventful year 2009, in particular, was marked, before and after the June presidential ballot, by an explosion of unprecedented and typologically new Shiite/Sunni violence, through a series of assassinations of first-rank Sunni personalities answered by a succession of bloody attacks in the

---

[3] For previous contributions by the same author on this subject, see: Stéphane A. Dudoignon, 'Sunnis and Shi'ites in Iran since 1979: Confrontations, Exchanges, Convergences', in *Sunni & Shi'ite Islam: Their Relations in Modern Times*, Brigitte Maréchal & Sami Zemni (eds), London: Hurst, forthcoming; idem, 'Un tropisme indo-pakistanais? Le sunnisme en Iran', *Outre terre, revue européenne de géopolitique*, 28, 2011, pp. 329–40; 'Zahedan vs. Qom? Les sunnites d'Iran et l'émergence du Baloutchistan comme foyer de droit hanafite, sous la monarchie Pahlavi', in *Misceallanea Internae Asia: Festschrift in Honour of Françoise Aubin*, Denise Aigle et al. (eds), Sankt Augustin: Monumenta Serica Institute, 2010, pp. 271–313; 'Un *mawlawi* contre les pasdaran?', *La pensée de midi*, 27, 2009, pp. 92–100; 'Sunnis online: The Sunni Religious Internet in Iran', *Asiatische Studien / Études asiatiques*, 63(1), 2009, pp. 27–66.

[4] Remarks by Ladan Boroumand at the colloquium 'L'Iran face aux défis du XXIe siècle', Geneva: Graduate Institute of International and Development Studies, 18–19 June 2010.

south-east of the country, attacks whose *modus operandi* is inspired by modern-day anti-Shiite organizations and movements of the Indus River valley. During the months that followed the election, the successes of Tehran's terror politics against the Green Movement and, in February 2010, the spectacular and mysterious arrest of 'Abd al-Malik Rigi (c. 1983–2010), the charismatic spokesman of the Baluchistan-based armed resistance group Jundollah, have suggested that Tehran was taking back political initiative. The situation remains however to be assessed as to the realignments produced by the acts of violence of 2009, in particular within a newly self-conscious Sunni community, the emergence and consolidation of which remains one of the most paradoxical features of the recent history of the Islamic Republic of Iran.

State Violence Instead of Pogroms

Geopolitics of the Sunni Revival

Since the early 2000s, with the military presence of the United States and its allies first in Afghanistan and then in Iraq, and the overall growth of the conservatives' power in Iran since 2003, Sunni/Shiite tension has given way to outbursts of open violence, of a type hitherto unknown in the country's modern history. The emergence since 2002 of Sunni guerrilla movements like the Jundollah in Iran's south-eastern province of Sistan and Baluchistan has gone in parallel with assassinations or executions of Sunni confessional leaders, principally in Kurdistan and in Baluchistan. The situation has deteriorated to the point that the Sunni populations of Iran are now cemented by a new sentiment of common interests and of a common destiny. In such a context, the main Sunni religious schools and mosques of the country have been playing the role of defenders of the community as a new entity. Such a posture has constituted an important factor of unification and concurrence between several of our 'villains' from the country's periphery against the central state's encroachments. Among the main protagonists of the Sunni religious field must be mentioned the Deoband School, a neo-traditionalist movement born in British India in the 1860s which advocates the return to the juridical norms of the pre-Mongol period of the history of Islam, and the modern Salafiya, a loose conglomeration of Sunni movements acting for the re-Islamicization 'from the bottom' of Muslim-background societies. The Deoband School has been prospering in Iran since as early as the 1930s, starting in Sistan and Baluchistan and expanding through a network of religious teaching institutions set up since the 1990s into a formal hierarchy. As to the Salafiya, one of its main cradles in the country has been Iranian Kurdistan, where it developed more recently, in the 2000s, under Iraqi influence and through the multiplication of self-segregated Salafi rural communities (*jama'at*s).

Confrontations and Transfers

In parallel, a number of cultural transfers from the Shiite majority to the Sunni minority can also be observed. Such is the case for instance of the Shiite notion of *marja'iyat* (the personal guidance of a religious master), which is now largely diffused in the Deobandi madrasas of eastern Iran as well as in the Salafi *jama'at*s of Iranian Kurdistan. In some cases the degradation of Shiite/Sunni relations has even been intensifying these transfers, as in the case of the notion of martyrdom, which since the 1990s has become central to the religious culture of Iran's Sunni populations. In his works on Islamism and death, sociologist Farhad Khosrokhavar has developed the concept of a 'culture of organized sorrow' practised by the Islamic Republic of Iran during the first two decades of its history. He emphasizes the impact of the dislocation of traditional family structures and warns specialists against an exclusively cultural and theological reading of such a phenomenon.[5] Indeed, as we shall see, Sunni Islam in Iran possesses rich substrata of its own as far as the culture of martyrdom is concerned. However, the activation of these substrata since the 1990s (notably through the memory of the jihads of olden days) appears as the direct product of a transfer from the Shiite majority—among whom formerly omnipresent references to martyrdom tend to vanish in the 2000s—to the Sunni minority, which has developed it with unprecedented intensity in the same 2000s in connection with a series of assassinations of its confessional leaders, and with the general rise of political pressure on Sunni confessional institutions since the election of Ahmadinejad to the Iranian presidency in 2005.

The Scarcity of Pogroms in Iran and the Risks for Their Multiplication

Still, a key feature of inter-confessional relations in modern and present-day Iran remains the statistical weakness of pogrom practice. The study of Iranian national archives shows the existence of a diffuse violence centred mainly on the Baha'i Faith, regularly accused of collusion with foreign powers,[6] and the object of sporadic coercion from the Muslim majority in almost every region of Iran in the Qajar and Pahlavi periods. Since 1979, state repression has hit this community even during the Khatami presidency (e.g., during the September 1998 campaign against Baha'i religious activists on account of their 'Zionist activities').[7] In another domain, the security organs of both the Pahlavi monarchy and the Islamic Republic have distinguished themselves by their common prejudice against the presence of Protestant missions on the western and eastern marches of the national territory, again on account of their

---

[5] Farhad Khosrokhavar, *L'islamisme et la mort: le martyre révolutionnaire en Iran*, Paris: L'Harmattan, 1995, notably pp. 305–30.
[6] As regularly recalled in anti-Baha'i literature printed in Iran since 1979: see for example Bahram Afrasiyabi, *Tarikh-e jame'-e baha'iyat* [A General History of Baha'ism], Tehran: Nashr-e Mehr-e Fam, 1382[/2003], pp. 323–45 (on the alleged links between Baha'ism and Great Britain in the late Qajar and Pahlavi eras), pp. 557–75 (on the contribution of Baha'is to the creation of the State of Israel).
[7] E.g., available: http://www.bahaindex.com/en/news/human-rights/271-mrruhollah-rowhani-executed-in-iran-21-july-1998 (accessed 18 July 2011).

possible links with foreign powers.[8] During the past thirty years, however, Christian converts and preachers of Iranian origin have been exposed to permanent intimidation and violence, culminating in the late 2000s with campaigns of assassinations. As to the attitude of the Islamic Republic towards its historical Christian minorities, Armenian and Assyrian (between 0.4 and 0.8 of the country's population, according to the available statistics), they continue to come up against the issue of school teaching.

A New Typology of Violence

Other communities, some numerically small, have preferred to leave Iran in the course of the nineteenth and twentieth centuries, in particular towards the Ottoman Empire or the subcontinent under British rule and, at later dates, towards Europe or North America. Beside generations of Baha'is, such was the case of the Isma'ilis in a period from the 1840s to the 1910s, and of the smaller community of Zikris of Baluchistan after the jihad launched against them by a Deobandi preacher of the Baluch market town of Sarbaz in April 1936.[9] (In this matter, the Deoband School in Iran has for long been reproducing, at a more modest scale, the intolerant attitude of the Shiite majority against the Baha'i minority: still another case of cultural transfer from the centre to the periphery.) From the viewpoint of the Sunni attitude towards the Shiite majority, it is to be noticed that the hostility expressed locally, for instance in Iranian Baluchistan, towards Shiite Islam and the Shiites has long focused on officials and agents of the Iranian state – those called in Baluchi *gajar* since the succession of military campaigns of the Qajars against their unruly south-eastern marches in the second half of the nineteenth century. In such peripheral regions of Iran, the main new development of the 2000s has consisted of the appearance of sharper tensions between the ever growing numbers of Shiite-background migrants and the Sunni local populations. Since 2007, after the destruction by local authorities of the Sheykh Fayz Sunni mosque of Zabol, the main city of the district of Sistan, the situation has further deteriorated as the Jundollah has imported models of violence practised by the Taliban in Afghanistan, in the Tribal Areas of Pakistan, and in the Indus River valley by such extreme anti-Shiite organizations as the Sipah-i Sahaba and the Lashkar-i Jhangvi, which are still active despite having been outlawed in the early years of the Musharraf era (1999–2008).

---

[8] As for the two reigns of the Pahlavi period, see for instance: Organization for the Archives and National Library of Iran, Tehran, file Nr. 24 0000 60 99 (*Ijad-e ekhtelaf va nefaq-e mazhabi tavassot-e 'ommal-e Engelis dar Sistan va Baluchistan, 1314 sh.* [The Creation of Confessional Divergence and Conflict by Agents of Great Britain in Sistan and Baluchistan], 1314[/1935], pp. 2 ff.; ibid., file Nr. 29 000 3607 (*Tabligh-e din-e masihiyat tavassot-e hey'at-e misiyun-e amrikayi dar beyn-e 'ashayer* [The Propagarion of the Christian Faith among the Tribes by the American Committee for Missions], 1334[/1955], pp. 22 ff.; etc.

[9] On this event, see Dudoignon, 'Zahedan vs. Qom?', pp. 293–99.

'National Unity and Islamic Concord'

In recent years the ideology of 'National Unity and Islamic Concord' (*vahdat-e melli va ensejam-e eslami*) has been promoted by Supreme Leader Ali Khameneh'i in view of this potentially fatal degradation of the situation. It is not a coincidence that the proclamation of the solar year 1386 (2007–2008) as the 'Year of National Unity and Islamic Concord' in March 2007 followed the first spectacular attacks organized in February of that year by the Jundollah against the IRGC in the centre of the city of Zahedan, the capital of the province of Sistan and Baluchistan. Frequently touring, during this eventful period, diverse Sunni-majority regions of Iran, Khameneh'i endlessly denounced the hand of foreign powers in the worsening of relations between the country's two main communities of faithful. Since that date a growing number of institutions and forums have been assembling Shiite and Sunni clerics and favouring their permanent dialogue, sometimes on the margins of the IRGC-held state administration. It is true that both Shiite and Sunni religious establishments are confronted with the emergence of new forms of political Islam questioning the traditional authority of the Shiite *hawza*s and Sunni madrasas: in Shiite Islam the messianic movement personified by Ahmadinejad himself, and among Sunnis the rapid progression of the Salafiya. Like Perestroika in Mikhail Gorbachev's Soviet Union, Islamic concord has become in Iran the ideological common place of the moment: it would not be proper to oppose it.

The Taboo of Proselytism

Aware of the state of balance of power between opposing forces, the Sunni religious establishment of Iran has adopted a moderate discourse on relations with the Shiite majority – in fact a non-discourse, the subject being carefully avoided on the public platforms of the Deobandi movement, in sharp contrast with the outbursts of aggressiveness of the non-institutional Persian-language Sunni internet.[10] The relations between the two communities permanently come up against the thorny issue of proselytising activity, at a time when conversion takes on significant symbolical and strategic dimensions. Even an organization like the Pakistan-based Tablighi Jama'at, introduced in Iran since at least the 1970s through Sistan and Baluchistan, but placed under the control of the Supreme Leader through his Representation (*Namayandagi*) in this region, has been keeping a low profile.[11] Such a restraint contrasts with the anti-Shiite deliriums of the Iranian Sunni internet, as well as with those of Iranian Sunni clerics established outside of Iran, either in the lower Indus River valley or in 'Londonistan'. Such is the case of Mawlana 'Abd al-Rahim Mollazadeh, born into one of the most prestigious Sunni religious lineages of Iranian Baluchistan, and the author in 2009 of a Persian-language pamphlet distributed in PDF format from London. In this work, the Baluchistani cleric

---

[10] Dudoignon, 'Sunnis online', pp. 41–45.
[11] Dudoignon, 'Sunnis and Shi'ites in Iran since 1979'.

draws associations between Shiism and the 'international Zionist plot'[12]—a clear if paradoxical and especially oxymoronic illustration of the current transfer of extreme language from mainstream to marginal culture within the Islamic Republic.

Sunni Islam, Iranian Way: An Exception and a Paradigm

The Issue of the Sunni Minority

One peculiarity of the Sunni population of Iran, compared with the country's other confessional minorities, is its relative numerical significance: between eight and twenty per cent of a population of roughly 71 million inhabitants (the figure varies greatly according to the origin of statistics at our disposal, the Sunnis being not accorded the status of a distinct minority endowed with special rights and representations). Another peculiarity of this population, which contributes to blur the figures at our disposal, is the non-equation between ethnic and confessional belonging: significant segments of the Persian population of the Gulf littoral and of central Khorasan traditionally adhere to Sunni Islam; they also have been playing a leading role during the past decade in the propagation of both Deobandi and Salafi schools of thought throughout the Iranian national territory. The Persian Gulf littoral and Khorasan are two regions with a strong tradition of mutual exchange.[13] Their role must be underlined in the exportation of Iranian Sunni revivals towards the Arab world in the southwest and towards Central Asia in the northeast. Conversely, the same populations have also been playing the role of intermediaries for foreign inputs, for which reason they are often considered by Tehran as unreliable and potentially disloyal to the Iranian state. This is all the more significant in that in Iran Sunni Islam remains associated with several ethnic groups traditionally seen in Tehran as tempted by national irredentism, the essential part of their population being located in neighbouring countries (partly Sunni Western Azerbaijani Turks as well as Kurds, Arabs, Baluch, and Turkmens).

Centrality of the Marches: Baluchistan and Kurdistan

Having dominated the Sunni Islamic religious field of Iran until the 1970s, Kurdistan has since then been replaced by a newcomer to the country's religious history: Iranian Baluchistan. Of course, first-rank Kurdish Sunni clerics

---

[12] Doktur Mawlana 'Abd al-Rahim Mollazadeh, *Virangarha-ye tashayyo' dar eslam va naqsh-e yahud dar tahrif-e an* [The Destructive Character of Shiism in Islam and the Role of Jews in Its Falsification], London: s.l.: s.n., c. 2006; on the Mollazadehs, see Dudoignon 'Un *mawlawi* contre les *pasdaran*?' passim and idem, 'Zahedan vs. Qom', pp. 292–93, pp. 299–301.

[13] See for instance the historical remarks by prominent Iranian geographer and ethnographer Mahmud Zand Moqaddam, *Afaq-e jazireh-ye Qeshm* [The Horizons of the Island of Qeshm], Tehran: Anjoman-e Asar va Mafakher-e Farhangi, 1383/2004, pp. 27–29 and 35.

like Mamusta Muhammad, the *Sheykh al-Islam* of Sanandaj, have continued playing a role in the highest authorities of the Islamic Republic such as the Assembly of Leadership Experts, but he was assassinated in September 2009. Nor was his death an isolated case: many Sunni Kurdish imams have been murdered since the mid-2000s for having set themselves up as defenders of their coreligionists, which demonstrates *a contrario* how important they are considered to be by the country's main political authorities and special services. However, the growing weight of the Deobandi School in Iran's Sunni religious teaching institutions has reinforced the positions of a Baluchistan-centred network of madrasas, imposing Zahedan instead of Sanandaj as the centre of Sunni teaching in Iran, making it a Sunni equivalent of Qom. For at least twenty years, until the emergence of the Internet in the late 1990s, Deobandi religious schools and mosques were favoured by the paucity of alternative forums within Iran's civil society. If many of these institutions were established during the last decade of the Pahlavi period and have continued to be set up since the revolution of 1979, it is of course because neither the monarchy nor the Islamic Republic ever hampered their construction, but also because these places were and remain a rare available tribune for the expression of discontent. From this viewpoint, remarkable continuities can be observed in the location of dissent within religious schools between the Pahlavi and the current periods. The capacity shown by these schools' headmasters to surround themselves with teams of young and talented webmasters has also allowed them to overcome the challenge posed at the turn of the twenty-first century by the irruption of the Internet and by the rapid development of a rich but elusive Sunni Persian confessional blogosphere.[14]

Indo-Pakistani Impacts

Contrary to religious developments in other Sunni-majority provinces and districts of Iran, the religious revivals that have been affecting Iranian Baluchistan, before and after the arrival of the Internet, have taken a pan-Iranian dimension, and as such have paradigmatic value. Three influences from India and Pakistan come together in the modern Sunni revival that has found its main cradle in Iranian Baluchistan: the vast network of madrasas of the Deobandi School, already mentioned; a political party, the Jam'iyat al-Ulama-ye Islam—a major proponent of the Islamicization of public life in Pakistan since 1947, its consistently modest electoral results notwithstanding; and the Tablighi Jama'at missionary society, created in Delhi in 1926, initially for struggling against Hindu proselytising activity among the subcontinent's Muslim tribal populations. As well as in India, then Pakistan, and more recently Afghanistan, the Deobandi movement in Iran has been recruiting a substantial part of its adherents in the tribal milieu since the 1930s, this recruitment having acquired special vigour since the early 1970s. This explains

---

[14] Dudoignon, 'Sunnis online', pp. 48–52.

the role of a geographical hub played by Iranian Baluchistan in the diffusion of the movement westwards. Baluchistan's tribal substratum expresses itself in two ways in the Deoband School. First, strong clientele links connect the major tribes with the leading madrasas, as revealed, for instance, by the role played since the 1930s by the Shahbakhsh tribe (renamed Isma'ilzayi since 1979) in the diffusion of the Deoband School on Iranian territory,[15] and second, the reinvention – rather than transmission – of a literary culture of jihad nourished by the memory of the Khanate of Kalat (which in the late eighteenth century had federated, against the Sikhs among others, a mosaic of ethnic groups west of the Indus River valley).[16] Whilst the pan-Iranian diffusion of the Deobandi movement has been putting Zahedan at the centre of the confessional map of Iran, the movement's tribal substratum also contributes to cement a growing identification between Sunni Islam and Baluch national identity.

Is Kurdistan back? Iraq, the Internet and Islamic Communities
The establishment of Deobandi mosques and madrasas has not remained unchallenged within the Sunni populations of Iran since the end of the Pahlavi period. Besides the emergence of the Internet, the newly established hierarchy of Deobandi Sunni minbars has had to contend with the diffusion of the modern Salafiya. One of the origins of the movement must be sought in Iraq, where it has been expanding since the end of the Kuwait War of 1991 and diffused since the mid-2000s towards the Sunni-populated districts in the north-western part of Iranian Kurdistan (still a *terra incognita* of modern religious history). Beyond their relative inner diversity (on the issue of jihad, notably), the nascent Kurdish Salafiya try to appear as a credible answer to the recent failure of Islamist parties and movements of Iraqi Kurdistan like the *Ansar al-Islam* and the *Maktab al-Qur'an*. In Iranian Kurdistan it also endeavours to respond to Tehran's exclusively Shiite rhetoric, as well as to the still dominant secular Iranian Kurdish political organizations. This trend's common practice of *takfir wa'l-hijra* ('anathema and self-exile', on the model of the Prophet Muhammad leaving infidel Mecca for Yathrib, a move that is the starting point of the Islamic calendar) has brought about, in the 2000s, the appearance of alternative rural communities (*jama'at*s). These embryonic 'ideal cities' have become new centres of Salafi teaching in Iranian territory, and rivals to the traditional networks of Sunni madrasas. Though often rejecting ethnic affiliations, the Salafiya are becoming in certain spheres a significant element of Kurdish identity, similar to the Deoband School in the case of some Baluch. Contrary to the latter, however, the Kurdish Salafiya do not

---

[15] Dudoignon, 'Zahedan vs. Qom?', 298–99.
[16] On the impact of this polity's memory on the structuring of a modern Baluch political identity, see Martin Axmann, *Back to the Future: The Khanate of Kalat and the Genesis of Baloch Nationalism, 1915–1955*, Karachi: Oxford University Press, 2008, in part, pp. 129–39.

Inter-Confessional Relations in Iran 105

seem to propagate their teaching to the entire Iranian territory, new positions having been gained mainly in Khorasan. Generally speaking, the Salafiya's recent appearance, their regional if not local dimensions, their infra-political stance and their lack of interest in elections, have permitted them to suffer less pressure from the Islamic Republic, which does not seem to see a major threat in this essentially reactionary movement, culturally and socially still more conservative than the ruling regime itself.

Three Turning Points: 1993, 2003, 2007

The First Outburst of Violence (1993–1997)
In the early days of the Islamic Republic, prominent Shiite but also Sunni religious leaders, among whom Sheykh 'Ezz al-Din Hoseyni in Mahabad and Mawlana 'Abd al-'Aziz Makki in Zahedan, had opposed the principle of *velayat-e faqih* and the establishment of Khomeini's dictatorship. During the years of war against Iraq (1980–1988), the Sunnis of Iran were the object of permanent scrutiny on account of their alleged links with the Saddam Hussein regime and their very limited enthusiasm for joining the ranks of the Basij. Since the 1990s, the growing weight of the IRGC in the political and economic spheres, and the fact that the Islamic Republic has adopted an ideology made of Aryanism and political Shiism, have aroused disappointment outside of the Persian and Shiite 'citadel' of the central Iranian plateau.[17] This disappointment was expressed in an escalation of tensions—briefly interrupted by the beginning of the Khatami presidency—until the municipal elections of 2003. Among the most telling events of this period were the ransacking by a Shiite mob of a newly built Sunni mosque in Sanandaj in 1993, and the reaction to the demolition of the Sheykh Fayz Sunni mosque in Mashhad in February 1994, an event that provoked street demonstrations in Zahedan and in the eastern parts of Iran. Characteristic of the post-war decade, these tensions have favoured the emergence of new Sunni confessional leaders with nationwide appeal, such as Mawlana 'Abd al-Hamid, Mawlana 'Abd al-'Aziz Makki's successor since 1987 as the *Shaykh al-Islam* of Zahedan, who has managed to transform the latter's madrasa, the Dar al-'Olum 'Makki', into Iran's most authoritative Sunni religions teaching institution.

The Situation since 2003
In the aftermath of the occupation of Afghanistan and Iraq by US-led coalitions, and of the first electoral successes of the conservative reaction in 2003, the ingredients of a major crisis seemed to have come together. To make matters worse, in the western and eastern peripheries of Iran, nationwide eco-

---

[17] The term of a 'Shiite citadel' has been coined by geographer Bernard Hourcade for designating the central regions of Iran giving majorities to Ahmadinejad in the presidential elections of 2005 and 2009; see notably 'In the Heart of Iran: The Electorate of Mahmoud Ahmadinejad', *MERIP Report*, 36/241, 2006, pp. 10–11.

nomic difficulties are aggravated by a durable underdevelopment, deepened in Khuzistan by the slowness of reconstruction after the war against Iraq and in Sistan and Baluchistan by a decade of drought. To these realities must be added the traditional underrepresentation of the ethno-confessional minorities in the local and regional power structures, and ongoing repression with a strong confessional dimension, characterized since 2005 by numerous assassinations of Sunni imams (attributed by the Sunni media and opinion to the ministry of intelligence). The election of Mahmoud Ahmadinejad to the presidency of the Islamic Republic has only deepened the divorce of 1979 between the Shiite majority and the Sunni minority. It must be noted that among the assassination attempts perpetrated since his election against Ahmadinejad himself, one of the most serious ones (it cost the life of one of the president's bodyguards) took place as early as December 2005 in Sarawan, a predominantly Baluch city located on the Pakistani border. The newly elected Iranian president had come to this town ravaged by unemployment, a pivot of international smuggling, for speaking on the situation in Gaza. 'We aren't in the UN here, and he could have come to speak of our problems' was the oral comment made by several Baluch witnesses some days later, at my own arrival in Zahedan.

In the Long Term: A Shiite 'Colonization?'

This conjunction of factors is made more volatile in the long term by the ever-growing significance of a still understudied demographic phenomenon: the increase of the part of Persian or Azerbaijani Shiite-background migrants coming from the central plateau for settling down in the country's western and eastern peripheries. In newly built cities recently encircled by shanty towns populated by the drift of Sunni-background populations from abandoned areas, two worlds have come to coexist, separated by a strong and careful spatial segregation. In Iranian Baluchistan, Sunni mosques and madrasas recently constructed in Bollywood style try hard to rival in dimensions and splendour the neo-Safavid pomp of the slightly older *hoseyniya*s erected in the central neighbourhoods of newly expanded cities like Zahedan, Iranshahr, and Chahbahar. In most cases, these Shiite places of worship have been built by migrant traders who have arrived since the 1930s from neighbouring Sistan and from cities like Yazd and Kerman on the edge of the Great Desert, or from Birjand in southern Khorasan, a bridgehead of Shiite power in eastern Iran since the sixteenth century.[18] This set of modern demographic factors has been reinforcing among the Baluch a double sentiment of abandonment and deprivation. Rarely since the Safavid period have mutual expectations and

---

[18] Cf. Mohammad-Reza Behniya, *Birjand, negin-e kavir* [Birjand, the Pearl of the Desert], second ed., Tehran: Entesharat-e Daneshgah-e Tehran, 1381/2002, pp. 347–60; Jamal Reza'i, *Birjand-nameh: Birjand dar aghaz-e sadeh-ye chahardahom-e khorshidi* [The Book of Birjand: Birjand in the Twentieth Century], Tehran: Hirmand, 1381/2002, pp. 121–57, pp. 235–39, pp. 243–52, pp. 462–65, pp. 467–69, pp. 603–26.

mistrust reached such a height between the two communities, and between the Iranian state and the religious leaders of the country's main Sunni marches. Demographic and political conditions seem to have been set up for an outburst of inter-communal violence unprecedented in the country's modern history. Attempts to evict the inhabitants of such a potentially troublesome neighbourhood have also contributed towards the appearance of the already mentioned segregated rural communities, through the implementation of the Salafi principle of anathema and self-exile. This implementation can take the form of Salafi villages in Iranian Kurdistan, or take place through rejuvenation of ancient cities as in the case of Kh^{v}af. Lying in a Sunni-populated district of central Khorasan, Kh^{v}af has been endowed since 1946 with a Deobandi madrasa created by two Sunni ulema and Sufi masters who had returned from the subcontinent. The Sunni madrasa of Kh^{v}af recently affiliated with the Dar al-'Olum Makki of Zahedan.[19] Let us also note the existence, in the eastern provinces of Iran, of Salafi rural communities associated both with a local Deobandi institution and with one or several trans-border traditional Sufi orders. A good example is the saffron-producing new market town of Heydarabad in central Khorasan, a town that is absent from the maps of the Iranian National Institute of Geography, but that is endowed with a madrasa that welcomes hundreds of pupils, among them boarders from Tajikistan some of whom are affiliated with Central Asian branches of the Naqshbandiya-Khufiya Sufi order.[20]

The 2009 Events: A Peak or a Turning Point?

Contrary to the Arab guerrillas of Khuzistan, the Baluchistan-based Jundollah (like the south-eastern Iranian networks of Deobandi madrasas) has constantly looked for possibilities to expand beyond regional boundaries towards the Iranian hinterland. From 2006 onwards it used to introduce itself as

---

[19] For a history of the Muslim clerisy in Kh^{v}af and its Khargerd neighbourhood see Ebrahim Zanganeh Qasemabadi, *Tarikh va rejal-e sharq-e Khorasan: Velayat-e Kh^{v}af* [History and Notables of Eastern Khorasan: The District of Kh^{v}af], 2 Vols., Mashhad: Nashr-e Khatereh, 1370/1991 and 1378[/1999], in part. vol. 1, pp. 125–31; 'Abd al-Karim Ahrari-Rudi, *Kh^{v}af dar gozar-e tarikh* [Kh^{v}af in the Path of History], Torbat-e Jam: Entesharat-e Sheykh al-Eslam-e Ahmad-e Jam, 1383/2004, pp. 45–51. Elements of history of the Ahnaf Madrasa of Kh^{v}af can be found in Zanganeh, *Tarikh va rejal*, pp. 131–44; in Ahrari Rudi, *Kh^{v}af dar gozar-e tarikh*, pp. 113–25; and in one of this madrasa's fanzines: see notably Hoseyn Ahmad Shahidi, 'Tarikhcheh-ye howzeh-ye 'elmiyyeh-ye Ahnaf-e Kh^{v}af [A Short History of the Ahnaf Religious School of Kh^{v}af]', *Naghmeh-ye towhid* 1/1 (1422 *q.*/2001–2002), pp. 25–27.

[20] Information collected notably during my visit of the market town and madrasa of Heydarabad, January 2006; see also my paper 'From Tribal to Global . . . to Tribal? Iran's Eastern Provinces: a New Hub for Neo-Traditional Sunni Islam', presented at the conference on 'Muslim Identities and Imperial Spaces: Networks, Mobility, and the Geopolitics of Empire and Nation (1600–2011)', Stanford University, 7–8 April 2011.

nothing less than the 'National Resistance Movement of Iran'. Two years after the first urban attack against the IRGC in Zahedan in February 2007, the spectacular attacks of spring and autumn 2009 in Baluchistan have signified a major turning point. On 28 May 2009, two weeks before the first (and last) round of the presidential election, a suicide attack was carried out in Zahedan against the 'Ali ibn Abi-Talib Shiite mosque, whose congregation is the second-largest in the city and includes a number of IRGC officers. On 18 October of the same year another suicide attack occurred in the border town of Pishin, tragetting a meeting of staff officers of the IRGC with Baluch tribal chiefs, which claimed 44 casualties. The National Resistance Movement of Iran claimed responsibility for both events, which shows that Taliban-type political violence had irrupted on Iranian territory, a violence that is essentially different from the more diffuse violence that was exerted in the region since the early 2000s. Coming as a reaction to the attempts by the Ahmadinejad administration to establish firmer control over the Sunni confessional institutions of the country, these unprecedented attacks expressed a will to sever all links with the highest authorities of the Islamic Republic. The organization led by 'Abd al-Malik Rigi was then finding itself in the forefront of the armed struggle against the regime, at a time when Deobandi madrasas were mobilizing the electorate in favour of the alternative candidates to the presidency of the republic, Karrubi and Musavi, and explicitly backing the Green Movement. Presidential elections campaigns had constituted a rare political safety valve for the Sunni minority, and so the official results of the June 2009 ballot brought about a major break with the past, as the overt rigging of the votes has inserted a certain unpredictability into the future attitudes of the Sunni minbars towards the country's political process. It also makes it more difficult for the Sunni religious establishment to confront the more radical trends, such as the expanding Salafiya.

The Game of Persophonia

Geographically peripheral, ethnically heterogeneous, and prone to import religious trends and political practices from abroad, the Sunni populations of Iran appear, when seen from Tehran, excessively exposed to alien influence. There are, however, other aspects of the Sunni revival in Iran that stir more mixed feelings among the country's authorities, namely its *Persian* dimension and its ability to project its influence beyond the Iranian territory towards the Arab world, Afghanistan, and Central Asia. The translation offices in the big madrasas of Iranian Baluchistan translate books of the Urdu-language Deoband School into Persian, which thus becomes a transnational vehicle for their diffusion. This has led the Iranian government since the 'Year of Islamic Concord' in 2007 to promote a dual policy so typical of the Islamic Republic: control and repression within, laissez-faire without, for the diffusion of the Deoband School by the Sunni religious establishment of south-eastern Iran contributes towards the projection of Iranian cultural power towards countries with a strong Sunni majority, such as the former Soviet republics of Central Asia. That is how a first-rank Sunni religious leader like Mawlawi 'Abd al-

Hamid, the *Sheykh al-Islam* of Zahedan and rector of that city's prestigious Dar al-'Olum Makki, came to act as an ambassador for Iran at the celebrations of the jubilee of Imam Abu-Hanifa (the founding figure of one of the four modern schools of Sunni Islam) in Tajikistan on 5 October 2009, a mere 13 days before Jundollah's bloody attack in Pishin. Persian-speaking Tajikistan has been sending students in religion towards eastern Iran since the end of its civil war in 1997. This illustrates the contradictions inherent in Iran's current policies vis-à-vis the Sunni world, which are due to the diversity of the protagonists and to the moving geopolitical context created by the upheavals of the past decade in the whole region. The situation is made even more complex within Iran by the recent evolution of the relations between the Supreme Leader, who is the artisan and main beneficiary of the concord policy, and President Ahmadinejad, whom many identify as the key agent of the strategy of tension. In the immediate aftermath of the war with Iraq, Mohammad-Reza Djalili observed that the Islamic Republic's diplomacy was that of a state actor that is overwhelmed by a radical movement.[21] It would seem that more than twenty years later, this radical movement has acquired an internal pluralism that complicates Iranian foreign policy even more.

Conclusion

The Possibility of a 'Sunni Card'
Although it is difficult to handle, the 'Sunni card' is worth trying for the Iranian government, all the more so since Sunni Islam, Iranian style, does not threaten Iran's territorial integrity, contrary to the Kurdish or Baluch separatisms of the 1950s to 1970s. The problem posed by the most radical Sunni militants comes from the relations they maintain with some violent anti-Shiite movements typical of the early Musharraf era such as the Sipah-i Sahaba and the Lashkar-i Jhangvi and their present-day successors in the Indus valley. More generally speaking, this issue originates in the intimate historical links between the School of Deoband, the Jam'iyat al-'Ulama, the Tablighi Jama'at, and the Taliban movement, a recurrent *bête noire* of the regime in Tehran. To these ties one must add those between the Jundollah and the People's Mojahedin: until Rigi's arrest in February 2010 the National Resistance Movement of Iran constituted the main threat for the Iranian authorities on their eastern flank, a region where endemic instability creates difficulties for such projects as a hydrocarbon pipeline to the subcontinent, and the opening up of Iran's Baluch littoral to commerce with Central Asia.

A Dual Policy
Of course the politicization of the Deobandi discourse in Iran, through the demand for full citizenship rights for the Sunni minority, the denunciation of a Shiite 'colonization' of the country's western and eastern peripheries, and the

---

[21] Djalili, *Diplomatie islamique*, p. 201.

growing structuring of a Sunni vote in presidential elections, also constitute immediate challenges for Tehran. Since 2007, the Islamic Republic has opted for a double line made of stricter firmness inside the country (and towards Pakistani authorities long accused of indulgence towards the Jundollah), and of relative openness outside (leaving the Deobandi madrasas to play a role of projection of Iran's cultural power beyond the country's boundaries). It remains to be seen, in the context of a growing chasm between the Supreme Leader and the president, whether the awkward attempts of the Ahmadinejad administration to tighten control over the world of Sunni madrasas—one of the very rare relatively open forums of present-day Iran—will not jeopardize an unstable political balance after years marked by Jundollah's imported violence.

The Risks of Militarization

Whilst the Sunni establishment of the Deobandi madrasas continues its effort for finding a modus vivendi with the regime, through negotiations with the Supreme Leader's apparatus and with Shiite confessional institutions, the course of the June 2009 presidential ballot prefigures a possible future confrontation. But in 2010 Tehran managed, through political terror, to retake the initiative that it had lost in the previous year. The Islamic Republic has also benefited from the unfavourable geopolitical situation created by the US military presence east and west of its frontiers, obtaining in 2010 the interruption of Pakistan's tacit support to the Jundollah. At the same time, the growing military nature of the regime makes room for further political instrumentation of the country's main and most problematic confessional cleavage within a military logic. Iran's leaders would do well to heed the warning of Catholic general and memorialist Blaise de Monluc (d. 1577), who, in the middle of Europe's own wars of religion, wrote: 'Other quarrels can easily be brought to peace, but religious quarrels have long sequels; moreover, although men at arms are not very religious, they take sides, and having become engaged in the conflict, they follow through.'[22]

---

[22] 'Les autres querelles se pacifient aisément, mais celle de la religion a longue suite ; et encore que les gens de guerre ne soient pas fort religieux, ils prennent parti, et étant engagés, ils suivent puis après.' Blaise de Monluc, *Commentaires (1521–76)*, Paul Courtault (ed.), Paris: Gallimard (Bibliothèque de la Pléiade), 1964, p. 629.

Chapter 6

Political Culture, Use of History, and Democracy in Iran

Firouzeh Nahavandi

> The strongest are still never sufficiently strong to ensure them continual mastership, unless they find means of transforming force into right, and obedience into duty.
> —Jean Jacques Rousseau, *Du Contrat Social*, I, 1.3

Iran has experienced much turmoil throughout the twentieth century, stemming from policies of modernization and Islamicization. Many of these policies have been analysed by Mohammad-Reza Djalili, especially those related to the Islamic Republic of Iran.[1] Djalili has extensively used the tools of political science and international relations to clarify the on-going changes occurring in Iran. This chapter will add to those contributions by focusing on the political culture of Iran.

Introduction: Political Culture and Legitimization

We consider here that in politics, perceptions may be more important than reality, so much so that they may even become reality. Moreover, regardless of whether an action has been proven true or not, what matters is what people *believe* to be true. Reality may become what the shared beliefs of actors do with it.[2] (For example, no matter how impossible it is that the image of Kho-

---

[1] Among others see: *Histoire de l'Iran contemporain*, Paris: La Découverte, 2010, with Thierry Kellner; *L'Iran de A à Z*, Bruxelles: André Versaille, 2010; *Géopolitique de l'Iran*, Bruxelles: Complexe, 2005; *Iran: l'illusion réformiste*, Paris: Presses de Sciences Po, 2001; *L'Iran en transition. Entre espoir et incertitude*, Paris: La Documentation française, *Problèmes politiques et sociaux*, 1998; *Diplomatie islamique: stratégie internationale du khomeynisme*, Paris: Presses Universitaires de France, 1989, and *Religion et révolution: islam shi'ite et l'État*, Paris: Economica, 1981.

[2] Dario Battistela, *Théories des relations internationales*, Paris: Presses de Sciences Po, 2003.

meini has been on the moon, the matter is that some Iranians saw his image and considered it to be the sign of his legitimacy.) This is why political culture plays a key role in the worldview of people and how they perceive power. Beliefs, symbols, and myths structure the attitudes of both the ruled and the rulers, or at least they give meaning to their actions. In this framework, concepts such as interest or national identity should be regarded as social constructs.

Political culture, though it has become a central theme in contemporary political science, has not long been mentioned as such, and its meaning and role have been the subjects of considerable debate among political scientists. Political culture has been referred to indirectly as customs and traditions,[3] ideology,[4] or national spirit, but the idea as such really emerged in the 1950s with the studies of Gabriel Almond and Sidney Verba and opinion surveys on the attitudes of voters which focused particularly on the political socialization of the governed and led to studies on the civic culture. 'The political culture is a set of knowledge and skills, of emotional and evaluative orientations towards the elements of political system. It is the subject realm that underlies and gives meaning to political actions.'[5] Marx and Engels in *The German Ideology* postulate that the ideas of the ruling class are the ruling ideas, meaning that the social class that has the material power also has the dominant spiritual power. The French sociologist Pierre Bourdieu speaks of symbolic power exerted on the dominated classes to make them accept the same principles of knowledge and assessment of the world and encourage their adherence to the established order.[6] These interpretations lead to the issue of legitimacy and legitimization of power, taking into account that legitimacy and legality differ: the law does not necessarily guarantee that a power is respected. Bertrand Badie provides a critical review of political culture and the weaknesses of its use in political science and refers to the need for a historical approach. He argues that cultural analysis can be conducted only in relation to history, because any structure of meaning implies a set of historically situated actions that by definition cannot be perfectly reproduced elsewhere.[7] The trajectory of change for each society has a specific cultural content that only a historical approach is able to highlight.[8] In turn, Reinhard Bendix offers an analysis of the historical foundations of authority.[9] He postulates the existence of a culture of authority in each society and reveals that the major political systems

---

[3] See Edmund Burke, *Reflections on The Revolution in France*, 1791.
[4] See Karl Marx and Friedrich Engels, *L'idéologie allemande*, Paris: Nathan, 1998.
[5] Gabriel Almond and Sidney Verba, *The Civic Culture, Political Attitudes and Democracy in Five Nations*, Boston: Little Brown Company, 1965.
[6] Pierre Bourdieu, *Langage et pouvoir symbolique*, Paris: Seuil, 2001.
[7] Bertrand Badie, *Culture et Politique*, Paris: Economica, third edition, 1993.
[8] Ibid, pp. 62–63.
[9] Reinhard Bendix, *Kings or People, Power and the Mandate to Rule*, Berkeley: University of California Press, 1978.

Political Culture 113

have sought to establish their authority based on an appeal to the sacred. Culture and legitimacy are thus assimilated.

In this chapter, I consider the issue of legitimization of power and action by referring to political culture in order to get to its link to democracy. In that framework, the role of history and religion will be stressed as a mode of legitimization worth studying. Some historical references used in the process of legitimization in Iran in the twentieth century will be emphasized and the common themes will be highlighted. Using historical references in politics allows for identification of the central values of a society and its ideals. It will be argued that in twentieth-century Iran, references to history and its interpretation have played a key role to legitimize actions. It is crucial to a ruler (or a government) that a large number of people believe that he has the authority, which leads to his legitimacy. Legitimization 'is a form of meaning which ideally integrates disparate institutional processes and sub-universes of meaning, thereby making sense of the entire social order. It has both a cognitive and a normative dimension. It provides information, explanation, rationalization, and justification.'[10] Sources of legitimacy are diverse. Legitimacy can be acquired by results, by habit, by procedures, or by links to historical, religious, or ethnic identity. In twentieth-century Iran, history and religion have been favoured in the process of legitimization. In the case of history, some references have been more valued than others, as is the case in religion. Key historical or religious personalities have been heavily mobilized. However, democracy has not been emphasized and has often been disregarded. That is why going beyond these representations can be considered a path to democratization, a point that will be developed in the conclusion. Thus, it will be argued that if geopolitics may explain the behaviour of a state and the options that are available to it, political culture also plays an important role, especially in the choice of available options. This does not imply that there is a mechanical relation between history and political choice; however the reference to history and culture provides the key for understanding situations and actions that seem 'irrational' and confused. 'The power of cultural interpretations of politics lies less in their inner coherence, rhetorical plausibility, or aesthetic appeal, than on their being well grounded sociologically.'[11]

Political Culture of Iran

By 'political culture' I mean the set of values, myths, traditions, and references mobilized to legitimize either the exercise of power or the opposition to it, which leads in turn to the representation of reality. Ernest G. Bormann speaks of rhetorical vision, which refers to 'composite dramas, which catch up

---

[10] Myron J. Aronoff, 'Conceptualizing the Role of Culture in Political Change', in *Culture and Political Change*, Myron. J. Aronoff (ed.), New Brunswick: Transaction Books, 1983, p. 1.
[11] Aronoff, 'Conceptualizing', p. 3.

large groups of people in a symbolic reality'.[12] The political culture of Iran is rooted in the foundation of the Persian Empire, as evidenced by an analysis of references and arguments that have supported and still support both domestic and internationally directed Iranian political discourse. In recent times, these references have gained new salience as part of the so-called 'nuclear issue'. These references are highly interesting and unusual, given that the Islamic Republic of Iran was built in opposition to the ancient history of Iran, which was dismissed as an era of *jahiliyya* (ignorance). However, one can discern many references to this history in all discourses on the nuclear issue. The following statements by President Mahmoud Ahmadinejad are telling: 'The Islamic Republic is not afraid to re-establish relations with Western powers, but we have to consider how to do so it in order that the independence, pride, and self-esteem of the Iranian nation do not suffer...'; 'to acquire peaceful nuclear technology is a requirement of the entire Iranian nation ...'; 'we are told that Iran must not have access to nuclear technology. This is not a good word for Iran, with an old civilization...'; 'the people of Iran, who are at the origin of a great civilization, will support such a programme (i.e., nuclear).'[13]

Furthermore, recently, President Ahmadinejad, speaking at a ceremony held to unveil the Cyrus Cylinder in Tehran, said the artefact has been an invaluable yardstick to evaluate the performance of politicians and rulers throughout history. In his discourse he lauded the Cyrus Cylinder as the embodiment of human values and a cultural heritage for all humanity. One of his interviews on the return of the Cyrus Cylinder is characteristic of the mobilization of history:[14]

> One of our kings replaced that dictatorship with a just regime. His name was Cyrus. The people in the Babylon of that time wanted assistance from Cyrus. They said, 'You preach justice, come and help us out. The dictator won't let us pray, he won't let us do anything.' I want to make a historical parallel here. Cyrus conquered Babylon and freed people from the brutal regime of Babylon. However, while going there to free the people, he did not hurt a soul. He did it in a way that the dictatorship in Babylon fell apart. And then he issued the Declaration of Human Rights. We know many nations themselves came and asked to be protectorates of the Iranian king. He said, 'I will never wage war only to be a king.' At that time it was said if you go north, south, east, or west, it was all the Iranian empire. He didn't allow any cruelty to anyone, he would confront cruelty, and he would punish cruelty. He said, 'I will not allow anybody's wealth to be taken away from him without compensation. For as long as I am alive, I won't allow anyone to enslave anyone. Everyone is free, everyone is free to live where he likes and choose any job he likes and spend the money he likes (...)'

---

[12] 'Fantasy and Rhetorical Vision: the Rhetorical Criticism of Social Reality', *The Quarterly Journal of Speech*, 58, 1972, pp. 396–407.
[13] Ahmadinejad congratulating President Barack Obama for his election in 2008.
[14] Interview with two Islamic Republic of Iran Broadcasting (IRIB) reporters televised on Friday 17 September 2010.

We have even more interesting points. He said, 'Everyone is responsible for his own actions.' In other words, if anyone commits a wrong, you cannot punish the entire family, whereas in the past if someone in a tribe did something wrong, members of the opposing tribe thought it gave them the right to kill whomever they liked from that tribe or from that family. He said, 'I will not allow human beings to be traded as slaves... and slavery must be wiped off the face of the earth.' Now let's go to the UN issue. Some people say Cyrus was a prophet. We don't say so. We just say that he was a good person. When we celebrate him, this isn't nationalism. He was just an outstanding character who did positive work for humanity, but part of the fact is that he was an Iranian. It also doesn't mean that during the rule of Cyrus there were no wrongs. We believe that the Islamic Republic is the best in the world and it has to dispense justice and take care of spirituality, but when you take into account the extent of the system, wrongs are committed. (...) In those days Iran was the only power in the world, and they conquered Babylon. But once he becomes the conqueror, injustice and aggression are outlawed. This is very important. Now let's see how this Cyrus goes to Iraq and frees the people of Babylon without bloodshed, without destruction of property, without any damage to infrastructure, and orders the abolishment of slavery and cruelty toward people and allows people to worship God the way they please in complete freedom. (...) Even the person who becomes the caretaker of a school wants to exert his authority. But look at other countries and look at Cyrus. He had taken over the whole world, but he said, 'If anyone does anything unjust, he will have to come and face me'. He said he would do everything within this Declaration of Rights.

Interestingly enough, Ali Motahhari, a member of the conservative hardline block in parliament, criticized the interview of Ahmadinejad:

Although there are some positive points in Human Rights Charter of Cyrus, the actions of Cyrus were not in line with the prophets' teachings (...) It seems that the President has made the remark under the influence of his advisor Esfandiar Masha'i, who recently proposed that Iran promote the Iranian School of thought instead of the Islamic School of Thought. The President should be aware that he is obliged to promote Islam and not ancient Iran.[15]

The speaker of parliament, Ali Larijani, went one step further: 'In our school, we have His Holiness the Prophet Mohammad and Imam Ali who ruled and provide infallible role models. Why don't you speak of them and talk instead about Cyrus? If we want to author a human rights declaration it should be inspired by the words of Imam Ali.'[16]

---

[15] *Tehran Times*, 19 September 2010.
[16] *Iran News Digest*, 21 September 2010, available:
http://www.irannewsdigest.com/2010/09/21/Ahmadinejad-under-fire-over-cyrus-remarks/ (accessed 4 September 2011).

A multiethnic country, Iran is considered by the majority of its population as primarily a historical and not an ethnic nation.[17] This common understanding and sense of history is what fuels the deep essence of being Iranian (*iraniyat*). It is also the main feature of Iranian political culture. This sense of belonging to one of the oldest nations in the world feeds the culture, as it provides an opportunity for many types of manipulation.[18] 'The extraordinary continuity of Iranian and sophisticated civilization has provided Iran with a multifaceted and tangled national experience and a legacy of a particularly rich and complex national culture.'[19] Iranians have not forgotten that their history goes back to two millennia before Christ. So far as it may seem, the Achaemenid Empire, founded in 550 BC, which included in its heyday a vast territory going from Egypt to part of modern Greece and included Sudan, Libya, and Asia Minor, still echoes in the minds of Iranians and is actively used in the speech of their leaders. There is a similar awareness of the great achievements of the Islamic civilization with the best architectural works, a great literature, and scientific progress.

Cyrus the Great, Imam Ali, and Imam Hoseyn: Mythical Figures of Political Culture

If we focus on the history of the second half of the twentieth century, two references are heavily used to legitimize power. The first is the ancient history of Iran, and especially the character of Cyrus, in the old regime (but not only in that regime, as evident in Ahmadinejad's aforementioned speech) and the second is Shiite Islam, imposed in the sixteen century by the Safavid dynasty, with a special emphasis on the characters of Ali and Hoseyn in the Islamic Republic of Iran. In that sense, Dariush Shayegan stresses that Mohammad Reza Shah and Ayatollah Khomeini are the two sides of the same coin, both referring to two mythic periods of history, that of Cyrus and that of the Prophet and Ali.[20]

Promoting the 'Great Civilization' by Reference to the Millennial History of Iran under the Old Regime

The Pahlavi regime was the instigator of the modernization policy of the early and mid-twentieth century. Reza Shah, the founder of the dynasty, laid the foundation that his son, Mohammad Reza Shah, followed. The latter added his own vision of the Iranian future and its place in the world. In the policy of modernization of the Pahlavis, pre-Islamic history of Iran was heavily used, probably to reduce the influence of religion considered as a barrier to modernization, and to legitimize chosen policies. To begin with, Reza Shah's

---

[17] Raoul Delcorde, 'Iran, Geopolitics and Regional Environment', *Studia Diplomatica*, 40(2), 2002, p. 44.
[18] Guy Spitaels, *La triple insurrection islamiste*, Brussels: Luc Pire, 2005, p. 289.
[19] Graham Fuller, *The Center of Universe, The Geopolitics of Iran*, Boulder: Westview, 1991, p. 8. See chapter one for the political and social culture of Iran.
[20] 'L'Imam et le Shah, deux Irans juxtaposés', *Libération*, 5 June 1989.

choice of 'Pahlavi' to name the new dynasty is quite evocative of the reference to history.[21] Moreover, Reza Shah not only began the secularization of the educational and legal systems, but created institutions designed to rehabilitate ancient history. Amongst them was the foundation of the Iranian Academy with Mohammad Ali Forughi as its first director. One of the missions of the academy was to create words to replace Arabic and Turkish ones, which were, and still are, common in the Persian language. The Academy was further charged with inventing an adequate vocabulary for modern and scientific terms. Additionally, Reza Shah instigated the Ferdowsi millennium as the symbol of the Persian language and created the Society for the Protection of National Patrimony, whose task was to find the tombs of famous Iranians and build mausoleums for them. This was accomplished for prominent poets, scholars, and kings including Sa'di and Hafez in Shiraz, Ibn Sina in Hamadan, Baba Taher in Hamadan, Omar Khayyam in Neyshapur, Sa'eb in Isfahan, and Nader Shah in Mashhad. The building of statues was also a task of the Academy, such as those of Ferdowsi, Sa'di or Ibn Sina. Reza Shah further replaced the Muslim lunar calendar with the Malek Shahi or Khayyami calendar, which is still in use today. In turn, his son Mohammad Reza Shah attempted to legitimize his regime politically by mobilizing the myth of 'the Great Civilization'. Among others, the 'Imperial' calendar was established introducing a time reset in accordance to imperial history. Overnight, Iranians found themselves driven from 1355 (1976) to 2535, as the beginning of the calendar was moved from Muhammad's journey from Mecca to Medina to the coronation of Cyrus the Great. The late Shah also began a policy valuing ethnic and religious minorities. The culmination of all these policies was the Persepolis celebrations in 1971. The last ruler of Iran saw 'Iranian Civilization' as the country's heritage. He thus tried to restore the latter to counter what he thought to be the ignorance of the Iranian people caused by a lack of modern structures due to the predominance of Islam, and shifted the nation's sense of *iraniyat* toward its heritage from ancient history. Thus, pre-Islamic history and traditions were promoted. This was achieved through the establishment of libraries and universities, proliferation of cultural initiatives—in particular the publication of a rich literature on the past, by the extensive reliance on Persian-centric television and radio programmes, and the rehabilitation of traditional Persian music. The celebration of 2,500 years of Iranian Empire was particularly rich in this sense. During the same period, history books dealing with the Iranian past and explaining the consequences of multiple invasions multiplied. Among them is Adolhoseyn Zarrinkub's well known *The History*

---

[21] The term is said to be derived from the Parthian language word *parthav* or *parthau*, meaning Parthia. If this etymology is correct, *Parthav* presumably became *pahlaw*. The term has been traced back further to Avesta. Common to all Indo-Iranian languages is a connotation of 'mighty'. Webster Online Dictionary. Avalaible: http://www.websters-dictionary-online.com/definitions/PAHLAVI?cx=partner-pub-0939450753529744%3Av0qd01-tdlq&cof=FORID%3A9&ie=UTF-8&q=PAHLAVI&sa=Search#906 (accessed 2 September 2011).

of *Iranian Nation*, published by University of Tehran Press, later republished during the Islamic Republic of Iran under the title of *The History of Iranian People*. The author characterizes the two centuries of Arab domination as dark ones in a chapter untitled 'Two centuries of silence'. On Cyrus, let us only cite *Cyrus the Great, Life and World-view of the Founder of Iranian Empire* by Shapur Shahbazi, also published by University of Tehran Press. Also worth quoting is *The Eternity of Iran*, by Sayyed Taqi Nasr,[22] which provides a view into how the late Shah conceived the history of Iran. Meanwhile, many books on Iranian history before Islam were translated.[23] In the main cities, monuments were built celebrating the past as columns with the Cyrus Cylinder. Finally, the Shahyad memorial in Tehran, with its 8,000 square metre museum devoted to the history of Iran, is one of the best demonstrations of the reference to millennial Persia.

The 'Great Civilization' was clearly inspired by Zoroastrianism to allow for continuity of the monarchy with its roots in ancient Persia; and in that way, reference to ancient history became the basis of propaganda and legitimization.[24] Mohammad Reza Shah wrote in his memoirs 'The idea that everything that belongs to the past is reactionary, anti-progressive or outdated...had led to denigrate authentic Iranian culture and neglect ancient works.' The goal of the Shah was to speed up development and reconstruction, maintaining a balance between technological advance and social growth by reference to the glorious past and Iranian values. For example, talking about the White Revolution (his reform programme begun in the early 1960s), he stated: '[t]he most important characteristics of this Revolution are that it has drawn inspiration from no source other than Iranian and is based totally on national interests, Iranian values, and the need of the society.'[25] The Great Civilization is one 'in which the most startling scientific discoveries and inventions will intermingle with the highest moral values and the greatest possible social justice. It is a civilization which will be planned on the foundation of creativity and all that is good in human nature and under it every individual will enjoy maximum welfare, social justice, and spiritual and world wealth.'[26]

In 1971, Mohammad Reza Shah's celebration, in Persepolis, of the 2,500th anniversary of the founding of Persian Empire and his tribute to Cyrus at Pasargadae, represented the culmination of this legitimization process. The Persepolis ruins were chosen as the authentic site for historic re-enactments and ultimate symbols of Iranian monarchy and civilization. According to the Shah, the location and event had to 're-awaken the people of Iran to their past and re-awaken the world to Iran.' His famous speech in front of Cyrus's tomb demonstrated the appropriation of fragments of ancient arte-

---

[22] Tehran: Keyhan edition, 1350/1971.
[23] See amongst other, R. Ghirshman, *Iran, des origines à l'islam*, Tehran: BTNK, 1976 or M.A. Dandamayev, *Iran under the Early Achaemenids*, Tehran: BTNK, 1973.
[24] 'Toward the Great Civilization', *Tehran Journal*, 9 March 1978.
[25] Ibid.
[26] Ibid.

facts: 'O Cyrus, great King, King of Kings, Achaemenian King, King of the land of Persia. I, the Shahanshah of Persia, offer thee salutations from myself and from my nation. Rest in peace; for we are awake, and we will always stay awake. And we will watch your glorious heritage.'

Cyrus thus represents this ancient and glorious past. Iranians hail him as a landmark. His origins are not clearly established, but they are mystified. His childhood may be considered part of the legends that follow a model of popular beliefs about the superhuman qualities needed for the founder of a dynasty. According to legend, Astyages, the king of the Medes and Persians, gave his daughter in marriage to a vassal, a prince called Cambyses. From this marriage Cyrus was born. Astyages, after dreaming that the baby would grow up to overthrow him, ordered him to be killed. However, the man who had to fulfil the task gave Cyrus to a shepherd and saved him from death. Later, the exceptional qualities of young Cyrus came to the ears of his grandfather who, despite the dream, let him live. As he reached adulthood, Cyrus rebelled against Astyages, who organized an army to subdue the rebels, but eventually submitted to Cyrus. Cyrus is the perfect example of a mythical personality. As a champion of tolerance, in the Bible, he is quoted as the one who delivered the Jews of Babylon. King Cyrus showed great tolerance towards the conquered peoples (as admitted by Ahmadinejad, as quoted above), supported local customs and even tolerated different communities' gods. But above all, he unified the Medes and Persians. The largest source of information about his life comes from the Greek historian Herodotus. Xenophon also composed a biography intended to present the ideal ruler to the Greeks. Sources tell us that Persians called him 'father of the people'. Cyrus was born between 590 and 580 BC. His reputation has survived throughout history as a great man, symbolizing the qualities expected from a leader. He is courageous, bold, tolerant, and magnanimous.[27] According to Aeschylus 'The sky was at peace with him because he was a wise.'[28] In the Torah, 'He is the shepherd and he will complete my joy.' According to Plato 'At the time of Cyrus, the kingdom was in progress in all areas, because people were free and the goodness and familiarity reigned among them.'[29] For Herodotus, 'His value is so high that the Persians do not give as much credit to their own children.' The qualities of a Cyrus are stated in Ferdowsi's epic book, the *Shahnameh*: integrity, humility, loyalty, justice, moderation, courage, forgiveness, knowledge, and patriotism,[30] although Cyrus himself is not mentioned in the *Shahnameh*. These

---

[27] See Richard Frye, *The Heritage of Persia*, Cleveland: World Club, 1963; and 'The Charisma of Kingship in Ancient Iran', *Iranica Antiqua*, 4, 1964, pp. 36–54. Dominique Lenfant, 'Les Rois de Perse vus par Athènes', in Actes du Xe colloque Poznan-Strasbourg, Nov. 1998 : *Les grands hommes des autres*.

[28] *Les Perses*.

[29] *Les Lois*, livre 3.

[30] See Mohammad Ali Foroughi's, Introduction to *Montakhab-e Shahnameh-ye Ferdowsi beh ehtemam-e jenab-e aqa-ye Mohammad Ali Foroughi va Aqa-ye Yaghmayi*, Tehran: Publications of the Ministry of Education, 1321, pp. 1–45; Forouz Djahan-

qualities correspond to what is interestingly enough also admired in Ali, as we will see later. Through this example we can see how ancient history and myth are closely linked.

Promoting Velayat-e Faqih *by Reference to Shiite Faith in the Islamic Republic of Iran*

By 1979, in the name of Islam, Ayatollah Khomeini took power, even though in the first days of the revolutionary movement religion was not the only reference for mobilization. He organized the system he had developed in his doctrine of *velayat-e faqih* (Islamic Government) while in exile in the early 1970s his thoughts became highly radicalized. *Velayat-e faqih,* a collection of lectures given in 1971, enshrines the political authority of the clergy, often discussed since the establishment of the Shiite faith as Iran's state religion in the sixteen century, but never achieved until the Islamic revolution. The monarchy is presented as illegitimate, and as an obstacle to the establishment of an Islamic order. The treatise became the foundation for post-revolutionary Iran's political order.

Using one of the mandatory teachings of Islam, namely 'enjoining the good and forbidding the evil' (*al-amr bi'l-ma'ruf wa'l-nahy 'an al-munkar*)[31] and defining what is good (Khomeini) and evil (the Shah) by drawing on symbolic and mythic dimensions of Shiite Islam, Khomeini succeeded in convincing a whole country to move towards revolution. According to Khomeini, the prerogatives of the Prophet and Imams should be granted to the clergy as natural leaders of an Islamic state. *Velayat-e faqih* is a political ideology legitimated by religion.

> In order to attain the unity and freedom of the Muslim peoples, we must overthrow the oppressive governments installed by the imperialists and bring into existence an Islamic government of justice that will be in the service of the people.[32]

Elsewhere he states: 'Islam is a political religion. It is a religion in which politics can be seen in the instructions and rituals.'[33]

---

shahi-Brélian, *Histoires légendaires des rois de Perse*, Paris: Imago, 2001 and Afsaneh Nahavandi, 'Cultural mythology and global leadership in Iran', in *Cultural Mythology and Global Leadership*, Eric H. Kessler, Diana J. Wong-MingJi (eds), Cheltenham: Edward Elgar Publishing, Inc., 2009, pp. 242–56.

[31] For the development of this idea see, Susan Zickmund, 'Constructing Political Identity, Religious Radicalism and the Rhetoric of the Iranian Revolution', *Poroi*, 2(2), November, 2003, pp. 22–41.
[32] Ruhollah Khomeini, *Islam and Revolution: Writings and Declarations of Imam Khomeini*, Hamid Algar tran., Berkeley: Mizan Press, 1981, p. 49.
[33] Ruhollah Khomeini, *Selected Messages and Speeches of Imam Khomeini*, Ministry of Islamic Guidance, Tehran: Hamadani Foundations Publishers, 1980, p. 22.

Khomeini mobilized the myths and symbols of Shiite Islam and made extensive use of martyrdom, thus giving to the deaths of Imam Ali (the first Shiite Islam) and Imam Hoseyn (the third Shiite Imam) a political significance transforming them from acts of holiness to revolutionary sacrifices. His speeches were characterized by a very personal rereading of ancient Persian history and Shiism, legitimizing his power as being the right one, justified by the victory of justice and good over evil. Thus, revolution became a redemptive act.

When Khomeini took power, the tools of legitimization were the same as in the time of Mohammad Reza Shah: publications, building monuments and statues, and renaming of towns and public spaces. Furthermore, under the Islamic Republic of Iran, to the use of mythical figures from the past was added the reference to some controversial figures of twentieth-century history who were rehabilitated and to whose actions new meanings were given. That was the case of Sheykh Fazlollah Nuri. Khomeini claimed 'enemies of Islam executed him by cleverly fooling the public as well as other grand ayatollahs.'[34] Nuri had opposed the Constitutional Revolution of 1906 by contrasting *mashru'eh* (conform to Shari'a) to *mashruteh* (conform to Constitution) and had encouraged the ruler of the time, Mohammad Ali Shah, to bombard parliament ruthlessly. However, when Mohammad Ali Shah saw how his monarchy was on the verge of collapse, he abandoned the sheykh. He claimed he had bombarded the parliament because the latter had convinced him that the constitutionalists would spread heresy. By claiming that he had been a puppet in the sheykh's hands, Mohammad Ali Shah was able to cling to his throne a little longer. Later, Nuri was hanged.

A 2006 article gave another interpretation:

> The largest fraction of the parliament was formed by aristocratic pseudo-intellectuals who did not want to lose their ancestral powers. They violently attacked the clergy. Some of their new newspapers attacked religion and its sacraments. To stand up to these violent and unjustified attacks, the other wing of the opposition, that is to say, the clergy, headed by Sheykh Fazlollah Nuri, slammed pro-Westerns that did not take into account the ideal of the revolution...to guarantee the country against the disastrous influence of colonial powers. As the criticism did not work, they returned to the religious shrine of Shah Abdol Azim. They required a constitution in accordance with the rules of Shari'a. This voluntary exile scared the court, which responded to that request. A supplement was prepared and signed by the king. According to this text, five learned theologians should verify compliance of draft laws with the Shari'a. This addition was developed thanks to the courage and obstinacy of great Sheykh Fazlollah Nuri, who paid with his blood his firmness. Indeed, he was executed a few months

---

[34] Ervand Abrahamian, *Khomeinism*, London: I.B. Taurus, 1993, p. 94.

later, after a pseudo trial as an enemy of the Constitutional Revolution, which would however not have happened without him.[35]

In the process of rehabilitation of clerical leaders of the past, Seyyed Hasan Modarres was also presented as a hero, as was Ayatollah Abolqasem Kashani, who had confronted Mohammad Mosaddeq after having been his ally. According to the *Ettela'at* newspaper, Modarres is 'the embodiment of the clergy's struggle against despotism and imperialism.'[36] Modarres had strongly opposed Reza Pahlavi's plan for deposing the Qajar dynasty in 1925. After an assassination attempt, he was exiled first to Kh^{v}af and then Kashmir, and was finally killed in a prison in 1937. Khomeini had been among Modarres's students. A picture of Modarres appears on the Iranian 100 rial banknote. Kashani joined the campaign to nationalize the Iranian oil industry in 1951 and served as the speaker of parliament during the oil nationalization. Political allies against the Shah and the British at first, Kashani and Mosaddeq parted ways in 1953 after emergency powers were granted to Mosaddeq and he instituted secular reforms. Following his break with Mosaddeq, Kashani gave support to his former adversary, Mohammad Reza Shah, and declared that Mosaddeq deserved to be executed because he had committed the ultimate offence: rebelling against the Shah, betraying the country, and repeatedly violating the sacred law. Curiously, despite his assistance in the 1953 coup, Kashani is often portrayed as a victim of the coup in the Islamic Republic of Iran today on the grounds that the coup was a prime example of American aggression in Iran, and that politically active clergy act as bulwarks of Islam against Western predation. The hard-line *Entekhab* newspaper, for example in 2002 asserted that the coup was launched against Mosaddeq and also Kashani.[37]

In the beginning of the revolutionary process, we find many references to Seyyed Jamaleddin Asadabadi, better known as al-Afghani, the famous thinker of the late nineteenth century, and to his anti-imperialist and pan-Islamic thought. At the same time, the symbol of the lion and sun was prohibited, and statues of Ferdowsi were taken down (though they will later be put up again). A huge statue of Modarres was built in front of the parliament building. The names of mosques containing the word shah were changed and became Isfahan mosque, Imam Khomeini mosque, Motahhari mosque, etc.

In the same way that Cyrus the Great was mobilized in the process of legitimizing Mohammad Reza Shah's modernization policies, the history of the Imams of Shiism was widely mobilized for legitimating the revolution and subsequent Islamicization. Just as myths can be used as control mechanisms

---

[35] 'Arefeh Hejazi, 'The Constitutional Revolution of 1906', *Tehran Review*, 10 September 2006.
[36] Quoted in Abrahamian, *Khomeinism*, p. 101.
[37] Stephen Kinzer, *All the Shah's Men: An American Coup and the Roots of Middle East Terror*, Hoboken, NJ: John Wiley and Sons, 2003, p. 224.

to inhibit political change, so they can also play an important role in bringing about political change.[38]

Imam Ali as a Mythical Icon
Ali, the first Imam of Shiite Muslims, was born around AD 600. He was the husband of Fatima (daughter of the Prophet) and son of Abu Talib, an uncle of the Prophet Muhammad in whose house the Prophet grew up after the age of six. According to the Shiite account, Ali was the first male to accept Islam and to have pledged himself to assist the Prophet. There are many indications put forward by Shiites to demonstrate that the prescribed and proper succession of the Prophet was to go to Ali.[39] Early in his prophetic mission, Muhammad announced at a gathering: 'The first among you to believe and accept my faith shall succeed me!' He repeated this sentence three times and each time Ali was the only person who professed his faith. On the night of the migration from Mecca to Medina, or *Hijra*, Ali took the place of the Prophet in his bed and slept there, as the Quraysh had plotted to kill the latter that night. He thus demonstrated his loyalty to him. According to Shiite teaching, the Prophet considered Ali as his own brother and, on return from his last pilgrimage, at Ghadir, publicly declared Ali the guardian of the Muslims and administrator of their affairs. Ali was the companion of the Prophet in his lonely days and his aide in hardships and dangers. After the third caliph, 'Othman, was assassinated, Ali was elected as the fourth caliph. However, opposition grew quickly, and a group whose interests were threatened, pretending to avenge the blood of the third caliph, set off bloody internal wars that lasted during the entire period of Ali's rule, until, finally, he was assassinated while he was praying. According to both Shiites and Sunnis, Ali was a learned, generous, pious, devoted, eloquent, noble, courageous, and brave person. He was just and humble. He became the model for both Islamic nobility of character and charity. To his name are attached countless poems, stories and anecdotes. But he is also a mythical personality. The story of his birth is especially telling, since his mother gave birth in Mecca, in the sacred house, the Kaaba itself, an event not repeated in Islamic history.[40]

His death symbolizes all the same qualities. Like so many other mythologized characters, Ali had foreknowledge that he was to be slain shortly before his death. The next day while going to mosque, he recognized his murderer and even roused him, as he fell asleep, inviting him to come and pray with him. That is when he was stabbed with a sword in the forehead. When stuck by his assassin, he cried 'O God, most fortunate I am.' His death took three days in which he urged Muslims not to punish the family of Ibn Muljam, his

---

[38] Aronoff, 'Conceptualizing'.
[39] See Michael, M.J. Fischer, *Iran, From Religious Dispute to Revolution*, Cambridge, MA: Harvard University Press, 1980, pp.13–14.
[40] Simon Ockley, *History of Saracens*, London, printed for R. Knaplock, J. Sprint, R. Smith, B. Lintott, and J. Round, 1718, p. 331.

murderer, and to be just with him. The qualities of Ali resonate in the minds of Iranians as does his legendary sword, the Zulfiqar.

Imam Hoseyn, Lord of Martyrs

The same is the case with Imam Hoseyn's qualities. He is considered the Lord of Martyrs. Hoseyn ibn Ali was born in AD 626. He succeeded his brother Hasan after the latter's assassination. Much persecution and opposition to the caliphs Mu'awiya and Yazid characterize the lives of the second and third Imams. When Yazid became caliph, he tried to force Hoseyn to pledge allegiance to him, but he refused and opposed Yazid, declaring that Umayyad rule was not only oppressive, but also religiously misguided. He finally was martyred at Karbala, in today's Iraq. How this happened is not quite clear. According to some sources, the people of Kufa called him to establish a caliphate and free them from Yazid's tyranny. Others emphasize that Hoseyn headed to Kufa as Yazid had plotted to kill him during the Hajj. This would have desecrated the holy place. In order to avoid this sacrilege, Hoseyn took along his wives, children, a few friends, and relatives and headed towards Kufa. Whatever the reason, on his way towards Kufa, he had to face the army of that city's governor. Like Ali, Hoseyn had foreseen his martyrdom. He is reported to have said: 'Don't you see that the truth is not put into action and the false is not prohibited? The believer should desire to meet his Lord while he is right. Thus I do not see death but as happiness, and living with tyrants but as sorrow.' On 10 October 680, Hoseyn, his followers, and family members had to confront an army of 30,000 men under the command of 'Omar ibn Sa'ad, son of the founder of Kufa. Hoseyn and all of his men, 72 in total, were killed and beheaded. The bodies were left for three days without burial and survivors were taken as prisoners to Yazid.

The Karbala episode is considered the most tragic one by Shiites and is commemorated with sorrow during the lunar month of Muharram. Processions begin on the first of the month and climax nine days later on Ashura, the day on which Imam Hoseyn was slain. Ashura is thus considered as a cosmic battle, the confrontation of good and evil. The Imam's battle at Karbala has become the historically defining moment for Shiite identity. To this day, Imam Hoseyn's martyrdom epitomizes the path of justice and defiance against oppression. Michael Fischer speaks of the 'Karbala paradigm', preferring the term to 'passion' as it 'focuses attention upon the story as a rhetorical device rather than on either the (albeit important) emotional component or the theological motifs common to Islam and Christianity. The story can be elaborated or abbreviated. However, in either case, it provides a model for living and a mnemonic for thinking about how to live.'[41]

Fischer further prefers the term 'paradigm' as it provides a way to clarify demarcating the Shiite understanding from the Sunni understanding of Islam and Islamic History. Regardless of what happened, Khomeini used Imam Hoseyn's martyrdom to legitimize the battle against the Shah, who was equat-

---

[41] Fischer, *Iran*, p. 21.

ed with Yazid, and against the monarchy, considered as illegitimate. By fighting them, the believers fought against evil, as did Hoseyn at Kerbala. They would get some form of redemption. Thus in the process of legitimization of the revolution and his power, Khomeini had recourse to one of the most potent episodes of the Shiite history of martyrdom.

Conclusion:
Political Culture, the Struggle for *Iraniyat*, and Democracy

Political culture has been presented above as a social construction, shaped in a given context. How actors use symbols and historical references has an effect on the latter and completes their meanings. We stressed for example how Khomeini used the martyrdom of Imams Ali and Hoseyn, giving them new meanings. The instrumentalization of historical references is used to legitimize political action. According to Bendix:

> Every country develops its own culture and social structure, but once the basic pattern of institutions is formed under the circumstances of early kinship, it is difficult to change. In order to understand the modern world, one must take into account the traditional practices of a nation and their unique elaboration.[42]

In the Western world, 'authority in the name of the people only gradually became an alternative to the authority of the kings.'[43] In Iran, authority in the name of the people has rarely been invoked. Instead, authority in the name of history and 'authentic' identity (*iraniyat*) has been favoured. Within that framework, there has been a struggle for *iraniyat* presented as rooted either in Iran's ancient history or in Twelver Shiism. When rival definitions of reality are used to legitimize opposition to the dominant definition, the latter is undermined. Thus, while leaders like Mohammad Reza Shah and Khomeini identify with their Iranian heritage, the point of identification was different.[44] Heisey and Trebing refer to a rhetorical battle,[45] as Iranian leaders were attempting to build a social reality by means of a rhetorical reality.

> The composite dramas planned by the Shah over a period of almost two decades and those envisioned by the Imam from his home in exile were contradictory in substance and method. The Shah's movement was a sustained drive from the top to make Iran distinctively 'Persian'. The

---

[42] Bendix, *Kings or People*, p. 3.
[43] Ibid.
[44] M. J. Aronoff, 'Conseptualizing'.
[45] D. Ray Heisey and J. David Trebing, 'A Comparison of the Rhetorical Visions and Strategies of the Shah's White Revolution and the Ayatollah's Islamic Revolution', *Communication Monographs*, 50, June 1983, pp. 158–74.

Ayatollah's answer to this vision was, by appealing to the Shah's enemies and to the masses, to make Iran uniquely 'Islamic'.[46]

The two authors describe Pahlavi rhetoric as a 'resurgence rhetoric', trying to bring to life latent Persian principles and ideals that were in the nation's past but not yet fulfilled. The Khomeini rhetoric is termed as 'holy war rhetoric', because it was designed to fight to the end, in the name of Islam, all that was corrupt, evil and satanic.[47] The two leaders tried to bring Iranians into their worldview by offering their own reading of the past and their own definition of the future. Both believed to be divinely guided and both had a paternalistic approach.

'In Iranian culture, monarchy means the political and geographic unity of Iran in addition to the special national identity and all those unchangeable values which this national identity has brought forth'...'In Iran, during the era of Great Civilization, there will be nothing left of such age old and destructive factors as: poverty, ignorance, illiteracy, corruption, discrimination and the like...'[48]

In the acknowledgements of his last book, *Response to History*, Mohammad Reza Shah refers to *Towards the Great civilization*, and writes that the latter

> was a book of hope, where I presented to my people, my views and my projects for the future. A future that I wanted glorious, happy and prosperous, worthy of the millennial history of a country which has always been one of the master builders of universal civilization. I wanted, on the eve of third millennium, a perfectly modernized, progressive Iran, highly advanced with a prosperous economy, a sophisticated education system and strong democratic structures.[49]

Both Mohammad Reza Shah and Khomeini were convinced that they were actors in a cosmic battle between good and evil:[50] modernization against poverty; Islamicization against *jahiliya*. Their ideologies have been elaborated in numerous texts either written by themselves or by 'court intellectuals', academics and others from the fields of political science, philosophy, economics, religion, law, literature and art. They were further propagated by political

---

[46] Ibid, p. 160.
[47] Ibid, p. 172.
[48] Mohammad Reza Pahlavi, *Beh su-ye tamaddon-e bozorg*, Tehran, Ketabkhaneh-ye Pahlavi, 1978, quoted in Ali M. Ansari, *Modern Iran since 1921: The Pahlavis and After*, London: Longman, 2003, pp. 190–91. See also, Mohammad Reza Pahlavi. *Answer to History*, New York: Stein and Day, 1980.
[49] Mohammad Reza Pahlavi, *Réponse à l'Histoire*, Paris: Albin Michel, 1979. For the late Shah's view see also, *Hoshdarha-ye nashenideh*, Bonn: Zartocht, 1360 and *Ma'muriat bara-ye vatanam*, ed. Siavosh Bachiri, Paris: Parang, 1987.
[50] For more on the cosmic battle, see Mark Juergensmeyer, *Terror in the Name of God*, Berkeley: University of California Press, 2003.

parties, media state institutions, and cultural associations: Rastakhiz party, Foundation of Martyrs, Ministry of Culture and Islamic Guidance. In a way their ideology was intended to replace a modern democracy by alternatives justifying their authoritarian rule – although the Shah claimed he wanted democracy for the future while Khomeini wished to banish it forever. 'A highly humanitarian and democratic social order will prevail in Iran during the era of Great Civilization' (Mohammad Reza Shah). In the constitution of the Islamic Republic of Iran, democracy is not mentioned.[51]

> 'In the revolution that was achieved in Iran, people were screaming that they wanted Islam; these people did not rise up so their country could have democracy'. (Khomeini in a meeting with the Islamic Republic Television and Radio Committee, Qom, 10 December 1979) 'In the world there is no democracy better than our democracy. Such a thing has never before been seen'. (Khomeini statement to the Minister of Finance, Qom, 23 June1979). 'Don't listen to those who speak of democracy. They all are against Islam. They want to take the nation away from its mission. We will break all the poison pens of those who speak of nationalism, democracy, and such things'. (Khomeini in a meeting with Iranian students and educators, Qom 13 March 1979).

Both leaders based their project on myth-making about the human condition and history by an anachronistic reading of the past. By reference to history, quotations, and appeals to national pride through past glories or battles, the invention of history becomes therefore an important facet of the hegemonic project.[52] The construction of cults is thus a key to understanding self-legitimization. The reference to the past is to support the particular conception of ideology and national development. Naturally, all ideologies tend to treat history instrumentally, as a resource for explaining, justifying, and giving meaning to the present.[53] In this chapter, it has been shown how Mohammad Reza Shah validated his idea of a strong and prosperous country through the myth of Cyrus and how Khomeini validated his idea of *velayat-e faqih* through the myth of Ali and Hoseyn.

In these social constructions, democracy is rarely mentioned. For Iran, in the coming years the transition to democracy will be a major challenge. This issue has already characterized the history of the twentieth century in the

---

[51] See the analysis of Daniel Brumberg, *Reinventing Khomeini*, Chicago: University of Chicago Press, 2001.
[52] For a parallel of the use of history see, Andrew F. March, 'The Use and Abuse of History: "National Ideology" as Transcendental Object in Islam Karimov's "Ideology of National Independence"', *Central Asian Survey*, 21(4), 2002, pp. 371–84.
[53] Amongst others: Pierre de Sernaclens, *Le nationalisme*, Paris: Armand Colin, 2010; Anthony D. Smith, *Nationalism and Modernization*, London: Routledge, 1998; Ernest Gellner, *Nations and Nationalism*, Ithaca: Cornell University Press, 1983; Walker Connor, *Ethnonationalism*, Princeton: Princeton University Press, 1994 or Adrian Hastings, *The Construction of Nationhood*, Cambridge: Cambridge University Press, 1999.

country. The constitution of 1906, while making Iran a constitutional monarchy rather than a monarchy of divine right, did not give birth to a democracy. Only a few classes could vote; women, the indigent, and the insane were excluded. Similarly, the Pahlavi dynasty was not a real example of democracy, because of its authoritarian regime. The Islamic Republic with the sovereignty of God is similarly far from being a democracy. Therefore one of the main challenges of the twenty-first century in Iran, if it is to become a real democracy, is to switch to a new political culture based on the rights of the people and not the past. The more a political culture is 'rationally' evaluated by people, the more it is questioned. A political culture fails to the extent that it does not meet the existential and societal needs of a country. We therefore need to evaluate whether Iranians perceive the manipulation of political culture and if so to what extent, so we can begin finding a solution to one of the main conundrums of twenty-first-century Iran: the path to democracy.

Chapter 7

Nationalism, Myth, and History in Modern Iran

Ali M. Ansari

During a visit to Iran by the Russian President Vladimir Putin in late 2007, one of the striking aspects of the official press conference in which he participated with President Mahmoud Ahmadinejad was the back drop provided by his hosts. Ahmadinejad, famous for his unorthodox religious views, had organized for a larger-than-life reconstruction of a frieze from Persepolis, the ancient Achaemenid (559–334 BC) capital, to adorn the setting and provide a symbolic back drop to the proceedings. The Iranian press lapped up the symbolism which proudly proclaimed an imperial heritage far predating the Islamic conquests of the seventh century. Indeed, there was hardly any Islamic representation at all. What was perhaps most striking about the use of Achaemenid imagery in an Iranian context was the fact that in the Islamic Republic such associations had been tarnished in official eyes by their extensive appropriation and exploitation by the Pahlavi dynasty and the last Shah, Mohammad Reza Pahlavi, in particular. Indeed in the early years of the Islamic Revolution, officials sought to debase and distance themselves from Iran's pre-Islamic heritage. Some even went so far as to argue that the Achaemenid part in particular was part of a European mythological narrative imposed upon the Iranians, and that Cyrus the Great had never in fact existed. Unsurprisingly however, as revolutionary fervour settled, the draw of the ancient monuments, especially Persepolis, continued, as they have done over the centuries to a series of aspirant dynasts and curious travellers. There was of course an initial reluctance, as if the monuments represented a temptation to be resisted, and the first senior-level visits by officials were couched in terms of moral lessons, particularly the consequences of political and moral decadence.

Ordinary Iranians however had no such qualms, and indeed one of the more striking developments of the post-revolutionary period has been the dramatic rise in interest in ancient Iran among Iranians. This social change, unsurprisingly, was to have its effect on the political class who sought to adjust themselves to the demands of their constituents. Interestingly, this adjustment proved neither reluctant nor slow, and Ahmadinejad has arguably been the most enthusiastic in its adoption, even going so far as to lodge a formal protest against the film '300'.[1] What is quite apparent from these developments is that thirty years after the revolution, Iranian 'nationalism' is back with a vengeance and part of the official ideology of the state. This paper will seek to chart the rise of modern Iranian nationalism from the nineteenth century to the present looking at the way in which an official state ideology has become over time socialized and the reciprocal impact this has had on the way in which the state has defined itself. It will be argued that Iranian nationalism, once the purview of the elites and the intelligentsia, has been transformed in the post-revolutionary period into a broad-based social ideology with dramatic consequences for its development and political life.

Traditional narratives of Iranian nationalism tend to locate its origins in the late nineteenth century as a direct consequence of the penetration of European powers and the dissemination of European ideas of nationalism. Iranian nationalism was thus conceptualized both as a reaction to European influence but was also very much driven and shaped by an intellectual agenda defined by European intellectuals. This latter aspect – the logic of Europe—is arguably only being challenged by Iranian intellectuals today. This European paradigm was defined by the idea of modernity—nationalisms were modern phenomena which witnessed the replacement of transnational religious loyalties with that of the nation defined around a single ethnicity. What constitutes an ethnic group has been a matter of some considerable debate among social scientists but at the high-tide of European nationalisms in the late nineteenth century, ethnicities were generally considered to revolve around biological determinants and were defined on pre-determined, fixed categories of race. It was in fact this belief that Europeans and Iranians shared a common heritage—defined by the late nineteenth century in racial terms—which encouraged European scholars to (re)discover Iran. Iran was indeed central to the development of the Aryan myth, and if racially obsessed theoreticians were disappointed with what they found, they explained the 'decay' of Iran in staunchly racial terms.[2] The consequence of such thinking upon Iranian intellectuals was to encourage them to think of their national identity in contradistinction to religion – in this case Islam – and in racial terms.[3] Mirza Aqa Khan

---

[1] For a sense of the indignity created and the occasionally mixed popular reaction to the government response see *Baztab.com* 22 Esfand 1386/12 March 2007. See also '300 Sparks outcry in Iran', *Time online*, 13 March 2007; 'Iran condemns Hollywood war epic', *BBC online*, 13 March 2007. The Iranian UN mission formally protested on 22 March.

[2] See in this regard, Tony Ballantyne *Orientalism and Race: Aryanism in the British Empire*, New York: Palgrave, 2002; Joseph-Arthur de Gobineau was of course one of the central figures in the development of this narrative; see Arthur, Comte de Gobineau *The Inequality of the Human Races*, Adrian Collin (trans), New York: Howard Fertig, 1967.

[3] For more detailed if differing readings of the role of race theory see Reza Zia-Ebrahimi, 'Self-Orientalisation and Dislocation: the Uses and Abuses of the Aryan

Kermani, an early nationalist ideologue writing in the late nineteenth century, was among the more explicit:

> The root of each of the branches of the tree of ugly character of Persia that we touch was planted by the Arabs and its fruit [sprang from] the seed sown from the Arabs. All the despicable habits and customs of the Persians are either the legacy and testament of the Arab nation or the fruit and influence of the invasions that have occurred in Persia.[4]

The belief that religion was inherently opposed to progress, and that ethnicity was biologically determined, were the two great, and durable, legacies of nineteenth-century European nationalism. Long after Western theoreticians had debunked or modified these particular ideas, they were only just beginning to take root in Iranian society. It would be a long gestation and the path of implantation would not be smooth with nationalist ideology in Iran having to contend, and engage with both Marxism and Islamism. Significantly, even these contests took place within a narrative constructed by the Europeans. In other words since the frame of reference was European, so too the debates about the shape of that frame took place within it, and no one thought to step outside the paradigm.

The traditional narrative of Iranian nationalism thus begins in the late nineteenth century, and it is generally accepted that it was conceived among intellectual elites and took its first tentative steps during the Tobacco Revolt of 1892. With an economic depression adversely affecting the traditional merchant classes (*bazaar*), the award of monopoly rights over the sale and distribution of tobacco throughout the country—the latest in a long list of economic concessions to foreigners—galvanized the Iranian elites into action, and with the important backing of the Shiite ulema, who issued a *fatwa* banning the use of tobacco products across the country, forced the Shah to cancel the concession. It was the first revolt of its kind and mirrored those which had taken place in Austrian Italy in 1848, themselves a reflection of emergent Italian nationalism.[5] This parallel may have lent itself to a more deliberate analogy than the events themselves warranted. Nonetheless, the revolt, against British, and generally foreign economic exploitation was discerned even by contemporary writers, including most significantly in terms of the development of (Western) narrative, the British scholar Edward Browne. For Browne, one of

---

Discourse in Iran', *Journal of Iranian Studies*, 44(4), 2011, pp. 445-72; David Motadel, 'Iran and the Aryan Myth', in *Perceptions of Iran: History, Myths and Nationalism from Medieval Persia to the Islamic Republic*, Ali M. Ansari (ed.), London: I.B. Tauris, forthcoming; and Ali M. Ansari, *The Politics of Nationalism in Modern Iran*, Cambridge: Cambridge University Press, 2012, pp. 22-33, 105.

[4] Quoted in Shaul Bakhash, *Iran: Monarchy, Bureaucracy and Reform under the Qajars: 1858-1896*, London: Ithaca Press, 1978, p. 345.

[5] See George Macaulay Trevelyan *Manin and the Venetian Revolution of 1848*, New York, H. Fertig, 1974 (reprint of 1923 edition published by Longman), p. 61. Macaulay argues that the boycott was in 'direct imitation of the Boston tea-party'.

the staunchest supporters of an Iranian national awakening,[6] the Tobacco Revolt was the precursor to the far more momentous Constitutional movement which emerged in 1905. In Browne's view, the intellectual progenitor of this movement was the Pan-Islamist thinker Jamal al-Din al-Afghani (who despite his name was Iranian), reflecting the fact that Browne recognized that Iranian identity had a religious dimension which could not be so easily distinguished and discarded.[7] Browne however was in many ways arguing against the dominant trend emerging in Iran, which was (publicly at least) avowedly secular, and if not irreligious, then certainly against organized religion and its pervasiveness in the public sphere. Indeed, although a broad coalition of intellectuals, ulema and bazaar had agitated for the adoption of a constitution which would limit the powers of the Shah and establish a national parliament (Majles), it was the liberal intellectuals who would soon come to dominate the process, and position themselves against the 'reactionary clerics'. The contest between the secular nationalists and the religious nationalism espoused by the more progressive clergy therefore originated in this period, and each side enthusiastically blamed the other for all the ills which befell them. After the Russian Revolution of 1917 they were to be gradually joined by a new cadre of zealous Marxists. This trilateral contest to define the direction of Iranian nationalism was to continue for the better part of the next century.

In the meantime, the practical failure of the Constitutional movement, the inability to achieve a working consensus in the new parliament and the havoc wreaked by the onset of the Great War, persuaded the country's intellectuals that Iran's salvation lay with a 'strong man'. The search for a saviour to come and rescue the country from itself has a profound historical pedigree in Iran, but in this case the myth was modernized and justified on the grounds that the country needed to be dragged out of its inherently conservative stupor. The new leader would thus be vigorously nationalist and break through the bonds of traditional (religious) loyalty, enforcing a new cohesion and national senses of purpose. Poets and writers drew on the glorious past to shame Iranians into action, and to justify the urgency which necessitated a turn towards dictator-

---

[6] Mansour Bonakdarian, 'Edward G. Browne and the Iranian Constitutional Struggle: From Academic Orientalism to Political Activism', *Iranian Studies*, 26, 1993, pp. 7–31.

[7] Browne produced the first study on the Constitutional Revolution in 1909. He was a staunch supporter and active lobbyist in its favour in London. His enduring popularity among Iranians is reflected in the fact that he still has a street named after him in Tehran. See Edward Granville Browne *The Persian Revolution of 1905–1909*, Washington, DC: Mage Publishing, 1995. For an alternative reading of al-Afghani's political philosophy see his letter to Ernest Renan, reproduced in Nikki R. Keddie, *An Islamic Response to Imperialism: Political and Religious Writings of Sayyid Jamal al-Din "al-Afghani"*, Berkeley: University of California Press, 1968, pp. 181–87.

ship.[8] Salvation was at hand with the emergence of the brusque figure of Reza Khan in the coup of 1921, led by the journalist and intellectual, Seyyed Zia Tabataba'i. Reza Khan, the commander of the Cossack Brigade, soon disposed of the intellectual leadership and took control himself in a series of moves which were in fact largely supported by an intelligentsia eager to see some progress. Reza Khan provided the coercive power to weld together a disparate country on the basis of a new nationalism which was fully supported by the intellectual elite. It is a matter of debate among scholars whether his actions were in practice much different from dynastic founders of previous ages, though most agree that his justifications were different and the state he sought to construct was at one level quite distinct, with its ministries, developed bureaucracy, centralized administration, and state-led economic development. As will be seen later in this chapter, there is now increasing dispute about how innovative his 'national' ideas were, but there can be little doubt that even if his methods were not necessarily different and the ideas historically grounded, the tools he had at his disposal were quite distinctly modern. For the first time, nationalism was being systematically implemented, and this in turn made the particular nationalism he espoused and promoted quite distinct in terms of its social reach and penetration. One of his greatest contributions was the development of education, particularly the foundation of the University of Tehran in 1934. This, along with greater centralization, and the advance of technology, ultimately ensured an unprecedented level of cultural cohesion. In 1924, as prime minister, Reza Khan introduced some of the most dramatic changes into Iranian society, including the introduction of surnames (a good ten years before Mustafa Kemal introduced them in Turkey),[9] the introduction of a two year period of conscription to expand the army,[10] and the reform of the country's calendar.[11]

Conscription and education were aimed at creating a cohesive and unitary nation, a process which was assisted by investment in communications, in particular the construction of the Trans-Iranian Railway which bound the Caspian provinces to the southwest of the country. The changes in nomenclature were intended to frame the debate within a distinctly Persian national narrative. The reform of the calendar for example institutionalized the Iranian solar calendar over the Muslim lunar calendar although the year was still measured from the date of the Prophet's *hijra* from Mecca to Medina. What was more significant however was the adoption of Zoroastrian month names as part of the official state calendar. Language reform was also pursued, and

---

[8] See, S. R. Shafaq 'Patriotic Poetry in Modern Iran', *Middle East Journal*, 6(4), 1952, pp. 426–28.
[9] H. E. Chehabi, 'The Reform of Iranian Nomenclature and Titulature in the Fifth Majles', in *Convergent Zones: Persian Literary Tradition and the Writing of History: Studies in Honor of Amin Banani*, Wali Ahmadi (ed.), Costa Mesa: Mazda, 2012, pp. 84–116.
[10] Stephanie Cronin, 'Conscription and Popular Resistance in Iran, 1925–1941', *International Review of Social History*, 43(3), 1998, pp. 451–71.
[11] FO 371 [...] E2431/455/34 dated 16 February 1924.

while the script was never changed, efforts were taken to replace Arabic loan words with more authentic Persian ones. A difficult process, but one nonetheless pursued by reference to that great repository of Persian vocabulary, Ferdowsi's epic poem, the *Shahnameh* (Book of Kings), which had been compiled in the tenth century in the aftermath of the Arab conquest in a bid to preserve the Iranian historical memory and the Persian language.[12] During this period, the *Shahnameh* was used largely for its literary merit as the historical mythology it portrayed was regarded by Iran's Western-educated nationalists as incidental to the real historical record being uncovered by archaeologists. Indeed the development of the discipline of archaeology in the nineteenth century and the gradual decipherment of the ancient inscriptions had a profound impact on the development of national narratives in Iran.[13] Achaemenid Iran was being rediscovered and Iranian nationalists, keen to impress their Western counterparts, saw the Achaemenids as a vital bridge to Western acceptability. As much as the Achaemenids were seen as opponents to the Greeks, they were nonetheless accepted by many Western scholars as part of the Western inheritance.[14] This was particularly true among Jews for whom Cyrus was the 'Lord's Anointed', and with the discovery of the 'Cyrus cylinder' in Babylon in 1879, Iranians rejoiced in the archaeological confirmation that the founder of the Persian Empire was also a humane 'liberator'.[15] That said, the Achaemenid domination of the narrative would only reach fruition under Reza Shah's son and successor, Mohammad Reza Shah (r. 1941–1979). During this formative period of Iranian nationalism, Reza Shah and his supporters drew on a wide range of historical analogies, many of which were Sasanian rather than Achaemenid and reflected sympathy with the *Shahnameh*. Thus in selecting a surname for his family and dynasty, Reza Khan chose 'Pahlavi', a term traditionally used to denote the Middle Persian language spoken from around third century BC to the seventh century AD. It also suggested an association with the Parthian/Sasanian eras inasmuch as the 'Pahlavis' were thought to have been one of the seven great aristocratic clans.[16]

---

[12] On the place of Ferdowsi in early Pahlavi nationalism see Afshin Marashi, 'The Nation's Poet: Ferdowsi and the Iranian National Imagination', in *Iran in the 20th Century: Historiography and Political Culture*, Touraj Atabaki (ed.), London: I. B. Tauris, 2009, pp. 93–112.

[13] For an excellent survey of the impact of archaeology on nationalism, see Kamyar Abdi, 'Nationalism, Politics and the Development of Archaeology in Iran', *American Journal of Archaeology*, 105(1), 2001, pp. 51–76.

[14] See for example, Georg Wilhelm Friedrich Hegel *The Philosophy of History*, New York: Dover Publications, 1956, p. 173.

[15] The identification with 'human rights' would come later. This view remains contested as much as it is vigorously promoted by Iranians, it is certainly true that Cyrus the Great's approach to the conquered was more humane than that of previous empire builders.

[16] See Donald N. Wilber, *Riza Shah Pahlavi: The Resurrection and Reconstruction of Iran, 1878–1944*, New York, Exposition Press, 1975, notes on p. 229 that Reza Shah asked the German archaeologist Ernst Herzfeld what the name actually meant.

Furthermore in insisting that foreigners use the name 'Iran' rather than 'Persia'—in effect demanding that foreigners call the country by the name used by its inhabitants—Reza Shah was mirroring developments in Sasanian Iran when the term Iran was first used in an explicitly political sense.[17] Just to emphasize this association, the Pahlavi crown was modelled on Sasanian crowns, and Reza Shah insisted on the ancient title *Shahanshah* (King of Kings).[18] This Sasanian analogy was more relevant because of Reza Shah's understanding of Iran as a centralized state rather than a tribal confederacy, which historians had generally ascribed to the Parthian era. Centralization therefore could be sold as a return to Sasanian norms when Iran was strong and a worthy opponent to the Roman Empire.

This process of centralization was in many ways Reza Shah's undoing. Central control encouraged the peripheries to rebel, not only in geographic terms but also intellectual. Many of Reza Shah's original supporters fell away as they found his monarchy stifling and repressive, and this sentiment grew more pervasive as the development of industry and education led to the growth of a new middle class eager for more political participation. Reza Shah's attacks on the religious classes had also engendered a backlash with the consequence that by the end of his rule, he had succeeded in uniting a disparate group of opponents. Yet what is striking about the reaction to Reza Shah which emerged with some energy following the Allied invasion and his abdication in 1941 was how much they were defined by the dominant nationalist narrative. Although few shed tears over Reza Shah's departure, the realization that centrifugal forces might tear the country apart resulted in the newly empowered parliament essentially pursuing the same policies of central control and rigorous nationalism.[19] But perhaps even more interesting is the fact that the separatist movements in Azerbaijan and Iranian Kurdistan, as they moved from demanding greater autonomy to full independence, themselves sought to implement centralizing, nationalist policies including the much hated conscription.[20] Indeed it was in part the realization that they had replaced one controlling government in Tehran for another in Tabriz, which dampened popular enthusiasm for independence and ensured that when Soviet troops finally withdrew in 1946, Tehran was able to re-establish control with minimal effort. The most explicit expression of nationalism came during the battle

---

[17] FO 371 18988 E3505/305/34 dated 29 December 1934, FO 371 18988 E952/305/34 dated 23 January 1935. Contrary to general assumptions, these demands were originally made of the Turkish Republic in 1924, see Mohsen Rusta'i *Tarikh-e nakhostin farhangestan-e Iran beh ravayet asnad* [A documentary history of the first Farhangestan], Tehran: Nashr-e Ney, 1385/2006, p. 83.

[18] This title had been revived by previous dynasts but it was generally regarded by foreign commentators as pretentious given the state of Iran's development, see FO 371 17890 E56 dated 6 December 1933.

[19] FO 248 1409, file 39, dated 13 April 1942. See also, FO 248 1409, file 39, – Letter from the Boir Ahmadis, dated 7 April 1944.

[20] FO 248 1463 file 69, Situation report 69/50/46, dated 23 February 1946.

over the nationalization of the Anglo-Iranian Oil Company in 1951. The National Front movement, headed by Mohammad Mosaddeq, succeeded for a brief time to unite the three main strands of nationalist ideology, the secularists, the religious nationalists and the left. The only group excluded were the monarchists, in large part because of the prevarication of the young ruler, Mohammad Reza Shah, and his personal antagonism with Mosaddeq. Mosaddeq had succeeded in injecting some popular enthusiasm into what had hitherto been an elite- and state-led nationalist agenda. He achieved this by focussing on a common and immediate enemy (Britain) and drawing to him the left and the religious groups, both of which enjoyed extensive popular constituencies. The frictions which had emerged between the various groups during the Constitutional Revolution, emerged with somewhat more vigour and definition on this occasion (the left after all came with a well-defined and pre-prepared ideology of their own). Ultimately these fissures tore the movement apart, and they were amply exploited by the US and British intelligence agencies, which facilitated the overthrow of Mosaddeq in a coup d'état in 1953. Mohammad Reza Shah now ruled as well as reigned.

The stigma of having been restored to his throne in a Western-orchestrated coup would haunt Mohammad Reza Shah for this rest of his life. He sought to compensate for this by appropriating as much of his opponents' ideologies as possible, taking from the left their enthusiasm for welfare and revolution; from the religious groups, a heightened sense of Divine providence and mandate; and from the secular nationalists, a keen sense of the idea of Iran, which in his case was centred upon the institution of the monarchy.[21] But in his own conception of nationalism he pursued the parameters established by his father in even more depth. If his father had outlined a national narrative which focussed broadly on the pre-Islamic past, his son narrowed this down more emphatically to the Achaemenids and to Cyrus the Great in particular. This in part reflected the further developments in archaeology and the logic of the developments initiated half a century earlier. But there can be no doubt that Mohammad Reza Shah added to this particular momentum a personal interest all his own. Mohammad Reza Shah was especially keen to associate his dynasty with that of the Achaemenids by hosting a lavish celebration in commemoration of the two thousand five hundredth year of the foundation of the Persian Empire and monarchy by Cyrus.[22] If the date was to be taken from the accession of Cyrus the Great to the throne in 559BC, then the 2,500th anniversary would have fallen in 1941—an auspicious year for the Shah since that was the date of his own accession but clearly of no use for the purposes of a commemoration. After several years were selected and then set aside (largely due to logistical reasons), the decision was taken to celebrate in 1971 with a

---

[21] Mohammad Reza Pahlavi *Beh su-ye tamaddon-e bozorg* [Towards the Great Civilization] Tehran, Ketabkhaneh-ye Pahlavi, 1978, p. 244.
[22] BBC SWB ME/3641/D/1 23 March 1971 - Shah's Now Ruz speech dated 21 March 1971.

monumental party and parade in Persepolis.[23] There was considerable opposition to the proposed festivities not only from the usual suspects among the left and the religious groups, but also from staunch secular nationalists who were critical of the intimate association with monarchy but also interestingly because some felt that the Shah had bought into a Western narrative that truncated Iran's history. In short, some bemoaned the apparent curtailing of Iranian history and civilization noting that it predated the Achaemenids and should at the very least account for the Median kingdom.

The narrative conception of those who criticized the limiting of Iranian history to 2,500 years was drawn from the *Shahnameh*, which Mohammad Reza Shah had relegated, far more emphatically than his father had done, to the realm of literature. While large portions of the national epic were obviously mythical, it still suggested a far more developed culture which predated Cyrus and the Achaemenids. Such a view was not anathema to the Shah, and remarkably when President Richard Nixon visited Iran in 1972, he commented that Iranian history was not limited to 2,500 years but 'goes back even 6,000 years'.[24] Indeed, the Shah would toy with these ideas in an interview with the Indian journalist R. K. Karanjia during which he alluded to apparently direct links between his own family and the great dynastic clans of the pre-Islamic past, and even went so far to reintegrate the mythological past into the standard historical narrative.[25] Be that as it may, such comments could be regarded as indulgent asides and the Shah remained fixated on the 2,500-year chronology going so far as to announce somewhat peremptorily that from March 1976, the dating of the Iranian calendar would begin with the accession of Cyrus the Great. This new imperial calendar would replace the reformed calendar introduced in 1924, and Iranians found themselves no longer in 1355 but in 2535. It was a remarkable conceit, and the imperial calendar was one of the first changes to be discarded as the revolutionary storms gathered.

The Islamic Revolution which erupted onto the world stage in 1978–1979 appeared by all accounts to be the antithesis of the nationalism espoused and promoted by the Pahlavis. Certainly the eager young revolutionaries did all they could to distance themselves from the monarchy they had just overthrown and the ideology associated with it, especially its predilection for the pre-Islamic Iranian heritage. This distinction was likewise encouraged by the victims of the revolution, monarchists and other exiles who sought to delegitimize the revolution by emphasizing its Islamic and hence 'Arab' character. One of the most extensively used quotes in this regard was Ayatollah Khomeini's apparently nonchalant answer to a reporter on the flight back from exile. When asked how he felt returning to Iran after fourteen years, the Ayatollah reflected briefly and dismissively responded to the seemingly intru-

---

[23] FCO 57/323 'The Dynasty Blessed by the Gods', diplomatic report no, 479/71 dated 11 October 1971.
[24] Toasts of the President and Mohammad Reza Pahlavi, Shah of Iran, at a State Dinner in Tehran, 30 May 1972, Nixon Library, document no. 181.
[25] R. K. Karanjia, *The Mind of a Monarch*, London, G. Allen & Unwin, 1977, p. 31.

sive journalist, 'nothing'. Few answers of such brevity have been used to such great effect to characterize an entire revolutionary movement. In truth for all its immediate pretensions about the rights of the *umma*, or the oppressed in general, the Islamic Revolution altered the nationalist discourse but left the frame of reference very much intact. In fact in reacting to the secular nationalism of the Shah, the religious nationalism of the Islamic revolutionaries operated within much the same parameters as that which had emerged from Iran's encounter with Europe in the nineteenth century, and unsurprisingly the 'West' featured prominently in the discourse, although on this occasion the relationship was generally antagonistic. Nonetheless some Islamic revolutionaries saw themselves very much as heirs to a European tradition of intellectual development, improving it by transcending the conceit of secularism (the focus of their antagonism), and moving beyond to reintegrate the spiritual dimension of national life. For example, according to one of their leading ideologues, the Islamic Republic, was in effect a 'post-modern state':

> While an Islamic society is not at ease with technical rationality, it finds itself quite in harmony with the authentic one. Therefore, Islamic modernity goes far beyond historical modernity and is basically a post-modern phenomenon.[26]

Consequently much of the nationalist discourse of the previous century was simply dusted down and provided with an Islamic veneer most obviously seen in the transition of the Islamic Revolution to an *Iranian* Islamic Revolution. The national distinction remained, and if the revolutionaries sought to distinguish themselves as Islamic, they were equally keen to distance themselves for the many other Islamic movements which were emerging around the world. There was in short, a pecking order, and it remained quintessentially national. This distinction was of course assisted by the fact that Iran was a Shiite country and instinctively treated with suspicion by the majority of the Sunni Islamic world. It was further facilitated by the war with Iraq, which was defined by the Iraqis in starkly ethnic terms, and if the Iranians officially let it be known that they were fighting to rid the world of Ba'athist heresy, it was also quite clear that they were fighting for their motherland. The focus of the historical narratives may have been Islamic rather than Achaemenid Iran, but if anything this allowed for a greater focus on the Persian language, which had emerged in its current form in the aftermath of the Islamic conquest. Perhaps most strikingly, the new Islamic Republic was no less keen on promoting a centralized state than the Pahlavis had before them. Indeed, events were to prove that the Islamic Republic would in time become a far more intensely Persian and centralized state than any of its predecessors.

To appreciate this development one must step back from the state, and turn instead towards society. The Islamic Revolution arguably inaugurated the

---

[26] Mohammad Javad Larijani, 'Islamic Society and Modernism', *The Iranian Journal for International Affairs*, 7(1), 1995, p. 58.

most democratic process in modern Iranian history. Not in the sense of political liberties or institutionalized participation, still less in any legal sense, but in a social and popular sense. In the aftermath of the collapse of the highly centralized and tightly knit monarchy, power became very suddenly socially diffuse and broadly based, centralized only in the charismatic authority of Ayatollah Khomeini. The new state was thus centralized but loosely bound. The elite became larger, was more diffuse and was certainly more disparate, a process which was further facilitated by the war and the casualties this induced. There was a high rate of turnover within the elite. Added to this were the technological changes which ensured greater continuous contact with the outside world, better educational access, and the development of genuine mass media. Devout Muslims had been warned not to watch television. Now after the revolution, Khomeini, keen to exploit this highly effective tool of communication, provided the necessary Islamic legitimacy. Combined with developments in education, which saw literacy continue to improve throughout the country, these changes ensured that Persian became the definitive *lingua franca* throughout the country. What the Pahlavis had aspired to, the Islamic Republic achieved by default. Technology centralized power and facilitated the dissemination of the ideological discourse and the linguistic structure. But technology also allowed for greater choice and access for a public hungry for information. This social revolution, combined with an antipathy to the imposed 'religious nationalism' of the state, was to inaugurate one of the most dramatic changes in nationalist ideology in Iran.

In the aftermath of the war against Iraq, Iranians returned from the front dissatisfied with the situation around them. Less deferential than previously, they began to question their government, their relationship with their government, and in short, their identity. Unhappy with the reassuring religious certainties repeated in official state sermons, many began to question the causes of Iranian under-development.[27] One popular lay religious philosopher suggested that Iranian complexity and plurality, a source of national strength which should be celebrated, had been bastardized and simplified by a succession of nationalist governments anxious to impose their particular reading of Iranian nationalism upon the people. The consequence of this had been alienation and a crippling of the national drive, as if the nation had been limited to firing on one or two cylinders. On the contrary, argued Abdolkarim Sorush, national salvation lay in recognizing and appreciating the complex inheritance which underlay Iranian identity. In fact:

> We Iranian Muslims are the inheritors and carriers of three cultures at once. As long as we ignore our links with the elements in our triple cultural heritage and our cultural geography, constructive social and cultural action will elude us....The three cultures that form

---

[27] A good example is Sadeq Zibakalam, *Ma cheguneh ma shodim? Rishehyabi-ye 'elal-e 'aqab-mandegi dar Iran* [How did we became who we are? The roots of backwardness in Iran], Tehran, Rowzaneh, 1374/1995.

our common heritage are of national, religious, and Western origins.[28]

Sorush of course emphasized that the country's Islamic heritage was the most important of the three, but by drawing attention to two other distinct inheritances, without which there could be no national equilibrium or harmony, Sorush, had within a simple formulation, legitimized the integration of both Western ideas and the legacy of the ancient Iranian world. One could argue that he simply rationalized a reality, but be that as it may, his popularity, especially among students, provided the necessary philosophical credence to an emergent nationalist movement which sought to look at origins. This time, however, the emphasis was not on the Achaemenid period, which while not wholly neglected, had been politically discredited by association with the Pahlavis, but on the subsequent Parthian and Sasanian periods. Indeed in the 1990s Iranians became reacquainted with their ancient roots for a number of diverse if converging reasons. On one level, young Iranians, increasingly disaffected with the imposition of Islamic morals by the state, registered their protest by seeking out and studying subjects related to ancient Iran. This was a simple reaction which reflected the rediscovery of an Islamic identity under the Shah. However, a more interesting process was a direct consequence of policies adopted by the state itself, for in the initial phases of the Islamic Revolution, great efforts and intellectual investment had been directed towards the study of Islam, its origins, and especially its early impact upon Iran.

One of the more significant debates related to the initial impact of the Arab conquest, and the ulema were keen to negate the argument that the Arab/Islamic conquest had not been entirely benign, and argued on the contrary that it had been welcomed by an oppressed Iranian populace. Books that had argued otherwise were either suppressed or rigorously critiqued.[29] As with religious history in the West, scholars and students gradually moved from this focus to look at the context of the Islamic conquest and this took two forms. On the one hand, scholars examined the religious background and the influence of Zoroastrianism, while on the other scholarly attention was drawn to the political legacy of the Sasanians, much of which could be located in Arab and Persian histories written during the Islamic period. These studies yielded information which tended to contradict the official narrative of a sterile state captivated by a dogmatic religion easily overturned by a vigorous young new religion, and enthusiastically welcomed by a grateful Iranian population who proved only too eager to convert. On the contrary, the conquest proved a protracted and at times bloody affair, in which the collapse of central authority

---

[28] Abdolkarim Soroush, 'The Three Cultures in Reason', in *Reason, Freedom, & Democracy in Islam: Essential Writings of Abdolkarim Soroush*, Mahmoud Sadri and Ahmad Sadri (trans. & eds), Oxford: Oxford University Press, 2000, p. 156.
[29] A significant debate for instance revolved around Abdolhoseyn Zarrnkub's *Do qarn sokut* [Two centuries of silence], first published before the revolution but since reissued by Sokhan, Tehran, 1378/1999, complete with a new 'critical' introduction.

and the defection of key notables ensured that political change at the top came at the price of considerable social and cultural continuity and a slow rate of conversion.[30] This continuity could be seen in both in the political and the religious spheres, [31] where Iranian influence was arguably profound and which ultimately resulted in new Persian becoming the *lingua franca* of the eastern caliphate.

The consequence of this was a renaissance in interest in the Sasanian period and its legacy, most interestingly in the histories of Iran which had been compiled during that period and the myths of descent which these encapsulated. This rediscovery of mythological history was perhaps best expressed by President Mohammad Khatami in an address to Iranian expatriates at the United Nations in 1998, during which he argued that:

> Mythology describes the spirit of various nations. And there is no nation or people whose history is free from myth. Of course, in conformity with the weight of civilization and the history of a nation, the myth of the nation is deeper and more complicated. And civilized nations usually have myths. The ethical myth and the myth epic indicate the spirit of Iranians...the Book of Kings [is] the symbol of Iran.[32]

This was a remarkable statement to make, since it not only suggested that the *Shahnameh* was no longer off the official syllabus of the state, but far from simply having a literary value it was of political importance to the identity of Iranians and to the concept of the Iranian nation. This moved far beyond the literary approach espoused by the Pahlavis and reflected a rehabilitation of mythic history.[33]

During the period of Reza Shah, the Sasanian legacy had been interpreted in somewhat simplistic terms which saw the Sasanian state as vigorously centralized, with militaristic tendencies, but increasingly dogmatic and sterile. This explained the rapid collapse of the state in the face of the more dynamic Arab conquerors, and while staunch nationalists may lament this, it was explainable and allowed for a fresh start. Indeed, nationalists would take up the

---

[30] For a recent, excellent contribution to this increasingly rich debate see Parvaneh Pourshariati, *Decline and Fall of the Sasanian Empire: The Sasanian-Parthian Confederacy and the Arab Conquest of Iran*, London: I. B. Tauris, 2008.
[31] For the influence of Zoroastrianism on the Semitic religions see Norman Cohn, *Cosmos, Chaos and the World to Come: The Ancient Roots of Apocalyptic Faith*, London: Yale University Press, 2001.
[32] President Khatami addresses Iranian Expatriates in USA, BBC SWB ME/3339 MED/1, dated 23 September 1998, New York, 20 September 1998.
[33] See in this regard, Paul Ricoeur, 'Myth as the Bearer of Possible Worlds', in *A Ricoeur Reader: Reflection and Imagination*, Mario J. Valdés (ed.), London, Harvester Wheatsheaf, 1991, p. 484. 'For it is only when it is threatened with destruction from without or from within that a society is compelled to return to the very roots of its identity; to that mythical nucleus which ultimately grounds and determines it.' See also in this regard, Aristotle, *Poetics*, London: Penguin, 1996, chapter 9, p. 16.

thread a few centuries later, with the emergence of the Persian language and ultimately the rise of the Safavids in the sixteenth century, all of which were interpreted as a 'national' history defined in terms of 'cultural resistance'. Looking at Islamic history through Arab eyes, the Iranians became marginal to the central narrative. In Iran itself, the rehabilitation of the Sasanian state was achieved through an emphasis of its particular religious qualities. Zoroastrianism was the official state religion under the Sasanians, it was argued, and religion remained important to the Iranian idea. The relevance of this debate to the current situation is obvious inasmuch as it tries to show that Iranians are naturally inclined towards religion. But even this assessment crumbled in the face of further research which began to show that the Sasanians had presided over a sophisticated state, with a complex, cosmopolitan, and highly plural social structure, built upon an inheritance stretching back almost a millennium to at least the Parthian era. In this state religious views which could not be described as orthodox co-existed. Far from being reducible to rigid dogmatism, Zoroastrianism in fact provided a frame of reference rather than a dogma. Occasional persecutions aside, Christian and Jewish communities flourished and were fully integrated: at least one king was held to have a Jewish mother, while another had a Christian queen.[34]

The consequences of this historical revolution on contemporary national identity have yet to be fully appreciated and while the influence of such revisionist studies on domestic politics have yet to make themselves felt, there are already international reverberations in terms of Iran's approach to the region. But what these early studies are doing is to provide an alternative narrative of Iranian history which steps outside the European paradigm which remains fixated on the idea of an ethnocentric nation. In many ways Iranians are returning to a pre-nineteenth rendition of their history which replaces a European construct of ethnicity with one that is more fluid and integrative.[35] That is not to say that the concept of ethnic groups is removed altogether from the narrative, but it is imagined differently and the distinctions created by Europeans, for instance between 'Iranians' and 'Turks', do not operate in quite the same way. The Iranian commonwealth of nations, as envisaged in the indigenous historiographical tradition, can include many diverse *ethnies*, including Turks, Kurds, Lurs, Armenians, and Georgians. All are part of an Iranian oecumene. Significantly, the only ethnic group that is excluded is the Arabs (al-

---

[34] For more detail see Touraj Daryaee *Sasanian Persia: The Rise and Fall of An Empire*, London, I B Tauris, 2009, pp. 69–97. The Sasanian kings with Jewish mothers are held to have been Narseh and Wahram V. Meanwhile, Khosrow II had two Christian wives one of whom, Shirin, was known for her propagation of Christianity. Ibid., p. 34.

[35] For the Iranian adherence to the *Shahnameh* see John Malcolm, *The History of Persia from the Most Early Period to the Present Time*, London: John Murray, second Edition, vol. 1, 1829, p. 475. Sir Percy Sykes, *A History of Persia*, vol. 1, London: Macmillan & Co, 1921, p. 133. See also Vita Sackville-West, *Passenger to Teheran*, London: Hogarth Press, 1926, pp. 105 and 121.

though even this exception is not absolute), and the implications of anti-Arabism are already being felt within Iranian society.[36]

Iranian nationalism is in the process of redefining itself away from the dominant European paradigm. It is a process which is being driven by society rather than the state and which seeks to draw on myth in support of historical fact. The relationship between myth and history has always been a complex and dialectical one, and in Iran's case, the return of a sophisticated mythological base is providing Iranian history and identity with a new lease of life.[37] Scholarship has been revitalized and nationalism re-energized. The consequences for the future of Iran and the region are likely to be dramatic. Perhaps the most interesting aspect of this rediscovery has been a renewed interest in the Sasanian concept of *Iranshahr,* the Iranian commonwealth whose cultural reach extends far beyond the current political borders of Iran. The dream of *Iranshahr* is amongst the most potent nationalist myths of contemporary Iran. To appreciate its importance one has to understand nationalism as defined by the Iranians themselves. It is time to move beyond the logic of Europe.

---

[36] For the debate especially as it pertains to historical mythology, see, See, Hamzeh Hoseynzadeh, *Zahhak: az ostureh ta vaqe'iyyat* [Zahhak: from myth to reality], Tehran: Tarfand, 1384/2005, pp. 196–213. In 2002 parliamentary deputies were so vexed by the idea that the head of the judiciary was an Iraqi, and hence an 'Arab', that they demanded to see his nationality certificate. See 'Majlis Deputies see letter on nationality of Judiciary Head', *Nowruz* website, 20 January 2002, BBC SWB Mon ME1 ME-Pol.

[37] For critical discussions of this relationship see, M. I. Finley, 'Myth, Memory, and History', *History and Theory* 4(3), 1965, pp. 281–302; Ben Halpern, '"Myth" and "Ideology" in Modern Usage', *History and Theory* 1(2), 1961, pp. 129–49; H. Tudor, *Political Myth*, London: Macmillan 1972. Tudor's book has recently been translated into Persian. The importance of myth to identity is also highlighted in Hoseynzadeh, *Zahhak*.

Chapter 8

The Short-Term Society: A Comparative Study in the Problems of Long-Term Political and Economic Development in Iran

Homa Katouzian

In 1997 Mohammad Khatami unexpectedly won a landslide victory in Iran's presidential election. Many believed that that was 'the beginning of the end' for the Islamist regime. Khatami was re-elected in 2001, and while he brought about significant changes in domestic and foreign policy, he had few friends left in the last two years of his presidency, since the conservatives and fundamentalists used all in their power to limit his options, while at the same time most of his constituents accused him of lack of faith for not delivering the moon.[1] During an address in November 2004 at a meeting at the University of Tehran, Khatami was booed and heckled, some students shouting 'Khatami, you liar, shame on you'. Yet when he went there again in 2007—the second year of Mahmoud Ahamdinejad's presidency—the crowd were shouting 'Here comes the people's saviour'.[2]

Khatami's changing fortunes and the fact that the reversals in his popularity have occurred in such short time spans are emblematic of a deeper structural feature of Iranian society that can be detected all the way back to the mythological origins of the Iranian nation, namely that Iran has been a *short-term society* in contrast to Europe's *long-term society*.[3] Consequently, in Iran

---

[1] For an early analysis of the structural impediments to the success of the reform project, see Mohammad-Reza Djalili, *Iran: l'illusion réformiste*, Paris: Presses de Sciences Po, 2001.
[2] Homa Katouzian, *The Persians: Ancient, Mediaeval and Modern Iran*, New Haven: Yale University Press, paperback edition, 2010, chapter 14.
[3] See, for example, Homa Katouzian, 'Problems of Democracy and the Public Sphere in Modern Iran', *Comparative Studies of South Asia, Africa and the Middle East*, 18(2), 1998, pp. 31–37, reprinted in *Iranian History and Politics, The Dialectic of*

change, even important and fundamental change, has tended to be a short-term phenomenon. In this chapter I present a theory to explain this phenomenon, and my findings may well be relevant to other countries of the Middle East and North Africa as well.[4]

The short-term nature of Iranian society was due to the absence of an established and inviolable legal framework which would guarantee long-term continuity. Over any short period of time, there could be notable military, administrative and property-owning classes, but their composition would not remain the same beyond one or two generations, unlike traditional European aristocracies, even merchant classes. In Iran, property and social positions were short-term, precisely because they were regarded as *personal privileges* rather than inherited and inviolable *social rights*. The situation of those who possessed rank and property—except in very rare examples—was not the result of long-term inheritance (say, beyond two generations before) and they did not expect their heirs to continue in the same positions as a matter of course. The heirs could do so only if they managed to establish themselves on their own merits – merits being the personal traits necessary for success within the given social context. There thus was a high degree of social mobility, unthinkable in mediaeval and much of the modern European history. This did not exclude the position of the shah himself, since legitimacy and the right of succession were nearly always subject to serious challenge, even rebellion.[5]

The most visible example of the short-term nature of Iranian society is the habit of declaring a building—especially a residential building—as a 'pick-axe building' (*sakhteman-e kolangi*). Most of these buildings are no more than thirty (even twenty) years old, and they are normally sound in foundation and structure. In a few cases they may be run-down and in need of renovation, but the feature that results in their condemnation as such, and incidentally wipes off the value of the structure and only leaves the price of their site, is that their architecture and/or interior design is unfashionable according to the latest forms, concepts, or whims. Therefore, rather than building a new house, thus adding to the stock of existing physical capital, it is demolished by the owner or purchaser, and a new building is erected on its site. Therefore, I have described the short term Iranian society alternatively as 'the pick-axe society',

---

State and Society in Iran, London: Routledge, paperback edition, 2008; Homa Katouzian [Katouzian],'Dar Ta'assob va khami, va tajalli-ye an dar jame'eh-ye kolangi' in *Kiyan* reprinted in idem., *Tazadd-e dowlat va mellat: Nazariyeh-ye tarikh va siyasat dar Iran*, Tehran: Nashr-e Ney, 2001.

[4] The present chapter is a revised and extended version of my 'The Short-Term Society: A Study of Long-Term Problems of Political and Economic Development in Iran', *Middle Eastern Studies*, 40(1), January 2004, pp. 1–22.

[5] See Homa Katouzian, *State and Society in Iran, The Eclipse of the Qajars and the Rise of the Pahlavis*, London: I. B. Tauris, 2000, pp. 1–3; idem., *Iranian History and Politics*, passim; idem., 'Farr-e izadi va haqq-e elahi-ye padshahan', in *Ettela'at-e Siyasi-Eqtesadi*, 129–30, summer 1998; idem., 'Legitimacy and Succession in Iranian History', *Comparative Studies of South Asia, Africa and the Middle East*, 23(4), December 2003, pp. 234–45.

the society where many of its aspects—political, social, educational, literary, etc.—are constantly in danger of receiving the pick-axe treatment by short-term whims of fashion.[6]

Lack of long-term continuity, by definition, resulted in significant change from one short period to the next, such that *history became a series of connected short runs*. In this sense, therefore, change was more frequent—usually also more drastic—and as noted, social mobility across various classes considerably higher than in traditional European societies. But, also by definition, it rendered very difficult *cumulative* change in the long term, including the long-term accumulation of property, wealth, capital, social and private institutions, even the institutions of learning. These did normally proceed or exist in every short term, but they had to be reconstructed or drastically altered in the following short terms.

Evidence of the short-term nature of society as described above is to be found virtually in all of its aspects almost throughout Iran's long history, both pre-Islamic and post-Islamic. Here we shall present a brief analysis of three of its main features closely related to one another: problems of legitimacy and succession, and the toll that this took of rulers, other royal persons, and ministers and military commanders; the tenuous nature of 'life and possessions' (*jan o mal*); and problems of accumulation and development. We will end with a brief discussion of how the issues raised affect Iran's political current situation.

Problems of Legitimacy and Succession

The testability of the criteria of legitimacy and succession, and the toll this took of rulers, other royal persons, ministers and military commanders, was a major feature of 'the short-term society'. Both in the feudal states of Europe and the absolutist states which succeeded them through and after the Renaissance, the rules of legitimacy and of succession were normally secure and inviolable. Primogeniture was the principal rule that in both the late feudal and the absolutist state governed succession, a rule which was also firmly in force in the case of landed estates. The duke's or earl's first in line was as firmly entitled to inherit his wealth and title, as was the king's first in line to inherit his kingdom. The 'first in line' in both cases would be the first son or the nearest surviving male relative (although, since the sixteenth century, there were a few female monarchs in the absence of a clear and convincing male heir apparent in those states that did not have Salic law). James VI of Scotland (later James I of England) was the legitimate successor to Elizabeth I through a distant and complicated relationship, which none the less made him first in line to the English throne.[7]

---

[6] See Katouzian, 'Problems of Democracy' and 'Dar ta'assob va khami'.
[7] See, for example, Neville Williams, *Elizabeth Queen of England*, London: Sphere Books, 1971; Antonia Fraser, *Mary Queen of Scots*, London: Panther Books 1970; S.

It is important to emphasize that strictly speaking neither the king nor aristocrats could have any say over the rules of succession, whereas merchants and other capitalists had the freedom of will over the bequest of their estates. And this was not surprising since the survival of manorial feudal estate ownership depended on it (and on the Law of Entail), and since—unlike the merchant classes—it was extremely difficult for those of non-aristocratic descent to be elevated into the ranks of the aristocracy and impossible for a commoner to become king. Even in the odd case of Poland where the habit grew of 'electing' the king, the election was made only from royal or old aristocratic families: in the early 1570s they elected Henry, Duke of Anjou, first in line to the French throne, who, barely having arrived in Warsaw, returned to Paris as Henry III upon the untimely death of his brother Charles IX.[8]

Thus, royal succession according to established procedures was the most basic requirement for a king's legitimacy, not only in the feudal period, but also under the absolutist state, which governed Europe for a maximum of four centuries (1500–1900) for the continent taken a s a whole. Apart from that, the support or co-operation of the church was also necessary, despite the fact that its powers had been trimmed in the latter period. The power of the established church was less after Reformation than before even in Catholic Latin countries. Still, it was one of the pillars of legitimacy for the absolutist government. Indeed, in countries like Spain, Austria, France and England which (unlike most of Germany, the Low Countries and Switzerland) were united under a single monarch, the existence of an established as well as episcopal church was seen as necessary for the strength of the king's authority. James I, who ruled a fundamentally Protestant country and, besides, fancied himself as a theorist of pure despotic rule, was at the same time fond of saying 'no bishop no king'.[9] It is important to note that while the principal of 'no bishop no king' emphasizes the usefulness of an established, indeed episcopal, church, for the king's power and authority, at the same time it clearly shows his formal dependency on a class of people outside of himself.

The aristocracy provided the other main pillar for the king's authority, once again as in the feudal period but at a reduced scale. The merchant or bourgeois classes were by now another principal social base for the state, such that in the early Renaissance period the state used their support to reduce the aristocratic magnates, perhaps the biggest single example of this being the

---

T. Bindoff, *Tudor England*, London: Pelican, 1952; Christopher Morris, *The Tudors*, London: Fontana /Collins, 1973.

[8] See H. W. C. Davis, *Medieval Europe*, London: Thornton Butterfield, 1936; R. H. C. Davis, *A History of Medieval Europe: From Constantine to St Louis*, London: Longman, 1974, Part II, V-IX; Herbert Butterfield et al, *A Short History of France*, Cambridge: Cambridge University Press, 1959; H. A. L. Fisher, *A History of Europe*, London: Edward Arnold, 1936.

[9] See C. H. McIlwain (ed.), *The Political Works of James I*, Cambridge, MA: Harvard University Press, 1918; Hugh Trevor-Roper, 'James I and the Bishops', in H. R. Trevor-Roper, *Historical Essays*, London: Macmillan 1957.

triumph—in the fifteenth century—of Louis XI over the so-called League of the Public Good, led by Charles the Bold of Burgundy.[10] Yet, not long afterwards the aristocracy (and gentry) became once again the state's principal social base next to the church, and they jointly underpinned the legitimacy of absolutist rule. It would be quite reasonable to argue that Charles Stuart's greatest misfortune was that both of these two pillars of the state were divided in their attitude towards him, at least until his trial and execution in January 1649.[11] It was in the same decade that, upon the death of Louis XIII and Cardinal Richelieu one after the other, the rebellion of some of France's grandest aristocrats as well as the judicial authorities of Paris (known as the Paris *Parlement*) in the two successive *Frondes* caused great disruptions for the rule of the very young Louis XIV and his regent and minister, Queen Anne and Cardinal Mazarin.[12]

In Iran there was no law or entrenched tradition, which made succession predictable and/or legitimate before the event. The most fundamental rule for succession and legitimacy was *not* primogeniture, although being a son or relative of the ruler was helpful. It was possession of *farr-e izadi* or God's Grace. Anyone in possession of the Grace would have the right to succeed or accede to the throne, and his rule would therefore be regarded as legitimate.

The theory or myth of the Grace, and the consequences of its possession and loss in practice, are spread virtually all over Ferdowsi's *Shahnameh*, including the purely mythological, the heroic or epic and the 'historical' parts of the poem. Significantly, the Grace takes a physical form on one occasion, and perhaps even more significantly this occurs in the 'historical' part, the story of Ardeshir, son of Babak, descendent of Sasan, and founder of the Sasanian empire. When Ardeshir is running away from the last Arsacid emperor, Ardevan, and is being chased by him, the latter reaches a 'town' (*shahr*) through which the former has passed. He asks if people had seen Ardeshir there and is told that they had seen:

> A ram galloping after a rider
> More beautiful than fabulous pictures

---

[10] See Sir George Clark, *Early Modern Europe, from about 1450 to about 1720*, London: Oxford University Press, 1966; Fisher, *A History of Europe*, Book II; A. G. Dickens, *The Age of Humanism and Reformation: Europe in the Fourteenth, Fifteenth, and Sixteenth Centuries*, London: Prentice-Hall International, 1977.

[11] See C. V. Wedgwood, *The Trial of Charles I*, London: World Books, 1964; *The King's War*, London: Fontana, 1966; Christopher Hill, *The Century of Revolution, 1603–1714*, London: Cardinal, 1974; J. P. Kenyon, *The Stuarts: A Study in English Kingship*, London: Fontana, 1966.

[12] See, for example, Maurice Ashley, *Louis XIV and the Greatness of France*, London: The English Universities Press, 1966; David Ogg, *Louis XIV*, London: Oxford University Press, 1967; Arthur Hassall, *Mazarin*, London: Macmillan, 1903; C. V. Wedgwood, *Richelieu and the French Monarchy*, London: The English Universities Press, 1958.

Ardevan's counsel then tells him it would be useless to go on chasing the man, because the Grace in the form of the Ram is accompanying him. The relief in Naqsh-e Rostam shows Ardeshir receiving the Grace or *farr* from Ahura Mazda in the form of a diadem. Both man and god are shown mounted on horseback while Ardeshir is being invested with the Grace. All this shows the supernatural as well as mythological nature of the Grace.

It is clear then, (a) that the Grace and its possession is a gift of God which carries paranormal or mysterious qualities, and (b) that it is the crucial and fundamental test for succession and legitimacy over and above any other, including primogeniture or indeed royal descent. The problem however is that, whereas in a mythological world supernatural feats may be performed, or tests conducted, to determine a claimant's legitimacy, in the world of reality there will not be any public test for it, a test, that is, which like primogeniture may be observed commonly by all concerned.

The last observation is absolutely crucial. The legitimate ruler was one who was anointed by God to act as his vicegerent on earth. Two fundamental differences emerge between the God's Grace theory and the European rule of primogeniture. First, that in the real world there cannot be an objective test of legitimate succession and rule. Or, in other words, this was possible to know merely by virtue of the fact that a pretender or claimant succeeded and maintained power. Primogeniture unambiguously conferred legitimacy to the first in line to the throne, a rule that the king (or for that matter the feudal lord) himself did not have the power to contradict. There could be argument about it as that between William of Normandy and Harold of England, and even though ultimately the sword determined this case, first there had been a legal battle in which the Pope had cast his vote in William's favour. Otherwise, rebellion was treasonable and even if it succeeded it could not confer legitimacy, unless it was successfully led by a prince or high aristocrat, and was supported by a sizeable portion of the ruling classes, the aristocracy and (later) gentry. That would be civil war like the successful revolt of Bolingbroke, Henry IV, against his cousin Richard II, or Wars of the Roses, and even the rise of Henry Tudor against Richard III, the last of the Plantagenets.[13] Or, from French history, the unsuccessful rebellion of Henry Duke of Guise, against Henry III, and the successful revolt, at the same time, of Henry of Bourbon, King of Navarre, against the same King of France, the last of the Valois.[14] Whereas on the basis of the myth, tradition or theory of *farr-e izadi*, virtually anyone could hold power, thus claiming that he had the *farr*, and

---

[13] The hereditary claim of Henry IV was not as good as the boy Earl of March, great-grandson of Clarence, elder brother of John of Gaunt, but he was told not to base his accession on the right of conquest since he would then be regarded as a rebel. See, for example, Sir George Clark, *English History: A Survey*, Oxford: Clarendon, 1971; E. L. Woodward, *History of England*, London: Methuen, 1947; Johan Harvey, *The Plantagenets*, London: Fontana, 1976.

[14] See Dickens, *The Age of Humanism and Reformation*; Clark, *Early Modern Europe*; Fisher, *A History of Europe*.

anyone could be claimed to have lost it by virtue of a successful rebellion against him.

The second fundamental difference between the two traditions follows directly from the first. Since Iranian succession and legitimacy were entirely determined by a divine gift which almost any one could be deemed to possess by virtue of attaining power and maintaining it, he was in no way bound by any entrenched tradition or (written or unwritten) legal framework. And *ipso facto,* he was not dependent on the consent—other than enforced submission—of any part of the society, whether high or low, which is contrary to various European traditions from the classical through mediaeval to modern and contemporary times.

Plainly it appears from the evidence that the real test of holding the *farr* was success itself, i. e., the fact that the ruler actually held and maintained supreme power. For apart from the mythological examples of Ardeshir carrying the Ram—the symbol of *farr*—on horseback, or Fereydun and Keykhosrow riding through wide and turbulent rivers, or the latter's father Siyavosh riding through fire, it is clear that the holding of the *farr* was recognized *ex post facto,* i. e., by the rule of *post hoc ergo propter hoc*: in a real world, he had the *farr* and was therefore legitimate as ruler who was actually in power and ruled effectively.[15] The position resembles some recent theories that the *vali* or Leader in an Islamic state emerges as a manifestation of the will of God, and would therefore lose authority and/or fall by divine will alone, the society or people, or any of their parts, not having any say in the matter.

The absence of any established rules of succession had a dialectical effect on the position of the ruler. On the one hand, and contrary to the position even of the absolute rulers of Europe, he was not bound by any earthly law, tradition or restraint, and could exercise authority at will up to the limits of his actual physical power, which, for prudent rulers, included consideration of limits to which the society would tolerate their actions. On the other hand, he almost constantly faced the fear of palace coups and potential rebellions—and he would never know with a reasonable degree of probability who would succeed him after his death—because, unlike in Europe, virtually all that potential rebels needed for taking power with at least as much 'legitimacy' as him was to succeed. In fact the 'legitimacy' of the successful rebel was nearly always greater at first than that of the fallen ruler, since (for reasons arising from these and other features of arbitrary rule) Iranian society normally disliked its rulers and wished them to be replaced by one who was 'more just', or at least 'less unjust'. Predictably, arbitrary state and arbitrary society, *unaccountable government and ungovernable society,* were two sides of the same coin. That was another principal dialectic of Iranian history.[16]

---

[15] See further, Katouzian, 'Farr-e izadi va haqq-e elahi-ye padshahan'.
[16] For greater details see Katouzian, *Iranian History and Politics*; and idem., *State and Society in Iran,* especially chapter 1.

The myth of God's vicegerency of the ruler was not limited to ancient, pre-Islamic, times.[17] The term *farr* itself was also used to confirm the divine legitimacy of post-Islamic rulers. Ferdowsi himself applies the term to Mahmud of Ghazna and his rule in a number of his prefatory verses to various books of the *Shahnameh*. For example: 'World Ruler Mahmud, owner of *farr* and generosity…The Book has begun with his name / His *farr* whitens dark hearts like ivory'[18].

No doubt Islamic concepts and theories of legitimate worldly authority emerged from the Koran, various bodies of Hadith (the traditions of the Prophet), and the theological and jurisprudential arguments and decisions based upon them. The comparison here made refers simply to the practical implications of the pre-Islamic and Islamic concepts, not their strict religious or metaphysical origins. The sultanate and, even more so, the caliphate were concepts that emerged and were justified on the basis of Islamic doctrine and tradition, but it would be difficult to deny their practical resemblance—sometimes down to small detail—to pre-Islamic Iranian traditions.

The problem of succession persisted down to the nineteenth century. Fath-'Ali Shah chose his grandson Mohammad Mirza as his successor after the death of his son Abbas Mirza, the prince regent and Mohammad's father, though he knew that it would cause serious dissent among his other sons and so delayed its announcement for as long as it was possible.[19] Yet, some of Mohammad's uncles rebelled against him when he succeeded to the throne.[20] Later, Mohammad Shah himself was known to favour his younger son Abbas Mirza (Nayeb al-Saltaneh, later Molk Ara) in preference to his eldest son, Naser al-Din, the heir apparent. When the latter managed to succeed his fa-

---

[17] For a statement of this myth expressed in post-Islamic terms, see Abolfazl Beyhaqi, *Tarikh-e Beyhaqi*, ed. Ali Akbar Fayyaz, Tehran: Ershad, 1995, pp. 116–17; Nezam al-Molk Tusi, *Siyar al-Moluk* or *Siyasatnameh*, ed. Hubert Darke, Tehran: Bongah-e Tarjomeh va Nashr-e Ketab, 1961.
[18] *Shahnameh*, vi, 1554, just as Ferdowsi resumes his own writing after the 1,000 inserted distiches of Daqiqi come to an end.
[19] See Ann K.S. Lambton, *Qājār Persia*, Austin: Texas University Press, 1988, p. 14.
[20] See, for example, Mehdi Bamdad, *Sharh-e hal-e rejal-e Iran*, four volumes, Tehran: Zavvar, 1992, on the killing, blinding and/or imprisonment of Mohammad's brothers and uncles, either because of their open rebellion or because of mere suspicion against them. See, for example, the entries in vol. 1 for Hoseyn Ali Mirza, Hasan Ali Mirza, Khosrow Mirza and Jahangir Mirza, but there were a few others as well. Mohammad Shah also had his able minister, Mirza Abu al-Qasem, the younger Qa'em-Maqam, suddenly arrested and strangled to death a few months after mounting the throne with the latter's indispensable help. This is a famous episode. What is not so well known is that, like most ministers in Iranian history, Qa'em-Maqam was unpopular, and that he had also played a leading role in the demise of those princes, whether guilty or merely suspected. See for example, Ali Asghar Shamim, *Iran dar Dowreh-ye Saltanat-e Qajar*, Tehran: Ibn Sina, 1964, chapter 8. It must be emphasized that Mohammad Shah was one of the least blood-thirsty of Iranian rulers. Indeed, he displayed strong Sufi sympathies.

ther, the nine-year-old Abbas Mirza would have lost his life, or been blinded, if foreign envoys (and Amir Nezam) had not intervened on his behalf. But his court was looted on official orders, and later he spent much of his life as a refugee in Ottoman Iraq and Russia. Permission for him to go to Mesopotamia as an exile was obtained as a result of persistent interventions of both the British and Russian ministers in Tehran to stop him from being killed at the age of thirteen by his brother the Shah on the mere supposition that he might be regarded as their alternative candidate for the throne by some unknown, imagined, intriguers.

The correspondence between the two foreign envoys and the chief minister makes fascinating reading. At one stage when the British minister wrote that they should not sacrifice 'fairness' to mere imagination (that there is a plot centred around the boy), the chief minister revealed the logic of arbitrary justice, by pointing out that in that country one should act on mere supposition, for otherwise one may end up by losing the game. And this was so precisely because 'legitimacy' always belonged to the winner. He wrote that he had reported the British minister's letter to the Shah. The Shah had agreed with the minister that he meant well, but had added that:

> Your Excellency must pay attention to some peculiar Iranian customs and traditions and realize that, in Iran, the things that Your Excellency has in mind will not work, and one cannot be immune from the evil intent of seditious and rebellious people. If the leaders of the Iranian state wish to act on the basis of fairness and justice to maintain order and security for all their subjects, *they would have no choice but at the slightest thought, imagination or supposition of rebellion, irrespective of who it might be, to try to put it down forthwith and not to hesitate even for a moment.*[21]

At any rate, the disputes over royal succession eventually came to an end as a result of Great Power guarantees of the succession of the heir-designate to the throne. Yet it is extremely instructive that Naser al-Din Shah—who was by no means the worst example of an arbitrary ruler of Iran—almost withdrew the right of succession from his son and heir-designate, Mozaffar al-Din Mirza and sold it to his other son, Zell al-Soltan. He wrote to the former that the latter had offered him two (Persian) crore—roughly a million—tumans for the position. Zell was well known both for his shrewdness and lack of scruples. Mozaffar was lucky, therefore, that, in reply to the Shah his father, his able secretary, Amir Nezam Garrusi, warned that Zell might well spend another ten crores for the Shah's position itself.[22] It was, of course, an open secret that

---

[21] See *Sharh-e hal-e Abbas Mirza Molk Ara*, ed. 'Abd a-Hoseyn Nava'i, 2nd edition, Tehran: Babak 1982. The letters have been published from the Iranian archives in 'Abbas Eqbal-e Ashtiyani's introduction to the book; see pp. 29–31. Emphasis added.
[22] See Mohammad Ebrahim Bastani Parizi, *Asiya-ye haft sang: Majmu'eh-ye maqalat-e tarikhi va adabi*, Tehran: Donya-ye Ketab, 1988, p. 644.

Zell was doing everything possible (including offering subservience to the British) to overthrow his father. There could be no better evidence at any rate for the unpredictability of succession in Iranian history that, not much longer than a hundred years ago, it looked quite normal for the Shah to sell the succession for money.

Legitimacy and succession being so much determined by mere success, by the mere fact of gaining and holding power by virtually anyone, it is not surprising that there was so much filicide, fratricide and parricide within the royal household. Apart from outright killing, the blinding and/or permanent incarceration of princes within the women's compound (*haram* or *andarun*) was a favourite Safavid device. It was from the *andarun* that Shah Safi emerged to claim the throne of his grandfather, Abbas I, and ruled with exemplary cruelty. And it would not take much imagination to think of the magnitude of insecurity in which ministers, chieftains and magnates lived and worked—and sometimes died. The familiar story—from ancient to modern times—of the long line of such powerful persons who (alone or together with their family and clan) perished on the order of their rulers, told in detail, would fill several volumes of chilling history.

There were few chief ministers and important high officials, and especially very few of the most able of them, who survived the suspicion, wrath or treachery of their masters, either because they feared their ability and strength or wanted to plunder their wealth and property or both. A few relatively recent cases of officials who did not survive their loyal service are well known, such as Amir Nezam Farahani, better known as Amir Kabir. But, like so many other features of arbitrary state and society, this too was structural and systemic. The names of Abu al-Fazl Bal'ami, Abu al-Fath Bosti, Abu al-'Abbas Esferayeni, (Ahmad son of) Hasan Meymandi, Hasanak the Vizier, Amid al-Molk Kondori, Nezam al-Molk Tusi, Ahmad Zia' al-Molk, the brothers Shams al-Din and Ata Malek Joveyni, Rashid al-Din Fazlollah, Emamqoli Khan, Hajj Ebrahim Kalantar, Qa'em-Maqam Farahani, Amir Kabir, Mirza Aqa Khan Nuri, Abd al-Hoseyn Teymurtash, Sardar As'ad Bakhtiyari, Nosrat al-Dowleh Firuz, among so many others, readily spring to mind, from the Samanids down to recent times.[23]

The Tenuous Nature of 'Life and Possessions' (*jan o mal*)

This feature of Iran's 'short-term society' followed directly from the first. The ruler being God's vicegerent on earth and in no way answerable to anyone or

---

[23] See, for example, Beyhaqi's *Tarikh-e Beyhaqi*, Ravandi's *Rahat al-sudur*, Rashid al-Din's *Jame' al-tavarikh*, Hamdollah Mostowfi's *Tarikh-e gozideh*, Abdollah Shirazi's *Tarikh-e Vassaf*, Mirkhand's *Rowzat al-Safa*, Kh^{v}andmir's *Habib al-siyar*, Aqili's *Athar al-vozara*, Eskandar Monshi's *Tarikh-e Alam Ara*, Rezaqoli Khan Hedayat's *Rowzat al-Safa-ye Naseri*, Lesan al-Molk's *Nasekh al-Tavarikh*, Mokhber al-Saltaneh Hedayat's *Khaterat va Khatarat*, Ebrahim Kh^{v}ajeh-Nuri's *Bazigaran-e Asr-e Tala'i*. See further, the entry on 'wazir' by Ann K. S. Lambton in *The Encyclopaedia of Islam*, new edition, xi, 2001, pp. 192–94.

any social class, however high by virtue of descent, position or money, had complete dominion over the life and property of all of his subjects or 'flock' (*ra'iyat*). When the ruler as the personification of the state is completely independent from the society, there can be no rights independently from him. That is, in the final analysis, no person or class of people is able to claim any rights except those that are bestowed or reaffirmed by the ruler. And what is bestowed by a ruler may be taken away by him or his successors, so long as they have the power to enforce their will. It follows that there will not be any legal code or procedure that may limit the power of the state, or be invoked against its transgressions. Indeed the very term 'transgression' could not be used in the normal sense, for where there is no independent right it cannot be legally violated, although some arbitrary moral and ethical sense may be used to describe an act as transgression.

This is the simple reason why there was not and there could not be private property in Iran in any sense that that word conveys in the history of Europe. *Khasseh, khaleseh*, and *divani* lands were directly or indirectly owned by the ruler and state.[24] Their definition and extent changed from one era to the next, from one dynasty to another, sometimes even from one ruler to the next.[25] The revenue assignment systems—*eqta', toyul, soyurghal,* etc.—also varied among themselves, and within each category through time. Frequently, there were different types of each of the categories at one and the same time. This itself is evidence for the absence of a well defined legal framework, showing that not only government was arbitrary, but so was its administrative system.

The most important aspect of the system—if this be the appropriate term—was that those who held land or enjoyed its revenue one way or another had no independent right to it. It was a *privilege* rather than a *right* which the state (i.e., the ruler, or local governors backed by him) could take away from him at will, so long as they had the physical power to carry it out. Willem Floor refers to the adage 'All that a slave owns belongs to his master' as the logical explanation for such confiscation.[26] Another version of that adage is 'The slave and all that he owns belong to his master'.[27] This is a more appropriate version because (as we shall see below), not only the property but also the person of a subject, however high, was ultimately at the disposal of the

---

[24] For a theoretical discussion of the nature and causes of these developments, see Homa Katouzian, 'The Aridisolatic Society: A Model of Long-Term Social and Economic Development in Iran', *International Journal of Middle East Studies*, 15(2), June 1983, pp. 259–81, reprinted in idem., *Iranian History and Politics*, pp. 61–76. See also Homa Katouzian, *The Political Economy of Modern Iran*, London and New York: Macmillan and New York University Press, 1981.

[25] See Ann K. S. Lambton, *Landlord and Peasant in Persia: A Study of Land Tenure and Land Revenue Administration*, London: Oxford University Press, 1953; Willem Floor, *A Fiscal History of Iran in the Safavid and Qajar Periods: 1500–1925*, New York, Bibliotheca Persica Press, 1998.

[26] Ibid., p. 335.

[27] Respectively: *al-'abd ma fi yaduhu li-mowlahu* and *al-'abd wa ma fi yaduhu kan-i li-mowlahu*.

ruler, or of those who acted within his authority. Since government was not based in law, power, position, possession and life itself could be taken away at short notice and without any formal procedures. The structure of insecurity ran through all the orders of society, from the village headman through the local craftsman, the merchant and trader, to the state's agents, the governor and governor-general, the *mostowfi*, the vizier, and not least the shah himself.

The primary sources of Iranian history are packed with innumerable examples of acute insecurity of not only property but also life itself. As already noted, countless viziers and other high officials of the state were killed or otherwise destroyed, and/or their entire property was confiscated, without any legal procedure and leave to appeal. Moreover, the plunder of the nobles' and notables' property did not happen only when they fell from office and grace. It could happen at any time.

Master Secretary Bunasr-e Moshkan was a very important and highly respected high official of the state under both Mahmud and Mas'ud of Ghazna. He was also very fortunate to die in bed. Beyhaqi, who wrote his history several centuries before the Safavids, relates that shortly before Bunasr died, the Sultan, prompted by a lesser official, had demanded a number of horses and camels from each of the Persian (*tazik*) notables, including Bunasr. Every one of them humbly complied. But Bunasr lost his equanimity, says Beyhaqi, solely because he thought that that lesser official had aimed this scheme at him personally. He sent a list of everything he possessed to the ruler, saying that he had earned them all in his long service to the state, and they were all there for Mas'ud to take and grant him an abode in a prison-citadel. The Sultan was angry but decided to overlook the matter and drop his demand in Bunasr's case. Shortly afterwards the latter died, 'and they told all sorts of tales about [the causes of] his death, which I shall not mention'. At any rate, he was mourned in honour. Nevertheless, all of his possessions were transferred to the state. And it is clear from Beyhaqi's text that this was normal practice:

> And they took his good well-trained slave boys to the Sultan's compound, and put the Sultan's brand on his horses and camels. And [a Treasury official] was told to draw up a list of whatever the man had for the treasury.[28]

The example is important for some fairly obvious reasons, but most important of all because it shows that the appropriation of the estate of a man such as Bunasr, even though he had died in honour, was a normal practice.

There are countless examples of this kind of official requisition in Iranian history, showing that a man's property, dead or alive, was always in danger of confiscation, in part or as a whole, even if he had not incurred the wrath of the shah, or whoever could exercise arbitrary power over him. Here are a few examples, from the nineteenth century—in fact, all except the first one from the late nineteenth century—when many leaders of the state and society, in-

---

[28] See *Tarikh-e Beyhaqi*, pp. 791–99.

cluding at times the shah himself, were convinced that the country's salvation was in establishing orderly, responsible and lawful government. After death in office (under Mohammad Shah) of Manuchehr Khan Gorji, Mo'tamed al-Dowleh, the very powerful governor-general of Isfahan, his estate 'was confiscated by the state, and his body was buried in Qom, in his own special tomb'.[29]

Asef al-Dowleh, one-time governor of Khorasan, who, because of a major rebellion against his injustices, had been withdrawn from his post, appeared to have gone mad. He had a large fortune, and rumour had it that he was pretending to be mad for fear that Naser al-Din Shah would take his wealth from him. When he died, Amin al-Soltan, the grand vizier, had his personal treasury sealed off on the Shah's orders, so that there was no access even to the special shroud he had purchased for himself, but in the end they opened the seal, got the shroud, and sealed the treasury again. Eventually, they got a total of 150,000 tumans from his heirs.[30]

Mostafa Khan-e Amir Tuman, governor of Ardabil and Khoy, died. 'The Shah expressed much regret. I have subsequently heard that he sent a man to seal off his house, because they say he has a lot of money.'[31] Yahya Khan Khajeh Nuri had endowed most of his property for fear that the shah would take them after his death.[32] Mehdi Khan was an official who had amassed a large fortune. When he died, the Shah had his house sealed off, and took a large amount of his wealth.[33]

Kamran Mirza, the Shah's third son and minister of war, jailed the wife of the commander of artillery after his death to obtain money from her. She refused to pay 70,000 tumans, and he eventually accepted 3,000. Having heard this, Nezam al-Dowleh, who was then the richest commander in the army, endowed the whole of his property.[34]

On the eve of the Constitutional Revolution, Mirza Mahmud Khan Hakim al-Molk, Mozaffar al-Din Shah's long-standing physician and favourite, and recently minister of the royal court, who was hated by Amin al-Soltan, then chief vizier and chancellor, died as governor of Gilan. He was believed to have amassed a fortune of about two and a half million tumans. Rumours were rife that he had been poisoned. His entire fortune was sealed off on the orders of Amin al-Soltan.[35] Once again, it is important to bear in mind the logic of the system for, according to Mokhber al-Saltaneh, since much of the

---

[29] See Mehdi Bamdad, *Sharh-e hal-e rejal-e Iran*, vol 4, p. 162.
[30] See Bamdad, *Sharh-e hal*, 2, pp. 301–17; *Ruznameh-ye Khaterat-e E'temad al-Saltaneh*, ed. Iraj Afshar, Tehran: Amir Kabir, 1966, pp. 345–545.
[31] E'temad al-Saltaneh in ibid., p. 543.
[32] See Bamdad, *Sharh-e hal*, 5, p. 333.
[33] Bamdad, *Sharh-e hal*, 5, p. 303. For a somewhat different, though not contradictory, version see E'temad al-Saltaneh, *Ruznameh*, p. 601.
[34] Bamdad, *Sharh-e hal*, 5, pp. 291–92; 1, pp. 151–53.
[35] See 'Abd al-Hoseyn Khan Sepehr, *Mir'at al-waqayi'-e Mozaffari va Yaddasht-ha-ye Malek al-Movarrekhin*, ed. 'Abd al-Hoseyn Nava'i, Tehran: Zarrin, 1989, 2, p. 28; Bamdad, *Sharh-e hal*, 4, pp. 35–38.

riches amassed by state officials were themselves due to 'plunder', confiscation from their property by the state was not viewed as an extraordinary violation of their rights.[36]

These are just a few examples of plunder of property when the victim had not fallen from office or grace, and was not an object of wrath by the ruler. They are examples of cases when the ruler demanded money from an otherwise 'innocent' notable. But there were other occasions when the ruler traded the life of an 'innocent' notable or official for money, 'innocent' here meaning that the ruler himself did not have the slightest anger or grudge against the notable.

Ravandi writes that Sultan Mohammad of the Seljuks was a good-natured ruler 'but he had a great love for accumulating riches'. Zia' al-Molk, son of Nezam al-Molk and currently the Sultan's vizier, had offered him 500,000 dinars, to put a very important man (who was also a seyyed) 'at his disposal' (meaning that he could dispose of his life and wealth as he saw fit) and the Sultan had agreed. Having got wind of the situation in time, however, the seyyed quickly saw the sultan and offered 800,000 dinars to the Sultan if he put Zia' al-Molk at his disposal instead.[37]

That was nine hundred years ago. At the close of the nineteenth century, Rokn al-Dowleh, a brother of Naser al-Din Shah, had been governor of Fars for only seven months when he heard that the Shah was thinking of giving his post to someone else who was offering a bigger *pishkesh* (a gift offered to secure a favour). He took various steps— most effective of all, using the influence of the Shah's favourite wife—to prevent that.

Rokn al-Dowleh bore a deep grudge against Qavam al-Molk, the biggest landlord and most important magnate in the province, had the soles of his feet beaten with sticks and thrown him in jail. He had then offered 100,000 tumans to the Shah and 30,000 to the grand vizier, Amin al-Soltan, to 'sell' Qavam al-Molk to him. They did not accept, partly because of the influence of his uncle, and partly – perhaps mainly – because of likely adverse comments by Europeans. E'temad al-Saltaneh writes in his diaries:

> After entering Shiraz, Rokn al-Dowleh had [Qavam al-Molk] bastinadoed and imprisoned, after which he had written a letter to Tehran saying that he would pay 100,000 tumans to the Shah and 30,000 to Amin al-Soltan if they sold Qavam to him, that is, to put Qavam's life and property at his disposal. But he did not manage to buy Qavam, since the latter is a nephew of Sahab-Divan, and, apart from that, this is not like the age of Fath-'Ali Shah, where it was possible to buy and sell

---

[36] See Mokhber al-Saltaneh, Mehdiqoli Hedayat, *Khaterat va Khatarat*, which is a good, fairly detached, source on the political culture of the Qajar and early Pahlavi period.
[37] See Mohammad ibn Ali Soleyman Ravandi, *Rahat al-sudur*, ed. Mohammad Eqbal, London: Luzac, 1921, pp. 162–65.

magnates and notables; the Europeans would make a fuss. He did not manage to buy Qavam.[38]

This happened in the early 1890s. The reference to the sale of important people by Fath-'Ali Shah is not spurious, for Amin al-Dowleh writes in his memoirs quite independently:

> The Shah [i. e., Fath-Ali] even used to sell the court officials and state dignitaries to each other . . . [since], as Iranian sycophants keep repeating, life and private possessions were the rightful property of the Shahanshah.[39]

As the above example from the Seljuk period shows, this was by no means a Qajar invention. In fact such things had been part of the country's social structure and it is difficult to believe that there had been any length of time in which they had *not* been practised. For that reason, it would be a mistake to attribute them to the personal moral dejection of rulers, viziers, governors, or whoever. No doubt some of these were less kind or more greedy than others. But the matter was deep-seated and systemic. It is succinctly captured by the above-quoted adage, 'The slave and all that he owns belong to his master.'

Problems of Accumulation and Development

If there is one point on which all the major theories of economic development are agreed it is that the industrial revolution occurred as a result of long-term accumulation of, first commercial, then industrial capital. Long-term accumulation of capital was a necessary though not sufficient condition for modern industrial development. Without it, the necessary investment would have taken place neither in the commercial sphere, resulting in the unification of the internal market and virtually continuous expansion of foreign trade, nor in the goods which made the innovation and application of modern techniques and processes possible in agriculture and industry.[40]

The simple but highly acute point about the necessity of long-term accumulation of capital was discovered by early classical economists, who observed that in order for the firm to expand it needed to accumulate, and in order for it to accumulate, it had to save first. This was what they sometimes described as the process of 'ploughing back capital'. Turgot described the process more clearly than any one before. But it was Adam Smith who put forward a memorable argument for the necessity of prior saving for the expansion of the firm, hence the industry and therefore the whole economy. He

---

[38] See E'temad al-Saltaneh, *Ruznameh*, p. 821; Bamdad, *sharh-e hal*, 3, p. 403.
[39] See *Khaterat-e siyasi-ye Mirza Ali Khan Amin al-Dowleh*, ed. Hafez Farmanfarma'ian, Tehran: Amir Kabir,1991, p. 6.
[40] See Alexander Gerschenkron, 'The Approach to European Industrialization', in *Economic Backwardness in Historical Perspectives*, Cambridge MA: Harvard University Press, 1962.

said with a certainty—perhaps even dogmatism—uncharacteristic of his even-tempered approach to most matters of theory and policy that it was not so much technical progress, but saving and investment, making its innovation and application possible that were the principal cause of industrial development. He therefore concluded that every saver was a friend, and every spender, an enemy of the society.[41]

In other words, aggregate saving is the sum of the savings of all firms and individuals. Furthermore, he said, it is saving, not production, which is the initial cause of investment, of capital accumulation.[42] It follows that savers compensate for the habits of the spendthrift in preventing economic decline. Savers therefore help the society, while spendthrifts hinder it.[43]

To sum up the fundamental points made above, capital accumulation required significant and continuous saving for long-term investment. Finance for investment was supplied directly by the savings of propertied classes, by banks, the state or—in the last century and a half—by all of them. Since the twentieth century, development finance has also been supplied by advanced industrial countries for investment in Third-World economies. The classic and earliest example of long-term accumulation was the accumulation of—first commercial then industrial—capital in England, mainly by the bourgeoisie, the commercial classes, although 'enlightened landlords' also participated in the process from mid-seventeenth century onwards.

Yet, to save continuously and at a significant rate would be *rational* only in a social framework where there was no endemic fear of plunder and confiscation. Even in Europe, long-term capital accumulation was greatly encouraged, first by the emergence of free towns—burgs, etc. —which afforded protection from feudal encroachments; and, secondly, by the rise of the Renaissance and absolutist monarchies, with the full blessing of the commercial and middle classes, which gave them protection vis-à-vis the great aristocratic magnates. It was the accumulation of financial capital which made possible the financing of technical innovations, and, through time, this led to modern technological development and industrial expansion—i. e., what used to be generally known as 'the industrial revolution'.

There used to be a puzzle posed by classical economists, and later economic historians and development economists, to which apparently no solution satisfactory to themselves and others has been offered. It was this: Why did the process of capital accumulation not begin in societies like Iran in their rich and technologically advanced times, say in the early mediaeval period. The clearest answer to that question is that it was not safe to engage in long-term saving for fear of plunder and confiscation; and that in a small number of

---

[41] See Adam Smith, *An Inquiry into The Nature and Causes of The Wealth of Nations*, ed. Edwin Cannan, London: Methuen & Co., 1950, 1, ii, 3, 'Of the Accumulation of Capital, or of productive and unproductive labour', p. 320.
[42] Ibid.
[43] Ibid., pp. 321–23. See further, Homa Katuzian [Katouzian], *Adam Esmit va Servat-e Melal*, Tehran: Amir Kabir, 1979, pp. 95–97 and 153–57.

cases where such attempts were made, or for other reasons a very large commercial fortune was amassed, later plunder and confiscation put an end to the process.

Max Weber's solution to that old puzzle was that the other, non-accumulating, societies lacked something corresponding to Protestant ethics. Weber's theory of the crucial role played by these ethics in shaping 'the spirit of capitalism' in Europe is intelligent, though it has also been subjected to serious criticism.[44] Notwithstanding that, the question in the context of our inquiry is whether such ethics could have become widespread in societies where, at least in practice, there was no right of long-term property ownership; and, if they had, and even lasted, for reasons which are difficult to envisage, whether they would have resulted in long-term accumulation of capital.

Even if significant saving *had* taken place in such highly discouraging circumstances, it would not have resulted in long-term accumulation in view of the fact that savings were perennially plundered. There can be little doubt that Protestantism, and especially its more radical sects, actively encouraged frugality and hard work (even in spite of Luther's emphasis on salvation by faith, and Calvin's doctrine of pre-destination).[45] But, from a scientific point of view, it is virtually impossible to know whether this was primarily a cause or consequence of the growth of the bourgeoisie and rise of commercial capitalism in Western Europe, i.e., the familiar scientific problem of determining the direction of causation—what is colloquially called 'the chicken or egg argument'. However, even assuming—as does Weber, virtually—that it was a cause, it is unlikely that it would have been such, if the European bourgeoisie had not had legal protection for their property, a protection which was much enhanced by the emergence of the Renaissance absolutist states with their blessing and support.

Long-term accumulation of capital was indeed one necessary condition for industrial development. But there were other conditions, other coincidental changes that made the emergence of modern state and society possible, not least the rise of the absolutist state in Europe which made capitalist property freer than before from the encroachment of the old aristocratic magnates. This factor both helped and was helped by the 'spirit of capitalism' which sought to please God by low consumption, high saving, and hard work.

---

[44] See Max Weber, *The Protestant Ethic and the Spirit of Capitalism*, London; Allen and Unwin, 1930; R. H. Tawney, *Religion and the Rise of Capitalism*, London: Allen and Unwin, 1937. For a short but poignant critique of Werner Sombart, as well as Weber, in whose spirit he wrote his *The Jews and Modern Capitalism*, see Hugh Trevor-Roper, 'The Jews and Modern Capitalism', in *Historical Essays*, London: Macmillan, 1957. See also his 'The Medieval Italian Capitalists', ibid.

[45] See further, Dickens, *The Age of Humanism and Reformation*; Joel Hurstfield, *The Reformation Crisis*, London: Edward Arnold, 1965; V. H. H. Green, *Luther and the Reformation*, London and New York: Batsford and Putman's Sons, 1954; Margaret Mann Phillips, *Erasmus and the Northern Renaissance*, London: The English Universities Press, 1949.

It might have been a common place if the fundamental point had not been constantly in danger of being missed about long-term development that it is a process which marks a total transformation of the society from one state into another. It is total transformations of this kind—changes which required a long and continuous process, in some cases taking a few centuries to transform the society—that seldom took place in Iran, and on the few occasions that they did for some time, the basic norms of arbitrary state and society led to their disruption, sometimes followed even by decline and retrogression, thus turning history into a series of 'connected short terms'.[46] And that is why, despite such commercial, cultural, and technical achievements in certain periods, traditional Iranian society did not reach stages of development corresponding to post-Renaissance Europe.[47]

Development requires not only *acquisition and innovation*, but also, and especially, *accumulation and preservation*, whether of wealth, of rights and privileges, or of knowledge and science. European society was a 'long-term society'. Major change, whether the fall of feudalism, the rise of capitalism and the emergence of the liberal state, whether the rejection of Aristotelian physics, Ptolemaic cosmography and the Greco-Roman political thought, or the Roman Catholic hegemony—all of these took a long time and a great deal of effort and struggle to occur, but when they finally did, the change was irreversible, and a new social framework, a new law, a new science, even a new religion was established that would once again take much time and effort to change, even to reform.[48]

As noted, the long-term society makes possible long-term accumulation, precisely because the law and traditions that govern it, and its institutions, afford a certain amount of security by making the future reasonably predictable. At the same time, and for the same reason, it makes major change in the

---

[46] See, for example, Homa Katouzian, 'Arbitrary Rule: A Comparative Theory of State, Politics and Society in Iran', *British Journal of Middle Eastern Studies*, 24(1), 1997, pp. 49–73, and idem., *State and Society in Iran*, chapter 1.

[47] For more detail see Katouzian, *Iranian History and Politics*.

[48] This discreet and long-term process of change in science as well as society had been well known. In the case of society it had been well documented and subjected to much theorizing. In the case of knowledge and science, it had once been discussed in the original sense of Hegelian and Marxian concepts of ideology, i. e., 'ideology' as consciousness bound by the limits of moral and/or material development in its various 'stages'. Thomas Kuhn offered a new model in the case of 'scientific revolutions', though he overlooked the fact that the theory was a tautology as it was equally valid for the history of all, not just scientific knowledge; and he implied that it was necessarily the best procedure for the advancement of science. See his *The Structure of Scientific Revolutions*, Chicago: The University of Chicago Press, 1970. For a critique of Kuhn's model see Homa Katouzian, 'T. S. Kuhn, Functionalism, and Sociology of Knowledge', *British Journal for the Philosophy of Science*, 45(2), June 1984, pp. 166–73, idem., 'The Hallmarks of Science and Scholasticism, A Historical Analysis', *The Yearbook of the Sociology of the Sciences*, Dordrecht, Boston and London: D. Reidel, 1982, idem., *Ideology and Method in Economics*, London, Mcmillan, 1980, p. 4.

short run very difficult. In the long-term society, revolution, whether in law, politics or science is a rare and extraordinary occurrence, but when it does happen it is non-reversible and therefore has long-term effects.

Some Observations on Recent Developments

It would make at least another full chapter to discuss more recent Iranian history in light of the foregoing. But let me just make a few rapid observations. In the 1970s many if not most Western journalists, analysts and academics used to describe Iran as 'an island of stability' and 'Japan of the Middle East', one Western economist even going so far as to predict Iranian GDP, rate of growth, etc., in the year 2000. In the late 1970s the entire Iranian society rose against the state and overthrew it.[49]

In 1997, 1999, and 2000 reformists won landslide electoral victories in presidential, local, and parliamentary elections, respectively, leading many to believe that an end to the Islamic regime was around the corner. Eight years later, a fundamentalist was elected president, and although there were some complaints about electoral irregularities, hardly anyone doubted that he had received a large share of the votes.

Let us begin with a brief account of the background to the present situation. In 1979 all shades of opinion combined to bring down the state. No social class and no political party stood against the revolutionary movement, and 98 percent of the people voted for the establishment of an Islamic republic. But almost at the same time fundamental differences began to emerge among the revolutionary forces such that by 1982 all but the Islamists had been eliminated from politics. There were conservative and radical tendencies among the Islamists themselves but their differences rarely led to conflict and confrontation in the 1980s, partly because of the necessities of the long war with Iraq, but mainly perhaps because of the unifying role of Ayatollah Khomeini who acted as the regime's supreme arbiter.[50]

The end of the war in 1988 and Ayatollah Khomeini's death in the following year began a new era in the politics of the Islamic Republic. At first the union of the conservative Seyyed Ali Khameneh'i as supreme leader and the pragmatist Ali Akbar Hashemi Rafsanjani as president seemed to work fairly well but, especially in Rafsanjani's second term of office (1993–1997), the conservatives began to show dissatisfaction with his policies. Apart from the conservatives and pragmatists, however, two other distinct factions had emerged in the 1990s: the fundamentalists and the reformists. The fundamen-

---

[49] See Katouzian, *The Persians*, pp. 10–12; Fahkreddin Azimi, *The Quest for Democracy in Iran: A century of Struggle Against Authoritarian Rule*, Cambridge, MA: Harvard University Press, 2008; Ervand Abrahamian, *A History of Modern Iran*, Cambridge: Cambridge University Press, 2008; Nikki R. Keddie, *Modern Iran: Roots and Results of Revolution*, New Haven: Yale University Press, 2003.

[50] Katouzian, *The Persians*, chapters 11–13; idem., 'The Iranian Revolution at 30: The Dialectic of State and Society', *Critique* 19(1), Spring 2010, pp. 35-53.

talists— mainly representing the traditional lower and lower middle classes—tended to emphasize the Islamist nature of the regime, advocated an anti-Western foreign policy, and championed the cause of 'the downtrodden': 'death to the capitalist' was a favourite slogan in their street demonstrations. The reformists, on the other hand, displaying an Islamic social-democratic outlook, believed in a more open society and (later) better regional and international relations. The conservatives were closer to the fundamentalists on their religious and foreign policy views; the pragmatists were more in line with the reformists on both domestic and foreign policy issues, although in more moderate and accommodating terms.

Contrary to all the predictions, the 1997 presidential election resulted not in a conservative but a reformist-pragmatist victory. Yet it was not, and could not be, an Iranian 'Thermidor', as some of the more historically conscious Western commentators rushed to describe it, if only because the Revolutionary Guards (Pasdaran), the ultimate legislative authority (Council of Guardians), the judiciary, and considerable business and property interests were on the side of the conservatives. Khatami won another landslide victory in 2001, but the reformists were ultimately thwarted.

Ahmadinejad was a fundamentalist and the candidate of a fundamentalist-conservative coalition, later forming the parliamentary group called 'Principalists' (*osulgarayan*),[51] and his election once again caught many of the Iran observers in the wings. Posing as a man of the people and promising increased welfare for the lower strata of the community, he won most of their votes while at the same time attracting the support of powerful conservatives who wanted to be rid of the reformists at all costs. That is why while the conservatives generally applauded Ahmadinejad's reversal of the reformist trends in domestic and foreign politics, they not infrequently displayed their displeasure at his economic policies and millenarian views.

Four years of Ahmadinejad's government taught the reformists and the secularists a hard lesson and made them nostalgic about Khatami's time as president. Under great pressure, Khatami first came forward but then stepped down in favour of Mir Hoseyn Musavi, a radical prime minister of the 1980s. Backed by the pragmatist faction as well, Musavi's campaign started late through a very slow process and—as further proof for the short-term nature of the society—it was only about three weeks before the election day that it began to take off the ground. And even as late as that, no-one could have predicted anything remotely close to the imminently unfolding events.

The electoral dispute that followed is now well-known history and need not be recounted in this brief. It was however a major turning point in the history of the Islamic Republic as it had not experienced anything like it since the power struggles of the early 1980s. The factional struggles during the Khatami years were at most a crisis of authority. But now there was a crisis of legitimacy as well, since the Islamic Republic had split down the middle, each

---

[51] For more on this faction see Walter Posch's contribution to this volume.

side claiming legitimacy and—at least implicitly—denying legitimacy to the other side.

At the political-cum-ideological level the reformist leaders stressed the representative and republican features of the system, whereas the fundamentalists put the emphasis on the authority of the supreme leader as representative of the Hidden Imam's, and thereby God's, authority, rather analogous to the ancient Iranian God's Grace theory described above. This brought up to the surface the unresolved dichotomy between the 'republican' and the 'Islamic' features of the constitution.

'The politics of elimination', as I have termed it, is also a long-standing feature of Iranian politics. For example, after the coup d'état of 1953, a dictatorial regime came into existence which eliminated the National Front, the Tudeh party and their supporters from politics. But the regime still maintained a social base, largely consisting of the political and the religious establishment. There was no democracy but nevertheless there was some degree of consultation, representation and participation, and there was a certain amount of freedom of expression. However, the regime jettisoned its social base in 1963 in the wake of the shah's White Revolution and the revolt of June that year, without replacing it with any other section of the society. Therefore, politics was altogether abolished and power became both absolute and arbitrary. That was the basic reason why the state had no social force or political party to defend it during the revolution.[52]

Things are never absolutely the same as before but, by way of a simple analogy, it may be observed that—apart from the secularists who had been dispossessed since the early 1980s—the reformists and pragmatists are now on the verge of being eliminated from legitimate politics, leaving it almost solely to the fundamentalists and conservatives, and making the situation look like the period 1953–63.

Forecasts which promise the imminent fall of the Islamic regime, or 'the beginning of the end' for it, are premature and often based on optimistic sentiments even when they come from otherwise serious analysts. There is at the moment no major external threat to the regime, and as for the domestic forces, the ruling parties have under their command the armed, police and intelligence forces, the economy, the parliament and the judiciary, not to mention the fact that they too have a base in society.

However, things can always happen to Iran and Iranians which are beyond rational expectations. It is not for nothing that Iranians themselves call it 'the country of possibilities' *mamlekat-e emkanat*.

---

[52] Katouzian, *The Persians*, chapters 10–12 and idem., 'The Iranian Revolution at 30: The Dialectic of State and Society'.

Chapter 9

How to Transform a Rent-Seeking Economy: The Case of Iran

Thierry Coville

Since the revolution of 1979, Iran has aspired to become the dominant regional power of the Middle East.[1] Nevertheless, these geopolitical ambitions will never be realized without real economic development. In this regard, Iran is still a paradox. The Iranian economy has huge potential, with considerable natural resources, an important internal market, an educated workforce, and an industrial base. Moreover, its geographical situation, between Europe and Asia, close to Central Asian and Gulf Cooperation Council countries markets, could make it an attractive location for foreign investment. However, Iran is still a less developed economy. The question of the types of reforms that should be applied to allow this economy to reach its potential has been debated since the Islamic revolution. This question is again on the frontline as the Iranian government has started to implement a privatization programme since 2004 and a massive programme of subsidies reduction since 2010. Will these present reforms allow the Iranian economy to reach its potential? After having looked at the present situation of the Iranian economy, this chapter will analyse these economic reforms and discuss their possible impact. The third part will consist of some remarks about the types of economic policies that would be adapted to the present economic problems of the Iranian economy.

A Deteriorating Economic Situation Since 2007

The Iranian economy has gone through a very tense situation over the last few years.[2] According to the IMF, growth has slowed down from 7.8 per cent in 2007 to 1 per cent in 2008. The brutal deceleration in 2008 was the result of several factors. An over-stimulating economic policy having led to a brutal

---

[1] Mohammad-Reza Djalili, *Géopolitique de l'Iran*, Bruxelles: Complexe, 2005.
[2] Unless otherwise indicated, the source of the data is the Central Bank of Iran.

acceleration of inflation—which went from 10.4 per cent in 2005 to 25.5 per cent in 2008—the government had to implement a complete U-turn in terms of monetary policy. The growth of M1 went from +29.2 per cent in 2007 to -1.9 per cent in 2008. The other explanatory factor was the consequences of the fall of the oil price during the summer of 2008. Due to declining oil revenues (the price of the barrel of Brent went from US$ 135 in July 2008 to US$ 40 at the end of 2008), the government had to adjust its expenditures, lowering them from 28.3 per cent of GDP in 2007 to 27 per cent in 2008.[3] Furthermore, the agricultural sector experienced a sharp fall of its production due to a severe drought. Since 2008, growth has been accelerating under the effect of increasing oil revenues and a less restrictive economic policy. According to the IMF, growth has reached 3.5 per cent in 2009 and 'the positive growth momentum continued in 2010'. It is true that the monetary policy has been more stimulating with an increase of M1 of 14.5 per cent in 2009. In 2010, oil revenues have increased: oil exports have reached US$ 60.3 billion during the first 9 months of 2010, which represents an increase of 18 per cent compared to the same period of the previous year. Due to higher oil revenues,[4] government expenditures have increased (+32 per cent according to the approved 2010 budget) and supported the economy. Nevertheless, despite this rather positive narrative since 2008, there is evidence that the economy is suffering.

The Impact of Sanctions

It is clear that the sanctions applied against Iran due to the nuclear issue have been more effective since 2010. The United Nations adopted resolutions imposing economic sanctions on the Iranian economy in 2006, 2007, 2008, and 2010. These sanctions have had an impact on the Iranian economy by forbidding the export of goods or services that could have a dual use (civil and military) and prohibiting business dealings with Iranian companies like Khatam al-Anbiya, a construction company belonging to the IRGC, or banks like Bank Melli, Bank Saderat, and Bank Mellat. Moreover, the United States imposed additional bilateral sanctions in July 2010 which aimed at avoiding any business dealings with the Iranian energy sector and prohibiting foreign exchange and banking transactions with Iran.[5] Then, in September 2010, the European Union approved its own sanctions aiming at energy, financial, and transport sectors, and at entities connected with the Iranian government. Among all these sanctions, the financial measures seem to have been the most effective. Due to US pressure, most of the European banks have limited their business with Iran, making it very difficult for Iranian companies to finance

---

[3] Source: IMF. Islamic Republic of Iran: 2009 Article IV Consultation, March 2010.
[4] According to the IMF, oil revenues represented 50 per cent of government revenues in 2008.
5 Kenneth Katzman, *Iran Sanctions*, Congressional Research Service (2011). Available:
http://fpc.state.gov/documents/organization/155592.pdf (accessed 2 September 2011).

their imports.[6] The volume of imports from Europe has decreased by 20.4 per cent in 2010, which has resulted in a lower level of imports in real terms in 2010 compared to 2009 (-12.7 per cent). Moreover, the increase in the value of Iranian imports during the same period (+16.4 per cent) meant higher import prices. These financing difficulties explain the sudden depreciation of the exchange rate of the rial against the dollar in October 2010.[7] This lower volume of imports has clearly had an impact on production and has exacerbated the difficulties of Iranian industry, which was already suffering due to inadequate economic policies. For example, the fiscal indiscipline of the Iranian government has increased delays of payments and put some sectors working as suppliers of the government in real trouble.[8]

Nevertheless, the sanctions have not led to a complete isolation of the Iranian economy. Iranian trade has now been redirected towards Asia, which has become the first exporter to Iran (18 per cent), China being the second exporter to Iran (9 per cent of market share).[9] Turkey has also enormously increased its exports to Iran in 2010 (+ 97 per cent). One can also notice that the UAE are still the first exporters to Iran with a market share of 33 per cent, which indicates that some European companies are still doing business with Iran. At the same time, Iran's non-oil exports have reached a historical level of US$ 26 billion in 2010, the main markets being China (17.3 per cent) and Iraq (16.9 per cent). In fact, these sanctions are taking place at a time when Iran is earning more foreign exchange due to increasing oil revenues and booming non-oil exports. All in all, Iran has quite a strong external position. The country had a current account surplus of US$ 17.1 billion for the first nine months of 2010. The level of foreign debt is low at around 8 per cent of GDP, and the government announced US$ 100 billion of foreign exchange reserves in April 2011.

A Deteriorating Labour Market

The lower growth regime since 2008 has led to a deterioration of the labour market. According to the Statistical Centre of Iran, the unemployment rate has increased from 9.6 per cent in the spring of 2008 (March 21–June 21) to 14.6 per cent in the spring of 2010. The young have been especially affected, with the unemployment rate of the population aged 15–24 increasing

---

[6] One notices that all these financial sanctions have been applied by non-US entities under US pressure. This seems illegal according to WTO regulations. In 1997, the European Union threatened the United States to complain to the WTO if there were any sanctions against Total for having invested in Iran.
[7] Thierry Coville, 'Iran's Dive against the dollar', *World Policy Journal*, 5 October 2010.Available:http://www.worldpolicy.org/blog/2010/10/05/irans-dive-against-dollar and http://www.worldpolicy.org/blog/2010/10/05/irans-dive-against-dollar (accessed 2 September 2011).
[8] Interview of Mohammad Parsa, director of the Federation of the Electrical Industries (*khabaronline*, 10 May 2011). In this interview, he points out the delays of payment of the state which put the suppliers of the electrical industry in financial difficulties.
[9] See Thierry Kellner's chapter in this volume.

from 23 per cent in 2008 to 29.6 per cent in the spring of 2010. These difficulties derive partly from demographic trends. Due to the high population growth rates after the revolution, the active population has been increasing in recent years, mostly because the generations born after the revolution are now arriving on the labour market. From 1996 to 2006, the average annual growth rate of the active population was 7.9 per cent against 1.7 per cent during 1991–96. On average, there have been around 1.2 million persons arriving each year on the labour market during the 1996–2006 period.

Table 1. Annual growth rate of the active population

1976-1986	1986-1991	1991-1996	1996-2006
2,7	2,8	1,7	7,9

Source: Statistical Centre of Iran

Moreover, this population is more educated. The literate population constituted 84.6 per cent of the population aged 6 years and over in 2006, as against 47.5 per cent in 1976, and university students constituted 6.5 per cent of the population in 2008 as against 0.3 per cent in 1986. Another important issue is the increasing number of women who want to work. The part of women in the active population, which had reached a low point of 10.2 per cent in 1986, had climbed up to 15.5 per cent by 2006. At present the Iranian economy does not have the ability to create the necessary jobs required by a young and educated population: it is still too dependent on oil export revenues, which represent around 80 per cent of total export revenues, and around 50 per cent of government revenues. Nor does Iran possess a competitive non-oil sector capable of creating the required jobs. With oil prices booming, the government tried to stimulate the economy in 2005–07 by increasing its expenditures from 22.7 per cent of GDP in 2004 to 29.8 per cent in 2006,[10] and decreasing the level of interest rates of the public banks: interest rates on facilities for the manufacturing sector went from -0.2 per cent in 2004 to -4.4 per cent in 2007.

Despite this stimulus, the unemployment rate has rather increased from 10.3 per cent in 2004 to 11.9 per cent at the end of 2007. That means that this stimulus has mostly benefited imports—which have increased from US$ 50.1 billion in 2004 to US$ 72.9 billion in 2007—and that the private sector did not respond to this economic policy. According to the Statistical Centre of Iran, the private sector provided 74 per cent of employment in 2006. The government policy was to support job creation by providing finance to the private sector. For example, from 2005 to 2007, all state banks had to provide

---

[10] - Source: IMF.

an important amount of loans to small businesses.[11] Due to the lack of supervision and to widespread corruption, the private sector has used this financing support to develop business in the import or the construction sectors. Private investment in machinery decreased from 21 per cent of national income in 2004 to 17.5 per cent in 2007, while private investment in construction was stable at around 7 per cent of the national income during this period. Thus, the stimulus failed to induce the private sector to create jobs. Moreover, it led to an acceleration of inflation from 15.2 per cent in 2004 to 25.4 per cent in 2008, which obliged the government to implement more restrictive fiscal and monetary policies since 2007. In sum, the economic stimulus did not lead to job creation because the private sector did not respond to it. Worse, this economic stimulus led to an acceleration of inflation, which obliged the government to harden its economic policies. This did not leave any room for supporting the economy when the oil price fell in 2008.

The Structural Problems of Iran's Economy

All these developments since 2005 are characteristic of the structural problems of the Iranian economy. Due to its oil dependency, the Iranian economy is completely unstable, which does not sustain private sector confidence. At the beginning of the 2000s, the Iranian government tried to limit this oil dependency by creating an Oil Stabilization Fund (OSF), which would have given the opportunity to save oil revenues surpluses when oil prices were high and to spend these savings when oil prices fell. This policy did not yield any significant result, as the Ahmadinejad government in 2005 did not respect OSF regulations and used this fund to finance part of its expenses at a time when oil revenues were booming.[12]

This instability of the Iranian economy leads to a preference for short-term commercial activities among Iranian companies.[13] The dependence on oil revenues has led historically to a high level of state intervention in the economy, and the nationalizations after the 1979 revolution amplified this. Public-sector companies were not competitive, as high transaction costs[14]

---

[11] In 2007, state banks had to provide loans to small businesses for 50 per cent of their deposits. See Zahra Karimi, *Financing Job Guarantee Schemes by Oil Revenues: the Case of Iran*, Working Paper 527, The Levy Economics Institute, 2008.
[12] Thierry Coville, 'Le gouvernement d'Ahmadinejad face aux conséquences économiques de sa politique clientéliste', *Les Cahiers de l'Orient*, 99, 2010, pp.113–20.
[13] For an interesting exploration of the effects of short-term thinking on Iranian society in general, see Homa Katouzian's chapter in this volume.
[14]Transaction costs are costs incurred in making an economic exchange. One refers usually to search and information costs, bargaining costs, policing and enforcement costs. See Ronald Coase, 'The Nature of the Firm', *Economica*, 4(16), 1937, pp. 386–405; Ronald Coase,'The Problem of Social Cost', *Journal of Law and Economics*, 3, 1960, pp. 1–44 ; Oliver E. Williamson, *The Economic Institutions of Capitalism: Firms, Markets, Relational Contracting*, New York: Free Press, 1985.

prevented the development of the private sector.[15] This could explain the constraints on the development of private sector firms in Iran (in 1996, 97 per cent of Iranian companies had between one and five employees). The importance of oil revenues is also a factor explaining the lack of integration of the Iranian in the world economy.[16] Despite the recent increase of non-oil exports,[17] Iran's foreign trade is still dominated by oil exports, which accounted for around 80 per cent of total exports in 2010, while manufactured products constituted only 5 per cent of total exports in 2009.[18] It is clear that this low level of integration in the world economy is amplified by the present economic sanctions. Even if the general economic conditions of the Iranian economy are a decisive cause of the low level of foreign direct investment in the Iranian economy during the recent period, it is also clear that a number of foreign investment projects in the energy sector have been stopped. In any case, a difficult environment for foreign investors and the sanctions have led to a very low level of FDI in Iran compared to neighbouring countries (See Table 2 below).

The Scourge of Rent-Seeking

Another explanation of Iranian economic difficulties is the importance of rent-seeking activities. Rents can be defined as economic activities that do not create any value but extract value from others by taking advantage of government regulations.[19] The economic cost of the rent-seeking activities is due to the fact that resources will be used in non-productive ways (lobbying, bribery, etc.) just to get access to these resources. Iran seems to be a fertile ground for this syndrome for two reasons. First, given the sheer volume of oil revenues belonging to the state (representing 50 per cent of government revenues), the volume of rents which can be extracted from the government is huge: between 2005 and 2010, the Iranian government received around US$ 440 billion in oil revenues. Second, the expansion of state intervention in the economy has amplified the possibilities of having access to diverse types of rents. This results in a situation where the public and private sectors of the Iranian economy are more willing to engage in rent-seeking activities than in

---

[15] Mohsen Ranani, *Bazar ya nabazar: barrasi-ye mavane'-e nahadi-ye kara'i-ye nezam-e eqtesad-e bazar dar eqtesad-e Iran*, Tehran: Entesharat-e Sazman-e Barnahemh va Budjeh, 1997.

[16] Hadi Salehi-Esfahani, and Hashem Pesaran, 'The Iranian Economy in the Twentieth Century: A Global 'Perspective', *Iranian Studies*, 42, 2009, pp 177–211.

[17] And this non-oil exports surge does not represent per se a sign of an improved competitiveness, as the level of competition in Iran non-oil main export markets (Afghanistan, Iraq) is still limited.

[18] *Annual review*, Central Bank of Iran, 2009. Petrochemical products, derived from the oil sector, were not considered.

[19] See Anne.O. Krueger, 'The Political Economy of the Rent-Seeking Society', *The American Economic Review*, 64, 1974, pp. 291–303; Gordon Tullock, 'The Origin of Rent-Seeking Concept', *International Journal of Business and Economics*, 2, 2003, pp. 1–8.

productive activities. What is interesting in the case of Iran is that economic policy since 1980 has tried to support these rent-seeking activities, as they have been a means for the authorities to gain political support from certain social groups.[20] The fact that some social actors (Foundations, IRGCs) have become so powerful that they act as a 'state within the state' has led one scholar to characterize the economic and social organization of Iran as a 'destructive mode of coordination'.[21] Alternatively, one could consider the economic organization of Iran as a complex system in which rent-seeking activities co-exist with good governance, as shown by long-term investment in education, transport, electricity, etc.[22] These long-term investment policies have been very instrumental in the modernization of the Iranian society since the revolution.[23]

Table 2 – Foreign Direct Inflows in some Middle-East economies
(Billions of US$)

	2005	2006	2007	2008	2009
Iran	3.1	1.6	1.7	1.6	3
Qatar	2.5	3.5	4.7	4.1	8.7
Saudi Arabia	12	17.1	22.8	38.1	35.5
Turkey	10	20.2	22	18.1	7.6

Source: World Investment Report 2010

Nevertheless, the Iranian government has started to implement an important set of reforms during these last years by calling for a privatization plan and by applying since 2010 an ambitious programme of subsidies reduction. Will these reforms be able to solve these structural problems that have just been discussed?

**The Reform of Subsidies and Privatization Programmes:
A Real Revolution?**

Despite a tense political situation, the Iranian authorities have started to implement ambitious economic measures in recent years. The modification of

---

[20] Economic policy has tended to support bazaaris involved in import businesses. See Thierry Coville, *L'économie de l'Iran islamique : entre ordre et désordres*, Paris: L'Harmattan, 2002.
[21] Mehrdad Vahabi, 'An introduction to Destructive Coordination', *American Journal of Economics and Sociology*, 68, 2009, pp. 353–86.
[22] Thierry Coville, *L'économie de l'Iran islamique: entre ordre et désordres*, Paris: L'Harmattan, 2002.
[23] Fariba Adelkhah, *Etre moderne en Iran,* Paris: Karthala, 2006; Thierry Coville, *Iran: la révolution invisible*, Paris: La Découverte, 2007.

Article 44 of the constitution in 2004 paved the way for a large privatization programme. Even more strikingly, the Iranian government has created a real surprise by starting to apply in 2010 a five-year programme of subsidies reduction.

Privatization

According to the Article 44 of the constitution of the Islamic Republic of Iran, the Iranian economy is divided into three sectors: the public sector, the cooperative sector, and the private sector. The main industries, foreign trade, mining, the banking system, the insurance industry, the energy sector, dams, radio-television, the postal industry, air and maritime transport, roads and railways, belong to the public sector. Besides the cooperative sector, the private sector includes the sectors of agriculture, industry, trade and services, as long as these activities are not in the other two sectors. In 2004 Article 44 was modified in order to open all industries to the private sector, except strategic sectors like defence or oil and natural gas extraction. In 2006, the government proposed a plan of 'justice shares' that would make low-income people shareholders of firms that had previously belonged to the public sector. Many privatization operations were supposed to be realized through the Tehran Stock Exchange. Despite these plans, factual evidence demonstrates that a real privatization of the Iranian economy has not taken place. The sale of 'justice shares' has been implemented with a total lack of transparency. And, most of the time, public companies' assets have been bought out by organizations of the public sector (pension funds, banks, holdings), by Foundations (Bonyad-e Mostaz'afan, the most important of these foundations, bought out 5 per cent of the stock of the Bank Saderat, a public bank, in June 2010) or by the IRGC (in September 2009, they became the owners of 51 per cent of the capital of the Telecommunications Company of Iran, the largest firm in this industry).[24] In fact, this privatization programme has been 'used' by the authorities as an instrument to give financial advantages to 'insiders' of the Islamic republic. One could even argue that the privatization policy has been used for 'predatory' purposes by these insiders. Sadra, a private construction company, whose turn-over has hugely decreased due to the fact that most of the public contracts have been awarded to construction companies belonging to the IRGC (without any tender, which is technically illegal), has been finally bought by the IRGC.[25]

Subsidy Reform

In 2010, the Iranian government announced that it was going to phase out most of the present subsidies of the Iranian economy with a five-year plan. This has been considered a very bold initiative, as a lot of goods and services

---

[24] There are numerous examples of public companies having been bought out by the IRGC in the past few years.
[25] Coville, 'Le gouvernement d'Ahmadinejad', pp. 113–20.

are subsidized (gasoline, natural gas, electricity, telephone, etc.). This policy of decreasing the subsidies had several objectives. First, to decrease government expenditures as these subsidies created a huge financial burden for the state, given that the Iranian public sector has been in continuous deficit since the revolution. The subsidies were also unfair from a social point of view, as they benefited all social classes, irrespectively of their income. The new subsidy reform programme aimed initially at using the money saved by decreasing the subsidies to target the low-income classes with financial aid. This reform programme had also the objective of decreasing energy consumption in Iran, whose trend was not sustainable: the level of energy consumption per capita in Iran in oil equivalent has gone from 981 kg in 1980 to 2808 kg in 2008. Iran has an excessive energy consumption which does not match its level of its economic development (see Table 3). Such a trend will in the future lead to a depletion of Iranian energy resources such as oil, and excessive internal consumption could decrease the foreign exchange generated by exports. The high level of energy consumption had already led to increasing imports of gasoline. This put Iran in a vulnerable situation as economic sanctions were targeting these imports. This means that this subsidy reform programme was also considered as an answer to the economic sanctions. Finally, the idea defended by some economists was that setting prices close to their equilibrium level was the best way to decrease the incentives for rent-seeking activities and to increase the efficiency of the economic system.[26]

Table 3 Energy consumption and GDP per capital in Brazil, Iran and Turkey

	Energy use (a)	GDP per capital (b)
Brazil	1295	8230
Iran	2808	4540
Turkey	1232	8215

(a) Kg of oil equivalent per capita. Data is from 2008 for China and Iran, from 2009 for Turkey.
(b) Current dollars
Source: World Bank

The implementation of this programme started in December 2010. It has so far been quite successful, as the decrease of subsidies has not led to social disorders, as some feared. It has also led to a decrease of energy consumption in Iran. According to Iran's National Iranian Oil Refining and Distribution Company, the daily consumption of gasoline stood at 61.1 million litres at the

---

[26] Massoud.Karshenas and Hashem Pesaran, 'Economic Reform and the Reconstruction of the Iranian Economy', *Middle East Journal*, 49, 1995, pp. 89–111.

end of the Iranian year (19 March 2011), reflecting a 5.4 per cent decrease compared with the corresponding period in the previous year. Inflation has accelerated due to this programme. According to the Central Bank of Iran, the inflation rate has gone up from 12.5 per cent in October 2010 (compared to October 2009) to 19.7 per cent in March 2011. Nevertheless, price increases have not reached uncontrollable levels.

This does not mean that there are no uncertainties about the ultimate success of this programme. Initially, it was planned that the government would use the savings obtained to compensate for the costs of higher prices. 50 per cent of the savings should have been used to financially support the poorest households, 30 per cent to help the productive sector, and 20 per cent to flow into the government budget. According to Ahmad Tavakkoli, head of the research centre of the parliament, in 2010, most of the savings were directed to the households.[27] Moreover, each household received the same amount of money (44,500 tumans by person). One can suppose that the Iranian government, fearful of social tensions, chose to pay the same amount of money to each household. Nevertheless, the continuation of this policy in 2011 is associated with high risks. The government wants both to decrease the subsidies at a sustained pace and to compensate the whole population with financial aid.[28] If such a plan is carried out, it is clear that higher prices (due to decreased subsidies) combined with an injection of liquidities in the hands of consumers, could lead a very dangerous level of inflation. It is also possible that the government starts gradually to target the poorest social classes in its financial support.[29]

In conclusion, these reforms do not seem to be able *per se* to address the structural difficulties of the Iranian economy. The privatization plan has not led to tangible results. The subsidy reduction plan has in fact been implemented but there are still numerous uncertainties on its sustainability. Besides, it does not appear that this plan will be sufficient to solve the structural problems of the Iranian economy. True, this plan can lead to a decrease of some rent-seeking activities like illegal gasoline exports, and decrease waste and inefficiencies as the energy prices have a great impact on the types of technologies used.[30] Nevertheless, the disappearance of these subsidies will not lead to a decrease on oil dependency, an increasing competitiveness of the non-oil sector, and a decrease of rent-seeking activities like those related to the import business or the banking system.[31] So, what

---

[27] *Tabnak*, 9 May 2011.
[28] The budget for 2011 plans that 80 per cent of the savings will be used to support the households and 20 per cent the productive sectors.
[29] To obtain financial support, Iranian households had to register and to give information on their income. It is possible that the government will use this information in the future to focus its aid on the poorest.
[30] Karshenas and Pesaran, 'Economic Reform', pp. 89–111.
[31] The system of import licensing leads to huge financial advantages for those who can get these licences. Obviously, import can be considered as a rent-seeking activity as

directions should the reforms that could lead the Iranian economy to reach its potential take?

How to Reform the Iranian Economy

Change the Institutional Environment

If one considers that the main challenge for the Iranian economy is to go from an economic system that supports rent-seeking activities to a system supporting productive activities, the most important issue is to change the rules of the game.[32] All the policies which are not directed at transforming the institutional environment will fail because it is this institutional environment that is going to direct the activities and talents of entrepreneurs to productive or rent-seeking activities.[33]

The Iranian state has not been able to develop stable institutions.[34] The absence of protection of property rights, a dysfunctional judicial system characterized by frequent changes of rules and laws and the difficulty to apply these, ever-changing fiscal rules, and an underdeveloped financial system have led to a productive structure where a multitude of very small companies belonging to the private sector co-exist with a small number of large public firms (Table 4)

Table 4. Breakdown of Iranian firms according to their size

	1-5 employees	6-9 employees	10-49 employees	50-99 employees	≥ 100 employees
%	96.6	1.8	1.4	0.1	0.1

Source: Statistical Yearbook of Iran 1375 (1996–1997).[35]

There has been a public policy which has aimed at protecting these large public companies through privileged access to the banking system. The very small firms, which are often family businesses, often operate on monopolistic

---

the access to these licences leads to huge profits. On the same basis, the access to bank finance which depends often on political support can also lead to rent-seeking behaviour.

[32] William. J. Baumol, 'Entrepreneurship: Productive, Unproductive, and Destructive', *The Journal of Political Economy*, 98, 1990, pp. 893–921.

[33] Kevin M. Murphy, Andrei Shleiffer, Robert W. Vishny, 'The Allocation of Talent: Implications for Growth', *The Quarterly Journal of Economics*, 106, 1991, pp. 503–30; Harry P. Bowen, Dirk De Clercq, 'Institutional context and the allocation of entrepreneurial effort', *Journal of International Business Studies*, 39, 2008, pp. 747–67.

[34] Ranani, *Bazar ya nabazar*.

[35] These data are not up to date but there is a high probability that the results have not really changed since.

micro-markets and have few incentives for innovation. High transaction costs due to dysfunctional institutions and a very difficult access to the financial system have constrained the development of these companies. These constraints to the development of small companies are a common issue in transitional economies like Russia.[36] Although these institutional issues have always existed in the Iranian economy, they have been exacerbated since the revolution. One striking example is the fact that the number of returned checks cases in the judicial system in 1992 was 45 times higher than in 1976.[37] Iranian small companies are complaining about the lack of transparency and instability of their legal and regulatory environment. At the beginning of the 2000s, the creation of a company in Iran involved taking into account around 50 commercial laws.[38] The complexity and the inapplicability of numerous laws and regulations can explain part of the level of corruption in Iran. Besides, due to a difficult access to the banking system, these small companies can only use their own funds or go to the informal credit markets to finance their projects. That means higher costs for the small companies as interest rates on banking loans for the manufacturing sector were fixed at 12.1 per cent in 2010 when the interest rates in the informal sector were close to 20 per cent.[39] Companies that do not have the necessary finance to innovate in terms of process or product are not able to reach foreign markets. Iranian Small and Medium Enterprises (SME) refer to the instability of the institutional environment and the difficulties of having access to the banking system as the two factors constraining their international development.[40]

Since the Islamic revolution, there has been a marked preference for large companies among Iranian officials. This lack of concern for small companies is reflected by the fact that there is still no definition of a SME in Iran. According to the ministry of industries and mines and the ministry of agriculture, an SME has fewer than 50 employees, while the Statistical Centre of Iran considers that an SME has fewer than 10 employees. In fact, Iranian economic policy has always been based on the hypothesis that economic development is only driven by large companies.[41]

It seems that the Iranian authorities have recently realized that SMEs should not be neglected. The government, through the Export Promotion Centre (EPC) has developed diverse training programmes to support the

---

[36]Valentina Hartaska and Claudio Gonzalez-Vega, 'What Affects New and Established Firms Expansion? Evidence from Small Firms in Russia', *Small Business Economics*, 27, 2006 pp. 195–206.,

[37] Renani, *Bazar ya nabazar*.

[38] UNIDO, *Strategy Document to Enhance the Contribution of an Effective and Competitive Small and Middle-Sized Enterprise Sector to Industrial and Economic Development in the Islamic Republic of Iran*, Vienna: UNIDO, 2003.

[39]Central Bank of Iran (the Central Bank of Iran determines the deposit and lending rates for the public and private banks). For the informal sector, this source is an interview at the Iranian Chamber of Commerce in May 2010.

[40] UNIDO, *Strategy Document*, p. 63.

[41] Ibid., p. 91.

international development of SMEs. Due to the small size of Iranian SMEs, the EPC is also trying to encourage the creation of export managing companies, which would include different companies of one sector aiming at developing their exports.[42] The Iranian state is also trying to take into account the needs of SMEs in its economic diplomacy.

The Iranian authorities have also started to try to change the institutional environment. According to the World Bank's 'Doing Business' report, Iran improved its ranking in 2011 compared to 2010 going from the 131st rank to the 128th by implementing some reforms to support business creation. The Islamic Republic of Iran supported business start-ups by (1) installing a web portal allowing entrepreneurs to search for and reserve a unique company name and (2) making enforcing contracts easier and faster by introducing filing of some documents, text message notification and an electronic case management system. In 2005, the Iranian government promoted a programme of loans for 'projects with a quick return' which could have been an answer to SMEs' financing difficulties. The privatization of the banking system during the last years could also be considered as a way to change Iranian banks' policy to make them more sensitive to private- sector needs.[43]

These reforms still have a long way to go if the Iranian authorities want to change the institutional environment. According to the 'Doing Business' report of the World Bank, Iran is still at a very modest rank (128th of 183 countries). The financing programme for 'projects with a quick return' was applied from 2005 until 2007: about US$ 15 billion were allocated by the public banks.[44] The results have been disappointing: due to a lack of supervision and a high level of corruption, a large number of these loans have been allocated to inefficient projects leading to a high level of non-performing loans in public banks assets, or have been misused (real estate, personal enrichment, etc.). Moreover, it is perhaps an illusion to think that it will be easier for SMEs to get access to finance from private banks. It is possible that the privatization of banks in Iran was only implemented with the objective of escaping the sanctions imposed because of the nuclear issue: as an embargo had been applied against several public banks, it was considered that private banks could play a more active role. The recent experiences in Iran have demonstrated that SMEs' access to the banking system is not related to the public or private nature of the banking system. Very often, Iranian SMEs are reluctant for fiscal reasons to get finance from the banking system. The governance of the Iranian banking system does not have the right skills to work with SMEs. It has been mainly used as an instrument to redistribute the national income to insiders close to the regime: large public companies,

---

[42]In interviews realized at the EPC in May 2010, the Iranian authorities admitted that it was difficult to evolve from a logic of competition to one of cooperation.
[43] In July 2011, the website of the Central Bank of Iran indicated that there were eight public banks and 16 private banks active in Iran.
[44]Zahra Karimi. Avalaible:
http://www.levyinstitute.org/pubs/EFFE/Zahra.pdf (accessed 27 October 2011).

companies belonging to the IRGC, or the Foundations have usually the necessary political backing to have easy access to banking loans. Moreover, due to the instability of the business environment, Iranian public or private banks have more incentives to finance commercial or real estate activities than SMEs working in the productive sector. This indicates that to change this situation would imply an evolution in the governance of the Iranian banking system which itself would require that the Iranian economic system evolve from a logic of redistribution of the oil rent to a logic of value creation.

Moreover, to think that Iranian economic difficulties are just caused by institutional deficiencies is very simplistic. One of the main concepts used by the institutional school of thought is that transaction costs should be minimized by creating the right institutions in order for the economic exchanges to lead to the highest efficiency.[45] But it is also true that transaction costs in some emerging countries like Russia are not imposed on entrepreneurs but result from their willingness to increase their comparative advantages.[46] This is also the case in Iran where networking abilities are a common characteristic of most Iranian entrepreneurs. Thus it would be an error to try to eliminate all the transaction costs in Iran. It would be then a priority to determine the exact structure of transaction costs for Iranian entrepreneurs in order to precisely find the costs which are a real constraint on their development without eliminating the networking abilities of Iranian SMEs.

Another problem with the 'institutional view' of the Iranian economy is the absence of information on the mechanisms through which new institutions and property rights emerge. According to institutional economists,[47] the basic source of institutional change is fundamental and persistent changes in relative prices, which lead one or both parties in a transaction to ask for change in the institutions as they would be better off under this new arrangement. This gives the impression that more efficient institutions would appear 'as the parties involved come to appreciate the new benefit-cost possibilities.'[48] Alternatively, is the emergence of new institutions just a question of more efficient institutions taking the place of less efficient ones? There are enormous uncertainties about the collective action that will bring about these institutional changes. Will the social groups potentially benefiting from these changes be able to get their act together? In the case of Iran, such a scenario will be difficult to achieve due to the present complexity of the internal political environment. More generally, the operation of natural selection in social institutions does not really take into account the historical

---

[45] Coase, 'The Problem of Social Cost'.
[46] Vadim Radaev, 'Entrepreneurial Strategies and the Structure of Transaction Costs in Russian Business', *Problems of Economic Transition*, 44, 2002, pp. 57–84.
[47] Douglass Cecil North, *Institutions, Institutional Change and Economic Performance*, Cambridge: Cambridge University Press, 1990.
[48] Pranab Bardhan, 'The New Institutional Economics and Development Theory: A Brief Critical Assessment', *World Development*, 17, 1989, pp. 1389–95.

'small events' that can have a real impact on the larger course of structural changes early on.[49] In the case of Iran, the rich history since the Islamic revolution is a sign that potential unplanned events could disturb a process of selection of the 'fittest' institutions.

A New Role for the Iranian State?

In any case, it will be nearly impossible to change the institutional environment in Iran as long as the state practises a policy of 'political' redistribution of the oil rent. In terms of fiscal issues, the Iranian state should have a long-term, transparent, and careful fiscal policy. It is necessary that the policy of long-term investments, which has been decisive in supporting the modernization of Iranian society since 1979, should continue to be a priority, even if it leads to the decreasing importance of the fiscal policy of cronyism. Again, it seems unrealistic to consider that the Iranian state is going to suddenly change its political alliances. Nevertheless, it is also clear that the 'insiders' in the Iranian economic system have come to gradually realize that they could also benefit from a more open economic system. Some Iranian foundations have started to rationalize their economic activities since the 1990s. One can take the example of the Iranian Bank Sina, which was initially created in the 1990s as the Islamic bank of the Bonyad-e Mostaz'afan, the largest of the Iranian foundations. This bank has considerably changed and has recently become a private bank with an expertise in electronic banking services.[50]

The Iranian state should also try to create a more competitive economic system. This would be facilitated if the Iranian government clearly stated that World Trade Organization membership was an official objective. It has also been demonstrated that in an oil economy, the ability of the state, even if it is not democratic, to have a dialogue with the main social and economic groups to define the most appropriate economic policies, is a key factor a success. This was what allowed Indonesia to succeed in diversifying its economy away from oil.[51] It is then important for the Iranian state not to be the only actor to define economic policy, as this process should be the result of negotiations with the main representatives of the various social groups. Again, there are trends in Iran which could lead to this process. The Iranian private sector, for

---

[49] Ibid.
[50] Thierry Coville, 'Les fondations en Iran: un obstacle à la mondialisation de l'économie iranienne?', *La revue française de géopolitique*, 5, 2009 and Thierry Coville,'The Foundations in Iran: an Obstacle to the Globalization of the Iranian Economy?', presentation, Conference of the International Society of Iranian Studies, Santa Monica, USA, 2010, pp. 50–61.
[51] Ben Eiffert, Allan Gelb, and Nils Borje Tallroth, 'Managing Oil Wealth', *Finance and Development*, 40, 2003.Avalaible:
http://www.imf.org/external/pubs/ft/fandd/2003/03/eife.htm (accessed 27 October 2011). Nowadays, Indonesia is one of the very few cases of an emerging economy which has successfully decreased its oil dependency.

example, through the Iran Chamber of Commerce, has tried to be more active since 2005 in its lobbying with the government. Nevertheless, there has also been a systematic repression of independent trade-unionists in Iran since the election of Mahmoud Ahmadinejad.

All these reforms will be necessary for the Iranian economy to really become an emerging economy. But these will not be sufficient as long as there is not a clear perception among the Iranian actors that the rules of the game have changed. This change of perception seems to have been an important explanation of the success of the Chinese economic policies since the 1970s: thousands of family businesses in China have suddenly realized that the rules of the game had definitely changed.[52] The deep changes in the Iranian society since the revolution have led some actors to modify their behaviour towards more efficiency, and that could lead to a more competitive and productive economic system. This indicates that the Iranian state, by appropriate policies and an objective of further integration in the world economy, could support these evolutions of economic behaviour. But to really change the perceptions of Iranian actors would clearly also require a greater degree of confidence between the political system and the civil society.

---

[52]Victor Nee, 'Organizational Dynamics of Market Transition: Hybrid Forms, Property Rights, and Mixed Economy in China', *Administrative Science Quarterly*, 37, 1992, pp. 1–27.

Chapter 10

Energy Subsidies in Iran

Narsi Ghorban

Iran has the second largest hydrocarbon reserves of the world after Russia. With a population of nearly one per cent of the world it has over 10 per cent of the world's oil and around 16 per cent of the world's gas resources. But in spite of these enviable circumstances, the Iranian economy in the past sixty years (oil was discovered in 1908 and the oil industry was nationalized in 1951) has not been able to take maximum advantage from these God-given resources. For example the economic progress in Malaysia, which has a fraction of Iran's hydrocarbon and skilled human resources, has been far more impressive over the past 25 years. It might be argued that Iran confronted the major oil companies and their respective countries from 1951 to 1953, went through a revolution in 1979, and was attacked by Iraq, which resulted in eight years of human and material losses to the country. The fact remains, however, that the energy policies of the last twenty years (after the war with Iraq) have not allowed Iran to occupy a position in the regional and world energy scene commensurate with its resources.

One of the most damaging policies in this respect has been the continuing subsidies to keep energy prices down within the Iranian economy. Iran has the highest consumption of petroleum products and natural gas in the Persian Gulf and Caspian region. For twenty years the Iranian motorist has paid a fraction of the cost of production, refining, transportation, and distribution of oil and other petroleum products. Wrong policies with respect to energy prices have also resulted in a high rate of growth in demand for petroleum products, natural gas, and electricity. While experts were warning on the consequences of these policies and elected governments promised to rectify the situation, it was not until early 2010 that a bill was passed through parliament to address the energy subsidies in the economy. This chapter seeks to answer the following four questions: 1) What are the objectives of this legislation?, 2) What will happen to the windfall revenues?, 3) What are the main shortcomings of this bill? and 4) Will this legislation help to solve the problems facing the Iranian economy at present?

The Objectives of Legislation for Removing Energy Subsidies

One of the most important aspects of the legislation to remove energy subsidies from the Iranian economy is to utilize hydrocarbon resources more prudently. The price of gasoline, gas oil, natural gas, and electricity in Iran in the past four decades has been a fraction of the prices in other countries and even below their delivered costs. This has led to so rapid an increase in demand for gasoline, gasoil, natural gas, and electricity that succeeding governments have had difficulty to keep up with demand. Iran's use of oil increased by over 40 per cent (from 1.22 million barrels per day (mb/d) to 1.74 mb/d) from 1999 to 2010. During the same period, oil consumption in the United States, the United Kingdom, Germany, and Japan declined by around 4, 6, 14 and 21 per cent, respectively. According to recent figures by the International Energy Agency (IEA), Iran's energy intensity, which is defined as the amount of primary energy consumption per dollar of Gross Domestic Product using market exchange rates, is four times the world average and 12 times that of Japan. In the past 30 years, Iran's per capita energy consumption has increased five times while the population has only doubled.

Apart from rapid depletion of resources, consumption of primary energy at this level would bring about associated environmental problems. Air and water pollution are a major concern in almost all big cities of Iran. While it is true that environmental problems increase with rapid growth in almost all the countries of the world, in the case of Iran low energy prices have exaggerated this trend. The new legislation aims at reducing the burden of air and water pollution by making the public and industry utilize energy more efficiently through price mechanisms.

In January 2010 a bill was passed to deal with the subsidies in the Iranian economy. This bill deals with energy subsidies as well as other subsidies in the Iranian economy such as water, wheat, rice, cooking oil, milk, sugar, postal services, airline tickets etc. According to this bill the price of petroleum products (gasoline, gasoil, naphtha, and fuel oil) considering all associated costs (transport, distribution etc) must not be less than 90 per cent of the FOB (Free on Board) prices of these products in the Persian Gulf. It is envisaged that this increase would be gradually implemented during the fifth development plan ending in 2015. The price of crude oil and condensate to the Iranian refineries would be 95 per cent of their Persian Gulf FOB prices of the said products.

With reference to the price of natural gas, the bill indicates that the average price of natural gas in the domestic market must be set in such a way that by 2015 it would be at least 75 per cent of the average price of gas exported from Iran minus the cost of transportation. To encourage investment in natural gas-based industries, such as petrochemicals and oil and gas refineries, the bill allows the prices to be set for at least ten years at less than 65 per cent of Iran's gas export basket at the Persian Gulf origin minus the transportation costs.

The law says that the average sale price of electricity in the country by 2015 must reflect the true cost of production and distribution of electricity. The price is based on costs of production of electricity from the power stations with efficiency of at least 38 per cent, considering all standards applied in this industry. This efficiency in the generation of electricity must be increased to 45 per cent by the end of the fifth development plan. In the same period the losses in the network must be reduced to 14 per cent.

The bill indicates that the government must implement this law in such a way that the income generated from removing these subsidies from the Iranian economy in the initial year of its implementation is not less than 10 or more than 20 US$ billion (less than one hundred or more than two hundred thousand billion rials). The fact that the government has not increased the prices according to this law in the first half of the Iranian year means that all this revenue would be collected after its introduction in what remains of the Iranian year.

How the Revenues from Removing Subsidies Are to Be Utilized

Depending on what assumptions one uses in calculating the current subsidies in the Iranian economy, the revenues to the government out of removing them would be huge. It is estimated that removing subsidies would generate between US$ 75–100 billion per year. According to a survey by the International Energy agency (IEA), which was prepared for the G20 meeting in Toronto in June 2010, Iran topped the 37 countries studied with US$ 101 billion in subsidies. This is much more than what Iran currently receives annually for exporting 2.4 million barrels of oil per day. Energy subsidies are the lion share of this amount. Based on current Iranian consumption, i.e., an oil price of 80 US$/b and a gas price of US$ 0. 26 per cubic meters to Turkey, and assuming that subsidies are removed in one step, the revenues from adjusting prices would generate around US$ 6 billion from gasoline, US$ 9 billion from gasoil, US$ 5 billion from electricity, and US$ 12 billion from natural gas sales. Removal of food subsidies would probably bring another US$ 6 billion to the treasury, bringing the total to around US$ 38 billion. This would be a windfall for the government and a huge burden on the people, who would have to adjust their standard of living to the new prices of energy and other commodities. It is envisaged that in the first year the revenue would not exceed US$ 20 billion, as there would be a gradual increase in prices.

The recent legislation has very specific provisions on how the money generated by removing subsidies is to be utilized by the government. It allows the government to use up to 50 per cent of this money to help the people directly or indirectly. Following are the steps that the government must take in this respect:

Cash payments and indirect assistance to families based on their income
Providing funds for social security and health insurance
Assistance in housing and job creation

Expanding social services

30 per cent of the funds must be utilised to further the following goals:

-Efficiency in use of energy in industry, services and housing as well as encouragement for energy savings
-Improvement in efficiency of production units such as power stations, water resources, and renewable sources of energy
-Compensate the state companies involved in providing services such as electricity, water, natural gas, and petroleum products
-Improvement in public transport system
-Supporting Agricultural and Industrial Producers
-Supporting industrial bread producers
-Expanding electronic communication to reduce unnecessary commuting

Twenty present of the revenues would go to the treasury and could be used by the government within its budget to overcome the effect of removing subsidies.

The Major Shortcomings of the Bill with Respect to Removal of Energy Subsidies

Nearly all the analysts believe that the continuation of present energy subsidies would lead to disastrous economic consequences for Iran. Many argue that the removal of subsidies should have started fifteen years ago. The governments in power at that time avoided addressing this essential but politically sensitive issue. Continuing the energy subsidies would divert nearly one million barrels per day of oil from Iran's oil export to domestic consumption so as to satisfy high demand for petroleum products in the coming ten years. Iran's position in the Organization of Petroleum Exporting Countries (OPEC) would be weakened and less oil would be available for sale to international markets.

Furthermore, domestic consumption of gas would increase rapidly, preventing gas injection into the oil fields and utilization of gas in the gas-based industries, which create jobs and value added in Iran's economy. There would be less potential for export of gas to Europe and the Indian subcontinent. And there would be fewer incentives by international companies to invest in the oil and gas industry of Iran, which would supply the domestic market.

In addition to all that, high consumption of energy per head would create further environmental pollutions in a country all of whose major cities already face pollution problems. Iran's CO_2 emission, which is already the highest in the region, would increase even more if the energy subsidies were to continue.

Having said all that, the present bill has its own shortcomings that have to be considered. The most important issue is the price of gas, which constitutes more than 60 per cent of Iran's energy basket. If we take into account that most of the power stations in Iran are gas based, the importance of the price of gas, which determines the price of electricity, is even more evident. The amount of subsidies given to gas is calculated based on the difference between the prices of exported and domestically consumed gas. It is also envisaged that the removal of subsidies would increase gas prices to 75 per cent of the export price for household and commercial sectors and 65 per cent for some industries. I would like to argue that these criteria to determine the price of gas would lead to wrong figures for the gas subsidies envisaged and would not be conducive to future development of gas based industries.

Unlike oil, natural gas does not have an international price and prices differ in various regions of the world. These prices are determined, in addition to consideration for costs of production, refining and transport, by the bargaining power of the buyers and sellers as well as by strategic considerations. For example, the average spot price of natural gas in the United States (Henry Hub) was US$ 3.9 per million Btu (14 cents per cubic meter) in 2009. The price of natural gas in the United States is currently (September 2010) around the same figure. By contrast, the gas delivered to Japan, whose price is formulated based on Japan's crude oil imports (Japan crude Cocktail), is about 2.5 times this figure. The price of Iran's natural gas export to Turkey, which is currently the only gas export from Iran and is also based on oil and petroleum product prices, is estimated to be almost twice the current gas price in the United States. Turkey is currently getting spot Liquefied Natural Gas (LNG) at around US$ 6 per million Btu, which is 25 per cent cheaper than the natural gas imported from Iran, and has for that reason reduced its purchase from Iran to the minimum allowed under the contract. Consequently, by removing subsidies from natural gas prices based on this model, the Iranian industrial sector will have to pay a higher price for natural gas than that paid by US industries.

In the last Iranian year (March 2009–March 2010), Iran produced 174 billion cubic meters of gas (BCM) and consumed 142 BCM of gas in households and commercial enterprises (54 per cent), power stations (30 per cent), and the industrial sector (16 per cent). Gas consumed in operations amounted to 23 BCM and around 10 BCM of gas was flared. In the same period gas exported to Turkey and Armenia was 7 BCM (less than the associated gas flared) and Iran imported 6 BCM from Turkmenistan. To base the price of the entire domestic consumption on gas sales to Turkey, which account for less than 5 per cent of the gas consumed and 4 per cent of the gas produced, creates a major distortion. In addition to that, the sale and purchase agreement with Turkey is not transparent and has been subject to claim and counter-claim from both sides. The agreement and gas price formula has not been revealed. Consequently, adjusting natural gas price to a percentage of gas sales to Turkey is not transparent.

The logic behind linking the petroleum product prices to FOB prices of the similar products in the Persian Gulf is the fact that if the oil and petroleum products are not sold locally, they theoretically have a definite market, and therefore value, outside Iran. However, the same is not true for the natural gas. The huge amount of gas which is currently produced in Iran does not have a market or definite value outside Iran, as there are no means of transporting this gas to other regions. To transport only ten per cent of this gas to international markets in the form of LNG would require US$ 8 to 10 billion of investment, providing there are no restrictions on the technology and finance, and setting up the necessary infrastructure would take between seven to eight years. Here we have a distinct difference between petroleum products and natural gas, which means that we cannot use the same mechanism for both.

The best alternative would have been to calculate the true costs of gas production, refining, and transport, and use that as a base. In addition, the government would levy a tax (call it the 'intrinsic value of gas') to be added to these costs. The tax would be levied in such a way that waste and irrational use of resources in household and commercial sectors would be discouraged. The tax could be set much lower for the gas-based industries, which create jobs, contribute to the development of the country, and have to compete with Qatar and Saudi Arabia.

By the same token, basing the price of electricity on its real costs is also unrealistic, as the real price depends on the price of natural gas used in the power stations. Hence, the price of electricity for household and industry would be higher than in many other countries.

Will This Legislation Help the Basic Problems Facing the Iranian Economy?

Will the answer is Yes and No. It all depends on how the implementation of this bill is carried out by the government. The objective of the bill is to remove subsidies from the Iranian economy in order to rationalize the utilization of hydrocarbon resources, to increase economic productivity, and to improve Islamic social justice. These are all very difficult objectives that would be a challenge to any government even at the best circumstances when it has the cooperation of the world community in trade and investment.

The increase in the prices of petroleum products, natural gas, and electricity will no doubt result in less waste and more prudent use of energy by the Iranian consumers. But there is a limit to eliminating waste and reducing energy needs. There must be massive investment on behalf of the government to ensure better public transport and encourage the domestic car manufacturers to design and produce affordable vehicles that consume less petrol in order to replace the present fleet. The government must also engage in promoting design and development of materials needed to improve insulation in the buildings and update heating and cooling facilities that are more energy friendly in the household and commercial sectors.

To increase economic productivity is also another major challenge. The increase in the price of energy is likely to reduce the revenues of most industrial complexes and manufacturing units in the country and reduce economic activity. The first aim would be to stop this decline, which would lead to job losses and lack of investment, and to increase the production capacity of the firms. It must be realized that industry must invest heavily for changing its machinery and equipment to be able to cope with high energy prices at a time when its revenues have shrunk considerably. To overcome this problem, the government must come up with adequate long-term soft loans to help change the industry to more energy-efficient outlets. Tax incentives could also be used for those who invest to change their industry to become more efficient in their energy use. Special treatment must be given to the existing petrochemical and refining industries that are competing with Qatar and Saudi Arabia. The petrochemical units and the gas-based industry in those countries receive their gas at around 2 cents per cubic meter (similar to the conditions that prevailed prior to the implementation of this bill in Iran). If the price of natural gas to Iranian units is increased fourfold (as envisaged under this bill), the profitability of these units (considering that they have restricted access to finance and technology at present) would be jeopardized. Furthermore, future investment in Iran's gas-based industry, which would create job pay taxes and contribute to the national insurance, would be in doubt. To overcome this problem, a long-term transparent and rational formula for the price of natural gas (feedstock) has to be presented so as to allow Iran to compete with other producers in the region.

Finally, the bill aims to adhere to Islamic social justice. The situation in the past allowed the affluent sector of the population who had more cars, bigger houses, and more facilities, to enjoy the subsidies more than the people in need. Fifty per cent of the revenues to the government out of this bill are allocated to alleviate the pressure on the less well-to-do section of the population, whose expenses would be considerably higher after the introduction of this bill. Cash hand-outs are the most important element of government policy, and there are currently debates about how much must be given to those in need and on the basis of what criteria.

It is estimated that around 60 million people have applied to get the cash hand-outs. The cash allocated to each person being estimated to be around 500,000 rials per month (50 US$/month), the first year's hand-out would amount to US$ 36 billion. This will be much higher than the government allowance of US$ 20 billion for the first year and would mean that the removal of subsidies on energy and food would have to be implemented at a much quicker pace in the initial years of implementation. If the removals of subsidies are well spread out over five years, the government will face a high budget deficit unless the price of oil increases substantially in the coming years.

There is always the danger that the cash hand-outs would be used for food, housing, and education, leaving the family with big utility bills to pay at the end of the month. If large numbers of people cannot pay these bills over a year, cutting their water, gas, and electricity would become a major political rather than economic issue. It might be preferable to keep the amounts allocated to each family in their accounts, to be used only against those utility bills and expenses that have changed after the bill has been implemented.

Conclusion

Iran consumes and wastes more energy than any other country in the region due to very high subsidies given to all forms of energy. The country's Energy Intensity is one of the highest in the world, and the future economic prosperity of Iran depends on using energy more prudently. In 2010 a bill to remove energy subsidies was passed. This bill has been debated for over a year and it seems that a political compromise has been reached. The government is not happy with the changes and restrictions imposed by the parliament, which they claim would undermine their efforts to change the basic parameters in the Iranian economy.

However, critics of the bill believe that it will fail to achieve its prime objective of economic progress and Islamic social justice and that it will increase inflation. They claim that it will increase the costs to Iranian industry at a time that it suffers from lack of investment and technology. Furthermore, they argue that the bill will lead to more bureaucracy and increase public dependence on government hand-outs.

Natural gas is very important for the future economic prosperity of Iran. Governments must decide on a long-term policy for natural gas and a price formula for petrochemicals and industries in order to create jobs, obtain added value from gas, and attract domestic and foreign capital for the development of natural gas resources and gas-based industries. Similarly, gasoil is of particular importance for transport and industry. If the price of gasoil is to adjust to the provisions in the bill, it has to increase 40-fold in five years (assuming that the price of oil stays around 80 US$/b). This will be a major shock to the transport and industrial sector. The public would particularly be affected by the price increases in gasoil and natural gas.

Even the critics of this legislation admit that this step was essential for the prosperity of future generations. The success of the bill depends on how efficiently and wisely the implementation of its various sections is carried out over the coming five years. The current economic and political pressures on Iran make the task of the government even more difficult.

Chapter 11

The Role of Ideology in Iranian Foreign Policy

Mehdi Mozaffari

Since the Islamic revolution in 1979, Iran has become the privileged subject of impressive and *tous azimuts* studies which go in all directions and embrace almost every aspect of Iranian life. Iranian foreign policy is not exempted from this overwhelming interest. Works in this field are so numerous that they cannot be listed here. There exist, among them, valuable works dealing with Iranian regional, bilateral, multilateral, and security issues. On the nuclear issue alone, a massive, rich, and varied literature is already available. Having said this, we have to recognize, however, the insufficiency of some solid scholarly works as to providing a theoretical explanation rendering the whole nuclear issue understandable. The real theatre of life takes place on a vast scene of actions, reactions, discourses, symbolisms and so on. The utility and the beauty of theoretical works rely precisely on their making sense of disparate elements that cannot speak for themselves.

In this connection, and without exaggeration, Professor Djalili is among the first, and perhaps *the* first scholar to have focused on the critical role of ideology in Iranian foreign policy. Already in 1989, he published a book on *Diplomatie Islamique: Stratégie internationale du khomeynisme*.[1] In this pioneering work, Djalili goes carefully and systematically through the analysis of fundamental aspects and dimensions of the Iranian post-revolutionary foreign policy. The theoretical assumptions to the ideological foundations of the Islamic regime, the structure of power and the decision-making process, and the international and regional implications are all studied in the best scholarly tradition. More than two decades after the publication of Djalili's work, the role of ideology in Iranian foreign policy is still as visible as ever.

Nowadays, Iran represents a highly critical actor, both at the regional and at the international level. The policy conducted by the Khameneh'i-Ahmadinejad tandem is a matter of great concern to the United Nation, the

---

[1] Mohammad-Reza Djalili, *Diplomatie Islamique: Stratégie internationale du khomeynisme*, Paris: Presses Universitaires de France, 1989.

International Atomic Energy Agency, as well as to the highly sensitive region around Iran. A number of questions arise as to, for example, why it is so difficult, almost impossible even, to come to some accommodation, to some negotiable compromise with Iran on issues like the nuclear issue or Iran's visceral hostility towards the very existence of Israel. In this concise study, I will search for answers to these kinds of questions by looking at the place and role of ideology in Iranian foreign policy. The expectation is that by selecting 'ideology' rather than 'national interest' as the main factor, persistent patterns of Iranian foreign policy will come to the surface, showing their essence and their true nature.

The Assumption

Let us start with two postulates of a general character and one assumption of a specific character. The first postulate is that ideology plays a more critical role in closed societies than in open societies. The second postulate assumes that ideology has an influence on the conceptualization, formulation, and execution of foreign policy in general.

The specific assumption, which is the subject of this study, is the following: *The foreign policy of the Islamic Republic of Iran (IRI) is guided by a totalitarian ideology rather than by national interest.*

(a) That ideology plays a more critical role in closed societies than in open societies is evident. In open societies, ideas are fluid and inter-communicable, which makes the rise of a hegemonic ideology unlikely. In closed societies, however, where ideas are controlled and communication between these ideas is very limited, ideology is imposed much more easily as the instrument of power. In the same way that ideology plays an even more important role in totalitarian regimes than in dictatorial, but non-totalitarian regimes. The reason is that totalitarian regimes cannot be sustained without an ideology whereas ideology is not necessary to the existence of non-totalitarian, despotic regimes.[2]

(b) A brief remark on the second point. Foreign policy is a part of the actions that occur in accordance with a specific world view. In some circumstances, the ideas that compose the world view become rigid, inflexible, and imperative. When this happens, ideas become 'ideology'. That ideology, like culture and identity, plays a significant role in shaping the foreign policy of a state is not a matter of dissension among scholars. If there is dissension, this is about the degree of influence rather than about the influence as such. When a regime is ideological, ideology is of course more prominent than in a country

---

[2] As Homa Katouzian puts it: 'By definition, and in contrast to a modern totalitarian regime, traditional arbitrary rule does not require an ideology for social and intellectual legitimation and organization', in Homa Katouzian 'The Pahlavi Regime in Iran', in *Sultanistic Regimes*, H.E. Chehabi and Juan J. Linz (eds), Baltimore and London: The John Hopkins University Press, 1998, p. 189.

governed by a non-ideological regime. It is also obvious that under ideological regimes foreign policy is justified in ideological terms. When the ideology of a regime is religiously founded, this justification occurs in accordance with religious terms and by way of religious symbolism.

Now I shall focus on the assumption that *the foreign policy of the Islamic Republic of Iran is guided by a totalitarian ideology rather than by national interest*. This assumption is supported by a comprehensive series of facts that extend from discourse to symbolism, from institutionalization to decisions and actions. In the Islamic Republic of Iran, ideology has a religious character which both reinforces its mythical dimension and exempts decision-makers from presenting rational justification. 'It is the will of Allah' and 'it is what Islam wants' are often used as justification. The ideological character of the Iranian regime is embedded in the constitution which stipulates that

> [t]he mission of the Constitution is to realize the ideological objectives of the Revolution (*Nehzat*) and to create conditions conducive to the development of man in accordance with the noble and universal values of Islam. (Preamble)[3]

What matters here is the 'noble and universal values of Islam' and not so much the 'national values' or 'national interest of Iran'. And who has the authority to decide the primacy of 'Islam' or 'Iran'? These two elements are not necessarily identical or in eternal harmony with each other.

Let us take a concrete and a very open example: the question of Israel. It is obvious that the Islamic Republic of Iran from day one has conducted a very hostile and activist policy against the very existence of Israel. Is this policy necessary for preserving and promoting Iran's national interests? Is it at least compatible with Iranian national interest? I do not think it requires a long and

---

[3] The Iranian constitution offers an excellent instrument for studying the most fundamental characteristics of the Iranian Islamist regime. In this document, we find the regime's world views, principled beliefs and causal beliefs, all in the same document. What is the extent of the validity of the Iranian constitution? This question is legitimate on the grounds that the countries in the Middle East that have a constitution, stipulating principles such as human rights and free elections, usually violate these very principles. Furthermore, Iranians still remember the non-application – and outright violation – of the constitution under the Shah's regime. The current situation is quite different for one simple reason. The constitution of 1906, which remained formally valid until the revolution of 1979, directly delegitimized the absolutism of the Shah, and consequently, he systematically violated it. There were also repeated demands from various opposition groups in the period prior to 1979 for a full application of the constitution (*ejra-ye qanun-e asasi*). Today, the constitution, based on an ideologized religion, is fully applied, allocating legitimacy to the religious elites and their leadership as well as providing them with real power. Therefore, the groups in power have acquired a direct interest in implementing the constitution. Violating or marginalizing the precepts of the constitution would amount to political suicide. In the Islamist constitution, any and every right is in accordance with religion. Judgment in such questions is allocated to the appointed religious authorities.

elaborated argumentation to prove that the hostility against Israel is not motivated by the national interests of Iran. On the contrary, both Iran and Israel have an objective interest in avoiding a conflict with each other in so far as both of them have been and still are at conflict with some Arab countries. Therefore, we have to find the motivation of the vehement hostility of the Islamic Republic towards Israel not in the logic of 'national interest', but in the ideological character of Iranian foreign policy which is inherently alien to the notion of 'nation' and where the 'national interest' is not recognized as the primary goal. The justification of the active animosity against Israel subsequently occurs with non-national arguments such as 'Israel is the enemy of Muslims', or Palestine is 'Islamic territory' and so on.

The Iranian Regime is Islamist and Totalitarian

Ideologically, the Iranian regime is based on the notion of the *Islamic Umma (ommat-e eslam)* and not on the *Iranian Nation (mellat-e Iran)*.[4] Iranian leaders rarely talk about 'Iran' in neutral terms; instead, they usually tie the name of the country to Islam, talking of *Iran-e eslami* (Islamic Iran) *mihan-e eslami, vatan-e eslami* (Islamic homeland), and so on. The pre-Westphalian character of the Iranian regime is in reality the reminiscence of the classic Islamic state, the basis of which 'was ideological, not political, territorial or ethnical and the primary purpose of government was to defend and protect the faith, not the state'.[5] The Iranian case corresponds perfectly to the late Professor Lambton's description where the regime is precisely founded on *faith* in Islam alone, not on the *nation*. The Preamble of the Iranian constitution stipulates that

> [i]n the view of Islam, government does not derive from the interests of a class, nor does it serve the domination of an individual or a group. Rather, it represents the fulfilment of a political ideal of a people who bear a common faith and common outlook...Our nation ... now intends to establish an ideal and model society on the basis of Islam.

During the last thirty years when Khomeinists have been in power in Iran, attempts directly initiated from their side or encouraged and sponsored by them to systematically weaken the *Iranian* identity are far from being few. At the beginning of the revolution, voices were raised for the destruction (*sic*) of Persepolis, the prohibition of playing the Iranian national anthem, the abolition of *Nowruz* (Iranian New Year) and replacing it with a Shiite day (*al-Ghadir*), and so on. The Iranian army battalions were renamed with strongly

---

[4]'Le refus de référence à la nation-Etat comme à l'idéologie ethnico-nationale et par conséquent le rejet en bloc du concept de nationalisme est l'un des aspects les plus fondamentaux de la philosophie politique du régime islamique; c'est à partir de cette idée centrale que toute la politique extérieure de la République islamique est sensée être élaborée.' Djalili, *Diplomatie islamique*, p. 58.
[5] Ann K.S. Lambton, *State and Government in Medieval Islam*, Oxford: Oxford University Press, 1981, p. 13.

Islamic connotations like 'Muhammad, Rasul Allah' and 'Zulfiqar' (Imam Ali's sword). Many universities were named after Shiite Imams, e.g. the University of Imam Hoseyn, the University of Imam Ja'far Sadeq, or the University of al-Zahra for female students.

It is true that since the accession of Mahmoud Ahmadinejad to the presidency we have been witnessing a slow but continuous trend towards Iranian *nationalism*. This tendency is visible in Ahmadinejad's discourse, where terms like '*mellat/*nation' and 'Iran' without the frequent prefix of 'Islamic' appear with increasing frequency. References to Iranian poetry with clear national connotations, to Iranian symbols and monuments (i.e., Persepolis, the mountain of Damavand on election posters), are more and more frequent. Ahmadinezhıad's new nationalist tendency is not, however, a volte-face or a replacement of his strong Islamist ideological convictions. He remains a fervent defender of Islam and Muslims, as he often claims. More than this, he even announced a one-party system in Iran by saying that the 'Islamic Republic has only a single party: the *velayat* (a vague concept referring both to the Leader and to the Shiite Imams).[6] The new development in this process lies in the use of nationalism as background music, indicating the existence of something different from the Islamic ideology—but not as an autonomous category or identity, rather, as a pendant to the Islamic identity which is represented as the real, the true and the authentic identity. In a hypothetical perspective, we cannot exclude Ahmadinejad's purely political motivations behind the rediscovery of 'Iranian civilization' and its 'glorious past'. If the antagonism between the rising Revolutionary Guards (IRGC) behind Ahmadinejad on the one side and the Shiite clergy in power on the other becomes serious in the future, the IRGC can always use the nationalist card as an alternative to the clerical legitimacy.

During 2011, the confrontation between Ahmadinejad and Khameneh'i became direct and quite obvious. The tension became clear when Ahmadinejad abruptly dismissed his minister of intelligence on 17 April 2011 without having informed the powerful *Bayt-e Rahbari*, Khamenei's office. Together with the foreign ministry, the ministry of intelligence traditionally belongs to Khameneh'i's *domaine réservé* as Supreme Leader. When the minister of intelligence was removed without his consent, Khameneh'i considered this action an act of war which needed a quick response, publicly and directly. A short time after Ahmadinejad had dismissed his minister of intelligence, Khameneh'i reappointed the same Heydar Moslehi to the same function. Unmistakably, the objective of the Supreme Leader's decision was to demonstrate once again who still held real power. Ahmadinejad was of course humiliated. This power struggle reveals two things: first, that the confrontation at the top of the pyramid of power is real. Second, that the Revolutionary Guards remain divided between what can roughly be described as 'moderates' and 'radicals'. The moderates, who are generally also the most wealthy and

---

[6] Ahmadinejad's address to the Leader's commissaries at universities, 10 July 2010.

privileged, support Khameneh'i, while the radicals, particularly the Basiji (para-military forces), are in favour of Ahmadinejad. In the aftermath of this struggle, Ahmadinejad felt it necessary to tone down his nationalist discourse without replacing it with a new one. This confirms the remark formulated above that Ahmadinejad's use of nationalism was based on an opportunistic rather than an authentic adherence to Iranian nationalism.

Let us leave this hypothetical, though not irrational scenario to concentrate on the totalitarian character of the Islamic regime. I would like to make clear here that when I talk about 'totalitarianism' I am referring to the regime in power and not to the society as such. It is a well-known fact that no society becomes completely totalitarian.

One of the best examples of the totalitarian character of the Islamic Republic is found in Article 4 of the Constitution:

> All civil, penal, financial, economic, administrative, cultural, military, political, and other laws and regulations must be based on Islamic criteria. This principle applies absolutely and generally to all articles of the Constitution as well as to all other laws and regulations, and the *fuqaha'* [religious jurists] of the Guardian Council are judges in this matter.

The totalitarian character of the regime is reinforced by the institutionalization of an entirely religious leadership that commands total power (article 110, the longest article of the Constitution).[7] In totalitarian regimes, ideology plays a

---

[7] Article 110 [Leadership Duties and Powers]
(1) Following are the duties and powers of the Leadership:
1. Delineation of the general policies of the Islamic Republic of Iran after consultation with the Nation's Exigency Council.
2. Supervision over the proper execution of the general policies of the system.
3. Issuing decrees for national referenda.
4. Assuming supreme command of the Armed Forces.
5. Declaration of war and peace and the mobilization of the Armed Forces.
6. Appointment, dismissal, and resignation of:
a. the religious men on the Guardian Council,
b. the supreme judicial authority of the country,
c. the head of the radio and television network of the Islamic Republic of Iran,
d. the chief of the joint staff,
e. the chief commander of the Islamic Revolution Guards Corps, and
f. the supreme commanders of the Armed Forces.
7. Resolving differences between the three wings of the Armed Forces and regulation of their relations.
8. Resolving the problems which cannot be solved by conventional methods, through the Nation's Exigency Council.
9. Signing the decree formalizing the election of the President of the Republic by the people. The suitability of candidates for the Presidency of the Republic, with respect to the qualifications specified in the Constitution, must be confirmed before elections take place by the Guardian Council, and, in the case of the first term of a President, by the Leadership.

predominant role by shaping the perception of the world and designing operations in terms of ideological goals. Restrictions to this are accepted only reluctantly.[8]

Another totalitarian characteristic is the obsession with the presence of irreducible *enemies*, who are ceaselessly hatching conspiracies. In totalitarian regimes, the situation is never normal; a state of emergency is the rule. They deliberately give the impression that they are constantly facing important threats requiring mobilization and readiness. They justify their actions and decisions by the state of emergency. For the same reason, totalitarian regimes must create 'crises' or maintain existing crises. Normality, appeasement and tranquillity are the worst enemies of such regimes. Creating artificial and unnecessary crises therefore becomes a mode of government which is the case of the Iranian regime.

The hostage-taking at the US embassy in Tehran (4 November 1979) was altogether a provoked crisis. The prolongation of the war with Iraq after the Iraqi proposal for a ceasefire in 1982 was also deliberate. The Rushdie Affair in 1989 and the vehemently hostile posture towards Israel are solely motivated by the need for an enemy. Conducting an enigmatic and thoroughly ambivalent policy in the very delicate and highly dangerous area of nuclear energy once again demonstrates the almost vital need of the Islamic regime for crises.

Now, what does the totalitarian character of the regime have to do with foreign policy? The relations between them are strong and direct. Firstly, all totalitarian regimes are *expansionist*, territorially and/or ideologically. Therefore, they conduct an aggressive foreign policy. Secondly, the line of conduct of totalitarian regimes is *maximalist* in general. Compromise is a rare occurrence. The following quotation explains the reason for the non-compliance of totalitarian regimes:

> Again and again the cry is heard that some kind of accommodation must be found, some over-all agreement be reached, through a summit conference or through traditional diplomacy. Advocates of these projects never seem to realize that nothing worse could happen to a totalitarian system than such general pacification, since it would deprive it of its enemies. To appeal for peace while at the same time doing everything to prevent it from 'breaking out' is a key feature of the relations of a totalitarian dictatorship with the rest of the world.

---

10. Dismissal of the President of the Republic, with due regard for the interests of the country, after the Supreme Court holds him guilty of the violation of his constitutional duties, or after a vote of the Islamic Consultative Assembly testifying to his incompetence on the basis of Article 89.
11. Pardoning or reducing the sentences of convicts, within the framework of Islamic criteria, on a recommendation from the Head of judicial power.
The Leader may delegate part of his duties and powers to another person.

[8] Zbigniew Brzezinski and Carl J. Friedrich, *Totalitarian Dictatorship and Autocracy*, Cambridge, MA: Harvard University Press, 1965, p. 355.

These lines were written in 1965 by Zbigniew Brzezinski and Carl J. Friedrich.[9] More than seven years of unsuccessful dialogue with the Islamic Republic to find a kind of accommodation on the nuclear issue confirms the accuracy of Brzezinski and Friedrich's observation.

The fact is that totalitarian regimes give in only under severe pressure. In the Iranian case, the regime has been obliged on some occasions to demonstrate a certain degree of flexibility and to accept an outcome that was not the preferred solution of the regime. Let us briefly mention three cases in this connection. The first case is the Iran-Iraq war. In 1980, Saddam Hussein's attack on Iran was celebrated by Khomeini as a 'divine gift' (*ne'mat-e elahi*). Ultimately, however, due to the extreme war-weariness of the population and the lack of adequate armaments, this very divine gift turned out to be a 'bowl of poison' (*jam-e zahr*) that Khomeini had to take in accepting the UN resolution 598 of 20 July 1987 and the subsequent ceasefire with Iraq (August 1988). We witnessed a similar scenario in the Rushdie affair. Iranian authorities firmly rejected making any concession in connection with Khomeini's death decree. Faced with a unanimous decision of the then twelve members of the EU to recall their ambassadors from Tehran, the Iranian foreign minister declared that the Iranian *government* would not make any attempts on Rushdie's life (24 September 1998).[10]

Another example is the suspension of the uranium enrichment programme in 2003. According to the US Intelligence Council report from November 2007, there are indications that Iran suspended the military aspect of its nuclear programme in 2003. If this information can be verified, the year 2003 clearly indicates Iranian attempts at following a preventive policy in a bid to avoid being placed under unbearable pressure—perhaps even military aggression—by the United States as the consequence of the first year of military success during the invasion of Iraq. The situation in Iraq changed dramatically thereafter with events like the scandal of the Abu Ghraib prison which encouraged Iran to return to its usual recalcitrant position.

In all three cases, *pressure* was the real cause of change in Iranian attitudes. In the first case, exhausted resources forced Khomeini to end the war with Iraq. In the other two cases, strong international pressure and fear of retaliation were the decisive factors of the change in Iranian policy.

It is also worth noting that the Islamic Republic of Iran has actually pursued a prudent policy in some geographical areas and towards a few specific

---

[9] Ibid., p. 354.

[10] On 24 September 1998, the Iranian foreign minister publicly dissociated his government from the death threat imposed on the British author Salman Rushdie in 1989 by Ayatollah Ruhollah Khomeini, and Britain responded by restoring full diplomatic relations. 'The Government of the Islamic Republic of Iran has no intention, nor is it going to take any action whatsoever, to threaten the life of the author of 'The Satanic Verses' or anybody associated with his work, nor will it encourage or assist anybody to do so', the Iranian Foreign Minister, Kamal Kharrazi, said in a statement that he read to reporters today. *The New York Times on the Web*.

states. This is the case in the Caucasus where Iran did not support the Muslim rebellion in Chechnya. Similarly, in the Armenia-Azerbaijan dispute over Nagorno-Karabakh, it adopted more of a pro-Armenian policy than a pro-Azeri policy, despite the fact that Azerbaijan is a Muslim country. Nor has Iran supported Islamist movements in Central Asia. Different factors explain this 'anomaly'. Iran's then close relation with Russia, Azerbaijan's ambitions concerning the Iranian provinces of Azerbaijan, and the anti-Shiite character of pro-Wahhabi Islamist movements are among the elements that explain the Iranian policy on these specific issues.

Furthermore, to reinforce themselves, to avoid potential dangers and ensure their interests, totalitarian regimes establish close relations, even a kind of alliance, with non-totalitarian regimes with the only condition that they get sufficient support from them. This has happened in history on a number of occasions: Stalin's alliance with Western democracies against Hitler, and Maoist China's excellent relations with pro-western Pakistan or the Shah regime in Iran are two examples. Having close relations with non-totalitarian regimes does not reduce the totalitarian nature of a regime. Totalitarian regimes can be pragmatic in their foreign policy, without neglecting either their *revisionist* character or their ideological goals. In the case of Islamist Iran, its very close relations with secular Syria as well as with a number of Marxist leaders in Latin America have not in any manner affected the fundamental nature of the regime itself as Islamist, totalitarian, and even anti-secular.

Thirdly, totalitarian regimes are *revisionist* in their foreign policy. Bolshevism, Nazism, and Maoism were all revisionist. Revisionism affects the structures of the international system. Their aims included a complete transformation of the existing system, replacing it with an entirely different system. Khomeini's Islamist revolution challenged both the then USSR (the challenger) and the United States (the challenged).

Islamic Anti-Imperialistic Imperialism

The revisionist character of the IRI has led to an *anti-imperialistic imperialism*. The Islamist struggle against imperialism is not a principled struggle; the goal is not to put an end to imperialism as a harmful concept and as an erroneous political and economic construct. Rather, the real issue for Islamists is to *replace* Western imperialism with a new Islamic hegemony as a reminiscence of the golden age of Islamic world power ('single world community/*ommat-e vahed-e jahani*'). This line of conduct has produced a strange alliance policy with all kinds of extremists insofar as they struggle against the existing international system. The Iranian regime is in alliance with both the extreme left and the extreme right worldwide—Hugo Chávez and the Ku Klux Klan, at one and the same time.[11]

---

[11] George Michael, 'Mahmoud Ahmadinejad's Sponsorship of Holocaust Denial', *Totalitarian Movements and Political Religions*, 8(3–4), 2007, pp. 667–71.

To achieve the goal of the 'single world community', the Leader/*Rahbar* has an 'Ideological Army' (*artesh-e maktabi*) at his disposal. This is perhaps the only army (regular army and the Revolutionary Guards Corps) in the world with two duties: 1) 'guarding and preserving the frontiers of the country; and 2) fulfilling the ideological mission of jihad in God's way; that is, extending the sovereignty of God's law throughout the world' (Preamble). In bald terms, military jihad is a constitutional duty of the Iranian army. The constitution stipulates that

> [i]n the formation and equipping of the country's defence forces, due attention must be paid to faith and ideology as the basic criteria. Accordingly, the Army of the Islamic Republic of Iran and the Islamic Revolutionary Guards Corps are to be organized in conformity with this goal, and they will be responsible not only for guarding and preserving the frontiers of the country, but also for fulfilling the ideological mission of jihad in God's way; that is, extending the sovereignty of God's law throughout the world (this is in accordance with the verse from the Qur'an: 'Prepare against them whatever force you are able to muster, and strings of horses, striking fear into the enemy of God and your enemy, and others besides them' (Qur'an 8:60) (Preamble).

In order to realize its ambitions to build an Islamic empire, the Islamic Republic not only needs the necessary resources, but also two other elements: conquering a prestigious Islamic city and acquiring the knowledge necessary to fabricate a nuclear weapon. At the moment, Jerusalem is the only potential city available, so to speak. Saying that Jerusalem would be the Iranian target sounds unrealistic. It is perhaps also a utopian objective as well. But, as we have seen repeatedly in history, this does not reduce the importance of the utopia in a totalitarian regime, or the danger that would entail for the security of the region. The choice of Jerusalem is also motivated by two factual elements. The first element is inherent in the geographical and religious physiognomy of the Islamic Republic, and the second is related to the absence of any other tangible alternative. It is a fact that, as a country, Iran possesses an important number of favourable factors, including its geographical location between the Caucasus and Central Asia to the north and the Persian Gulf to the south, between Asia to the east and the Middle East to the west. It has a population of over 70 million people, most of whom are quite young, and the country possesses massive reserves of gas (the second-largest gas reserves in the world) and oil (third-largest in the world). Especially since Ahmadinejad became president, Iran has also gained significant popularity in the Arab countries. This popularity may rightly be interpreted as Iranian *soft power*. Benefitting from these favourable factors, Islamist Iran is entitled to view itself as the coming new Muslim superpower. President Ahmadinejad already pretends that Iran is 'the world's first power'.[12] At the same time, Iranian ambitions

---

[12] Speech on 28 February 2008 on the occasion of the 1980–1988 Iran-Iraq war (Tehran: AFP).

meet serious obstacles. These obstacles are not only in the form of other Muslim countries such as Saudi Arabia, Pakistan, Egypt, and Turkey, which nourish similar dreams; Iran also faces difficulties of another nature. Firstly, Iran is a Shiite country while a large majority of Muslims are Sunni (roughly 90 per cent). However, there has been a Shiite empire—the Fatimids (909–1171)—in Islamic history. But the Fatimids were only recognized as a Shiite dynasty of the Isma'ili sect, whereas the Sunni caliphate of the Abbasids (750–1258) was regarded as a truly *Islamic* empire. Shiite Iran may become the new centre of a Shiite empire at some point in the future, but not the centre of an Islamic empire. To sweep away this serious obstacle, Iranian Islamist leaders have tried to tone down their Shiite allegiances from the first days of the revolution. Khomeini systematically addressed all Muslims (except in particular ceremonies and events directly related to the Shiites), and he considered himself the supreme leader of the Islamic world. It was in this capacity that he delivered his fatwa containing the death decree against Salman Rushdie.[13] In the post-Khomeini era, Khameneh'i, the current Supreme Leader, argues that it is not Iran that is seeking war with Sunni Islam, but the United States that is seeking war with the entire Islamic world. In a speech in Qom on 8 January 2007, Khameneh'i emphasized that

> [t]he United States aims to portray the Islamic Republic of Iran as a Shi'a republic and try to set it against the great Sunni community. This is a very dangerous plot which their politicians are currently trying to carry out.[14]

Animated by the same ecumenical spirit, the Iranian government has tried to build a bridge between Shiite and Sunni believers by organizing inter-faith gatherings in Iran. One of the most recent gatherings of this kind took place in Tehran and involved representatives from 25 Islamic countries (10 October 2007). It was in prolongation of the same ecumenical policy that an Asian Interfaith and Intercultural Dialogue Seminar took place in Tehran on 11 September 2011.

In addition to all of these disputes, Shiite Iran faces a major obstacle: In the view of Muslims, Iran does not really represent a prestigious *Islamic* land. Tehran is a relatively new and trivial city; it is nowhere near as prestigious as cities like Mecca, Medina, Baghdad, Damascus, Cairo, or Istanbul. The two holy Islamic cities in Iran, Mashhad and Qom, are only holy in the eyes of Twelver Shiite believers. Aware of these handicaps, Khomeini and his successor have made considerable efforts to seize control over some of the Islamic centres recognized as holy by all Muslims. During the first years of the revolution, Khomeini's attention was primarily orientated towards Mecca and Me-

---

[13] Mehdi Mozaffari, *FATWA: Violence and Discourtesy*, Oxford: Aarhus University Press, 1998.
[14] Karim Sadjadpour, *Reading Khamenei: The world view of Iran's most powerful Leader*, Washington DC: Carnegie Endowment for International Peace, 2008, p. 25.

dina, the most sacred of the Islamic cities. To reach this objective, he tried to destabilize the power of the Saudi royal family by supporting unrest in the kingdom, e.g. in connection with the military occupation of the holy mosque of Mecca (20 November 1979) by Saudi Islamists and by provoking bloody demonstrations during the hajj pilgrimages. Together with various other terrorist actions allegedly perpetrated by Iran (e.g. the attack on US military personnel at Khobar in Saudi Arabia on 25 June 1996), these events created difficulties for the Saudi kingdom, but did not bring it down.

Parallel to these initiatives, Khomeini developed a Plan B consisting of the conquest of Jerusalem. During the Iraq-Iran war (1980–1988), Khomeini used to remind the Iranians that 'the road to Jerusalem goes through Karbala', which was a clear indication that the real objective was not so much the defeat of Iraq, but the conquest of Jerusalem. It is also worth noting that Iran is the only country with a 'Jerusalem Day' (*Ruz-e Qods*) and also the only country that has established a 'Jerusalem Army' (*Sepah-e Qods*) which was (according to American sources) operating in Iraq against the allied forces.

This is to say that a combination between hegemonic and almost utopian ambitions of the Islamist authorities in Iran on the one hand, and the lack of any other alternative on the other, has made Jerusalem a significant *objet désiré* of the Islamic Republic of Iran. It is in this context that we should understand the Iranian position to Palestine. As already mentioned, it is common knowledge that the Iranian government, since the revolution in 1979, has conducted a zealous and unconditional pro-Palestinian policy that it is unequalled in any other Muslim and even Arab country. Iranian assistance has been multidimensional: diplomatic, financial, and military. With this comprehensive assistance, the Iranian government has tried to convince everybody of its total involvement in favour of the Palestinian cause: the creation of an independent Palestinian state. However, when we look deeper, we discover that the Islamic Republic is not so much for a Palestinian state, but that its real intention is to destroy Israel. These two objectives are not necessarily the same. Iran only supports the Palestinian factions that both reject peace with Israel and work for the destruction of the Jewish state. Ismail Hanieyh and Khaled Mashal, the leaders of Hamas, are invited to Tehran, not Mahmoud Abbas and Salam Fayyaz, the leaders of the Palestinian autonomous authority. Consequently, Iran is not pro-Palestinian, but anti-Israel at almost any price. The 'destruction' of Israel has only one objective: control of Jerusalem.

The same hegemonic logic explains the so far unshakable Iranian ambition to acquire nuclear capabilities. In the nuclear age, it is inconceivable that a new Islamic empire can emerge without having the ultimate weapon. The point is not that Iran wants to or really can use a nuclear device against Israel or another nuclear power. The logic of dissuasion will prevent it from doing so, unless the Iranians were willing to accept their own annihilation. Rather, it is the prestige associated with possessing nuclear weapons that is interesting for a country with the ambition to become the centre of an Islamic world power. It is quite interesting that we find the difference between 'having' and 'deploying' the atomic weapon in the discourse of Ayatollah Khameneh'i and other leaders of the Islamic Republic. In their attempt to deflect the suspicion against them about the building of a nuclear bomb, they make a sophisticated differentiation between the 'deployment' and the 'possession' of nuclear weapons by insisting that 'in Islam, the 'deployment' (*este'mal*) of nuclear weapons is prohibited', while they remain silent about the 'possession' (*dashtan*) of such weapons. In this way, the post-revolutionary Iranians, who are masters at equivocal and ambiguous language, try to camouflage (*ketman*) their real intentions by using the classic Islamic stratagem (*hilah*) of spreading confusion among their opponents and critics.

Is Change Possible in Iranian Foreign Policy?

Since the 1979 revolution, the world has undergone dramatic changes. The Cold War has ended, the Soviet empire has imploded, apartheid in South Africa has been replaced by a democratic pluralistic regime, the countries of Eastern Europe have become democratic, and China is opting for a capitalist economy. Even Iranian society has been transformed: new classes have emerged, Iranian youth—female and male—is pushing for openings towards the modern world, and cultural plurality, or more correctly cultural schizophrenia, has become evident. Despite this vast array of changes, the Iranian *regime* (still different from *society*) remains almost as it was under Khomeini. It has retained its main revolutionary characteristics, its revolutionary institutions, and its revolutionary ambitions. The leader is still the leader of the *revolution* in addition to being the leader of the Islamic Republic of Iran and the leader of the Islamic Umma. One of his websites goes as far as to declare him the 'leader of the world'. The *revolutionary* tribunals are still functioning, the parliament has remained under Islamist control, and the *Revolutionary* Guards are today much more powerful than ever before. In the area of foreign policy, the main goals of the revolution have remained unchanged.

Among Iranian presidents, Mahmoud Ahmadinejad, is a very different type of person, prone to harsh rhetoric and undiplomatic behaviour. Adopting Mahdism[15] as his doctrine and conducting an 'apocalyptic foreign policy',[16] he claims to have returned to the authentic sources of Khomeini's revolution where 'building a model society and introducing *Islamic Revolution* are our nation's missions'.[17] What President Ahmadinejad is saying here is nothing but a repetition of what his former mentor, Ayatollah Khameneh'i, the leader of the revolution, has repeatedly emphasized. In his speech in Yazd (central Iran), for instance, Khameneh'i forcefully reaffirmed that '[t]o day, the ad-

---

[15] A. Savyon and Y. Mansharof, 'The Doctrine of Mahdism: The Ideological and Political Philosophy of Mahmoud Ahmadinejad and Ayatollah Mesbah-e Yazdi', Washington DC, The Middle East Media Research Institute, 2007.
[16] Mehdi Khalaji, *Apocalyptic Politics: On the Rationality of Iranian Policy*, Washington DC: The Washington Institute for Near East Policy, 2008.
[17] Ahmadinejad's speech on 28 February 2008 on the occasion of the 1980–1988 Iran-Iraq war (Tehran: *AFP*).

vanced socio-political doctrine of Islam, presented by the Islamic Republic of Iran, stands as a model and guide for the nations which keep thirst for spirituality and salvation' (5 January 2008). Two questions then arise: Firstly, is it realistic to expect Islamist Iran to distance itself significantly from its ideological roots in a bid to become a 'normal' state? Secondly, under what conditions will the Islamist regime revise its revolutionary, revisionist, totalitarian and pre-Westphalian foreign policy?

These questions lead us to consider the relational landmarks of the Islamist regime. The fact is that this regime, which is ideologically and institutionally monistic, is not monolithic, *politically* speaking. In fact, there are various voices, tendencies, and forces within the Iranian political system that are competing for a share in power. Roughly speaking, those who refer to themselves as *Principalists (osulgarayan)* and those who refer to themselves as *Reformists (eslahtalaban)*. Their differences, however, are limited to the *functionality* of the entire system. By 'functionality', I mean all of the practical aspects related to the exercise of power or, in Goldstein and Keohane's vocabulary, the struggle is about the 'causal beliefs' and the modality of implementation of the 'road map' rather than the substance of politics.[18] The dispute is about finding the appropriate policy to attain the goals. More specifically, the fundamentalists (the hawks) favour a more rigorous policy while the reformists (the doves) want to introduce a degree of moderation in the exercise of power. Apart from this, all agree on the fundamental aspects of the regime as well as the ideological goals to be pursued. Even if some voices are heard among reformists in favour of a more rational or less ideological foreign policy, these voices are not strong enough to help modify the main course of policy.

Parallel to the internal antagonism between fundamentalists and reformists, there is possibly a more important antagonism that may have considerable consequences in the future: the unprecedented success of the IRGC in gaining political power through a 'creeping coup d'état'.[19]

To assess the possible scenarios of a gradual, substantial change in Iranian foreign policy, the following factors should be taken into consideration. The change will happen when serious contradictions arise between the ideological creeds and tangible material interests of the current rulers. This has not yet happened. On the contrary, the election of Ahmadinejad to the presidency in 2005 has served to further radicalize the ideological nature of the Islamist regime. At the same time, however, the rise of a new radicalism and the proclaimed return to Khomeinism have provoked internal divisions and a new

---

[18] Judith Goldstein and Robert O. Keohane, 'Ideas and Foreign Policy: An Analytical Framework' in *Ideas and Foreign Policy: Beliefs, Institutions, and Political Change*, Judith Goldstein and Robert O. Keohane (eds), Ithaca: Cornell University Press, 1993, pp. 8–10.
[19] Ali Alfoneh, 'Iran's Parliamentary Elections and the Revolutionary Guard's Creeping Coup d'Etat', *American Enterprise Institute for Public Policy Research*, No. 2, February 2008.

political fragmentation. Faced with Ahmadinejad's harsh rhetoric and radicalization of the foreign policy in general, reformists had no other choice but to harden their criticism. This rift has occurred now as a result of Ahmadinejad's re-election to the presidency in June 2009. With the rise of the Green Movement, the dissension between Fundamentalists and Reformists has never been as profound as it is today. The Green Movement is a sort of umbrella covering different and even contradictory factions. But the two front figures of this movement, Mir Hoseyn Musavi and Mehdi Karrubi (two other presidential candidates), neither contest the existence of the Islamic regime nor its constitution. They only contest the legitimacy of the current Leader (Ayatollah Khameneh'i), who is criticized for being the leader of a clique instead of being the leader of the Islamic Republic as required by the constitution.[20] Since the Green Movement is the subject of study of other authors in this book, I shall limit my remarks to a few points on foreign policy that have been concisely outlined by one of the front figures of the Green Movement.

The Green Movement has not yet produced a clear and comprehensive programme on issues of foreign policy. Foreign policy is almost absent from Mehdi Karrubi's declarations. And what has so far (September 2010) been publicized from Mir Hoseyn Musavi on this issue in the form of interviews and communiqués has been allusive, cryptic, and ambivalent. Behind all these declarations, we get the impression of a person who describes himself as an authentic Khomeinist who is nostalgic about the 'illuminated era' (*'asr-e nurani*) under Khomeini, but who is also aware of the presence of a 'millenary Iranian identity'.[21] Musavi finds the foreign policy of Ahmadinejad's government 'erroneous and adventurous'.[22] In another declaration, he led us to believe that he is an adherent of the realist school in international politics by saying that 'due to the primacy of power (*esalat-e qodrat*) in international relations, every state is pursuing its national interest', adding immediately the following statement: 'We are.....against those [states] who do not respect our customs, religious and national beliefs.'[23] In a more thematic and structured declaration, Musavi tried to establish a synergy between Islamic and Iranian identities which is 'one and indivisible'. In the same document, he spoke in favour of a 'rational and dignified foreign policy, transparent interactions the purpose of which should be the promotion of.... Nation of Iran in the world'.[24] On the nuclear issue, Musavi's position remains ambiguous. On the one hand, he has criticized in harsh terms the government's conciliatory attitude at the Geneva meeting with the 5+1 delegations (October 2009), and on the other hand, when the government returned to its usual firm and reluctant

---

[20] Mehdi Mozaffari, *The Iranian Green Movement: One Year After*, Aarhus, Department of Political Science, June 2010, available: www.cir.au.dk (accessed 5 September 2011).
[21] Musavi's meeting with a group of his young followers', 30 April 2009.
[22] Communiqué No. 13, 29 September 2009.
[23] Communiqué No. 17, 1 January 2010.
[24] Communiqué No. 18, 15 June 2010.

position, Musavi criticized it again for conducting an 'adventurous and demagogic diplomacy'.[25]

Conclusion

Choosing *ideology* as the main factor in explaining the Iranian post-revolutionary foreign policy does not explain everything – but it explains a great deal. To the existing Westphalian system, post-revolutionary Iran represents an anomaly. By constantly focusing on its ideological identity, Iran has dramatically weakened its identity as a *nation-state*. Iran is standing as an actor that is struggling for a *faith* instead of the multi-faceted tasks that a state-nation may usually undertake: primarily the survival and security of the state. Important is also the pursuit of wealth and economic growth and power as well as the preservation of the nation's culture. In this connection, goals like 'the victory of Islam' or 'jihad in Allah's path' represent a struggle for the faith which is alien from the wealth and economic growth of Iran as a *nation*. Therefore, when one has to analyse the conduct of a literally *faithful* state, one has to interpret it according to this faith and not to the national aspect. This is what I have tried to do in the present study by emphasizing the crucial importance of ideology as a main explanatory factor in understanding the real sense and orientation of Iranian foreign policy.

When the fulfilment and implementation of a faith-based ideology becomes the state's proclaimed task, the emerging regime will inevitably be totalitarian. This study has demonstrated that the behaviour of the IRI can be better explained when the totalitarian character of the IRI is taken in account. I did not launch an elaborated discussion about totalitarianism as a political philosophy which is itself a vast domain. I based my analysis on some admitted and institutionalized characteristics of the Iranian regime which are akin to recognizable totalitarian features. Since the Iranian regime has overtly and deliberately made Islamism (or Khomeinism) its *raison d'être*, it has at the same time made itself a prisoner of its own ideology. This is why the ideology determines the conduct of the state and not vice versa. Bolshevism, Nazism and Maoism have not been particularly successful in accommodating themselves to hard realities and, at the same time, keeping their ideology intact. The Soviet empire failed by itself and was subsequently dissolved. Nazi Germany destroyed itself together with millions of human beings, leaving behind a continent in ruins. China became capitalist, keeping the communist party merely as an integrative apparatus and Mao's portrait as the reminiscence of independence. What will happen to the Islamic Republic of Iran will probably create a new and unprecedented scenario.

---

[25] Ibid.

Chapter 12

Iran's Cultural Diplomacy

Nadia von Maltzahn

Mohammad-Reza Djalili suggested in his January 1989 publication *Diplomatie islamique* that diplomacy is governed by ideology in every regime of totalitarian nature. The Islamic Republic's foreign policy was based on several factors, including geo-strategic concerns, the evolution of Iran's domestic politics, the international arena, and the ideology the state put in place. Of these, Djalili argues, ideology in the first revolutionary decade was proportionally more important than the other factors in guiding Iran's diplomacy. As such, exporting the revolution was one of the principles of the Islamic Republic's foreign policy. Islamic ideology dominated the official discourse of the revolutionary government, although regime opponents wrote off Iran's Islamic-revolutionary rhetoric as a 'smoke screen'. Ten months after the victory of the Islamic revolution, Djalili wrote, Iran's Islamic diplomacy was born.[1]

This chapter does not consider Iran's Islamic diplomacy per se, but rather Iran's cultural diplomacy. What role does culture play in Islamic Iran's foreign policy? What tools and institutions has Iran employed for promoting itself in other countries? Following the 1979 Islamic revolution, the Iranian revolutionary administration emphasized the need to propagate its culture abroad, stressing the Islamic nature of the revolution. A rising number of institutions and public organizations started to develop cultural activities outside Iran. On the institutional level, Iran's cultural work abroad lacked coherence and central organization in the first revolutionary decade. To have an integrated policy, the Islamic Republic set up the Islamic Culture and Relations Organization (ICRO) in 1995, and henceforth this organization had the main responsibility of coordinating Iran's cultural diplomacy. Its mission was to introduce the foundations of the Islamic revolution and the ideas of Imam

---

[1] Mohammad-Reza Djalili, *Diplomatie islamique: stratégie internationale du khomeynisme*, Paris: Presses Universitaires de France, 1989, Introduction and pp. 55f.

Khomeini, in particular in the Islamic world, realizing Islamic unity by strengthening cultural relations among Muslim states.

In the following, the concept of cultural diplomacy will be introduced, before turning to Iranian cultural policies in the first revolutionary decade, which were marked by Iran's efforts to export the revolution. Iranian cultural diplomacy took a more concrete form in the 1990s with the creation of the ICRO. The organization and its mission will be analyzed, and the vehicles for promoting Iran abroad—Iranian cultural centres—introduced. Through two case studies, Iranian cultural diplomacy in the Middle East and in Europe, it will become clear how Iran's cultural diplomacy works in practice. This chapter is far from comprehensive, but provides an insight into the work of Iran's official body for conducting cultural diplomacy, the ICRO. Something that lies outside the scope of this study, for instance, is the impact Iran's transnational media—such as the English language Press TV and Arabic language al-Alam—have on foreign publics. While the director of Iran's national broadcasting agency sits on the council of the ICRO, the latter is not responsible for the former. The study of media—despite the media's potential in reaching out to other countries—has thus been omitted.

Cultural Diplomacy

Attracting and co-opting the people of another state through the use of culture and political values lie at the core of cultural diplomacy. Culture is a vital component of public diplomacy, the latter being the way in which a country communicates with foreign publics. Public diplomacy is based to a large degree on communication, engaging people and building lasting relationships. Culture is one of the means through which these steps can be taken. Through the use of culture, a nation can promote understanding by transmitting its ideas and value systems, and build up lasting relationships through exchanges and educational activities. The term 'cultural diplomacy' will be understood as the efforts of a country's government to build up understanding and lasting relationships with the people of another country by way of official cultural relations.

Cultural diplomacy is an effort to gain soft power, that is the ability to attract and co-opt people rather than coercing them. Soft power is less easily controlled by government policies than cultural diplomacy, as it refers to the outcome of having the ability to attract others, which largely depends on perception.[2] This study is concerned with Iran's cultural diplomacy rather than its soft power, although the Islamic Republic clearly believes it has soft power.

Cultural diplomacy is an instrument that governments use to mobilize resources—resources that arise from values a country expresses in its cul-

---

[2] For a study on soft power, see Joseph Nye, *Soft Power: The means to Success in World Politics*, New York: Public Affairs, 2004.

ture—to communicate with and attract the publics of other countries.[3] Most programmes of cultural relations abroad are initiated and supervised by foreign ministries, which also carry a large proportion of the cost. In some cases—most notably the recent example of China's Confucius Institutes—education ministries are the instigators. Traditionally, cultural diplomacy is conducted through cultural institutes abroad, like the British Council or the Goethe-Institut. Important components of these cultural centres are language teaching, coordinating artists' exchanges and exhibitions, and organizing events such as concerts and lectures. Another important channel for cultural diplomacy are academic exchange programmes, as well as the exchange of technical experts and leaders in various fields of intellectual and artistic expression. How Iran conducts its cultural diplomacy and sets about promoting its ideas and values abroad will be discussed in the following.

The First Revolutionary Decade: Export of the Revolution
According to the website of the Supreme Council of the Cultural Revolution: 'Upon the victory of the Islamic Revolution in Iran, which was indeed a Cultural Revolution, Islamic Iran took up its historic mission to promote and deepen the cultural ties with other nations as well as presenting the world the true Iranian and Islamic culture.'[4]

Iranian cultural foreign policy in the first revolutionary decade was more marked by attempts to export the revolution than by the conduct of cultural diplomacy. From the outset, the revolutionary administration in Iran emphasized the need to promote the country's culture abroad, stressing the Islamic character of the revolution. At home, it set out to Islamicize Iranian society by attempting to eliminate any non- and anti-Islamic elements from Iran's national culture and making the teaching of the Arabic language, the original agent of Islam, mandatory in secondary school education.[5] Khomeini believed that the world was divided into oppressors and oppressed, and that Iran, as the only truly Islamic and non-aligned country, had the duty to lead the revolutionary movement and help Muslim and other oppressed nations to reach real independence.[6] To this end, an Iranian cultural official explained the change of goals in Iranian policy:

> The Islamic revolution is known to be a genuine revolution with the aim of freeing the oppressed in the world from the burden of the op-

---

[3] Joseph Nye, 'Public Diplomacy and Soft Power', *The Annals of the American Academy of Political and Social Science*, 616, March 2008, p. 95.
[4] www.iranculture.org/en/nahad/ertebatat.php (accessed on 09 May 2008).
[5] Shireen Hunter, 'Iran and the Arab World', in *Iran at the Crossroads: Global Relations in a Turbulent Decade*, Miron Rezun (ed.), Boulder CO: Westview, 1990; Anoushiravan Ehteshami and Raymond Hinnebusch, *Syria and Iran, Middle Powers in a Penetrated Regional System*, New York: Routledge, 1997, p. 89. Cf. the Iranian constitution, Article 16.
[6] Christin Marschall, *Iran's Persian Gulf Policy: From Khomeini to Khatami*, London: Routledge, 2003, p. 11.

pressors. It is a revolution with unifying and humane goals, wishing to defend Muslim identity, strengthening unity and fighting against any kind of division among Muslims. Its basic goal is to give a picture of genuine Islam.[7]

One of the main aims of Iran's foreign policy during the first decade—at least in theory—was thus to export its revolution in order to achieve Muslim unity, to confront the oppressor nations and gain Muslim sovereignty. In Khomeini's world view, the source of the Muslim world's problems lay in its drifting away from the divine path of Islam, the adoption of the corrupt ways of either the East or West, and its disunity. To solve their problems, Muslims had to return to Islam and divisions had to be overcome to achieve unity.[8] To this end, Khomeini called upon Muslims to rely on Islamic culture, resist Western influence, and be independent.[9] The export of the revolution required the breaking down of Persian-Arab barriers, for which the notion of Islamic unity was an important instrument. It was based on the idea that all Muslims share a set of basic convictions as well as face the same enemy—namely the 'militarily, economically and culturally expansive West, which threatens the political independence and cultural and religious identity of the Islamic world'.[10] As such, the revolution was publicly characterized as being neither Iranian nor Shiite, but rather Islamic and universal; Khomeini did not advertise the fact that the associates of the Islamic revolution abroad were generally Shiite figures connected to the Iranian clergy.[11]

The means by which the revolution should be exported were not clearly specified. The Iranian constitution had several stipulations on spreading the revolution. The armed forces of the Islamic Republic were instructed not only to guard the borders, but also to follow the new ideology and fight for expanding 'the divine sovereignty in the world'. The government had the duty to formulate its foreign policy according to Islamic values and fraternity with all Muslims.[12] Overall, it is clear that the Islamic Republic recognized the importance of communication in spreading its revolutionary message. As Khomeini stated in 1980, 'the greatest means by which the revolution can succeed here and be exported is *tablighat* [propagation, communication, and proselytization], in its proper form.' It has been explained that *tabligh* means 'propaga-

---

[7] Former Iranian cultural attaché to Damascus, Hoseyn Shafi'i, 'Al-mustashariya al-thaqafiya al-iraniya bi-dimashq khilala rub'a qarn' [The Iranian cultural chancellery in Damascus during a quarter century] in *al-thaqafa al-islamiya*, 100, 2006, p. 98.
[8] Shireen Hunter, *Iran and the World, Continuity in a Revolutionary Decade*, Bloomington: Indiana University Press, 1990, p. 40.
[9] Marschall, *Iran's Persian Gulf Policy*, p.12.
[10] Wilfried Buchta, 'The Failed Pan-Islamic Program of the Islamic Republic: Views of the Liberal Reformers of the Religious "Semi-Opposition"', in *Iran and the Surrounding World, Interactions in Culture and Cultural Politics*, Nikki Keddie and Rudi Matthee (eds), Seattle: University of Washington Press, 2002, p. 283.
[11] Djalili, *Diplomatie islamique*, pp. 63–66.
[12] Ibid, p. 64.

tion', but that 'its Islamic connotation derives from the word *balagha*, meaning "to reach", "to get", or "to affect", [and] also means "proselytizing".'[13] The Islamic Propagation Organization (*sazman-e tablighat-e eslami*) was set up in 1981 to promote the teaching of Islam, enhance people's Islamic knowledge, coordinate public propagation activities and explain the Islamic revolution.[14]

Khomeini allegedly told a group of diplomats who had been recalled to Tehran for consultation:

> It does not take swords to export this ideology. The export of ideas by force is no export. We shall have exported Islam only when we have helped Islam and Islamic ethics grow in those countries. This is your responsibility and it is a task which you must fulfil. You should promote this idea by adopting a conduct conducive to the propagation of Islam and by publishing the necessary publications in your countries of assignment. This is a must. You must have publications. You must publish journals. Such journals should be promotive and their contents and pictures should be consistent with the Islamic Republic, so that by proper publicity campaigns you may pave the way for the spread of Islam in those areas.[15]

Iran's cultural politics in the first revolutionary decade showed many characteristics of the concept of soft power. Recognizing the importance of culture and values, trying to set an example and introducing one's culture abroad, are all components of soft power. However, soft power and cultural diplomacy depend on legitimacy and how policies are perceived. The Islamic Republic's revolutionary propaganda in the early years was not successful in winning over followers. As long as Iran was still calling for an export of its revolution, regional neighbours in particular were extremely wary of Iran's intentions.

On the institutional level, Iran's cultural movement in the first revolutionary decade lacked coherence and central organization. While the department of international affairs of the ministry of culture and higher education was theoretically responsible for conducting bilateral cultural relations with foreign countries, following the revolution a rising number of Iranian institutions and public organizations started to develop cultural activities abroad. These included established institutions such as branches of ministries that were reorganized under the new administration, as well as newly formed bodies such as the Islamic Propagation Organization. These institutions acted independently from each other, and with an increase in numbers, Iran's cultural movement

---

[13] Farhang Rajaee, 'Iranian Ideology and Worldview: The Cultural Export of the Revolution' in *The Iranian Revolution, Its Global Impact*, John Esposito (ed.), Miami: Florida International University Press, 1990, p. 72.
[14] www.iranculture.org/en/nahad/tabligh.php (accessed on 09 May 2008).
[15] As quoted by Rouhollah Ramazani, 'Khumayni's Islam in Iran's Foreign Policy', in *Islam in Foreign Policy*, Adeed Dawisha (ed.), Cambridge: Cambridge University Press, 1983, p. 19.

abroad soon became fragmented. As there was no centralized policy or directive, every institution managed its activities at will. Money did not seem to be difficult to obtain; according to a senior cultural official, the government at the beginning of the revolution allocated budgets for revolutionary propaganda to all ministries.[16] Efforts mainly targeted Muslim communities, and aimed at spreading the principles of the revolution.

The ministry of culture and Islamic guidance evolved throughout this period by integrating several ministries. In March 1978, the ministry of culture and higher education was formed by merging the ministry of culture and art with the ministry of science and higher education. In May 1979, the ministry of information and tourism was renamed ministry of national guidance, which was in turn renamed ministry of Islamic guidance in 1980, acquiring a more religious character at a time when the factions around Khomeini secured their positions. A number of the departments of the ministry of culture and higher education were subsequently integrated into this ministry, until it was renamed the ministry of culture and Islamic guidance in March 1987.[17]

By the time of the death of Imam Khomeini in 1989, in particular after it had become clear during the course of the Iran-Iraq war that most Arab countries were more interested in Arab than Islamic unity, the revolutionary zeal of the early period had ebbed away. The drive for disseminating revolutionary propaganda transformed over time into a more subtle and organized effort to introduce Iran's culture and values abroad. To reassure Iran's regional neighbours, Ali Khameneh'i proclaimed the end of an active revolutionary export as part of Iran's policy, which President Ali Akbar Hashemi Rafsanjani confirmed.[18]

Iran's Cultural Diplomacy: The Islamic Culture and Relations Organization

While the Islamic Republic's foreign cultural policy in the first revolutionary decade was largely marked by its efforts to export the revolution, in the 1990s Iran started to build up its cultural diplomacy. In October 1990, Khomeini's successor as Supreme Leader, Ali Khameneh'i, founded two associations in Tehran: the World Assembly for the Rapprochement between the Islamic Schools of Thought (*al-majma' al-'alami l-il-taqrib bayn al-madhahib*, short: *Taqrib* Assembly) and the World Assembly of the *Ahl al-Bayt* (*al-majma' al-'alami l-il-ahl al-bayt*, short: *Ahl al-Bayt* Assembly).

---

[16] Interview with ICRO official, Tehran, 22/04/2006. For an idea about one aspect of Iran's cultural policies abroad in the first revolutionary decade, see Rajaee, 'Iranian Ideology and Worldview'.

[17] www.iranculture.org/en/nahad/ershad.php (accessed on 09 May 2008). For a discussion of the power struggles at the beginning of the revolution, see Nikki Keddie, *Modern Iran, Roots and Results of Revolution*, New Haven: Yale University Press, 2003, Chapter 10.

[18] Wilfried Buchta, *Die iranische Schia und die islamische Einheit 1979–1996*, Hamburg: Deutsches Orient-Institut, 1997, pp. 246f.

Iran's Cultural Diplomacy 211

Coming out of the 'World Conference on the *ahl al-bayt*' held in Tehran in April 1990, the idea behind the two associations was to foster unity between the Islamic schools of thought on the one hand, and on the other hand solidarity between Shiite communities.[19]

To have an integrated cultural policy, the Islamic Republic on the initiative of a group of cultural personalities set up the Islamic Culture and Relations Organization (*sazman-e ertebatat va farhang-e eslami*, short: ICRO) in 1995, by merging the main institutions engaged in Iran's cultural movement. The latter included the international affairs departments of the ministry of culture and Islamic guidance and the Islamic Propagation Organization, the *Taqrib* Assembly, the *Ahl al-Bayt* Assembly, and the Council for the Dissemination of the Persian Language and Literature (*shura-ye gostaresh-e zaban va adabiyat-e farsi*). While the *Taqrib* Assembly, the *Ahl al-Bayt* Assembly, and the Council for the Dissemination of the Persian Language and Literature were to preserve their own identity independent of the ICRO, their activities abroad were henceforth to be conducted through the ICRO.[20]

Having been approved by the Supreme Leader, the ICRO had the sole responsibility of coordinating Iran's cultural foreign policies. It was established as an independent organization affiliated to the ministry of culture and Islamic guidance, under the ultimate guidance of the Supreme Leader, and to work in cooperation with the foreign ministry. A higher council (*shura-ye 'ali*)—to include three cultural figures selected by the Supreme Leader, as well as the foreign minister, the head of Iran's national broadcasting organization (*sazman-e seda va sima-ye jomhuri-ye eslami-ye Iran*), the directors of the above-mentioned institutions, and a representative of the foreign affairs office of the Leader—was to oversee its policies under the leadership of the minister of culture and Islamic guidance.[21]

The ICRO's mission was to introduce the foundations of the Islamic revolution and the ideas of Imam Khomeini, in particular in the Islamic world, realizing Islamic unity by strengthening cultural relations among Muslim states. According to its constitution, Islamic thought and learning should be revived and spread in the world with the objective of 'awakening Muslims and communicating the message of the true Islam to the inhabitants of the world'. The ICRO was to strengthen and organize the cultural facilities of the Islamic Republic abroad, and to present Iran's culture and civilization. One goal was to spread the Persian language and its literature. Strengthening a sense of national and cultural identity amongst Iranians living abroad was another concern. The school of the *ahl al-bayt*—the Shiite school of thought that is—was to be introduced as the 'school of glory and perfection' (*madrasat al-'azza wa al-kamal*). Promoting and reforming the cultural, political, economic, and social situation of Muslims in the world—especially the fol-

---

[19] For more on both associations, see ibid., pp. 245 ff.
[20] Constitution of the ICRO (dated 21 November 1995), Article 7.
[21] Ibid, Articles 1 and 10.

lowers of the *ahl al-bayt*—was another goal.[22] Looking at the ICRO's objectives, one can clearly discern a focus on Islam in the direction of Iran's cultural diplomacy.

The ICRO, as the main organ supervising the Islamic Republic's cultural foreign policy, was from now on in charge of directing the content and reach of Iran's cultural diplomacy. It coordinated Iran's bilateral cultural programmes with foreign countries, provided the necessary background information for setting up cultural agreements and treaties, undertook and supported research in Islamic and Iranian studies, interacted with cultural and religious personalities and institutions in foreign countries, sought to increase Persian language teaching and strengthen chairs of Persian language at universities, organized cultural festivals and exhibitions, and was to be active in the field of writing, translating and distributing books and publications with the object of introducing Islamic and Iranian science, philosophy, culture and civilization.

The ICRO publishes over twenty journals in different languages inside Iran, to be distributed in the representations outside Iran; and over thirty of its cultural centres abroad have their own publications. This is clearly in line with Khomeini's urge to Iranian diplomats to encourage publications. The constitution also specified that the ICRO was to help establish and support the activities of *howzeh*s (Shiite religious schools) and universities outside Iran. Moreover, the ICRO was to establish and administer Iran's cultural representations abroad and appoint cultural and propaganda representatives, whose duties it supervised.[23]

The ICRO's work aimed at co-opting people rather than coercing them. Its activities were in line with the main goals of cultural diplomacy, namely increasing familiarity, increasing appreciation, engaging people and influencing people's behaviour. The guidelines for Iran's cultural policies and programmes were set by the organization's head office in Tehran. The Iranian public was informed about its policies by the ICRO's department for public relations and conferences, which also interacted with the media to hold news conferences, the idea being that having an informed domestic public opinion helps towards maintaining a unified picture to the outside. In practice, it is highly questionable to what extent the public followed the ICRO's policies.

Whilst no figures regarding the organization's budget are available, it does not seem to lack funds to organize and implement its cultural policies abroad. The ICRO's budget has several sources. The government allocates yearly budgets from the public treasury for the organization and each country in which the ICRO is active. Additional sources include income raised by cul-

---

[22] Ibid, Article 2; www.icro.ir; 'adawa' 'ala rabitat al-thaqafa wa al-'alaqat al-islamiya fi iran' (Lights on the Islamic Culture and Relations Organization) in *al-thaqafa al-islamiya* 89, p. 153; Shafi'i, 'Al-mustashariya al-thaqafiya al-iraniya bi-dimashq khilala rub'a qarn', p. 98; Interview with ICRO official, Tehran, 23 September 2008.

[23] 'adawa' 'ala rabitat al-thaqafa wa al-'alaqat al-islamiya fi iran, p. 154; Constitution of the ICRO, Article 3c.

Iran's Cultural Diplomacy 213

tural activities carried out by the ICRO in foreign countries, and assistance from people and places of religious legal funds. The remaining income's sources have to be approved by the higher council of the ICRO.[24]

Looking at the headlines published on the news section of the ICRO website, one can discern in what kind of activities the ICRO is actually involved. These include participating in cultural events abroad ('Iran participated in 90th anniversary of Baku National Museum', 'India Holding Shahnameh Exhibition', 'al-Hoda publication to attend Qatar Book Fair), being active in the field of translation ('Imam Sajjad's Treaties on Rights Translated into Italian'), promoting Iran's and Islamic culture abroad ('Iran commemorates Hafez in Berlin', 'Muharram Workshop to be Held in Zambia' by the Iranian cultural centre in Senegal, '"Self-purification and Islamic Education" Conference to Be Held in Belgium', 'French Shias to Mourn Martyrdom of Imam Hussein', 'Iranian Cultural Week opens in UAE', 'Festival of "Religion, Culture" to be held in Germany'), strengthening bilateral cultural relations ('Iranian, Turkish children's friendship festival opens in Istanbul', 'Tehran hosting Syrian cultural festival', 'Iran, Russia ink cultural MOU'), and organizing Islamic events at home ('Most exclusive wooden Quran unveiled', '2nd Meeting on Imam Musa Sadr Studies Planned in Tehran'). The news section also mentions items such as 'Wahhabism; reviewed from within', a book review of a recent ICRO publication in Moscow that assesses Wahhabism – 'the book is meant to reveal who is really damaging the Muslim society'.[25]

Iranian Cultural Centres

Iranian cultural centres abroad (*rayzani-ye farhangi-e jomhuri-ye eslami-ye Iran*) actively implement the official policies by promoting the Islamic Republic's ideas and values, building up relationships and teaching Persian language and literature. The ICRO set up these cultural centres across the world, in particular in countries with a Muslim majority or large Iranian expatriate community. In case the ministry of culture and Islamic guidance had established a centre somewhere prior to 1995, the ICRO took over responsibility for it. These centres, of which there exist around seventy worldwide, are formally attached to the Iranian embassy or consulate in each country. However, they have separate budgets administered by the ICRO, and refer back to the ICRO in Iran rather than the foreign ministry.[26] The ICRO plans to expand the number of cultural centres abroad to one hundred within the next three years, with a particular focus on Latin America and Africa. More than ten are to be set up in Latin America where Iran currently does not have any centre, and the number of cultural centres in Africa is to double from twelve

---

[24] Constitution of the ICRO, Article 8.
[25] www.en.icro.ir (events between 28 November 2010 and 8 December 2010).
[26] Interview with Ali Ansarian, Director of the Iranian cultural centre, Damascus, 19 April 2008.

to twenty-four, with some other centres added in regions were Iran already has a cultural presence.[27]

Cultural councillors (*rayzan-e farhangi*), as the directors of the cultural centres are called, are appointed through the ICRO. They often have an academic background or constitute a cultural figure in Iran; they can but do not necessarily come from inside the organization. Other than the directors, the centres generally employ a cultural attaché, a public relations officer, an IT manager, and a librarian, depending on the size of the centre. Employees are both sent from Iran and hired locally.[28] The centres' staff is subordinated to the Supreme Leader's office or his representatives rather than the ambassadors.

The Leader's representatives—usually clerics—are positioned in every important state ministry and institution, and in revolutionary organizations, amounting to a total of around 2,000 according to Wilfried Buchta. In terms of foreign relations, they ultimately supervise the work of the Iranian cultural centres and Islamic organizations. Their main function is to enforce the authority of the Supreme Leader, being more powerful than other government functionaries and even ministers, having the authority to intervene in any matter of state.[29] Political scientist Asghar Schirazi explains:

> The Representatives of the Imam are one of the most important institutions of supervision and propaganda. They act as a kind of extended arm of the leader in all chief educational, administrative and security agencies and other state institutions, and use their considerable power to intervene in the running of those organizations.[30]

In many cases, they were appointed by Khomeini himself and remained after his death to represent Khameneh'i.[31] As the Supreme Leader is ultimately responsible for Iran's cultural work abroad, the presidency does not have a great impact on the content of cultural diplomacy.

The means by which the cultural centres abroad try to accomplish their aims are manifold. Activities consist of exhibitions (of books, Koranic calligraphy, photographs, handicrafts), organizing cultural weeks, conferences and seminars, teaching Persian language and literature, cooperating with intellec-

---

[27] 'Afzayesh-e te'dad-e rayzaniha-ye farhangi-ye kharej az keshvar az 70 rayzani beh 100 rayzani', 9 December 2010, www.icro.ir. The number of countries in which there are cultural centres is lower than 70 as Iran has several cultural centres in some countries (such as India and Pakistan). Interview with ICRO official, Tehran 19 April 2006.
[28] Interviews with ICRO officials, Damascus April 2008 and Tehran September 2008, Constitution of the ICRO – employment regulations.
[29] Wilfried Buchta, *Who Rules Iran? The Structure of Power in the Islamic Republic*, Washington DC: Washington Institute for Near East Policy and Konrad Adenauer Stiftung, 2000, pp.47–49.
[30] Asghar Schirazi, *The Constitution of Iran. Politics and the State in the Islamic Republic*, London: I.B. Tauris, 1998, p. 154.
[31] Ibid, p. 74.

tuals and cultural institutions of the host country, and organizing events for Iranian residents abroad. The cultural centres in non-Islamic countries moreover aim to introduce the principles of Islamic thought through a programme of 'dialogue between religions'.[32] In the following, we will consider two case studies of Iranian cultural diplomacy. Looking at the work of cultural centres in selected countries in the Middle East (Syria, Lebanon and Tunisia) as well as Europe (France and the United Kingdom) will contribute to our understanding of how Iranian cultural diplomacy works in practice.

Iranian Cultural Diplomacy in the Middle East

While Iranian cultural diplomacy has a large focus on the Islamic world, its reach in the Middle East has been limited. As Djalili pointed out in 2007, one hurdle for developing deeper relations between Iran and Arab countries is the view Iranians and Arabs have of each other. Drawing on political scientist Hamid Enayat, he argues that although one would have expected good relations between the peoples due to geographic proximity, a shared religion and a mutual contribution to Islamic civilization, relations are in fact dominated by suspicions of the other side's intentions. The historical tensions between Iranians and Arabs did not disappear following the Islamic revolution in Iran.[33] Especially during the early period, governments in neighbouring countries were troubled by Iran's revolution and worried about what impact it might have on their own Islamic—and in particular Shiite—communities.

From the outset, Iran's cultural diplomacy in the Middle East was thus most dynamic in countries with which Tehran maintained good political relations. The Islamic Republic's most prolific cultural centre is in Damascus, where Iran organizes seminars and conferences, cultural weeks, book exhibitions, cinema weeks, and teaches Persian, against the background of the strong diplomatic relationship between Syria and Iran. The ICRO regards its work in Syria as exemplary, and often cites Syrian-Iranian cultural relations as a model for Arab-Iranian cultural exchange. Tehran maintains a large cultural centre in Damascus, and in 2006 opened a dependency thereof in the Syrian coastal city of Latakia.

The centre in Damascus, opened in 1983, is situated in the centre of the city and consists of several departments. It has two libraries, its own bookshop, a publishing department, one for cultural activities in Syrian provinces, a public relations department and a women's department. It used to run its own journal for over two decades, *al-thaqafa al-islamiya* (Islamic culture), which it stopped in early 2006 when the ICRO Damascus website (www.damascus.icro.ir) started to play a more active role. Now several cultural publications can be found online. Persian language teaching is one of its most important activities. Iran has also been involved in setting up depart-

---

[32] 'Adawa' 'ala rabitat al-thaqafa wa al-'alaqat al-islamiya fi iran', pp.155–63.
[33] Mohammad-Reza Djalili, 'La politique arabe de l'Iran', *A contrario*, 5(2), 2007, pp. 145–46.

ments of Persian language and literature at Syrian universities. Iran finds an audience in Syria, albeit to a large extent one that is already sympathetic to its ideas. It also reaches out to those who have an interest in cooperating with Iran due to professional circumstances. Iran's cultural diplomacy in Syria has to be understood within the context of the Syrian-Iranian alliance—the Islamic Republic is able to undertake activities in Syria due to the close political relationship between Tehran and Damascus.[34]

In Lebanon—a country that has much stronger historical cultural links to Iran than Syria has[35]—the ICRO is less active, as Lebanese-Iranian relations take place more on a popular than on a state level. While less dynamic than in neighbouring Damascus, the Iranian cultural centre in Beirut is nevertheless one of the biggest of the ICRO. The centre in Beirut was established in the early 1980s, and officially opened by then Minister of Culture and Islamic Guidance Mohammad Khatami on a trip to the region; he opened the centre in Damascus during the same trip.[36] The centre is located in the south of Beirut, an area dominated by Lebanese Shiites. According to the Iranian foreign ministry, one of the important activities of the Iranian cultural centre in Lebanon was the organization of conferences and festivals on different occasions such as Islamic holidays, Jerusalem Day,[37] and the anniversary of the Islamic revolution. Something with a particular reach in Lebanon was the implementation of different programmes during the month of Muharram, when on the anniversary of the martyrdom of Imam Hoseyn religious processions were organized for *sinehzani* and *zanjirzani* (flagellation processions to mourn for Imam Hoseyn). The foreign ministry regarded the participation of Lebanese Shiites in these processions as a symbol of religious, emotional, and cultural links between the peoples of the two countries following the Islamic revolution.[38]

Roschanak Shaery-Eisenlohr has analysed the work of the Iranian cultural centre in Lebanon. She argues that the centre's work aims to underline a sense of shared and continuous history with Lebanon's Shiites. Therefore most of the centre's activities

---

[34] For a detailed account of Iranian cultural diplomacy in Syria, see Nadia von Maltzahn, 'The Case of Iranian Cultural Diplomacy in Syria', *Middle East Journal of Culture and Communication*, 2, 2009, pp. 33–50. See also Jubin Goodarzi's contribution in this volume.
[35] See H. E. Chehabi (ed.) *Distant Relations: Iran and Lebanon in the Last 500 Years*, London: I.B.Tauris, 2006.
[36] Interview with Mohammad Hoseyn Hashemi, Director General, Artistic and Cultural Cooperations Department at the ICRO, former cultural attaché at the Iranian cultural centre in Damascus, and former director of the centre in Beirut, Tehran, 22 April 2006.
[37] Khomeini declared the last Friday of the month of Ramadan as Jerusalem Day, and called on all Muslims to celebrate this day to remind people of the occupation and the importance of the city for Muslims.
[38] *Lobnan [beh sefaresh-e] daftar-e motale'at-e siyasi va beyn el-melali*, new edition/4, Tehran: Foreign Ministry, 1995.

are organized around two main themes: the propagation of a narrative of Iranian-Lebanese Shi'ite history that justifies Iran's current official presence in Lebanon and the dissemination of the idea that Iran stands at the centre of Islamic civilization, and has contributed to its flourishing at least as much as have Arabs.[39]

The organization of seminars on Islamic occasions, and of activities during the month of Muharram, ties in with the propagation of these two themes. Unlike in pre-revolutionary cultural relations, the Islamic Republic emphasizes Shiite religious ties between Iran and Lebanon in its cultural diplomacy work, in line with the ICRO's mission to strengthen bonds between the followers of the *ahl al-bayt*. The re-opening of the Centre for Persian Language at the Lebanese University—created in 1956 but closed for more than two decades due to the civil war—by the Iranian cultural centre in 1999 was a further indication of this trend. The centre apparently interpreted the teaching of Persian in Lebanon as 'yet another example of long-standing Iranian-Lebanese Shi'ite relations', taking a particular interest in 'proving the specific Shi'ite connection between Iran and Lebanese Shi'ites through linguistic research'.[40] Shaery-Eisenlohr mentions another planned project: the establishment of several cultural centres for Shiites throughout Lebanon, instigated by Lebanese Shiite Islamists, funded by the *ahl al-bayt* Assembly and negotiated through the Iranian cultural centre in Beirut. These centres were to contribute to the empowerment of the Shiite community on a national level.[41] It is not clear what came of the proposed project.

While the ICRO is more present in countries with which it maintains good political relations, it also tries to establish a cultural presence in countries with which Iran maintains diplomatic ties but with which relations are less strong. In Tunisia for instance, an Iranian cultural section is maintained through the Iranian embassy. While it is not a *rayzani-ye farhangi* but rather a cultural section of the embassy (*al-qism al-thaqafi*), the centre in Tunis has existed in an independent building since 2007—until then it was physically integrated into the embassy. The current cultural attaché had previously worked for fifteen years at the *Taqrib* Assembly in Tehran, and then at the ICRO headquarters in Tehran, where he was director of the department for Islamic studies until he was sent to Tunis in 2007.

The Iranian cultural section offers Persian language classes, teaches calligraphy, and organizes joint events with Tunisian cultural institutions such as the *Dar al-thaqafa Ibn Khaldun*. Tunisian universities offer no Persian language teaching, with the exception of Zeitouna University—an Islamic university attached to the Zeitouna Mosque. The centre has a library with books about religion, Iranian civilization, and the revolution, as well as one book-

---

[39] Roschanak Shaery-Eisenlohr, *Shi'ite Lebanon. Transnational Religion and the Making of National Identities*, New York: Columbia University Press, 2008, p. 161.
[40] Ibid, p. 166.
[41] Ibid, pp. 183–85.

shelf of Iranian films and music. According to the Tunisian employee at the centre, the library is frequented by Tunisian intellectuals. It was empty when I visited.[42] While it is unclear to what extent Iranian cultural diplomacy manages to reach out to the Tunisian population, the fact that the Iranian cultural embassy maintains a cultural section in an independent building to conduct its cultural activities shows that Iran does not miss an opportunity to try to spread its ideas and values, as far as bilateral relations allow them to. Ironically, the Iranian cultural section in Tunis is situated in King Abd al-Aziz Al Saud Street, close to a mosque called after the Al Saud – both Saudia Arabia and the Islamic Republic are competing for hearts and minds in the Islamic world.

Iranian cultural diplomacy in the Middle East largely focuses on reaching out to Muslims, by promoting Shiism or emphasizing Islamic unity in countries with no Shiite communities. Its dialogue centres on Islamic issues, although concepts such as anti-Zionism and anti-Imperialism also feature. Even where Iran's cultural diplomacy attempts have a limited audience, Tehran's anti-Israeli and anti-American discourse is popular with the public in Arab countries. Ahmadinejad for instance is regarded as someone who has the courage to speak up to the United States.[43] In Europe, Iranian cultural diplomacy focuses largely on Iran's own nationals abroad as well as European Muslims before reaching out to Europeans more broadly. This will become clear by looking at the work of the Iranian cultural centres in Paris and London.

Iranian Cultural Diplomacy in Europe

The Iranian cultural centre in Paris gives priority to providing services to its own nationals before reaching out to the French public. It considers itself as an 'Iranian house' and strives first of all to become a place where Iranian residents in France can come and go, and wants to make them feel as though they are in a house in their own country. The second objective is to become a place to visit for those French who are interested in Iran and its culture. Strengthening a sense of cultural identity amongst Iranians living abroad is one of the aims of the ICRO, and the cultural centre in Paris has made this one of its main concerns since it was set up in 1998.[44]

Situated in a beautiful *hôtel particulier* in the sixth arrondissement of Paris, the university quarter in the heart of the city, the Iranian cultural centre has tried to accomplish its goals through a number of initiatives. A programme is set every three months, and copies are sent to Iranians resident in France. The

---

[42] www.tunis.icro.ir; Interview with Tunisian employee of the centre, Tunis, 6 November 2010; website of the Zeitouna University: www.uz.rnu.tn.
[43] Djalili, 'La politique arabe de l'Iran', p.136; Elaheh Rostami-Povey, *Iran's Influence*, London: Zed Books, 2010.
[44] All the information about the Iranian cultural centre in Paris is taken from its website (www.paris.icro.ir), both the Persian and the French version (accessed on 13 December 2010).

centre invites artists from Iran as well as Iranian artists resident in France to perform, and has set up a cinema club. One floor of the cultural house hosts a library and small room for research; the library comprises books in Persian, French, Arabic, and English about subjects such as history, art, Persian language and literature, tourism and geography, Islam and Shiism. The centre cooperates with other cultural centres in Paris and establishes relations with the municipalities. Amongst its activities are organizing academic conferences, conferences introducing Iran and tourism, cultural weeks, ceremonies for Islamic and Iranian festivities such as Ashura and Nowruz, Iranian cinema months, concerts of traditional Iranian music, and plays with theatre groups invited from Iran.

On its Persian website (www.paris.icro.ir) the Iranian centre provides services to Iranians such as listing Iranian companies and organizations in Paris, including Iranian doctors, airlines and travel agencies, businessmen, cultural organizations, Iranian restaurants, and more. The website also encourages people to call the centre and give feedback on how to improve their activities. In terms of courses for Iranians and non-Iranians, the centre teaches Persian, calligraphy and music classes—the latter focusing on Iranian instruments such as the Tar, Setar and Ney.

Iranian cultural diplomacy in France concentrates to a large extent on Iran's own nationals, as there is less of a market to promote Shiite and Islamic thought amongst the French. For the second group, Iran's cultural work has extended out in particular during umbrella events such as '*la semaine des cultures étrangères à Paris*' (the week of foreign cultures in Paris). During these weeks—organized by the *Forum des instituts culturels étrangers à Paris*, a federation of foreign cultural centres in Paris formed in 2002[45]—Parisians are encouraged to visit foreign cultural centres. During the weeks in 2004, for instance, all events put on by the Iranian cultural centre were attended by more people than the locations could host, with television screens showing events in neighbouring rooms. The event in 2010, a lecture by an Iranian researcher at the CNRS about the influences of the Persian language on Persian culture, followed by a poetry recital and tasting of Iranian food, seemed to have been equally well attended judging by photos taken at the occasion.

Similar to the Iranian cultural centre in Paris, the Iranian cultural centre in London has the responsibility to provide cultural services to Iranians resident in the United Kingdom.[46] Like France, the UK hosts a large Iranian expatriate community, which numbers several hundred thousands. The Iranian cultural centre organizes festivals for Iranians on different occasions, such as Nowruz. It moreover supports the establishment of Iranian associations and societies, and assists schools and organizations involved in Persian language teaching across the UK. Activities in the field of Persian language and literature are at

---

[45] www.ficep.info.
[46] All the information about the Iranian cultural centre in London is taken from its website (www.london.icro.ir), both the Persian and the English version (accessed: 13 December 2010).

the core of the Iranian cultural centre's mission. Another focal point is the wider Muslim community in the UK—together with Islamic centres and Islamic Studies' departments, the centre organizes joint fine arts and calligraphy exhibitions and seminars. The Iranian centre also participates in sending Koran reciters to various Islamic centres during the month of Ramadan.

In terms of introducing Iranian culture and values—and the Islamic revolution—to British society, the Iranian cultural centre in London cooperates with art and cultural centres across the UK. In partnership with universities and cultural centres it organizes events such as exhibitions (photography, arts, handicrafts), concerts, seminars and conferences as well as Iranian film festivals. The centre participates in international exhibitions such as the London Book Fair, Islam Expo and the International Tourism Exhibition, and takes part in the annual film festival in London. The Iranian cultural centre takes a special interest in Iranian Studies in the UK. It is in touch with those involved in Iranian and Islamic studies, and states as one of its aims sending students to Iran for further studies—something not always realized as the Islamic Republic does not easily grant study visas to British citizen.

Translating and printing works in the field of Persian modern literature is another stated objective of the Iranian cultural centre in London. The centre has recently started a new initiative to promote its values to those interested through an electronic fortnightly newsletter in English, emailed upon request. This newsletter, called ICN (Iran Cultural Newsletter), gives cultural and political news, speeches of the Supreme Leader and of the Islamic Republic's president, introduces new books in English, and gives details about seminars and cultural exhibitions taking place inside Iran.

Judging by the activities of the Iranian cultural centres in Paris and London, it can be argued that Iranian cultural diplomacy in Europe is largely directed towards Iranian residents, Muslim communities, and those interested in Islamic and Iranian studies. Introducing Iran's culture and values to Europeans more generally is most successful if working in cooperation with cultural institutions or as part of a wider cultural initiative such as the week of foreign cultures in Paris.

Iranian Cultural Diplomacy Confronting Twenty-First-Century Challenges

As the Islamic Republic struggles with internal tensions following the 2009 presidential election, the question arises to what extent Iranian cultural diplomacy is confronting twenty-first century challenges. Considering that the ICRO and its cultural diplomacy apparatus refer back to the Supreme Leader's office rather than the Iranian presidency, the content and direction of Iranian cultural diplomacy has not been affected as such by recent events. One of the main challenges of Iran's current foreign policy—the nuclear issue—does not come up in Iran's cultural work abroad. Where Iranian cultural diplomacy does face a challenge in the twenty-first century is how to win friends in an increasingly polarized environment.

The ICRO tries to tailor its cultural diplomacy activities to react to local characteristics, by studying to whom it can reach out in each region, finding points of commonalities—Iranian cultural diplomacy towards Southeast Asia for instance focuses on Islamic matters. In its regional policies towards its Eastern neighbours, Tehran attempts to strengthen its cultural reach by promoting the Persian language. As Djalili and Therme demonstrate, Iran, Tajikistan, and Afghanistan created a Persian-language Television channel as well as the 'Economic Council of the Persian-speaking Union' in 2008. Iran's cultural policies were not welcomed by all Afghanis, however—some were against Iranian attempts to homogenize the cultures of an ethnically diverse region.[47] In Europe, Iran reaches out to Iranians and Muslim communities in particular, and in the Middle East to Muslims, especially Shiites. The Islamic Republic's underlying goal of introducing an Islamic—and, if possible, more narrowly Shiite—message, limit its ability to build relationships on a larger scale, however. After all, *Islamic diplomacy*, the title chosen by Mohammad-Reza Djalili for his work on Khomeini's international strategy, may still be the more appropriate title for Iran's cultural diplomacy.

---

[47] Mohammad-Reza Djalili and Clément Therme, 'Le flanc Est de l'Iran: opportunités et vulnérabilités', *Politique étrangère*, No. 3, 2008, p. 6.

Chapter 13

'Dialogue' in the Foreign Policy of the Islamic Republic of Iran

Clément Therme

At the theoretical level, it is true that there is a close relationship between power and the dynamic of ideas in state behaviour.[1] Nevertheless, the case of President Mohammad Khatami's administration demonstrates that the correlation between discourse in public diplomacy and state action is, to say the least, only partially present. This disconnect must be understood through the structure of the political system of the Islamic Republic of Iran, which consecrates the Supreme Leader as the main decision maker regarding foreign policy issues. This made it impossible for a reformist president to implement his international agenda of *détente* and *rapprochement* with the West beyond the economic and cultural spheres. From a theoretical point of view, this failure is best explained by the effect of domestic and international factors on the decision-making process in foreign policy. Khatami chose to place more importance on domestic factors than on the international benefits that he would have gained with a genuine implementation of his *détente* agenda.[2] Consequently, the discourse of the president of Iran regarding dialogue and *détente* was more a change in rhetoric than in substance in Iranian foreign policy. The idea of dialogue was, at every moment, challenged by the confrontational foreign-policy discourse of the highest authorities of the Islamic state, notably the office of the Supreme Leader.

This idea of dialogue was also a means for the Iranian state to guarantee the survival of the Islamic revolutionary state in the context of a new international system dominated by the United States, in which it is no longer sufficient to rely on major powers such as China and Russia to avert regime change. The discourse of dialogue was a tool to open a dialogue with the West

---

[1] Shireen T. Hunter, *Iran's Foreign Policy in the Post-Soviet Era: Resisting the New International Order*, Santa Barbara: Praeger, 2010, p. xiv.
[2] Alex Minz and Karl DeRouen Jr., *Understanding Foreign Policy Decision Making*, Cambridge: Cambridge University Press, 2010, pp. 133–34.

"Dialogue" in the Foreign Policy 223

without altering the anti-Western nature of the Islamic revolutionary state. This international diplomatic campaign enabled the Islamic state to improve its image in the West. But the idea of dialogue of civilizations was not totally new, as claimed by some of Khatami's supporters. Indeed, this idea was introduced in Iran by the philosopher Dariush Shayegan in a book entitled 'Does the worldwide impact of Western thought make a true dialogue between civilizations possible?'.[3]

More generally, the idea of dialogue between cultures and/or religions has been recurrent in the Islamist discourse since 1979. It has been one of the key instruments of Islamic foreign policy during the last 33 years. After 1991, dialogue among civilizations became instrumental not only to integrate the Islamic Republic into the post-Cold War international context but also to defuse Western pressures against the Islamic Republic. This chapter first explores the historical background of the idea of dialogue among civilizations in the Iranian context. This is followed by an analysis of Iranian discourses regarding dialogue among civilizations during the presidency of Mohammad Khatami. Finally, the chapter introduces the idea of dialogue in the context of the rising factional divide between the reformist and the conservative factions during Ahmadinejad's presidency, with a particular focus on the religious dialogue between the Orthodox Church and the Shiite clergy.

The Idea of Dialogue of Civilizations in Iran: The Historical Background

According to Shayegan, the emergence of a research programme on dialogue of civilizations was initiated by Empress Farah Pahlavi through the creation of a research centre: the Iranian Centre for the Study of Civilizations (le Centre iranien pour l'étude des civilisations) in 1976–77.

> The Centre was founded in order to favour the dialogue between the main Asian great civilizations. Indeed, since the nineteenth century Iran has seen itself through the Western prism. To avoid a bilateral encounter, we chose to confront ourselves with the other Asian civilizations to analyze the common problems that we faced in the face of the West's assault and to determine if we had a common destiny. We wished to open branches of the Centre in India, in Japan (with the collaboration of Toshihiko Izutsu, the Japanese orientalist) and in Cairo. Finally, we published a collective book after an international conference that included, amongst others, Henry Corbin and Christian Jambet.[4]

---

[3] Centre iranien pour l'étude des civilisations, *L'impact planétaire de la pensée occidentale rend-il possible un dialogue réel entre les civilisations ?*, Paris: Berg International Editeurs, 1979.

[4] Dariush Shayegan, 'Présentation de M. Shayegan à l'ouverture du colloque le 20 octobre 1977' in Centre iranien pour l'étude des civilisations, *L'impact planétaire*, pp. 9–11.

Beyond the confrontation of the shared historical experiences of Asian civilizations, one of the main ideas that the Centre wanted to promote was to gauge the latest metamorphosis of Western thought. According to Shayegan, this was a necessary intellectual enterprise due to the inability of Iranian scholars to comprehend the metaphysical bases of Western intellectual domination which was, at this time, spread worldwide.[5] He pointed out that 'Westernization does not mean consciousness of Western thought; on the contrary, this is rather a passive and paralysing attitude towards its prodigious performances, the blinding amazement and the almost psychic inability to penetrate the spirit that enhanced dynamism.'[6] This Oriental difficulty to understand Western thought is due to the dialectic between dialogue and domination. Before the era of Western domination (sixteenth century), it was easier to organize a genuine dialogue between civilizations. The connection between Asian traditional civilizations and the West has always been through translation. In the context of the Shah's foreign policy, the research activities of the Centre were favoured by Empress Farah Pahlavi as part of her work to promote cultural activities inside Iran in the 1970s.[7]

Nevertheless, the Centre functioned for only two years (1977–1978), and its activities were interrupted by the Islamic revolution. The intellectual influence of the French philosopher Roger Garaudy was tremendous, given his innovative research activities regarding the topic of dialogue between civilizations which he said was designed in order to 'invent the future'.[8] To enable dialogue between civilizations, Garaudy insisted on the necessity of a 'cultural revolution' in the West.[9] This 'cultural revolution' entailed an increased study of non-Western civilizations, the need to put aesthetics in Western thought on an equal footing with the teaching of sciences and technics, and finally, the recognition that prospective thinking is not less essential than the study of history. As a result, from an educational point of view, the dialogue could not be avoided, particularly because of Westerners' unfamiliarity with non-Western civilizations.[10] Garaudy acknowledged the importance of his dialogue with Empress Farah Pahlavi and the philosopher Shayegan in his encounter with the meaning of Islam:

> From my point of view Islam is (…), in Iran, Farah Pahlavi, to whom I presented my project of 'dialogue of civilization' and who was the first who accepted to support me for carrying on this ideal; Dariush Shayegan, the poet philosopher who introduced me to the poetry of the Per-

---

[5] Dariush Shayegan, 'Transmutation et mutation en tant que phénomènes de rencontre dans le dialogue des civilisations' in Centre iranien pour l'étude des civilisations, *L'impact planétaire*, p. 356.
[6] Ibid., p. 367.
[7] Farah Pahlavi, *Mémoires*, Paris: XO Editions, 2003.
[8] Roger Garaudy, *Pour un dialogue des civilisations: L'Occident est un accident*, Paris: Denoël, 1977, p. 8.
[9] Ibid., p. 155.
[10] Ibid.

sian mystics from the eleventh century, to Rumi and Attar, to the romantic novels of Khosrow and Shirin by Nezami or Vis and Ramin by Gorgani.[11]

Indeed, Roger Garaudy's thinking is in line with the issues studied by the Institute of Philosophy which Farah Pahlavi chaired in the 1970s. The institute tried to address two key questions: what had the Persian civilization brought to the world? What could Iran still offer the world?[12] As early as the 1970s, the intellectual advocacy of the dialogue of civilizations was designed to tackle the issue of Western hegemony worldwide. As stated by Roger Garaudy, in the 1970s, there was a need to change the nature of the relationship between the West, on one side, and China, Africa, India, and Islam on the other; these relationships had to be grounded on a more equal basis. This theoretical framework seems to correspond to the diplomatic promotion of dialogue of civilizations during the Khatami's presidency in Iran (1997–2005). This similarity could seem paradoxical given the two regimes' different nature, but one has to consider that in 1976 the Shah and the Empress were at odds politically. At that time, Farah Pahlavi was surrounded by intellectuals critical of the imperial regime.[13]

Moreover, in 1977, Garaudy's dialogue of civilization was implemented in Iran through the political will of Farah Pahlavi and the academic research activities of Shayegan. The latter was significantly different in nature from Khatami's diplomatic enterprise.

Figure 1.1: Roger Garaudy and the Empress, Farah Pahlavi, in October 1977, during the opening of the *Institut Iranien pour le Dialogue des civilisations*, which was a continuation of the *Institut International pour le Dialogue des Civilisations*, launched by Garaudy at Neufchâtel in 1974.[14]

---

[11] Roger Garaudy, *Pour un dialogue des civilisations*, pp. 11–12.
[12] Farah Shahbanou d'Iran, *Mes Mille et Un Jours*, Paris: Stock, 1978, p. 104.
[13] Léon Zitrone, *Farah, une cruelle destinée*, Paris: Le Signe, 1979, p. 278.
[14] Available: http://rogergaraudy.blogspot.com/2010/08/images-dun-parcours-2.html (accessed 3 September 2011).

According to Shayegan, the Centre's budget was US$ 500,000 per year, compared to the US$ 4 million annual budget given to Khatami for his promotion of dialogue among civilizations. On top of the difference in budget, one of the main differences between the two projects is the Centre's focus in the 1970s on scholarly research for the study of civilizations compared to the broader political objectives of Khatami's enterprise.[15] It is also noteworthy that the political and diplomatic effectiveness of dialogue amongst cultures and/or civilizations was already in doubt in the 1970s. Ehsan Naraghi explored the reality of the diplomatic rhetoric in relation with 'dialogues' between the South and the North at UNESCO. He concluded by stating that 'all that is concrete has yet to become reality.'[16] One could draw a similar picture after analysing the effectiveness of the dialogue among civilizations promoted by Khatami on the international scene to tackle political issues at the beginning of the twenty-first century.

Indeed, since the presidencies of Ali Akbar Hashemi Rafsanjani and above all Mohammad Khatami, 'dialogue' has become one of the main pillars of Iranian revolutionary foreign policy. In the 1990s, the term *goft-o-gu*, which means both 'dialogue' and 'discourse', was widely used among academic quarterly titles published by Iranian intellectuals supporting the reformist movement.[17] It was also the main principle of the rhetorical change that characterized the discourse of Iranian public diplomacy during the Khatami presidency. Even the supporters of the reformist president acknowledged that the idea of dialogue of civilizations was not sufficient to address Iran's foreign policy concerns. Indeed, the philosophical nature of the project would not enable Iranian diplomacy to attain political objectives such as addressing historical grievances between Tehran and Washington, and solving political conflicts with the West, such as, for instance, the nuclear dossier and the Iranian-Hamas connection.[18] Ghoncheh Tazmini has pointed out the methodological hurdle that Khatami could not overcome in his attempt to implement his dialogue agenda, namely his inability to build a consensus inside the political elite to establish a dialogue with the West. He was not able to go beyond rhetoric in advocating his dialogue and *détente* foreign policy. In other words, 'substance needed to be added to the rhetoric' of dialogue of civilizations.[19]

---

[15] Personal interview with Dariush Shayegan, Tehran, 6 August 2008.
[16] Ehsan Naraghi, 'L'UNESCO et le dialogue des civilisations', in Centre iranien pour l'étude des civilisations, *L'impact planétaire*, p. 264.
[17] For instance: *Discourse. An Iranian Quarterly*, published by the Center for Scientific Research and Middle East Strategic Studies and *Goft-o-gu* (Dialogue) created, in 1993, by young Iranian intellectuals to promote a new thinking concerning political and intellectual issues inside Iranian society (the official website is available at: http://www.goftogu.net/?id=100 [accessed 3 September 2011]).
[18] Ghoncheh Tazmini, *Khatami's Iran: The Islamic Republic and the Turbulent Path to Reform*, London: I.B. Tauris, 2009, p. 92.
[19] Ibid., p. 93.

"Dialogue" in the Foreign Policy 227

Despites these limitations, the Iranian philosopher Dariush Shayegan and the reformist president Khatami in October 2009 received the Global Dialogue Prize, an award for research in the humanities.[20] The prize is awarded to persons 'excelling in research and knowledge presentation within the field of intercultural dialogue and the promotion of peaceful co-existence'.[21] In June 2011, Shayegan received the *médaille académique de l'Ordre de la Francophonie* in France for his long-standing intellectual contribution to French culture.[22] This intellectual success of his philosophical research regarding dialogue of cultures and civilizations will probably be a long-term achievement. By contrast, the political and diplomatic dimension of dialogue of civilizations seems to have been a short-lived concept in the field of international relations as well as among international institutions such as the United Nations.

Dialogue of Civilizations: The International Contribution of the Khatami Presidency

In 1998, the General Assembly of the United Nations declared 2001 the United Nations Year of Dialogue among Civilizations. According to Resolution 55/23 adopted in 2001, this acknowledgement

> will provide the opportunity to emphasize that globalization not only is an economic, financial, and technological process which could offer great benefit, but also constitutes a profoundly human challenge that invites us to embrace the independence of humankind and its rich cultural diversity.[23]

Khatami's initiative was implemented through the Islamic Conference Organization and more particularly the Tehran Declaration of December 1997 outlining the peaceful nature of the Islamic civilization and its ambition to 'dialogue' with 'representatives' of others civilizations.[24] Contemporary analysis of Khatami's discourse about dialogue of civilizations draws upon the

---

[20] Since Mohammad Khatami was 'not in a position to accept the prize', the Global Dialogue Prize 2009 was awarded to Dariush Shayegan alone. Available on the official website:
http://www.globaldialogueprize.org/page.php?idMenu=5&idSub=0&idMain=5 (accessed 3 September 2011).
[21] Available: http://www.au.dk/en/about/news/oldnews/2010/270110/ (accessed 3 September 2011).
[22] *Sharq*, 25 June 2011.
[23] Resolution 55/23, Resolution adopted by the General Assembly, 'United Nations Year of Dialogue among Civilizations', 11 January 2001, available: http://www.un.org/documents/r55-23.pdf (accessed 3 September 2011).
[24] 'Déclaration de Téhéran sur le dialogue des civilisations' in Le livre blanc sur le dialogue entre les civilisations, Rabat: Publications de l'Organisation islamique pour l'Education, les Sciences et la Culture, Deuxième édition, 2002, pp. 47–55.

theory of an emerging international public sphere or an international civil society as a renewal of international relations theories. Marc Lynch's theoretical approach was a valuable contribution to foreign policy in Middle Eastern states:

> Public deliberation can frame issues, articulate alternatives, interpret the meaning of policy of identity. In the absence of an effective public sphere, it seems plausible to assume that the state will enjoy a considerable degree of autonomy in the definition of the national interest, subject only to the constraint imposed by the fear of 'the street'. The more developed a public sphere, however, the more the state will be forced to articulate and justify its conception of the national interest against the counter-arguments of politically important forces.[25]

The Iranian case demonstrated, *a posteriori*, the validity of this outcome; in 2009, the emergence of an international public sphere contributed to the irruption of public discontent in the Iranian street. Indeed, the inability of the post-Khatami Islamic Republic to deal with public discontent inside the political system (*nezam*) reinforced the distance between the Islamist state and the public opinion. One of the main advantages of the discourse about the dialogue of civilizations was the ability of the Islamic Republic of Iran to address international criticism through dialogue. The rise of Ahmadinejad after 2005 deprived the Islamist state of the capacity to credibly respond to both international criticism and domestic discontent.

Furthermore, the discourse about dialogue of civilizations was, on the one hand, an opening of the Islamic Republic towards the outside world and, on the other hand, fully in line with the ideological tenets of the Islamic revolution. Khatami explained the rise of Islam and the decline of the West through the rhetoric of dialogue rather than open confrontation. This was the main innovative aspect of his foreign policy. Indeed, before his diplomatic success on the international level, he stated that:

> We wish to base our life on the tenets of Islam; we possess the will to create an Islamic civilization. At a time when modern civilization is going through its last days, or at least experiencing senility, we must ask, didn't Islamic civilization already emerge once and end centuries ago?[26]

His answer was 'no', and he added that 'while the old Islamic civilization has vanished, religion stands deeply rooted and can generate new civilizations'.[27] To fulfil the objective of a renewal of Islamic civilization, it was nec-

---

[25] Marc Lynch, State interests and Public Spheres: The International Politics of Jordan's Identity, New York: Columbia University Press, 1999, p. 21.
[26] Mohammad Khatami, *Hope and Challenge: The Iranian President Speaks*, Institute of Global Cultural Studies, New York: Binghamton University, 1997, pp. 9–10.
[27] Ibid., pp. 11–12.

"Dialogue" in the Foreign Policy 229

essary to find 'the proper way of confronting the West'.[28] According to the letter of Khatami's discourse, *dialogue* was a *means* to protect the Islamic renaissance rather than a *way* to reach an ideological reconciliation with the West. He considered the latter an impossible path given the existential challenge posed by the West—an enemy to the Islamic Republic.

Christian Minorities and the Discourse of Religious Dialogue

The integration of Iran's Armenian minority is one of Tehran's foreign policy tools, proof of the democratic and tolerant political nature of the Islamic Republic. This is very important to the Iranian government, which is often condemned by the United States and the European Union for its non-compliance with international standards on human rights. Iran's Armenian minority was down to 80,000 people by 2007 due to an increase in emigration since the turn of the twenty-first century, comparable to what occurred directly after the Islamic revolution.[29] However, the living conditions of Armenians in the Islamic Republic do not appear to account for most of the departures from Iran.[30] Rather, they are linked with the emigration campaign conducted by the Haiaz association, which since the start of the century has offered them the opportunity to emigrate to the United States via Austria for US$ 3,000. In fact, the Iranian authorities have often used the diplomatic alliance with Christian Armenia in connection with the policy of dialogue of civilizations promoted by Mohammad Khatami.[31]

This reformist diplomatic strategy is fully in accordance with traditional Khomeinist diplomacy. Since 1979, dialogue between Islam and Christianity has been one of the main tenets of the diplomacy of the Islamic Republic of Iran. Behind this recurrent idea advocated in the Iranian public diplomacy discourse of dialogue between religions, one can point out that the two major interventionist powers in Iran in the nineteenth century were Christian: the Russians and the British. As a result of these foreign interferences, an assimilation scheme emerged amongst the Iranian population: 'the Christians tend to identify with foreign Christians elements, which has placed them in the posi-

---

[28] Ibid.
[29] According to a representative of Tehran's Armenian community, the minority is divided between the cities of Tehran, 65–70,000, Isfahan, 5–6,000, and Tabriz, 2–3,000. Personal interview with an Armenian-Iranian citizen, Tehran, January 2008. According to the archbishop of the Armenians of Iran, they are 200,000 in number. However, this statistic is politically motivated, as the archbishopric wishes to preserve the seats of the two members who represent the community in the parliament. Finally, according to the Islamic Republic's own official figures, there are 150,000 Armenians in Iran.
[30] Anne-Sophie Vivier-Muresan, 'Communitarian Neighborhoods and Religious Minorities in Iran: A Comparative Analysis', *Iranian Studies*, 40(5), 2007, pp. 593–603.
[31] Clément Therme, 'The Irano-Armenian Alliance', *Journal of International and Strategic Studies*, 1, Spring 2008, p. 4.

tion of being both envied and hated by the majority Muslim population.'[32] In other words, there is an historical feeling of resentment towards Christians in general and Armenians in particular, due to the perceived favoured treatment that they received from the Imperialist powers to increase their influence on Iranian internal political and financial affairs. On a religious level, it is necessary to mention the Orthodox mission of 1897 in Urmia directed by Pope Victor Sinatsky to establish an Orthodox church. The presence in Western Persia of the new Orthodox Church was reinforced by the consular and military presence of the Russian in Azerbaijan after 1911.[33]

This feeling of resentment further intensified following Russia's proclamation of its policy to protect the Christians in Iran. This was compounded by the support of Christian minorities for the Kurds and the revolutionary Turks in Tabriz during the Soviet-sponsored autonomist governments in the northwestern provinces after World War II.[34] Given this hostile background, the historical significance of the start of a religious dialogue in 1997 between the Shiite clergy and the Orthodox Church should not be underestimated.

The idea of religious dialogue in Iran dates back more than fifty years with Ayatollah Hoseyn Borujerdi's initiative to establish a dialogue between Shiite clerics and the Sunnis, on the one hand, and between Shiite clerics and Christian churches on the other. Currently, Ayatollah Mohammad Ali Taskhiri, the head of the Islamic Culture and Communications Organization (*Sazman-e farhang va ertebat-e eslami*),[35] is one of the main personalities in charge of religious dialogue in the Islamic Republic. Before 2009, Mohammad-Ali Abtahi was also part of many initiatives for dialogue as the Director of the Center for Dialogue between Religions.[36]

From Mohammad Khatami's point of view, theological dialogues are not always relevant. Indeed, they are often a way to demonstrate one's religious positions as the only truth, rather than constituting a genuine dialogue.[37] Officially, the objectives of the meeting between, for instance, representatives of the Vatican and those of the Islamic Republic are the following: to enhance a 'comprehensive mutual understanding' and to compel the different parties to 'reciprocal esteem'.[38] More generally, in 1991, in his speech to the ambassa-

---

[32] Richard Merril Schwartz, 'The structure of Christian-Muslim relations in contemporary Iran', *Occasional papers in Anthropology*, No. 13, Halifax/Nova Scotia: Saint Mary's University, 1985, p. 24.
[33] Florence Hellot-Bellier, 'Les chrétiens d'Iran au XIXe siècle (1800–1918): une page se tourne' in *Chrétiens en terre d'Iran: implantation et acculturation, Studia Iranica*, Cahier 33, Paris: Association pour l'avancement des études iraniennes, 2006, p. 96.
[34] Schwartz, 'The structure of Christian-Muslim relations', p. 106.
[35] Available: http://www.icro.ir/ (accessed 3 September 2011).
[36] Personal website of Mohammad-Ali Abtahi, available:
http://www.webneveshteha.com/en/about.asp (accessed 3 September 2011).
[37] According to Amir Hoseyn Mehdizadeh, Administrative head, International Institute for Dialogue among Cultures and Civilisations, Tehran, 9 August 2008.
[38] Declaration of Mohammad Masjed, Ambassador of the Islamic Republic of Iran at the Vatican, speech during the conference 'Dialogue between Islam and Christianity',

"Dialogue" in the Foreign Policy 231

dor of the Islamic Republic, Pope John Paul II expressed his conviction that 'today and tomorrow, religions have a major role in preserving peace and in building a society respectful of human dignity.'[39] He also expressed his hope that diplomatic ties between the Vatican and the Islamic Republic would be reinforced to achieve a better mutual understanding and increased collaboration.[40]

In 1999, Pope John Paul II met the Iranian President Mohammad Khatami in his private library in the Vatican. Viewed from Iran, this encounter was entirely compatible with the Islamic revolution's ambition to introduce the Islamic Republic worldwide as the defender of monotheism, ethics, and morality.[41]

As seen by a senior Iranian diplomat,

> The fall of the ex-Soviet and Eastern European regimes suddenly provoked the emergence of the Orthodox churches of these countries. The Church was a part of the historical and societal reality of these countries kept under silence during the last decades. The emergence of the Church was welcomed by the educated population and the nationalists, unsatisfied with Western interferences in their internal affairs.

He stated the need for increasing cooperation between Islam and Christianity to face the contemporary challenges to 'religious, moral, and familial values', and stressed the efficiency of cooperation between the Islamic Republic and the Vatican state in this regard.[42]

The intention of the representatives of the Islamic Republic to increase religious cooperation with the Russian Orthodox Church can also be explained by Tehran's diplomatic objective to reinforce the political entente between post-Soviet Russia and Iran. More generally, theological and cultural dialogues are a diplomatic method used by the Islamic political elite to project a tolerant image worldwide, and they are an occasion to denounce the Western demonization of the Islamic Republic.

Khartoum, 1996 quoted in 'Dialogue entre l'islam et le Christianisme: Imaginations et Réalités', *Le message de l'Islam*, No. 140, Tehran: Fondation de la pensée islamique, July 1996, p. 27.

[39] 'A l'ambassadeur de la République islamique d'Iran', Rome, 20 June1991 quoted in Conseil Pontifical pour le Dialogue Interreligieux, *Le dialogue interreligieux dans l'enseignement officiel de l'Église catholique du Concile de Vatican II à Jean-Paul II (1963–2005)*, Documents rassemblés par Francesco Gioia, Solesmes: Editions de Solesmes, 2006, p. 591.

[40] Declaration of Mohammad Masjed, p. 592 (see endnote 38 for full reference).

[41] James A. Bill, John Alden Williams, *Roman Catholics and Shi'i Muslims: Prayer, Passion, and Politics*, Chapel Hill, NC: The University of North California Press, 2002, p. 1.

[42] Declaration of Mohammad Masjed, p. 30. (See endnote 38 for full reference).

The Significance of Bilateral Cultural Dialogue between Iran and Russia

Iranian entente has also been a way for Moscow to appear as an independent power on the international scene, while also providing a tool to build a multipolar world. Both Iran and Russia are against Western-style democracy and Western human rights policies. They opposed US policy in favour of democratization in the former Soviet republics, the so-called Russian near abroad, and have refused, for different reasons, NATO expansion eastwards. For Russia, NATO policy is based on a strategic rationale and Moscow is reluctant to see American influence in the post-Soviet space. Although the Russian media did not hesitate to advance ideas such as 'NATO expansion targeting revolutionary Islam', Russian officials seemed reluctant to adopt such an ideological rhetoric.[43] On the other hand, Iran's attitude towards NATO expansion seems more motivated by ideological factors such as anti-Americanism than by strategic reasons. Nevertheless, opposition to NATO and more broadly to Western influence in the post-Soviet regions is a key pillar in the regional *entente* between Moscow and Tehran.

Both countries have decided to discuss cultural and religious issues in a bilateral way within the framework of diplomatic cultural cooperation, and have advocated cultural diversity as well as cultural and religious dialogue.[44] They insist on shared cultural values such as the importance of family, ethics, and education. They consider their dialogue as a joint cultural response to globalization and as means of confronting Western globalized cultural hegemony.[45] They also underline the necessity of dialogue among civilizations in a postmodern world.

This view is criticized by the French philosopher Régis Debray, who strongly condemns the academic view of dialogue among civilizations which sees it as a political necessity 'to oppose the monologue of empire' and as an alternative paradigm for international relations.[46] On the contrary, Debray perceives the dialogue of civilizations discourse of the European governments as a means to 'label religious many problems that are political [and] which have to be treated through political means'.[47] Elie Barnavi, a writer and former Israeli ambassador to France, considers that the dialogue of civilizations is an 'invention' to promote a debate between the societies respecting *laïcité*

---

[43] According to Izvestia, quoted in 'L'expansion de l'OTAN vise l'Islam révolutionnaire', *Le message de l'Islam*, No. 143, Tehran: Fondation de la pensée islamique, October 1996, p. 22.

[44] Mehdi Sana'i, 'Neshast-e goruh-e goft-o-gu-ye rahbordi Rusieh–jahan-e eslam', *Faslnameh-ye motale'at-e asiya'i-ye Qafqaz*, 54, 1385/summer 2006, pp. 226–30.

[45] Ibid., p. 229.

[46] For an overview of this view, for instance, Michális S. Michael and Fabio Petito, 'Imperial Monologue or Civilizational Dialogue?', in *Civilizational Dialogue and World Order: The Other Politics of Cultures, Religions, and Civilizations in International Relations*, New York: Palgrave Macmillan, 2009, p. 4.

[47] Régis Debray, *Un mythe contemporain: le dialogue des civilisations*, Paris: CNRS Editions, 2007, p. 14.

(the French version of secularism) – in other words, liberty – and those that do not understand the meaning of *laïcité*. He further categorizes these civilizational dialogues as hypocritical and irrelevant, given the absence of representativeness of those who claim to speak for the civilizations.[48] In Khatami's view, civilizations means the main monotheist religions.

Finally, in their meetings, the political elite of the Islamic Republic and Russia have expressed their disaffection with the hegemony of Western culture and unilateralism, going so far as to express their beliefs in conspiracy theories. In one of the meetings, the Iranian vice-minister for cultural affairs explained that 11 September 2001 was a cinematographic construction in which there were no aeroplanes but bombs. From his point of view, these events were used by the Americans to launch a new crusade in the form of war between religions.[49] The objective of countering Western cultural hegemony and plots against non-Western nations has been anchored in the Islamist political psyche, and this has been the case in Russia as well, although to a lesser degree. The ideological dimension to the diplomatic relationship is used with more flexibility in Moscow than in Tehran, and as a result, the Islamic Republic's authorities are more constrained by their ideological commitments toward an alliance with Moscow than Russian decision-makers are to Tehran. The latter also appear far more pragmatic in the implementation of their foreign policy objectives than Khomeini's successors.[50]

Finally, there is also the religious factor: the leadership in Moscow considers its relationship with Tehran to be a useful tool for improving its negative image in the Muslim world, brought about by the Chechen wars.[51] This strategy also includes Moscow's participation in the Organization of the Islamic Conference (OIC), which Russia joined as an observer in 2005. To further this policy, Moscow has chosen to open a religious dialogue between the Orthodox Church and the Shiite clergy. In 1997, a joint Russo-Iranian commission was put in place, meeting on a rotating basis in Tehran and Moscow. According to the Russian Patriarch Alexei II, the main objective of the commission is to define areas of agreement, such as opposition to 'values of secularization imposed from the outside in contradiction to religious values.'[52] As in the case of Russia's observer status in the OIC, the bilateral religious commission is also a means for Moscow to show its openness and good-will for

---

[48] In particular chapter 'Contre le "dialogue des civilisations"' in Elie Barnavi, *Les religions meurtrières*, Paris: Flammarion, 2006, pp. 135–39.
[49] Sana'i, 'Neshast-e goruh-e goft-o-gu', p. 221.
[50] The revolutionary dimension of Iranian foreign policy is highlighted by Saïd Amir Arjomand in *After Khomeini: Iran Under His Successors*, Oxford: Oxford University Press, 2009.
[51] Alexei Malashenko, 'The Islam Factor in Russia Foreign Policy', *Russia in Global Affairs*, 3, July-September 2007.
[52] Declaration of Alexei II in the course of a December 2005 visit to Moscow by the president of the Iranian parliament, Gholam-Ali Haddad-Adel; the last meeting of the committee was from 27 February to 4 March 2006 in Tehran with the theme 'eschatology from the point of view of Orthodoxy and Islam'.

dialogue with the Muslim world, with which its relations have been complicated by the Chechnya wars. From the Islamic Republic of Iran's point of view, these dialogues allow its diplomacy to go beyond the traditional Islamic sphere of influence and show that the Shiite clerics are theologically open to other monotheist religions. The representative of the Shiite clerics chosen by the Iranian authorities and the representative of the Russian orthodox clergy defend the superiority of moral values over the rights and freedom of human beings:

> The history of mankind shows that the destruction of moral foundations engenders a crisis of the individual and society, hostility and inner emptiness. Therefore, it is our duty to assert moral values, the foundations for which have been provided by the Creator, by way of education, the mass media, and the manifestation of believers' civil position.[53]

During the sixth session of the Joint Russian-Iranian Commission for the Islam-Orthodoxy Dialogue, which took place in Moscow in July 2008, the head of the Iranian delegation, Ayatollah Akbar Rashidi, pointed out that 'the world was quickly moving closer to spirituality and religion' after 400 years of attempts to exclude religion from the public life.[54] Thus, these dialogues are a means to underline not only the peaceful dimension of the message delivered by the traditional religions but also the dangers linked to the modernization process—by which Russian and Iranian official discourses mean Westernization most of the time.

The fear of a velvet revolution and what Moscow perceives as Western democratization in the post-Soviet region is the main ideological framework at work in the Moscow-Tehran connection.[55] Nevertheless, as in the case of Iranian-Syrian cultural cooperation,[56] state-to-state cultural activities have not had much of a mass impact—as shown by the spontaneous expression of anti-Russian feelings after the contested re-election of Mahmoud Ahmadinejad. Unsurprisingly, Iranian authorities accused a 'cultural NATO' of being involved in the post-June 2009 election popular protests, qualified by the Iranian state media, as a 'velvet revolution' (*enqelab-e makhmali*) and as a 'soft

---

[53] Final document of the sixth session of the joint Russian-Iranian commission for the Islam-Orthodoxy dialogue, Moscow, 17 July 2008 quoted in 'Russia Orthodox, Iranian Muslim clergy agree on need to assert moral values', *Interfax*, 17 July 2008.
[54] Ibid.
[55] During the Georgian crisis of August 2008, the Chief of Staff of Iran's Armed Forces, Hasan Firuzabadi, called Mikheil Saakashvili 'a product of an American velvet revolution', quoted by Jalil Roshandel in 'That tiny war: Iran, Russia and the Middle East', *Bitterlemons International*, Edition 35, Vol. 6, 4 September 2008.
[56] On this topic, Nadia von Maltzahn, 'The Case of Iranian Cultural Diplomacy in Syria', *Middle East Journal of Culture and Communication*, 2, 2009, pp. 33–50. See also her contribution to this volume.

war' (*jang-e narm*) of Western enemies against Islam.[57] Indeed, the Islamic political elite believe that since the fall of the Soviet Union the Islamic Republic has faced a double threat: military (the presence of NATO forces close to Iranian territory) and cultural/ideological. According to Tehran, the latter, coming from Western powers, is concerned with spreading Western values in the Islamic world.[58] This rhetoric used by the followers of the Supreme Leader, Ali Khameneh'i, and President Ahmadinejad is articulated along the lines of the intellectual discourse of clash/dialogue of civilizations.

Dialogue: A Reformist/Conservative Divide?

Cultural encounters between Tehran and non-Western powers such as Russia are not linked to the change of power in the Islamic Republic. Whether the reformists or the conservatives are in charge does not make any difference regarding their common objective of promoting the creation of an ideological alternative to the West. What changed in Iran after the rise of Ahmadinejad is the path chosen to confront the West: Khatami's administration preferred dialogue and Ahmadinejad aggressiveness. After 2005, this new orientation of Iranian foreign policy was based on the conviction that dialogue means weakness and that aggressiveness will prove to the West that Iran is strong. Finally, one should point out that the intellectual dimension of President Khatami contrasts strongly with the authoritarian behaviour of Ahmadinejad and his populist rhetoric. Khatami's quoted Hafez concerning the origin of conflict and war to the effect that they stem from ignorance of the truth: 'Excuse the war of the seventy-two sects, for they, having failed to see the truth, went astray.'[59] It would seem that Ahmadinejad's diplomatic posture does not consider Hafez's philosophy.

Paradoxically, despite the rise of Ahmadinejad in Iranian politics after 2005, the dialogue discourse was still a propaganda tool of the Islamic Republic as defined in the official discourse as a monotheist nation. Ahmadinejad's definition of dialogue between cultures and/or religions is clearly designed to prove to the non-Western world—in particular to the non-aligned movement—that Iran is a tolerant Islamic state demonized by the West. Nevertheless, his policy has failed in contrast to the success of the reformist intellectual enterprise on the international scene. After the end of the second Khatami administration, the former president created a non-governmental organization called the *International Institute for Dialogue among Cultures and Civiliza-*

---

[57] Declaration of Morteza Saffari, Commander of the Marine Force of the Sepah-e Pasdaran, about the creation of a 'cultural NATO', *E'temad*, 9 September 2009.
[58] Abdal Sadr Hidraf, 'Negaresh-e Iran beh gostaresh-e nato', *Faslnameh –ye motale'at-e asiya'i-ye Qafqaz*, 59, 1386/Fall 2007.
[59] Hafez quoted by Mohammad Khatami, 'Symposium: Islam, Iran and the Dialogue of Civilisations', *Global Dialogue*, 3(1), Winter 2001, p. 3.

tions which was launched in 2006.[60] But, as early as of 2008, the Institute was confronted with budgetary hurdles: the difficulties of fundraising in the face of cuts to public resources. The Institute refused foreign funding and its director, Mohammad Khatami, could not reconcile his own moral values with accepting the financial contribution of the Supreme Leader or other leading political figures of the Islamic Republic.[61]

According to the reformists, the Ahmadinejad administration used the rhetoric of dialogue of cultures without genuinely believing in dialogue. According to this view, it was merely rhetoric without any political will to enhance dialogue in Iranian foreign policy. The main difference with Khatami was that he truly believed that dialogue should be one of the main pillars of his political action. In 1997, a member of the Khatami administration, Mohammad-Javad Faridzadeh,[62] a former ambassador to the Vatican, was the first to propose the concept of dialogue of civilizations to President Khatami. At this time, the main objectives were (1) to enhance cooperation with European countries after the Mykonos crisis;[63] (2) to insist on the philosophical meaning of the word 'dialogue' in a discussion forum distinct from a forum in which states only express their interests; (3) to choose dialogue as the main tenet of the diplomatic strategy of the ministry of foreign affairs; (4) to increase mutual knowledge and deconstruct the *clichés* between the West and Muslim countries; (5) to improve economic cooperation with Western countries; (6) to diminish the number of enemies of the Islamic Republic and the military threat against Iran.[64]

In terms of diplomatic achievements, the strategy of civilizational dialogue promoted by the Khatami administration was more successful in defending Iran's national interest than Ahmadinejad's confrontational diplomacy. Indeed, even if the change in reformist strategy was limited in scope and in substance, one has to consider that after the end of the first term of Ahmadinejad's presidency (2009), the *détente* and dialogue agenda was more in line with the popular aspirations of a majority of Iranian public opinion. It was the failure of Khatami to implement his international agenda of reconciliation with the West that provoked the loss of credibility of the reformist faction from the point of view of his early supporters. In this political disarray, the role of the dialogue of civilizations was not significant except that it demonstrated the growing disconnect between the priorities of public opinion, such

---

[60] This private Institute has a branch in Geneva, the Foundation for dialogue among civilizations. Available on the official website: http://www.dialoguefoundation.org/ (accessed 3 September 2011).
[61] Personal interview with Amir Hoseyn Mehdizadeh, Administrative head, International Institute for Dialogue among Cultures and Civilizations, Tehran, 9 August 2008.
[62] For instance, this discourse of Javad Faridzadeh, available: http://www.unesco.org/dialogue/en/farid.htm (accessed 3 September 2011).
[63] When Lebanese terrorists linked to the Islamic Republic killed a number of Iranian oppositionists in Berlin in 1992.
[64] Personal interview with Amir Hoseyn Mehdizadeh.

as improving the economic situation, and the intellectual debates promoted by the reformist politicians on the international stage.

Conclusion

Engaging the West through dialogue was one of the key tenets of the public discourse of the Islamic Republic of Iran during the presidency of Mohammad Khatami (1997–2005). Engaging the Muslim world was then one of the main objectives of Barack Obama's administration (after 2009).[65] *Dialogue*, as a key priority of the US administration vis-à-vis the Muslim world, cannot be directly compared with the vision of *dialogue* defended by the leaders of the Islamic Republic. Even if dialogue is often the least bad option to solve international quarrels, one has to consider the irrelevancy of many of these 'dialogue discourses' when it comes to solving political issues such as the Israeli-Palestinian conflict, the Hezbollah question, or the terrorist activities of al-Qaeda and the Iranian nuclear issue.

In 2000 Mohammad Reza Djalili explained that, as far as the image of the Islamic Republic in international public opinion was concerned, one of the main diplomatic cards used by Khatami was his discourse on dialogue among civilizations.[66] He criticized this new diplomatic discourse of the Islamic Republic:

> To speak about dialogue of civilizations—confusing religion and civilization, as Huntington did—signifies choosing a fragmented world, abandoning the idea of a universal modern world, and forgetting the fact that most of the world's population lives between traditional culture, disappearing almost everywhere, and an unfinished modern world.[67]

Nevertheless, Djalili acknowledged that Khatami's discourse on dialogue of civilizations constituted progress compared to the confrontational discourse and the aggressive diplomatic line implemented by Khomeini.[68] In line with Djalili's opinion, Juan Cole explained that one of the main differences between advocacy of dialogue in the United States and in Iran is the role of religion. Cole further criticized the role of clerics and politicians from both sides in the escalation of tensions and anxiety between Muslim and Westerners:

> I have watched with dismay as the rhetoric about Islam and Muslims has become more strident, and as misinformation and disinformation have proliferated. Clerical leaders on both sides have stoked the fire.

---

[65] Juan Cole, *Engaging the Muslim World*, New York: Palgrave MacMillan, 2009, pp. 237–47.
[66] Mohammad-Reza Djalili, *Iran: l'illusion réformiste*, Paris: Presses de Sciences Po, 2001, p. 70.
[67] Ibid., p. 71.
[68] Ibid., p. 72.

> Pope Benedict XVI held Islam up as an example of religious fanaticism and intolerance, and Ayatollah Ali Khameneh'i, the Iranian theocrat, calls down imprecations on the West nearly every day. Secular politicians have also poured oil on the fire, whether former New York mayor Rudy Giuliani with his insistence on tying the religion of Islam to "terrorism," or Iranian president Mahmoud Ahmadinejad, complaining endlessly of what he calls Western "decadence" and its allegedly pernicious influence on Iranian youth.[69]

This description of the relationship between the West and Islam after September 11th is accurate and relevant. Indeed, ignorance on both sides has fuelled anger regarding Muslims in the West and resentment towards Westerners in the Islamic worlds. But, is dialogue a viable way to solve these anxieties and tensions? This article argued that dialogue as defined by the Iranian revolutionary political elite is first and foremost a means to *not* address political and ideological differences with the Western democracies' international agenda. Rather, as demonstrated by the religious dialogues between the Orthodox Church and the Shiite clergy, there is an attempt led by Iran to define an alternative ideological model to what they call the 'Western international order'. Until now, this attempt has failed—notably due to the unattractiveness of the Russian and Iranian political/cultural models worldwide. At the end of the day, even the rise of China is not likely to reverse the lack of success of Iran's efforts.

---

[69] Juan Cole, *Engaging the Muslim World*, p. 2.

Chapter 14

France and Iran:
Between Tensions and 'Critical Dialogue'

Denis Bauchard

In the past, the relations between France and Iran were not very significant. The French were fascinated by Persian civilization and interested in the fields of culture and archaeology, but France was not involved in the political game, especially in the so-called Great Game. It is only in the middle of the twentieth century, at the beginning of the 1960s, that France became more present in Iran, both politically and economically. I will focus on three significant periods of time before outlining the main orientations of France's current policy.

Three Turning Points

Active Cooperation: 1974–79
During the presidency of Valéry Giscard d'Estaing, France had very active relations with Iran, which became a 'special partner' after the 1973 oil crisis. In October 1974, Hushang Ansari, the Iranian finance minister, visited Paris and delivered three messages to his French counterpart, Jean-Pierre Fourcade: (1) the increase of oil price must be accepted by Western countries; (2) the Iranian government was aware that this sudden and dramatic increase had provoked serious problems for the French economy, but it was ready to help during this transitional period; (3) a dialogue had to be established, and a link fixed between the price of oil and the price of equipment needed by Iran. He stressed the nuclear ambitions of the Shah, who had just created the Iranian Organization for Atomic Energy. The objective of this body was to promote nuclear energy in the civilian field, but as early as 1975 the Shah did not exclude the possibility to switch to military applications: 'We are not contemplating acquiring nuclear weapons, but if others acquire this kind of weapons, Iran will be obliged to have some.'
In October 1975, President Giscard d'Estaing paid an official visit to Iran. Between 1974 and 1976, several important agreements were signed by Iran

and France: (1) Iran was to make a deposit of 1 US$ billion in an account at the Banque de France; (2) Iran was to obtain a 10 per cent share in the Eurodif project:[1] in return, it would receive 10 per cent of the production of enriched uranium; (3) Iran was to buy from Framatome five nuclear reactors of 1000 MW; (4) an agreement of nuclear cooperation was signed between the two countries. Iran, which had some difficulties in nuclear cooperation with the United States, considered France to be its main partner.

In January 1979, the Iranian prime minister, Shapur Bakhtiar, cancelled the agreements with Eurodif and Framatome for financial reasons. This decision was confirmed by the Islamic regime that took over in February, as it was not interested in nuclear cooperation. The financial dispute between the two governments was settled in October 1991, with Iran remaining a 10 per cent shareholder of Eurodif without receiving any further enriched uranium.

The 'Critical Dialogue' (1993–1998)

The dialogue between France and the Islamic Republic of Iran resumed after a long period of tensions. Diplomatic relations were broken between July 1987 and June 1988, at both European and bilateral levels.[2] The death of Ayatollah Khomeini in 1989 and the election of Ali Akbar Hashemi Rafsanjani as president in that same year provided an opportunity for an improvement of relations. This took the form of the so-called 'critical dialogue', which was initiated by France, Great Britain, and Germany on the occasion of the European Council meeting of December 1992. The objective was to make a political gesture, 'restore closer and confident relations', and develop economic relations. This dialogue, implemented at the level of the 'Troika', addressed different issues: (1) human rights and political prisoners; (2) the fatwa against Salman Rushdie who had been condemned to death by a fatwa pronounced by Ayatollah Khomeini in February 1989 with a reward of US$ 2.8 million; (3) cooperation in the field of terrorism; (4) political dialogue, especially on drug trafficking, Bosnia, Tajikistan, and Afghanistan. Some positive results were achieved, which contributed to easing the tensions between Europe and Iran. Concerning Rushdie, the Iranian government made a commitment not to implement the death sentence, but it rejected the idea of any written text.

Regarding French-Iranian relations, some bilateral visits took place, first at the level of high officials, then at the level of ministers. Ali Akbar Velayati met his French counterpart, Alain Juppé, in New York at the General Assembly session of the United Nations in autumn 1993. The first visit of a French minister to Tehran occurred only in 1997 with Hubert Védrine. The process culminated in the state visit of President Mohammad Khatami to

---

1 Eurodif is an international consortium led by France which built a plant which was in the 1970s the only one for enriched uranium outside the United States and the USSR.
2 For an analysis of Franco-Iranian relations in the years following the Iranian revolution see Mohammad-Reza Djalili, *Diplomatie islamique: stratégie internationale du Khomeynisme*, Paris: P.U.F., 1989, pp. 138–49.

France in 1999, which was quite positive, despite some sensitive protocol problems; Khatami returned to France in 2005, a few weeks before the end of his mandate. This dialogue yielded some positive results. On both sides there was a willingness to ease the tensions and even to cooperate on some issues. For example, a positive role was played by Iran to find a solution to the crisis brought about by the 'Grapes of Wrath' operation launched by Israel against Lebanon in 1996. Iran put some pressure on Hezbollah to convince it to accept the agreement which settled the crisis. A 'Surveillance committee', co-chaired by the United States and France, with the participation of Israeli, Lebanese and Syrian officials, was set up in order to defuse any incident in South Lebanon against Israel or its Lebanese allies. This agreement worked until the withdrawal of the Israeli armed forces in 2000. As far as economic relations were concerned, there was a strong increase of French exports to Iran: France became Iran's third or fourth supplier; Total developed its activities with the National Iranian Oil Company, and an agreement on the protection of French investments was signed.

New Tensions: 2007–2010
New tensions appeared in 2005 soon after the election of President Mahmoud Ahmadinejad—for obvious reasons. But the relations worsened dramatically in 2007 after Nicolas Sarkozy was elected president and immediately took a strong stand vis-à-vis Iran and its nuclear programme. The first reaction from Ahmadinejad was irony: he suggested that the freshly elected president had to learn his new job. But on 27 August 2007, President Sarkozy, at the yearly conference of the French ambassadors, underlined the choice between 'an Iranian bomb or bombing Iran'. On 16 September, the French minister of foreign affairs, Bernard Kouchner, was more specific, stating that the 'worst' had to be envisaged on the basis that an Iranian military programme is a threat for the whole world. Pleading for new sanctions, he demanded that French firms stop any new investment in Iran. The response, through the official Iranian press agency, was clear: 'we are determined to make a major revision of our relations with France, particularly in the economic and trade field'. The position of France was more and more criticized, and France more targeted than the United States, which in the meantime, especially after the election of President Barack Obama, was very cautious, proposing a genuine dialogue. France stood at the forefront of Western countries and became the main challenger against President Ahmadinejad and Iranian policies. The tensions grew regularly until 2008 when Nicolas Sarkozy decided to establish a naval base in Abu Dhabi, which Iran denounced as a threat against its security, and escalated further in June 2009, when he underlined the 'illegitimacy' of the re-election of Ahmadinejad. The following month, tensions increased again when a French student, Clotilde Reiss, was arrested, an act that was considered as a 'hostage-taking seizure' by the French president. Despite Clotilde Reiss's liberation several months later, relations continued to be very difficult. France took the lead in promoting not only UN sanctions through Security Council resolution

1929, but also strong European sanctions against Iran. Never since 1987 had such a climate of mistrust and tensions prevailed, due to a strong stand on the nuclear issue from the French side. But, on both sides, the declarations and sources of tensions had a personal dimension. Several factors played a role in the increase of tensions: the French approach to the nuclear issue, the personal conviction of President Sarkozy that there is an 'existential threat' against Israel, that harsh sanctions are absolutely necessary to avoid a military confrontation which could be disastrous for the region. In addition, the personal style of Nicolas Sarkozy upset the Iranian president. Obviously, the French position will not change and for the time being, no improvement is in sight: quite the opposite.

As we have seen, the French policy towards Iran was quite different during these three periods of time. Is there any main thread or *fil conducteur* in the French approach to Iran?

The Three Pillars of French Policy

The French approach towards Iran is based on three pillars:

Iran is a major country in a sensitive region of the world.
It is a major country because of the importance of its population—72 million inhabitants—with a sophisticated and educated people. It is a major country because of its geographical situation, at the crossroads of Central Asia, the Middle East and the Indian subcontinent, able to control the Persian Gulf and the Strait of Hormuz through which one third of the world oil trade is shipped. It has a strategic position and affirms its leadership as a regional power. Iran is also a major country because of its huge resources in oil and gas, with the second or third oil and gas proved reserves. It is an indispensable partner for the big oil companies. The economic potential of the country is quite impressive because of the quality of the manpower, the development of a middle class, and the richness in many natural resources: without the poor record in economic management, it could become an emerging power and could provide a large market for exporting countries.

Iran is presently a threat for Middle-Eastern countries, and even for the stability of the world.
Iran exports an aggressive and fundamentalist Islam and wants to be seen at the forefront of the fight against 'American and Israeli imperialism' and, more generally, against the Western world. Taking into account this situation, it manipulates the Shiite communities of the Arab world, especially in Lebanon and Iraq, and in the Gulf countries like Saudi Arabia and Bahrain. It supports militias such as Hezbollah, Hamas, and the Army of the Mahdi of Muqtada al-Sadr with financial resources and military equipment. Finally, Iran continues to export terrorism against the regime's opponents but also to supports terrorist groups which are acting against Israeli civilians or Jewish

interests. Its nuclear programme has a more obvious military objective: to build nuclear weaponry in the short term.

Iran is an unavoidable actor not only in the Middle East, but also outside this region.
(a) Iran is involved in many conflicts. In Afghanistan, Iran is interested in finding a solution in order to have a stable neighbouring country, to avoid a Taliban regime, and to protect Shiite communities. In Iraq its influence is obvious through different groups like the Sadrists, the Supreme Islamic Council, and the Dawa party: it supports a unified but weak Iraq and is strongly opposed to the independence of Iraqi Kurdistan. In Lebanon, Iran has historical and religious relations with the Shiite minority, which is more and more influential in the political life: traditionally Lebanese Shiite clerics have attended religious seminaries in Qom. The Islamic Republic is providing Hezbollah with financial resources, weapons, military training. In the Persian Gulf, Iran is active for many reasons: (1) presence of a large group of Iranians, especially in Dubai (about 400,000) and Shiite communities in Bahrain and in the Saudi Arabia's Eastern Province, (2) close historical relations with the Sultanate of Oman; (3) disputed islands with the United Arab Emirates; (4) control of the Strait of Hormuz. Dubai remains a hub for financial transactions and smuggling activities of goods that are not directly obtainable because of sanctions. In Gaza, Iran is actively supporting the Hamas government and other radical Palestinian groups such as the Islamic Jihad. The role of Iran was enhanced by the miscalculation of the Bush administration, which eliminated Iran's two worst enemies: Saddam Hussein's regime and the Taliban regime.

(b) Iran, despite its regime, remains a partner in the fight against drug trafficking and international mafias and gangs.

(c) The importance of its oil and gas reserves is making Iran a major supplier in energy, for Asian countries as for Europe.

France's Current Policy vis-à-vis Iran

The French strategy...
On the basis of these observations, France had until recently a strategy vis-à-vis Iran with three major objectives:

(1) Maintain the dialogue with the Islamic Republic of Iran and consider it as a regional power and a major partner, especially as an actor involved in the different crisis in the Middle-East. France was aware that the cooperation of Iran was needed to settle these crises.

(2) Preserve an economic presence in Iran through French companies with substantial interests (Peugeot, Renault, Total).

(3) Influence the Islamic Republic and facilitate its reintegration in the international community.

The idea of a global agreement ('grand bargain') was suggested on several occasions, notably in the report of the International Affairs Committee of the

French National Assembly. This deal could address the main issues at stake: nuclear programme, international sanctions, human rights, security agreements, WTO membership, cooperation on the Middle East crisis.[3]

....was drastically changed by President Sarkozy

This kind of deal seems more and more problematic, because of the radicalization of the regime after the presidential elections of 2009 and the rise of the Green Movement, and the hardening of France's already tough position. There is no doubt that the position of France is now focusing on the nuclear risk, with the belief that any cooperation with Iran is hopeless. The conclusion is that France is betting on the collapse of the regime, which is weakened by the Green Movement. From now on the objective is clearly a change of the regime. From the Iranian side, old disputes are recalled, like the choice of France to favour Iraq during the Iraqi-Iranian war and support the 'terrorist group', the Mojahedin-e-Khalq, which is hosted by France.

An assessment of French policy must take into consideration the fact that at the end of the day French economic and cultural interests are dangerously jeopardized in Iran because of an ineffectively aggressive position. Dialogue was replaced by confrontation without any concrete counterpart. Despite the sanctions which contribute to the economic difficulties, Iran's position on the nuclear programme remains unchanged. Obviously there are some serious tensions inside the regime, but the real danger for Ahmadinejad is not coming from the reformists but from other conservatives, led by Ali Larijani, the speaker of the Majles.

Conclusion

Relations between France and Iran are in a deadlock. This situation is quite the same for a number of France's partners, but France took the leadership in the nuclear dispute and was certainly the most active country in promoting tougher sanctions at the level of the United Nations and the European Union. As long as Ahmadinejad from one side, and President Sarkozy on the other side, will lead their respective countries, the climate of confrontation will go on, and perhaps worsen. But dialogue could possibly resume between the two countries and the two peoples, because it is in their interest to promote cooperation rather than confrontation. But, as so often in the Middle-East, no turning point is in sight for the moment.

---

[3] 'Rapport d'information', No. 1324., Commission des affaires étrangères de l'Assemblée Nationale. December 2008.

Chapter 15

Iran's Asian Strategy: The Importance of Economic Ties

Thierry Kellner

Since its founder passed away in 1989, the Islamic Republic of Iran has considerably reinforced its relations with numerous Asian countries. This phenomenon gathered momentum in the 1990s and 2000s under the presidencies of Ali Akbar Hashemi Rafsanjani and Mohammad Khatami before experiencing turbulence under the presidency of Mahmoud Ahmadinejad; yet the Asian dimension of Iranian foreign policy has not been called into question. Without overlooking its ties with other partners worldwide, Tehran puts a particular emphasis in its external relations on its political and economic connections with its Asian partners.

A Useful Reminder: Iran is an Asian Country

Even though it is often associated with the Middle East region alone, Iran is, geographically speaking, part of the Asian continent. Spreading out between the Caspian Sea and the Indian Ocean, the territory of Iran occupies the crossroads between Asia Minor, Central Asia, Southern Asia, and the Arabian Peninsula (Western Asia). Geography set aside, Iran also belongs to the Asian continent on account of its history. Indeed, over the long term, it has maintained intense political, economic, religious, and cultural relations with its neighbours in Asia Minor, Western Asia, Central Asia, the Indian subcontinent, the Caucasus, and the Persian Gulf, at times extending the reach of its foreign ties to Southeast Asia (Thailand), maritime Asia (the Malay and Indonesian sultanates), China, and Japan. Admittedly, the links with its close and more distant Asian neighbours have fluctuated throughout history. Thus, they shrank considerably in the nineteenth century, under the pressure and influence of the imperialist powers, mainly Great Britain and Russia. Yet, they were never completely severed and resumed at the first opportunity. In view of this long-term perspective, it could be argued that Iran has a natural propensity to foster relations with its Asian neighbours. Indeed, the development of Iran-Asia relations in the last decades owes a lot to this propensity.

Another factor complements this geo-historical perspective. The interest in Asian countries displayed by the Islamic Republic is not as new or original as it may seem at first glance. There was an 'Asian dimension' to Iran's external relations in the Pahlavi era, and when the Islamic Republic decided to resume or broaden its connections with Asian states, it could in fact rely on the existence of a whole series of ties established between Iran and some Asian countries under the former regime.

The Reasons Behind the Islamic Republic's Interest Toward Asia

As Mohsen Aminzadeh, former deputy minister of foreign affairs under Khatami, put it in an article published in December 2007, Iran is now 'more Asian than ever'.[1] What are the reasons behind the recent reinforcement of the relations between Iran and numerous Asian countries? Several explanatory factors can be put forward.

The first is related to the progressive rise of Asia on the world stage. In the economic realm, a large part of Asia has undergone a remarkable development since the 1970s–1980s, with a strong acceleration in the last years. Since 2001, this region alone secured approximately half of the global growth.[2] In this context, the emerging Asian countries are increasingly interested in the large countries of West Asia that constitute potential markets for their consumer goods. The existence of a market of over 70 million persons in Iran therefore has caught their attention. At the same time, they look after the raw materials and energy resources crucial to their economic development. In this area, too, Iran can offer attractive investment opportunities. Accordingly, their oil and gas interests have led them to pay a great deal of attention to the Iranian potential. This has materialized in the cases of Japan, China, India, South Korea, Pakistan, Malaysia, Indonesia, etc. From the opposite perspective, i.e., from Tehran's viewpoint, Asian countries offer very substantial markets for Iranian oil—which forms the basis of the Iranian economy—and gas. They also constitute potential investors in these sectors that should not be neglected. Furthermore, they are increasingly becoming suppliers of technologies, a role particularly important for Tehran, given its difficulties with the United States. Since the 1980s, Washington's policy of sanctions has significantly hampered the development of the hydrocarbons sector. Lastly, Asian countries offer outlets for other Iranian export products and potential investments. In the economic field, there are thus considerable common interests.

---

[1] Mohsen Aminzadeh, 'Iran, More Asian than ever',
www.irdiplomacy.ir, 2 December 2007. Available:
http://www.irdiplomacy.ir/en/news/31/bodyView/1128/0/Iran,.More.Asian.than.Ever.html (accessed 17 November 2011).
[2] 'The alternative engine. Asia and the world economy', *The Economist*, 19 October 2006.

In the political realm, the weight of Asia has also increased on the world stage in the last twenty years. This political rise, similar to the economic development of the region, constitutes a new dynamic in international relations that offers original and substantial opportunities to the Iranian diplomacy. Furthermore, the fall of the USSR opened up new Asian spaces as well as a new horizon to Iran's foreign policy, as Tehran could set up relationships with the new states resulting from the dissolution of the USSR in the Caucasus and in Central Asia. The existence of these states in itself has also opened up quite original possibilities to Tehran in its dealings with its other neighbouring Asian partners. In addition, intra-Asian relations have also grown denser, which contributes to the rapprochement between various Asian countries. In this context, it is quite natural that Iran intensified its relations with Asian countries, all the more because its connections with the West remained problematic as a result of the policy choices of the Iranian regime, notably its militant and continuous anti-Americanism. Mohammad-Reza Djalili has explained that Iranian political strategy with Asia forms part of the global response of Islamic foreign policy to Washington: 'the establishment of a Teheran–New Delhi–Beijing axis, with a possible extension to Moscow, would enable Iran to minimize its isolation and to gain support vis-à-vis the United States.'[3]

The Asian countries therefore offered Iran a natural counter-weight against the West. The Islamic Republic's foreign policy has been kept prisoner of its militant anti-Americanism for thirty years. After the end of the Iran-Iraq war, in the 1990s, the Iranian government tried to 'reset' its foreign policy to end its isolation and initiate the economic reconstruction the country greatly needed. Tehran outlined a rapprochement, notably with the European countries, so as to soften its isolation and use transatlantic divergences in its own interest. Yet, as it grew aware of the limitations of a policy that tried to play the European card against the United States, the Iranian regime increasingly looked east, although it never totally abandoned its European policy. The Iranian authorities paid particular attention to Asian countries in a logic of edging toward the West but also in a pan-Islamic strategy, with Malaysia or Indonesia as two cases in point.

Another political cause explaining the Iranian will to draw closer to Asian countries is the sanctions against Iran unilaterally imposed by the United States. These were first introduced in 1979/80, reinforced in the 1990s (*Iran and Libya sanctions act*, which turned into the *Iran sanctions act* in 2006), and then taken up by the UN Security Council beginning in 2006 in response to Iran's nuclear programme. Faced with American sanctions, Tehran naturally turned toward other European and Asian partners. In the context of the nuclear issue, as some European countries showed eagerness to put the sanctions into force, Tehran wished to soften the effects of these by getting closer to other partners. Once again, it was only natural that the Islamic regime

---

[3] Mohammad-Reza Djalili, 'L'Iran sur la scène internationale', *Questions internationales*, 25, May–June 2007, p. 39.

turned toward the less hostile Asian pole. Iran also sought support, both bilateral and multilateral, within the United Nations and the International Atomic Energy Agency in order to avoid becoming isolated in these institutions that deal with the question of its nuclear programme. There is therefore also a pragmatic dimension to Iran's policy vis-à-vis other Asian countries, which derives from its difficulties pertaining to the nuclear issue.

Another factor, of ideological nature, also justifies the renewal of Iran's interest for its Asian environment. Indeed, the main reproach formulated toward the Pahlavi regime by the Islamists in power in Tehran is its conservatism and its alliance with the West. This in part explains the new Iranian regime's policy which presented itself as revolutionary, opposed to the hegemonic powers—'Neither East nor West' was the most often heard slogan under Khomeini—in opposition to the West, favourable to non-alignment, and defender of the Muslims and 'oppressed peoples'. In this spirit, Iran progressively threw itself into the development and the reinforcement of its relations with the Asian states, mostly from the 1990s (under the slogan 'Both North and South' under Rafsanjani). The choice to lean more toward Asia also coincided with the historical opportunity presented to Iran by the crumbling of the Soviet Union and the attainment of independence of the three states in South Caucasus and the five republics in Central Asia, a situation which wreaked havoc on Iran's regional environment and brought in possibilities not seen since the nineteenth century. The dissolution of the USSR took place while Tehran's relations with its Gulf neighbours turned out to be disappointing, as these were increasingly tied to the United States. Iran then chose pragmatically to reorient its foreign policy towards less hostile partners, such as the republics of Central Asia and the Caucasus, Pakistan, India, Afghanistan, and China. Lastly, during the post-Cold war era, by denouncing the risks of an 'American hegemonism', by advocating 'multipolarity' in the international system, by initialling the 'dialogue of civilizations', and by denouncing American 'unilateralism' under the Bush administration, Iran found ideological common grounds with Asian countries such as China, Malaysia, and India, which further facilitated a rapprochement with Asian states.[4]

Lastly, the Iranian ambition to practise a foreign policy that would be global, multidirectional, and not solely anchored in a regional framework also explains in part its active implication in Asia. Tehran's immoderate objective of playing a role at the global level has a double origin. Firstly, this approach is articulated around a conjunction of various factors such as revolutionary internationalism, access to important financial resources in the wake of the rise in oil prices, and the reinforcement of its position in the Middle East after the toppling of Saddam Hussein and the Taliban. Secondly, the frenzied hunt for friends and allies is justified in the eyes of the Iranian stakeholders by a will to reach an international status that could lessen the isolation in which the Islamic regime finds itself.

---

[4] However, one can also adduce the counter-examples of Japan and Singapore, which do not find the Iranian disocurse regarding the United States attractive.

The Rapid Development of Irano-Asian Relations: A Few Milestones

In the restricted framework of this chapter, mapping the evolution of the relations between Iran and the Asian countries as a whole cannot be exhaustive. As early as the 1980s, in the aftermath of the Islamic revolution and in the difficult context of a conflict with Iraq that threatened the new regime, the Islamic Republic developed its relations with China and North Korea, notably to acquire arms. Pyongyang and Beijing rapidly became important suppliers to Tehran, which was much isolated on the world stage at that time. In the same way, the Islamic regime maintained the oil relations that had been already established under the Shah with South Korea, Taiwan, and Japan, despite the fact that they were close to Washington. With Japan, the Bandar Shapur joint petrochemical complex project that was underway was continued in spite of the regime change. This cooperation only ended because of military operations in the midst of the Iran-Iraq war. Japan pulled back and, due to the financial losses it suffered, abstained forthwith from investing directly in the Iranian hydrocarbons sector until the post-9/11 era. At that time, it regained interest in this field through the development of the Azadegan oil fields, a project eventually abandoned as a result of American pressure.

With India, even though economic relations began to develop, political relations in the Khomeini era did not yield any major results, as the Iranian regime's stances, favourable to Islamic causes (Muslims in India, Kashmir), annoyed New Delhi. Both countries also had a different analysis of Soviet policy in Afghanistan, while the proximity between India and Moscow constituted another obstacle to the further development of relations with Tehran.

In the 1990s, beginning with the death of Ruhollah Khomeini and the rise of Hashemi Rafsanjani, the Islamic Republic's foreign policy became more pragmatic and less ideological. Given the necessity of reconstructing and modernizing the country after the conflict with Iraq, Iran needed to end its international isolation and join the world economy. This orientation facilitated the establishment of political and especially economic relations with some countries in Asia. During the Rafsanjani presidency, Tehran deepened its ties with Beijing, including in the nuclear sector until 1997. With Japan, a close ally of the United States, relations remained more sensitive. No Japanese high-ranking official visited the Islamic Republic between 1991 and 1998. Economic relations were kept, but political contacts remained minimal until Khatami became president. The Islamic Republic also progressively got back in touch with its neighbours bordering the Indian Ocean, notably with India (visit of the Iranian minister of foreign affairs in 1992 and more importantly, the visit of the Indian prime minister in 1993, which constituted a turn in the bilateral relations; Rafsanjani also travelled to India in 1995), and to a lesser extent with Pakistan and Bangladesh. Tehran also reinforced its ties with the Muslim-majority countries of South-East Asia. The Sultanate of Brunei established official diplomatic relations with Tehran in 1990. Connections with Malaysia became closer; a situation shared by Indonesia after the visit of President Rafsanjani in 1994. Iran also developed relations with the non-Muslim states of the region, such as Thailand and Singapore. Among the new trends with regard to Asia that began during the Rafsanjani presidency, one can mention that bilateral political and economic ties were established with the newly independent republics of Central Asia and the Caucasus. The transformation of its regional environment in the north of its territory opened up the possibility for Iran to reaffirm its status of regional transit hub for inter-Asian (Persian Gulf/Indian Ocean toward Russia, Caucasus, Central Asia and the north-west of China) or Eurasian (north-west of China/Central Asia toward the Middle East of Europe) trade. Beginning in 1993, Tehran revived the Economic Cooperation Organization (ECO) so as to foster, in a multilateral framework, the development of ties with all of its close Asian neighbours, part of the Turko-Iranian oekumene. Besides Iran, the organization includes the five republics of Central Asia—Kazakhstan, Kyrgyzstan, Uzbekistan, Tajikistan, Turkmenistan—as well as Azerbaijan, Turkey, Pakistan, and Afghanistan. Based on foundations laid under Rafsanjani, Iran's Asian policy widened after the election in 1997 of Mohammad Khatami, whose 'reformist' orientation facilitated the strengthening of contacts with pro-West Asian countries such as Japan.

In the post-9/11 period, the trend toward the strengthening of political and economic Irano-Asian ties continued during Khatami's second presidential term. With the advent of the Ahmadinejad administration, however, Iran's new radical stances and the nuclear issue weighed heavily over these relations. Connections were kept, but at a lower level than the one they had been expected to reach based on the developments between 2001 and 2004. Numerous Asian states strictly applied the decisions adopted by the UN Security Council in the matter of the Iranian nuclear issue, i.e., sanctions. Yet, the door was kept open to relations with Tehran, notably in the economic field. That is why the economic and commercial relations between Iran and Asia in general were maintained even though they encountered some difficulties. With regards to political relations, visits, travels, and reciprocal exchanges of high-ranking officials were plentiful between 2001 and 2004. While these did not stop under the Ahmadinejad administration, they were reduced. The Iranian administration was diplomatically active under Ahmadinejad; in fact, 12 of his 19 official foreign trips in 2005–2006 took him to Asian countries: Saudi Arabia (OIC summit) in December 2005, Azerbaijan in December 2005, Syria in January 2006, Kuwait in February 2006, Malaysia in March and August 2006, Indonesia in May 2006, the summit of the Shanghai Cooperation Organization in June 2006, Turkmenistan and Tajikistan in July 2006, and Qatar in December 2006. During the year 2007, the Iranian president also threw himself into a series of new visits to the neighbouring Sunni-majority Arab countries, visits that were connected with the sectarian strife in Iraq. He visited Saudi Arabia in March 2007, the United Arab Emirates and Oman in May 2007. Mahmoud Ahmadinejad was also the first president of Iran to attend the summit of the Gulf Cooperation Council in Doha. Additionally, he visited Afghanistan, Azerbaijan and Turkmenistan in August 2007, Armenia in October 2007, Bahrain in November 2007, Iraq in March 2008, quickly stopped in Pakistan (first visit) and India in April 2008, and visited Sri Lanka in April

2008 as well as Turkey in August 2008. He maintained high-level contacts with Singapore and Thailand but here his radical stances produced some turbulence in bilateral relations. All these visits—and not all have been listed—provided international visibility of the Islamic regime and reduced its isolation, even though the results of Iran's Asian policy were not optimal, given that not all of Iran's Asian partners received the Iranian president.

In the economic sphere, generally speaking, the nuclear issue and the radical political leanings of Mahmoud Ahmadinejad have dampened the development of Irano-Asian relations. Though the volume of trade has not been hit—it has even kept on growing, mostly due to the rise of oil prices—the story is different for the development of investments in the strategic Iranian sector of hydrocarbons. In this sector, numerous officially announced projects have progressed very little, if at all. The project of an Iran/Pakistan/India gas pipeline, under discussion for two decades, has moved very slowly. India has remained reluctant to clearly commit herself and has finally withdrawn from the project. But this has not prevented Teheran and Islamabad from moving forward on a bilateral base. In spite of American pressures and instability in Baluchistan, a 25-year agreement for gas delivery was signed in June 2010. On the Iranian side the construction of the gas pipeline is nearly completed (800 km built out of the 960 km envisaged), but not on the Pakistani side.

In the projects concerning the exportation of Iranian liquefied natural gas (LNG) to Asian countries such as India, Malaysia, or China, progress has also been quite slow. For example, since 2004 Tehran and Bangkok have had discussions about possible LNG deliveries to Thailand. In 2006, the Thai company PTT signed a preliminary deal with Pars LNG Ltd—the joint-venture between Total, Petronas, and NIOC to develop the Phase 11 of the Pars field—to import annually 3 million tons of liquefied natural gas for twenty years, starting in 2011.[5] However, by 2008 there were such delays in the development of the Pars field that the Thai firm signed a contract with Qatargas in early 2008.

Although the Japanese are generally eager to maintain relations with Iran, given the uncertainties surrounding the nuclear issue and the new policy followed by Ahmadinejad, the Japanese company Inpex slowed down the work on the giant oil project of Azadegan. No significant progress was recorded between 2004 and 2006 in the development of the deposit, to the great displeasure, then to the irritation of Tehran. The deal signed between Tehran and Tokyo in February 2004 was finally reconsidered in October 2006. The Azadegan project with a Japanese stake did not become reality, which constitutes an important economic and political setback for Iran. It took a few years, until 2009, to see Beijing take the place of Tokyo and reach an agreement with Tehran to re-launch it. Other projects with China have progressed at a slow pace; contracts have admittedly been signed but their implementation takes a very long time.

---

[5] 'Thailand plans first LNG terminal after Iran deal', *Reuter's*, 7 July 2006.

What Results?

From a political perspective, thanks to the emphasis put on its relations with Asian states, Iran has broadened its diplomatic room for manoeuvre. Diplomatic exchanges with Asian countries slowed down somewhat under the Ahmadinejad administration, but started to revive from the end of 2008, only to come to a new halt in June 2010 in the wake of the new sanctions adopted by the Security Council. The controversial Iranian president has been welcomed a few times in Asia, but not in Europe. These visits provided him with forums and allowed him to reinforce the international visibility of the Islamic regime.

The Iranian participation in international regional organizations and regional forums that include Asian countries has also increased. Iran actively participates in organizations such as the Economic Cooperation Organization (ECO), having hosted a summit of this organization in Tehran in March 2009. This event indicated the Iranian will to give a new impetus to the organization by associating with new partners from the Persian Gulf and the Levant. The Iraqi president, the emir of Qatar, and the Syrian vice-president were indeed invited. Iran also acquired the status of observer to the Shanghai Cooperation Organization, whose members are Russia, China, and the four Central-Asian republics of Kazakhstan, Kyrgyzstan, Uzbekistan, and Tajikistan, while India, Pakistan, and Mongolia are observers. Moreover, Tehran acquired the status of observer in the South Asian Association for Regional Cooperation (SAARC) in April 2007.[6] In addition, it is a member of regional forums linking it to Asian partners such as the Asia-Middle East Dialogue (AMED) that is made up of fifty states of the Middle-East and Asia and whose first session was organized in Singapore in July 2005; the D8 group (Developing-8), an arrangement for the setting up of a development cooperation among members; and the G15 group, whose objective is to facilitate the national efforts toward development and economic progress. Tehran is also at the source of the creation of a summit among Persian-speaking heads of states of Iran, Tajikistan and Afghanistan.[7] Even if for some of these groupings the Iranian participation is rather cosmetic, the association of Tehran with these organizations is undoubtedly a considerable achievement for Iranian diplomacy, given that it reduces the isolation of the Islamic Republic and the ostracism that the current Iranian president faces in the West.

This association of Iran with regional organizations and forums is also an important element in terms of the image for the Islamic regime, as it confers a certain 'normality' to it and contributes to the idea that 'normal' relations can be fostered with Iran. This provides the regime with respectability and contributes to relay the message that it is with the West and only with the West

---

[6] Founded in December 1985 (seven founding members: Bangladesh, Bhutan, India, the Maldives, Nepal, Pakistan, and Sri Lanka). Afghanistan joined the organization in 2005.

[7] See the chapter by Frédérique Guérin in this volume.

that Iran has a problem. The view the regime wishes to convey is that nothing stands in the way of cordial relations between Iran and the rest of the world. This reinforces the 'anti-imperialist and revolutionary' image of the Iranian regime, which in turn provides it with an audience in the public opinion of several countries in the South (for instance in the Arab world or in Latin America), but also in some European left-wing circles. This 'anti-imperialist' image arouses the interest of some regimes hostile to Washington, in Asia but also in South America or Africa, and contributes once again to broaden the possibilities of the Islamic Republic in terms of diplomacy while admittedly limiting the possibilities to develop ties with more moderate states. The intensification of the relations with Asian states and the participation of Tehran in all these forums strengthen also the perception of Iran as a regional power in Asia.

As for the nuclear issue, thanks to its ties with Asian states, Tehran has gained the sympathy and the diplomatic support of numerous countries in that region (notably among the non-aligned countries), countries that are opposed to any military intervention against Iran and support Tehran's civilian nuclear programme. From a bilateral perspective, countries such as Indonesia, Malaysia, Laos, Thailand, Myanmar but also India have all lent Tehran their diplomatic support regarding the development of its peaceful civilian nuclear programme. Among international institutions such as the United Nations and the IAEA, Tehran also benefited from the sympathy of some of its partners. Thus, in June 2007 Indonesia rejected a draft declaration of the Security Council that condemned the comments of the Iranian president, quoted as saying that Israel would soon 'disappear'. In March 2007, though, Jakarta had voted in favour of the coercive measures of the Security Council against the Iranian nuclear programme, a vote that constituted a diplomatic setback for Tehran, which supports Indonesia's candidature to a permanent seat at the Security Council. Similarly, after providing Iran with support and despite the important political and economic ties it has with Tehran, India eventually voted twice against the Islamic Republic at the United Nations. However, on the nuclear issue, it is the diplomatic umbrella that Tehran obtained from Beijing—which admittedly implied compensations, in terms of economic contracts—that turned out to be the most important achievement of Iran in the international institutions, given China's international clout. Despite its cost, the value of this Chinese diplomatic umbrella is considerable for the Islamic regime, as it allowed Tehran to gain time and led to the restriction of the scope and severity of the sanctions adopted by the Security Council. The time gained in this way and the emphasis put on diplomacy allowed the Iranian regime to move forward with its nuclear project, notably in the matter of uranium enrichment. Ultimately, it could have offered to Tehran the possibility to reach a threshold in its nuclear programme by giving it the opportunity to choose the 'Japanese model' in this matter. Furthermore, the establishment of ties with large Asian states enables Tehran to find mediators in the future if it ever chooses to restore links with the United States. This task could be undertaken by Turkey, India, or even Japan.

In addition to the political sphere, it is in the economic realm that the benefits generated by the connections between Iran and Asia are particularly significant. By developing economic and commercial relations with Asian countries, Tehran has somewhat benefited from the globalization process, even if much more could have been done in the economic field if its ties with Europe and the United States were better. In terms of the geographic distribution of the Iranian trade, Asia is nowadays, with around two thirds of the total, the leading commercial partner of the Islamic Republic.

Geographical distribution of the Iranian trade in 2007[8]

Rank	Geographical area	Trade (in billion US$)	Percentage of the foreign trade of Iran
1.	Asia (total)	91.02	66.15
	East Asia[9]	59.4	43.17
	Australia/New-Zeland	0.33	0.24
	Indian sub-continent[10]	4.77	3.47
	South-East Asia[11]	4.69	3.41
	Central Asia	3.65	2.65
	Caucasus	0.67	0.48
	Turkey	7.54	5.48
	Persian Gulf[12]	8.71	6.33
	Others Middle East[13]	1.26	0.92

[8] IMF, *Direction of Trade Statistics Yearbook 2008*, Washington DC, 2008, pp. 266–268.
[9] China, Japan, South Korea, Taiwan.
[10] India, Pakistan, Afghanistan, Bangladesh, Sri Lanka, Nepal. Regarding Afghanistan, Iran is a major business partner of Kabul. But the statistical directory of the IMF used here does not give any figure for the trade between the two countries. The Iranian authorities nevertheless place the annual volume of exchanges between the two countries at US$ 500 million in 2008. 'Iran-Afghanistan transactions stand at US$ 500M: Official', *Payvand News*, 22 December, 2008. Available:
http://www.payvand.com/news/08/dec/1236.html (accessed 17 November 2011).
[11] Brunei Darussalam, Cambodia, Indonesia, Malaysia, Myanmar, Philippines, Singapore, Thailand, Vietnam.
[12] Bahrain, Kuwait, Oman, Qatar, Saudi Arabia, United Arab Emirates.
[13] Iraq, Jordan, Lebanon, Syria, Yemen. Iran is a very important business partner of Iraq, but the statistical directory of the IMF used here underestimates the trade between the two countries. For the year 2007, bilateral non-oil trade – primarily Iranian exports – seems to have reached US$ 2 billion. Gulnoza Saidazimova, 'Iran/Iraq: Trade Flow Increases, But Mostly From Tehran To Baghdad', *RFE/RL*, 5 March 2008. The first meeting of the Iran-Iraq common trade commission met in February 2009. It laid down the objective of US$ 5 billion of annual exchanges between the two countries. Accord-

2.	Europe		27.35
	European Union	31.86	23.16
	Russia	3.57	2.59
	Others Europe	2.17	1.60
3.	Africa	4.483	3.26
4.	America (including United States and Canada)	3.572	2.60

In the oil sector, which has the largest share in Iran's exports, its main clients are all Asian countries (Japan, China, India and South Korea). Asia is thus the first export market for Iranian oil.

Iran Oil Exports in 2007[14]

Country	Exports (in thousand barrels per day)	Percentage of total exports
Japan	523	21.28
China	411	16.72
India	374	15.22
South Korea	258	10.50
Italy	197	8.01
France	131	5.33
South Africa	128	5.20
Greece	113	4.60
Netherlands	93	3.78
Spain	79	3.21
Others	151	6.14
Total	2.458	100

---

ing to the IRNA agency, the non-oil exchanges could reach US$ 10 billion in the future. See 'Iran, Iraq set $5b target for annual trade', *Tehran Times*, 12 February 2009 and 'Iran's Non-Oil Exports To Iraq To Exceed 3 Billion US$', *Payvand News*, 2 June 2009. Available:
http://www.payvand.com/news/09/jun/1018.html (accessed 17 November 2011).
[14] EIA, 'Iran', EIA Country Analysis Briefs, February 2009. Available: www.eia.doe.gov/emeu/cabs/Iran/Oil.html (accessed 3 September 2011).

In the future, given its needs, this region could turn out to be an important market for Iranian gas if the projects under discussion between Tehran and its partners end up becoming a reality.

Iran Main Trading Asian Partners in 2007[15]

Rank	Country	Iranian exports to (in billion US$)	Iranian imports from (in billion US$)	Total (in billion US$)	Percentage of the foreign trade of Iran
1.	China	12.12	8.02	20.14	14.64
2.	Japan	11.60	1.47	13.07	9.49
3.	South Korea	5.89	3.59	9.49	6.90
4.	Turkey	6.01	1.53	7.54	5.48
5.	United Arab Emirates	0.75	5.17	5.92	4.30
6.	Taiwan	2.96	0.65	3.61	2.62
7.	Russia	0.32	3.25	3.57	2.59
8.	India	0.85	2.09	2.95	2.14
9.	Singapore	1.22	0.59	1.81	1.32
10.	Turkmenistan	0.23	1.48	1.71	1.24
11.	Kazakhstan	0.02	1.60	1.62	1.18
12.	Saudi Arabia	0.62	0.80	1.42	1.03
13.	Oman	0.09	1.02	1.11	0.80
14.	Malaysia	0.39	0.68	1.07	0.78
15.	Thailand	0.08	0.85	0.93	0.68
16.	Sri Lanka	0.77	0.13	0.90	0.65
17.	Pakistan	0.50	0.31	0.81	0.59
18.	Indonesia	0.07	0.52	0.59	0.43
19.	Azerbaijan	0.10	0.48	0.58	0.42
20.	Hong Kong	0.17	0.09	0.26	0.19

Asia is also the first destination of Iran's non-oil exports. Iran essentially exports petrochemical products, industrial, agricultural and mineral goods, as well as carpets. In 2010 China was the first export market for Iranian petrochemical products.

---

[15] IMF, *Direction of Trade Statistics Yearbook 2008*, Washington DC, 2008, pp. 266—268.

Iranian Non-Oil Exports (geographical distribution)
(March 2007/2008)[16]
(*in billion US$*)

Rank	Continent	Amount	Percentage of the total
1.	Asia and Oceania	12.641	83.3
2.	Europe	2.055	13.5
3.	Africa	0.284	1.8
4.	America	0.237	1.5
	Total	15.172	100

Iranian Non-Oil Exports (major clients)
(March 2007/2008)[17]
(*in million US$*)

Rank	Country	Amount	per cent of Iranian non-oil exports
1.	UAE	2153	14.2
2.	Iraq	1586	10.5
3.	China	1231	8.1
4.	Japan	927	6.1
5.	India	830	5.5
6.	South Korea	555	3.7
7.	Turkey	553	3.6
8.	Italy	518	3.4
9.	Afghanistan	442	2.9
10.	Germany	367	2.4
	Total	9165	60.4

The relative importance of trade with China is noteworthy. Capitalizing on the absence of American firms and on the progressive withdrawal of Westerners as a result of the sanctions policy enacted in response to Iran's nuclear policy, China has become a major economic partner of Iran. It pulled itself up to the first place during the post-9/11 period. With a bilateral trade reaching over US$ 20 billion in 2007, China in that year became the first individual economic partner of Iran, overtaking Japan. In 2009, China was second only to the European Union (and its 27 members) with 15.8 per cent of the overall trade of the Islamic Republic, and in 2010 Sino-Iranian trade reached US$ 29.3 billion. In contrast to the trade between Iran and East Asian industrialized countries such as Japan or South Korea, the volume of Chinese exports to

---

[16] Iran's Customs Administration (IRICA), *Iran's Non-Oil Exports Statistics*, p. 7. Available: http://en.tpo.ir/UserFiles/3-IranNonoilExportStatistics.pdf (accessed 3 September 2011).

[17] Ibid.,pp. 5-6.

the Iranian market is quite significant and increased rapidly, passing from a mere US$ 1 billion in 2002 to US$ 11.1 billion in 2010. The People's Republic was not only the first export market for the Iranian oil in 2009, it was also Iran's third economic partner in terms of imports with 14.7 per cent of the total Iranian imports, behind the European Union (27 per cent) and the United Arab Emirates (15.2 per cent). Dubai is a staging area for trade with Iran, and Chinese companies have taken advantage of that. In 2009, some 3,000 of them had established branches in Dubai. The volume of trade between China and the United Arab Emirates is quite substantial (around € 14.66 billion in 2009), and part of that trade is destined to the Iranian market. In 2009, direct imports of Chinese products into Iran somewhat shrunk to US$ 7.9 billion. Iranian estimates indicate, however, that an equivalent amount of Chinese goods went to Iran via Dubai.[18] Bilateral trading ties should continue rising in the future, Beijing gaining from the particular relation it developed with Tehran in the context of the nuclear crisis. China indeed declared that the sanctions adopted by the United Nations in June 2010 should not hit normal trade. While the sanctions were being discussed, Beijing kept strengthening its trading ties with Tehran. At the end of May 2010, Iran ordered six gas carriers from China to transport the liquefied natural gas (LNG) it hopes to export in the future. This order is worth US$ 1.2 billion.

It has also been noticed that there is an increasing presence of Chinese companies in the Iranian strategic sector of hydrocarbons, despite the diverse range of sanctions adopted by the UN Security Council. Important developments have to be noted in the matter of investments in this sector during the post-9/11 period. The most striking of these is related to the acceleration of the Chinese penetration. Generally speaking, Asian companies are very present in the Iranian strategic sector of hydrocarbons. Out of 41 firms listed by the US administration in March 2010 as being commercially active in the Iranian sectors of oil, gas, oil transportation or in the petrochemical industry between 2005 and 2009,[19] there were no fewer than 21 Asian firms, originating from South Korea (Daelim, Daewoo Shipbuilding & Marine Engineering, GS, Hyundai Heavy Industries), China (CNOOC, CNPC, Sinopec), Malaysia (Amona, Petrofield, SKS Ventures), India (Indian Oil Corporation, Oil India Ltd., Oil and Natural Gas Corporation, ONGC Videsh Ltd., Petronet LNG), Japan (Inpex, JGC Corporation), Thailand (PTT Exploration & Production), Turkey (Turkish Petroleum Company) and Russia (Gazprom, Lukoil). In the post-9/11 era, as nuclear-related sanctions were gradually adopted and American pressures were reinforced, Chinese companies adopted a long-term approach, in contrast to other Asian countries that maintain close relations with the United States (Japan and South Korea). As the United States kept discreetly lobbying with companies operating in Iran and brandishing the threat

---

[18] Laurent Maillard, 'China takes over from West as Iran's main economic partner', *AFP*, 15 March 2010.

[19] Available: http://www.gao.gov/new.items/d10639r.pdf (accessed 3 September 2011).

of sanctions against them, some Western and Asian governments favoured a 'wait-and-see' or even a 'pullback' policy for their companies. On the Iranian side, the authorities insisted that the investments promised by these companies would indeed be made, otherwise they would be put aside and replaced by other corporations. The Chinese side took advantage of this situation by substituting its firms for Western ones, thus reinforcing its positions in Iran. The Chinese state-owned oil companies maintained the development pace of their various projects in Iran while Beijing resisted any new sanctions in the energy sector. The China National Petroleum Corporation (CNPC) replaced Total, a French company that had been induced by political pressures to delay its decision to invest in the development of the Phase 11 of the giant gas field of South-Pars. This investment is valued at US$ 4.7 billion. At the end of 2009 CNPC expanded its staff in Iran, while Western firms that were still present on the Iranian market cut down their activities. Aside from South-Pars, in 2009, CNPC replaced Japan's Inpex Corporation in South Azadegan oilfield, a project with a needed investment of up to US$ 2.5 billion, and also committed to development of the oil deposit of Azadegan North, a project valued at US$ 2 billion. Sinopec is dealing with the Yadavaran field. According to a WikiLeaks cable, to ward off any risk of Washington's unilateral sanctions against them over their activities in Iran, Chinese oil executives are very 'careful to describe their firms' projects in Iran as service or engineering contracts that did not involve equity stakes or investment of capital'.[20] Chinese investments and progress on these new projects have been slow to materialize, but this slowness is seemingly more a result of the difficulty to work with Iranian partners and with the country's administration than of political pressures. Even the adoption of new sanctions in June 2010 did not seem to reduce Beijing's eagerness to be present in Iran. According to the Iranian deputy oil minister, Hoseyn Noqrehkar Shirazi, Beijing's oil companies should invest US$ 6 billion in the development of Azadegan North and South. Contracts for both fields have reportedly been signed in March 2011.[21] As the deputy minister put it, 'the volume (of Chinese investment) in upstream projects is US$ 29 billion', adding that 'Beijing had signed contracts worth another US$ 10 billion in petrochemicals, refineries, and oil and gas pipeline projects.' China would thus be in 2010 the largest foreign potential investor in the sector of Iranian hydrocarbons.

In addition to the investment to develop Iran's hydrocarbons, China buys it as well. In 2009, China imported around 460 000 b/d of Iranian crude oil, that is around 15 per cent of Beijing's crude oil imports this year. In 2010, China was only the second importer of Iranian oil, after Japan. Iran supplied Beijing with 9 per cent of its oil imports.[22] In the gas sector, China signed

---

[20] Quoted in Melanie Lee, 'How U.S. trying to wean China off Iranian oil', *Reuters*, May 2, 2011.
[21] 'China invests USD 6bn in Iran oilfields', *Iranian Government News*, 13 March 2011.
[22] 'China renews oil import pact with Iran', *Reuters*, January 21, 2011.

contracts with Iran to import LNG, but little progress has been made. While China can play a significant role in supplying Iran with the capital needed to develop its gas reserves, Chinese companies cannot provide the critical technology in the domain of liquefaction. Beijing could help in terms of constructing gas pipelines, but not with LNG technology. This factor impedes drastically its role in this particular sector. However, Chinese companies recently got involved in the country to fill the gap left by the withdrawal of Western companies trading in oil products. In this sector, Tehran is indeed not self-sufficient: its refineries are not capable of satisfying its domestic demand. In the gasoline business, the Chinese company Chinaoil, an arm of CNPC, had not delivered gasoline to Iran since January 2009, but in April 2010 it sold two loads to Tehran. The same month, Unipec—a subsidiary of Sinopec—revived its gasoline sales to Iran, after a hiatus of six years. Zhuhai Zhenrong also delivered one or two loads of gasoline to Iran at least during one year, sometimes in cooperation with the Russian firm Litasco, the trading arm of Lukoil. While supporting resolution 1929, adopted by the Security Council in June 2010, China explained that its companies would keep doing business in the energy sector with Tehran. Since June 2010, the United States, the European Union, Canada, and Australia have, for their part, enforced new sanctions against Iran, but Chinese officials maintained their meetings with their Iranian colleagues to discuss common projects. During the visit of the Iranian oil minister in China in August 2010, Beijing reiterated its wish to pursue bilateral cooperation with Tehran in this realm.[23]

More recently, China has also resorted to its new-found financial power by granting for instance a loan of € one billion to the municipality of Tehran for investments in infrastructure (notably roads), the construction of which would be undertaken in part by Chinese companies.[24] China has also an interest in the hydroelectricity (signature in March 2011 of a contract on the construction of a dam valued at US$ 2.5 billion), and railways. Beijing could thus invest up to US$ 13 billion in the modernization and the interconnection of Iranian lines (5,300 km) according to a deal struck in February 2011. Iran and China also plan to sign a cooperation agreement worth US$ 7 billion to develop two projects of oil refineries in the Iranian cities of Abadan and Isfahan (to produce 30 million litres of gasoline and diesel fuel per day). Beijing thus succeeded to become a very useful partner in the eyes of Tehran.

In addition to trade, Asian countries (India, China, Malaysia, Taiwan, South Korea) are also important suppliers of technology to the Islamic Republic. This has allowed Iran to find substitutive partners in areas where Europeans were reluctant to cooperate. Of course this is not an optimal choice in many sectors, and in the case of oil or gas technologies it is not even a second choice. However, if the technological rise of Asia continues, in the future Iran

---

[23] Available:http://www.iranenergyproject.org/iran-chinese-energy-partners.pdf (accessed 3 September 2011).
[24] 'Iran orders six Chinese LNG tankers', *Yahoo Business News*, 30 May 2010.

might be able to get rid of its European suppliers, were that to be deemed desirable by the regime.

Iran also takes advantage, but to a lesser extent, of its relations with Asia to secure investments. But possibilities in this area are limited, given that Asian investments in the sector of hydrocarbons, while sizeable, have been greatly restricted (Chinese investments excepted) by the UN Security Council's policy of sanctions and by the discreet lobbying of Washington with which a number of Asian countries such as Japan, South Korea, India, and Malaysia have more or less complied.

From a symbolic perspective also, Iran's relations with Asian countries have yielded positive results that have been rapidly instrumentalized by the regime's propaganda, for in the face of the Asian countries' will to maintain their independence with regard to their ties with Tehran the American policy of sanctions and isolation has shown signs of weakness. The Asian clients of Tehran have for instance agreed to pay their oil purchases in currencies other than the US dollars (i.e., euro or yen), thus lessening Iran's sensitivity to American sanctions and affording the regime an important propaganda victory. Overall, Iran's economic links with Asian countries have helped the Iranian regime to better resist to the American and international sanctions, ultimately enabling it to fortify itself.

Lastly, thanks to its ties with Asian countries, Iran has also gained militarily. Quite aside from past North-Korean, Pakistani, or Chinese assistance in the nuclear and ballistic fields, the scope of which is difficult estimate, deliveries of advanced Russian and Chinese weaponry has been significant. According to the Stockholm International Peace Research Institute (SIPRI), China was Iran's second-largest arms supplier between 1990 and 2010, after Russia.[25] According to John Garver, the Chinese sold Iran sophisticated equipment specifically designed to counter the naval and aerial power of the United States. China also transferred a large array of sophisticated industrial technologies to Iran in violation of its own rules on technology trading (which were formulated under the urging of Washington) and of unilateral US legislation.[26] All of this has substantially increased Iran's defensive capabilities and self-sufficiency in terms of arms production. This means that Iran's nuisance power, thus its bargaining power and its capacity to resist potential Western pressures, has also increased.

The Limits to Irano-Asian Relations

Broadly speaking, there are two types of limits to the development of Irano-Asian relations: political and economic.

---

[25] SIPRI, *TIV of arms exports to Iran, 2002-2010*. Available: http://armstrade.sipri.org/armstrade/html/export_values.php (accessed 3 September 2011)
[26] John W. Garver, 'Is China Playing a Dual Game in Iran? ', *The Washington Quarterly*, 34(1), Winter 2011, p. 76.

Political Obstacles

Political restrictions are numerous, as Iran's relations with a number of its close Asian neighbours are fraught with difficulties: Azeri nationalism in the relationship with Azerbaijan; the regional rivalry with Pakistan or Saudi Arabia, widespread suspicion in the Gulf states regarding Iran's policy towards Iraq, Afghanistan, Pakistan or even to the Central Asian republics. One of the most intractable obstacles to a further strengthening of Iran's ties with Asian countries is the nuclear issue. Iran's immediate neighbours are not alone to be anxious about its nuclear ambitions: countries such as Japan, South Korea, Taiwan, India, even China, are opposed to Iran acquiring nuclear weapons, and their strategic interests have a decisive influence on their political relations with the Islamic regime. No one among the Asian consumers of Iranian oil wishes to see Tehran's nuclear programme destabilize the Persian Gulf or contribute to the launch of an arms race in a region that is critical to the global energy supply. Proliferation in that zone would constitute a true nightmare for all of the oil consumers in the world, in Asia as much as in the West. Besides risks linked to the rise in oil prices in case of tensions, there are also fears that in case of an armed conflict, oil supplies would be threatened—and given the volume exported from the region, no other production zone would be capable of filling the gap left by a potential rupture of supplies originating from the Persian Gulf. Moreover, numerous Asian countries have aligned themselves with the sanctions policy decided by the UN Security Council. This is the case of Japan or South Korea, for instance. The nuclear issue thus constitutes a serious obstacle to the strengthening of their ties with Tehran. That is what Goh Chok Tok, senior minister in the prime minister's cabinet and chairman of the Monetary Authority of Singapore, declared during a visit to Iran in March 2007.[27] That being said, the UN sanctions—at last until June 2010—have remained limited and allow for a large array of ties with Iran. Still, the climate around the nuclear issue does not encourage the development of a political rapprochement, nor does it bolster economic connections.

In addition to the nuclear issue, the radicalism of Ahmadinejad's regime also displeases numerous Asian states. In terms of image, it is indeed quite

---

[27] 'However, we have to acknowledge that there are serious impediments to the development of our ties. Iran is under UN sanctions. Whether Iran agrees with the UN Security Council's decision or not, all UN members are legally obliged to comply with UNSC sanctions. Singaporeans are concerned about Iran's standoff with the international community over its nuclear programme and the risk of further UN sanctions. Singapore's view is that Iran has the right to develop atomic energy for peaceful purposes. But, to be frank, there are serious international concerns about Iran's intentions. Singapore hopes that Iran will comply with its obligations under the Nuclear Non-Proliferation Treaty (NPT) and the IAEA's safeguards regime. Iran has explained that its nuclear programme is a peaceful one. But the IAEA is not fully convinced. Singapore therefore hopes that Iran will take concrete steps to reassure the international community of its peaceful intentions by complying with its obligations under NPT and abiding by the relevant UN Security Council resolutions', in 'Senior Minister Goh Chok Tong's Interview with Iran Daily', *Iran Daily*, 11 March 2007.

delicate for countries that proclaim being responsible stakeholders on the world stage to be associated with a regime headed by a man like President Ahmadinejad. For instance, after the Iranian president's speech denying the Holocaust, the spokesman of the Singaporean ministry of foreign affairs, questioned by the press, declared 'we are shocked and appalled at President Ahmadinejad's comments, which are unacceptable. The history and facts of the Second World War cannot be denied.'[28]

The Israeli factor also has to be taken into account. Indeed, numerous Asian countries maintain important relations with Israel. This is notably the case of Japan, China, and India. Israel is the second arms supplier of India. Indo-Israeli cooperation is very important: India has for instance put an Israeli spy-satellite—mainly destined to survey Iran—into orbit. Israel has also developed important ties with China. The two countries established diplomatic relations in 1992, and Israel is an important supplier of the technologies required to the modernization of the Chinese army. It is also the second arms supplier to China behind Russia. As this is a critical sector of cooperation for China, the Israeli factor has a great influence on the Sino-Iranian ties. Just as in the case of Japan or India, Iran's anti-Israeli rhetoric, especially with Ahmadinejad, has annoyed the Chinese authorities. This Israeli factor is less important with regard to Asian Muslim countries such as Malaysia, Pakistan, or Indonesia but, but in these cases, the abovementioned image problem is still an issue.

Asian countries' relations with other oil-exporting countries in the Gulf also restrict their rapprochement with Tehran. Asia's oil-consuming countries all have more interests and closer relations with the Arab countries of the Gulf than with Iran. In numerous cases, Saudi Arabia is a more important oil supplier than Iran, not to mention the fact that its investment capacity is far more substantial than Iran's. These links are very important and Asian countries take them into account when dealing with Tehran.

Finally, the American factor remains the most important obstacle to the development of political and economic connections between Iran and Asia. The poor relations between Tehran and Washington have weighed on the development of ties with countries close to the United States, such as Japan, Australia, South Korea or Singapore. With regard to Central Asia, the bad state of US-Iranian relations is depriving Tehran of the benefits stemming from the opening up of hydrocarbons production in the Caspian basin. Even the Asian countries less close to Washington such as India or China take this factor into consideration in their dealings with Tehran. Despite its interests in energy matters (New Delhi imported 16 per cent of its oil from Iran in 2010) and regardless of its independent foreign policy, India—whose relations with Washington are blossoming—has considerably slowed the pace of its rapprochement with Tehran, compared with the beginning of the 2000s. Even China, which has chosen to protect its political and economic ties with Iran to

---

[28] MFA spokesman's comments, Ministry of Foreign Affairs, Singapore, 9 December 2005.

the maximum and which is probably the most influential international actor in Iran, bears in mind this American factor when dealing with the Islamic Republic. For that matter, Beijing has discreetly tried to undertake the role of go-between between Tehran and Washington, if cables released by WikiLeaks are to be believed.[29] At the end of the day no Asian country is really willing to risk a quarrel with the United States over Iran.

Economic Obstacles

One major economic obstacle to the further development of Irano-Asian relations is the weakness and the insularity of the Iranian economy. The economic choices of the Islamic Republic are not optimal. Contracts in the field of hydrocarbons are not attractive and, besides, in the Islamic Republic there are strict constitutional limitations to foreign investments in the hydrocarbons sector. The judicial framework is still incomplete. Projects signed with Asian states in the field of hydrocarbons are not implemented as a result of Iranian domestic problems. The unsettled internal debates, the propensity to change the contracts' conditions and renegotiate prices, etc., constitute as many factors that bother the Asian partners of Tehran. Besides, corruption- and graft-related difficulties, administrative delays, the lack of dynamism in the country, the limitation and the shortcomings in terms of transportation, communication, and interconnection with neighbouring countries, cultural differences, are all obstacles and hindrances to the development of economic relations between Iran and other Asian countries. From an opposite point of view, the weaknesses of some Asian economies are also impediments to the development of trade opportunities. This is the case of the Central Asian republics, the Caucasus, and also Afghanistan and Pakistan.

Finally, there are voices inside Iran that view further growth in Irano-Asian trade relations with ambivalence. Iran might become a simple supplier of raw materials, and entire sections of its economy might be endangered due to the competition low-cost Asian products bring to the industrial sector, to the retail sector, and even to the service sector. The influx of Chinese products and the industrial competition of China are particularly criticized. Others also condemn the choice of Asian countries as Iran's most favoured partners, arguing that this option, which is supported by the Islamic regime, is not always optimal for the development of the country. For instance, seen from Tehran, the connection in the automobile industry between China and Iran Khodro did not yield very positive results.

Conclusion

Since the passing away of its founder in 1989, the Islamic Republic of Iran has considerably reinforced its political and particularly its economic relations with numerous Asian countries. Given the benefits this reorientation has

---

[29] 'Secret documents show Chinese role on Iran', *CNN*, 29 November 2010.

yielded for Iran, the 'Asian dimension' now constitutes a long-range trend in Iranian foreign policy, notwithstanding the risks that these relations entail for the country's economy. In view of the benefits engendered, the current regime in Tehran will most likely continue to develop its ties with its Asian partners, chiefly China. Westerners cannot ignore this fact in their approach and their calculations with regard to the Islamic Republic of Iran.

Chapter 16

Iran and Syria: An Enduring Alliance

Jubin M. Goodarzi

'Our relations with Syria are strategic, and we view the political, economic, and cultural relations between the two countries as strategic.' Iranian Foreign Minister Ali-Akbar Velayati, 31 March 1983 'Syria remains firmly on the side of the Iranians, and will never depart from its solidarity with the Islamic Republic.'
—Syrian Foreign Minister Farouk al-Shara, 14 November 1987

There is no doubt that one of the most intriguing developments in modern Middle East politics has been the emergence and longevity of the Syrian-Iranian alliance. For more than three decades, the Tehran-Damascus axis has baffled many scholars. Pointing to differences in their respective ideologies, as well as their political foundations and structures, many analysts have been perplexed as to how a revolutionary, pan-Islamic theocracy such as Iran could ally itself with a secular, pan-Arab, socialist republic like Syria.[1] Moreover, while Ba'athist Syria claims to be an ardent supporter and the rightful leader of the pan-Arab cause, Iran advocates Islamic universalism and the export of its revolution.[2]

When Saddam Hussein invaded Iran in September 1980, many observers expected Syria to follow in the footsteps of other Arab countries, which rallied to the support of their Iraqi brethren in order to deliver a decisive blow against non-Arab Iran and blunt the intrusive edge of the Islamic revolution. Such expectations were partially based on the ideological and structural similarities between the two Ba'athist regimes. The leadership in both countries espoused

---

[1] Yair Hirschfeld, 'The Odd Couple: Ba'athist Syria and Khomeini's Iran', in *Syria Under Assad: Domestic Constraints and Regional Risks*, Avner Yaniv and Moshe Ma'oz (eds), New York: St. Martin's Press, 1986, p. 105; and Shireen T. Hunter, 'Syrian-Iranian Relations: An Alliance of Convenience or More?', *Middle East Insight*, June/July 1985, pp. 30–31.
[2] Hirschfeld, 'The Old Couple', p. 105.

pan-Arab socialism and had risen to power in military coups. However, to the dismay and surprise of many, the war contributed to the consolidation of the Syrian-Iranian nexus that had emerged following the Iranian revolution. Moreover, the alliance still stands today, in spite of the many challenges that it has faced, and the periodic strains in the relationship over the past thirty years. Unlike so many others, Mohammad-Reza Djalili has always emphasized the strategic dimension of the alliance between Iran and Syria, particularly in the Levant: 'In the long term, relations between Tehran and Damascus are the centre of gravity of all the architecture of the Iranian policy towards the Fertile Crescent region.'[3]

Overall, the longstanding ties between Syria and Iran continue to be of great interest at the beginning of the twenty-first century, particularly in view of major developments in the Middle East in recent years such as the 2006 Lebanon war which pitted Israel against the Syrian and Iranian-backed Lebanese Hezbollah movement, the controversy over Iran's nuclear programme, heightened cooperation between Damascus and Tehran since the 2003 Iraq war, and, beginning in 2011, the armed conflict between the Syrian regime and the opposition against it, a conflict in which Tehran firmly backs the former.

The purpose of this chapter is to provide an analytical and theoretical framework to understand the forces which have moulded and influenced the evolution of the Syrian-Iranian alliance. Furthermore, it will highlight the importance of the axis, and major myths and misconceptions concerning it. The chapter will also present an overview of the various phases in the evolution of the relationship, and its changing power structure.

Generally speaking, there are three important reasons to study and understand the Tehran-Damascus axis. Firstly, the alliance has had a significant impact on Middle East politics over the past three decades, as we have seen again over the past few years since the 2003 US-led invasion of Iraq. Secondly, it has proven to be an enduring relationship that has lasted over thirty years now, which is quite extraordinary when one takes into consideration the volatility and shifting political sands in the Middle East. Thirdly, the alliance is still misunderstood in certain respects by many regional and political observers. Hence, this has led to many inaccurate assessments on the aims and actions of the two partners, and gross oversimplification of the complex state of affairs relating to the alliance and regional politics.

The Importance of the Syrian-Iranian Alliance

To begin with, over the past three decades, the two partners have had some noticeable successes in frustrating the designs and policies of Iraq, Israel and the United States in the Middle East. Through their continuous collaboration, they played a critical role in stemming Iraq's invasion of Iran in September

---

[3] Mohammad-Reza Djalili, 'La politique arabe de l'Iran', *A Contrario*, 5(1), 2008, p. 135.

1980, and ensuring that Saddam Hussein's Iraq would not become the predominant power in the Middle East. They were also able to thwart Tel Aviv's strategy to bring Lebanon into its own orbit, following the June 1982 Israeli invasion of that country and occupation of almost half its territory. Through the use of Lebanese proxies—most notably Hezbollah—Syria and Iran were able to expose the limits of Israeli military power and forced Tel Aviv to withdraw from the territory it occupied between 1984 and 2000. Concurrently, in this same arena, they were able to inflict one of the very few foreign policy setbacks that Ronald Reagan suffered during his two terms in office as US president in the 1980s. Even in the post-Cold War era, with American predominance on the regional and world stage, the imposition of economic sanctions on both countries, and the 2003 US-led invasion of Iraq, Syria and Iran have been able to wield considerable power and influence in the Middle East, especially in Iraq, Lebanon and—directly and indirectly—on world oil markets, as recent events have demonstrated.

A Conceptual Framework and Theoretical Explanations to Understanding the Alliance

Contrary to prevailing views (due in large part to the authoritarian nature of the Syrian and Iranian regimes and their unpopularity in many quarters), the alliance has been primarily defensive in nature, aimed at neutralizing Iraqi and Israeli offensive capabilities in the region, and preventing American encroachment in the Middle East. While the initial impetus for the alliance came from the overthrow of Iran's conservative, pro-Western monarchy in February 1979, the Iraqi invasion of Iran in September 1980 served as a major catalyst in bringing Syria and Iran closer together, with Syria providing invaluable diplomatic and military assistance to help Iran stave off defeat and expel Iraqi forces from its territory by May 1982. In turn, when Israel launched its second invasion of Lebanon, and challenged Syria in its backyard a month later in June 1982, Iran lent its support to Syria, in part, by mobilizing Lebanon's Shiites to drive out Israeli and Western forces during 1983–1985. From 1988 to 1989, prior to the Kuwait conflict, the two allies cooperated in Lebanon to crush Michel Aoun's anti-Syrian revolt which was interestingly enough backed by Iraq, Israel, and other states. More recently, following September 11, the Bush administration's 'war on terror' and especially the US-led invasion of Iraq in 2003, raised concerns in Damascus and Tehran, ushering in a period of heightened cooperation and frequent consultations between the two allies. The two partners have also signed a number of defence agreements in recent years.

In general, defensive alliances which have set and limited objectives are more stable and durable.[4] This, in part, explains the longevity of the 34-year-long partnership. According to George Liska and Stephen Walt, defensive alliances are less fragile than offensive ones. Offensive alliances quite often

---

[4] Herbert S. Dinerstein, 'The Transformation of Alliance Systems', *American Political Science Review*, 59(3), 1965, p. 599.

fall apart once the opponent has been attacked and vanquished. The rationale for maintaining the alliance consequently ceases to exist for the members, and they frequently fall out and squabble over the fruits of their victory.[5]

Another simple but important reason for the strength and durability of the alliance is that it consists of only two members. It has never been a broad coalition of states with various and divergent interests. Since it is small, it is more viable.[6] In the words of Holsti et al., 'the smaller the alliance, the more cohesive and effective it is, and the more important the contribution of each member.'[7] For a number of years during the 1980s, Libya also aligned itself with Syria and Iran, providing diplomatic, military and economic support to Damascus and Tehran in the confrontations with Israel and Iraq. However, Libya for the most part was a junior partner in the grouping, and its contribution and importance diminished as the 1980s drew to a close. Essentially, Syria and Iran were and have always been the principal partners in the alliance.

Furthermore, it should be underscored that another reason that has contributed to the stability and longevity of the alliance is that the two partners' priorities differ in the two arenas in which they cooperation. For Iran, the Persian Gulf region is the main area of concern, while for Syria, it is the Levant. Over time, by continually consulting one another and modifying their aims, the two allies came to recognize this reality. Consequently, they tried to coordinate their policies and accommodate one another, while at the same time, protecting and furthering their own interests.[8] More specifically, after a number of crises in the relationship which erupted between 1985 and 1988, when Iran in particular was pursuing certain policies in Lebanon against the wishes of Syria, through continuous consultations, an understanding was eventually reached on key issues, whereby Syrian interests took precedence in the Arab-Israeli arena, while in the Gulf region, Damascus would defer to Tehran. Here again, Liska sheds light by stating that the more complementary the interests of alliance members, the more easily intra-alliance compromises and agreements can be reached.[9] Although, their interests and policies did not always converge, through regular consultations, the two allies gradually tried to resolve their differences, harmonize their positions and coordinate their actions.

In addition, on a related matter, the fact that Syria has carried the greater part of the burden in checking Israeli power, and Iran's main role has been to

---

[5] George Liska, *Nations in Alliance: The Limits of Interdependence*, Baltimore: Johns Hopkins University Press, 1962, pp. 39–40 and Stephen M. Walt, 'Why Alliances Endure or Collapse', *Survival*, 39(1), 1997, p. 159.

[6] Edwin S. Fedder, 'The Concept of Alliance', *International Studies Quarterly*, 12 (1), 1968, p. 83.

[7] Ole R. Holsti, P. Terrence Hopmann and John D. Sullivan, *Unity and Disintegration in International Alliances*, Lanham, MD: University of America Press, 1985, pp. 21 and 56–57.

[8] Liska, *Nations in Alliance*, p. 62. Liska argues that consultations strengthen alliance cohesion since they reinforce solidarity and equality among the members. Ibid., p. 69.

[9] Ibid., p. 82.

contain Iraq in the Gulf, has meant that the two partners fulfil different functions, thus reinforcing the rationale and utility of their strategic links. In other words, the more pronounced the differentiation of functions of the members, the more cohesive the alliance.[10] Both partners have tried to check American power in their respective backyards in the Levant and Gulf; at times jointly, and in other instances, on their own. For example, during 1983–1984, Syrian-Iranian collaboration proved instrumental in driving the United States out of Lebanon. However, Iran's gambit in the final stages of the First Gulf conflict during 1987–1988 to expel US naval forces from the Persian Gulf failed miserably. More recently, in the immediate aftermath of the US-led invasion and occupation of Iraq, Tehran and Damascus were extremely concerned that Washington would use Iraq as a springboard to attack them. Hence, Syria facilitated the passage of Arab and Sunni Muslim fighters from its territory into northern and western Iraq to tie down US-led forces. Similarly, from the east, Iran provided aid to radical Shiite Iraqi groups such as Muqtada al-Sadr's Army of the Mahdi in a bid to bolster armed opposition against US-led coalition forces in central and southern Iraq. Essentially, between 2003 and 2007, Washington and its allies came under intense pressure from a Syrian-Iranian pincer in Iraq. To a large extent, the tactical moves undertaken by Damascus and Tehran complemented each other, and helped their overall strategy in Iraq and the Middle East as a whole to thwart the ambitions of the Bush administration.

In terms of the longevity of the alliance, the mere fact that the Syrian-Iranian partnership has endured for so many years (a particularly rare occurrence in the Middle East), gives it considerable weight and importance. It is noteworthy that Robert Rothstein argues that 'once an alliance has been created, there is positive value placed on continuing it, even if it seems to perform very few functions.' Furthermore, Morton Kaplan builds on this point by postulating that longstanding alliances are characterized by greater unity and legitimacy.[11] It is also worth noting that if a member wishes to abandon an alliance that has become institutionalized, it is prudent to find another viable arrangement that has at least equal utility. In other words, the member will pay an opportunity cost unless it joins an alternative arrangement that is at least equally useful as the previous alliance. This holds particularly true in the case of countries such as Syria and Iran. With regard to the former, in his classic work, *The Struggle for Syria*, Patrick Seale argues that those who aspire to control the Middle East must first win over Syria. According to him,

> there are many reasons for this view: one is the strategic position of Syria, guarding the north-eastern approaches to Egypt, the overland

---

[10] J.R.P. French, 'The Disruption and Cohesion of Groups', *Journal of Abnormal and Social Psychology*, 36 (4), 1941, pp. 365–66.
[11] Robert L. Rothstein, *Alliances and Small Powers*, New York: Columbia University Press, 1968, p. 119, and Morton A. Kaplan, *System and Process in International Politics*, New York: John Wiley & Sons, 1957, pp. 108–09.

route to Iraq from the Mediterranean, the head of the Arabian Peninsula, and the northern frontier of the Arab world...Syria held the key to the struggle for local primacy...Whoever controlled Syria or enjoyed her special friendship could isolate [other Arab states] and need bow to no other combination of Arab states.[12]

As far as Iran is concerned, there is no doubt that it enjoys an extremely important geopolitical position; a large and populous country dominating the crossroads between the Middle East and South Asia, and the northern approaches to the Persian Gulf region. In addition to having the longest coastline along the Persian Gulf, Iran and its other Gulf neighbours possess two-thirds of the world's oil reserves. Iran's critical position is conveyed poignantly in the title of Graham Fuller's book on the geopolitics of Iran, *The Center of the Universe.*[13]

Another key factor which helps shed light on the nature and longevity of the Syrian-Iranian partnership is the role of ideology. Ironically, a crucial element in the relative success and durability of the alliance is that the political elites of these two authoritarian regimes espouse different ideologies; and herein lies the paradox. Quite often, alliances between states that adhere to the same transnational ideology are more likely to be short-lived than those in which ideology plays a secondary role. This is particularly true in the Middle East where authoritarian regimes predominate, and frequently use ideology as a tool to boost their political legitimacy and power base domestically and in neighbouring countries. Revisionist ideologies such as pan-Arabism and Islamic fundamentalism have quite frequently been divisive, because they are used to project power and influence, and to destabilize rival states.

In the Middle East, the record clearly shows that states sharing a common ideology compete for the mantle of leadership rather than form durable alliances. Each state may claim to be the legitimate leader, and may even demand others to relinquish their rights and sovereignty to form a single political entity. This was quite evident in the rivalries between the pan-Arab regimes in Egypt, Syria, and Iraq between the 1950s and 1990s, including the competition between the rival wings of the Ba'ath Party in Syria and Iraq. It should be underscored that Syria stands out as the first Arab country that relinquished its sovereignty in 1958 to join Nasserite Egypt in the ill-fated United Arab Republic. This pan-Arab project only endured for three years until 1961, and proved to be a bitter disappointment to the Syrians. Another poignant example of rivalries between states with similar ideologies was the animosity between the Islamic Republic of Iran and the Taliban-led Islamic Emirate of Afghanistan until 2001. It should not be forgotten that Tehran almost went to war with the Taliban in August 1998 after the massacre of thousands of Afghan civil-

---

[12] Patrick Seale, *The Struggle for Syria,* New Haven: Yale University Press, 1987, pp. 1–2.

[13] Graham E. Fuller, *The Center of the Universe: The Geopolitics of Iran*, Boulder, CO: Westview Press/RAND Corporation, 1991.

ians and a dozen Iranian consular officials in the city of Mazar-e Sharif, when more people were killed than in the September 11 attacks. Iran massed over 100,000 troops on the Afghan-Iranian border and held ground and air manoeuvres. According to Stephen Walt, the historical record in post-1945 era demonstrates that alliances among Arab states and communist countries that sought to form a single, centralized movement have been unstable and short-lived. In the final analysis, common ideologies have often served as an obstacle to unity, prompting states to compete with one another rather than form durable alliances.[14] Fred Iklé also recognized this point, explaining that in certain instances, alliances not characterized by doctrinal unity will more easily resolve internal differences without disrupting the partnership.[15]

When looking at Syria and Iran, it is evident that Iran (a non-Arab country) is not trying to be the standard-bearer of Arab nationalism, unlike Syria, which considers itself 'the beating heart of Arabism'. Syria, for its part, is not vying for leadership of the Islamic revivalist movement in the Middle East. Overall, there has been neither ostensible competition on the ideological level (except in Lebanon during 1985 to 1988) nor fear that one partner might upstage the other, precisely because of distinctly different ideological platforms. On this point, Herbert Dinerstein explains that 'ideological dissimilarities will not disrupt alliance cooperation if none of the members is intent on political revolution in the others.'[16]

It is noteworthy in this regard that Iran refrained from supporting the Syrian Muslim Brotherhood in their ill-fated effort to overthrow the Ba'athist regime in Damascus during the early 1980s. Between 1980 and 1982, as the struggle between the Muslim Brotherhood and the Syrian authorities intensified, Iran's state-controlled media maintained a news blackout on events in Syria. The situation in Syria presented the clerical regime with a major dilemma. Tehran could ill-afford to criticize its most valuable Arab ally, however, the Brethren were historically speaking an organization with solid Islamic credentials. Consequently, Iran continued to refrain from supporting or criticizing the Muslim Brotherhood. However, after the massive uprising in the city of Hama led by the Ikhwan in February 1982, which was ruthlessly crushed by the Syrian army, the Iranian government finally broke its silence, by publicly condoning the suppression of the revolt. The Iranian foreign ministry issued a statement condemning the Ikhwan for allowing itself to become a functional ally of the 'Zionist entity and Hashemite Jordan'.[17]

---

[14] Stephen M. Walt, *The Origins of Alliances*, Ithaca, New York: Cornell University Press, 1987, pp. 35–36, 206–12 and 'Why Alliances Endure or Collapse', p. 163.
[15] Fred C. Iklé, *How Nations Negotiate*, New York: Harper & Row, 1964, p. 236.
[16] Herbert S. Dinerstein, 'The Transformation of Alliance Systems', p. 592.
[17] Richard Cottam, 'Iran: Motives Behind its Foreign Policy', *Survival*, 28(6), 1986, pp. 488–89. It is noteworthy that since the late 1960s, the Syrian Ikhwan's principal source of support had been the Iraqi Ba'ath. See Hanna Batatu, 'Syria's Muslim Brethren', *MERIP Reports*, November/December 1982, p. 13. According to former Iranian President Abolhassan Bani-Sadr, and British author Patrick Seale in his book, *Asad:*

At the same time, it should be noted that both Ba'athist Syria and Islamist Iran have been fiercely independent states, whose political elites share certain perceptions and world views, and in fact their secular and fundamentalist ideologies overlap in certain respects. While Iran has tried to use its brand of revolutionary Islam to transcend nationalism, create Muslim unity in the region by surmounting Arab-Iranian political divisions and Shiite-Sunni religious differences, and demonstrate its solidarity by actively participating in the Arab-Israeli struggle, Syria, as the self-proclaimed birthplace and heartland of Arabism, has striven to overcome the political fragmentation of the Arab world by acting as a vehicle for Arab unity. Hafez Assad, Ruhollah Khomeini and their successors have viewed the Middle East as a strategic whole and regarded their alliance as a vital tool to assert themselves, to further what they see as in the Arab and Islamic interest, and to increase their room for manoeuvre by diminishing foreign— particularly American—influence in the region. As a result, to advance their common agenda over the years and decades, both regimes have put longer-term interests before short-term gains. This was clearly manifested in the period between 1985 and 1988 when the temptation to terminate the alliance may have been great, particularly for Syria, but instead the alliance was consolidated due to overarching strategic concerns and long-term interests.

The Foreign Policy Priorities of Syria and Iran
As staunchly independent states, it is important to understand the main foreign policy priorities and key objectives of the ruling elites in Damascus and Tehran. The core priority of course for both the Syrian Ba'athist and Iranian Islamist governments, in view of their authoritarian nature, is regime survival. The second priority is national security which in general terms means the maintenance of the territorial integrity and independence of their respective countries. With regard to national security, for Syria, its two main policy objectives are: 1) to regain the Golan Heights occupied by Israel since 1967; and 2) to have (at minimum) veto power over Lebanese affairs in order to ensure the government in Beirut does not adopt policies detrimental to Damascus's interests. With respect to Iran, its two major policy aims are: 1) to be the primary regional player in Persian Gulf affairs; and 2) to ensure that a government hostile towards Tehran does not eventually emerge in Baghdad. Finally, the third priority is the aim to protect and promote, in the case of Damascus, what it sees as Arab interests, and in the case of Tehran, what it perceives as Islamic interests in the region. With regard to the latter, this entails backing the Shiite Lebanese Hezbollah and Sunni Palestinian Hamas movements.

Misconceptions about the Syrian-Iranian Alliance
As previously mentioned, the Syrian-Iranian nexus has been consistently

---

The Struggle for the Middle East, the Syrian Ikhwan also received support from Jordan and its Western backers.

misunderstood in many respects throughout the years. A number of examples demonstrate this fact. First, since the inception of the alliance, one has consistently seen many scholars and observers writing off the Damascus-Tehran partnership as a short-term, opportunistic alliance or marriage of convenience against Saddam Hussein's Iraq that would dissolve rapidly once the Iraqi dictator was overthrown. Saddam Hussein was toppled in 2003, yet the alliance still stands today. It is evident that this line of thinking was too simplistic, requiring instead a more nuanced and sophisticated approach and understanding of the overall relationship. There are a number of factors that contribute to the existence and longevity of the axis. Iraq is crucial, but it is only one element in the overall equation.

A second misconception or myth has been to attribute the cooperation between the two regimes to the fact that the Syrian leadership is Alawite (an offshoot of Shiite Islam), and Iran's clerical regime is Twelver Shiite. This argument does not stand up under close scrutiny. The Syrian regime is secular, and its relationship with Tehran has been based on common political and strategic concerns. Furthermore, just as many orthodox Sunni Muslims may not consider Shiites to be true Muslims, there are those in Shiite Islam who do not consider Alawites to be true Muslims.[18] Various arguments have been put forth; for example that Hafez Assad did not visit Iran while Ayatollah Khomeini was alive because the latter did not consider the Syrian leader to be a true Muslim. Overall, the religious element has not been a determining factor and has had little, if any, salience.

A third misconception or myth is the belief that Iran in essence bought Syrian fealty during the 1980s with free oil shipments to Syria, particularly during a critical period between 1985 and 1988. However, with careful examination, one can confidently conclude that this argument is false. During the period between 1986 and 1987 when Iran was not forthcoming with oil shipments, Syria was under immense pressure from the Soviet Union, Saudi Arabia, Jordan, and other states to abandon its alliance with Iran in exchange for huge financial injections and oil deliveries amounting to billions of dollars in aid. At the same time, the economic situation in Syria was dire, and the country's foreign exchange reserves had fallen dangerously low – enough to finance only a few weeks of imports. Furthermore, there was the prospect of war and greater isolation in the aftermath of the Hindawi affair, with Israel engaging in sabre-rattling and the spectre of international sanctions. If economic and financial imperatives had been the key determinants in Syrian foreign policy formulation, the partnership would have collapsed, but this was not the case. Even today, many observers state that the relationship is only a tactical arrangement, and if the West extends economic incentives to Syria, Damascus will reorient its foreign policy. This is doubtful, unless perhaps this is part of an overall package that includes the restoration of the Golan Heights to Syrian sovereignty and specific security guarantees.

---

[18] Martin Kramer, 'Syria's Alawis and Shi'ism', in *Shi'ism, Resistance, and Revolution*, Martin Kramer (ed.), Boulder, CO: Westview Press, 1987, pp. 237–54.

Stages in the Evolution of the Syrian-Iranian Alliance

Relations Prior to the 1979 Islamic Revolution
Prior to the 1979 revolution, relations between Tehran and Damascus had been anything but cordial, fluctuating for the most part between cold peace and outright hostility. The Shah of Iran, who had reigned since 1941 and enjoyed close links with the United States and Israel, perceived Syria's Ba'athist regime which had seized the reins of power in 1963 as a menace due to its close ties with the Soviet Union, its hostility towards Israel and the West, and support for radical Arab nationalist movements in the Middle East. The Shah viewed the radical brand of Arab nationalism espoused by the Syrian regime as a threat to Iran's regional interests and national security. As far as Syria's Ba'athist leadership, including President Hafez Assad who had ascended to power in 1970, was concerned, Imperial Iran was a dangerous enemy of the Arab nation. He resented the Shah's close ties with Israel, and conservative, pro-Western, Arab monarchies, such as King Hussein's Jordan. The Iranian regime was considered to be an instrument of American and Western policy in the region to frustrate Arab aspirations, including the liberation of Palestine. Despite a brief thaw in relations between Damascus and Tehran following the 1973 Arab-Israeli war, full normalization of relations remained elusive.[19]

Relations in the Post-Revolutionary Era
Since the alliance has been an enduring feature on the political landscape of the Middle East in the post-1979 period, it has undergone several stages in its evolution, and also significant changes in its power structure, due to regional and international events. In terms of the different phases in the development of alliance, at least six distinct periods can be identified:

1) The Emergence of the Syrian-Iranian Alliance 1979–1982;
2) The Zenith and Limits of Syrian-Iranian Power 1982–1985;
3) Intra-Alliance Tensions and Consolidation of the Axis 1985–1988;
4) The Containment of Saddam's Iraq in the Levant and Gulf 1988–1991;
5) Alliance Cooperation in the Post-Cold War Era 1991–2003; and
6) The Reinvigoration of the Alliance since the 2003 Iraq War.

In general, the first three stages were crucial, and constituted the formative years of the alliance, leading to the consolidation of the relationship. If one understands the period between 1979 and 1988, particularly the phase between 1985 and 1988, one can then easily comprehend and decipher how the partnership has evolved since, in spite of the radical changes and transformations that have occurred on the regional and international level.

---

[19] See Ruhollah K. Ramazani, *Revolutionary Iran: Challenge and Response in the Middle East*, Baltimore: Johns Hopkins University Press, 1988, p. 181.

Phase One (1979–1982)

When the Shah of Iran was deposed in February 1979, Assad considered the change in government to be a positive development, and deemed it necessary to establish cordial ties with the new revolutionary regime which seemed sympathetic to the Arab cause and the plight of the Palestinians. In fact, Syria was the first Arab country to recognize the provisional government of Prime Minister Mehdi Bazargan, and overall the third, after the Soviet Union and Pakistan.

The warming of Syrian-Iranian relations during 1979–1980 coincided with the deterioration of Syrian-Iraqi and Iranian-Iraqi relations. After Egypt signed the Camp David Accords with Israel in spring 1979, Syria and Iraq held talks aimed at creating a political union between the two states. However, their efforts came to naught due to differences between the two sides, eventually resulting in mutual recriminations. Concurrently, relations between Baghdad and Tehran deteriorated markedly. On one hand, Iraqi President Saddam Hussein feared that Iran's brand of revolutionary Islam would destabilize his regime, and on the other hand, he interpreted the domestic turmoil in Iran as a sign of his neighbour's weakness. He believed the situation presented him with a golden opportunity to wage a short war to seize territory, overthrow the Islamist regime, and become a major regional power.

The Iraqi invasion of Iran in September 1980 was the main catalyst in transforming the Syrian-Iranian rapprochement into a formal alliance. Damascus condemned Baghdad for initiating the conflict, calling it 'the wrong war against the wrong enemy at the wrong time'.[20] Once it became evident that Saddam Hussein was not going to halt the hostilities, Damascus began to provide invaluable diplomatic and military support to Tehran in order to stem the invasion, and to turn the tide of the war. On the diplomatic front, Syria thwarted the emergence of a united Arab front against Iran at the Amman summit in November 1980 hosted by Saddam Hussein's staunchest ally, King Hussein of Jordan. Syria massed 30,000 troops along its border with Jordan and persuaded half-a-dozen Arab League members to boycott the meeting. In military terms, it served as an important conduit for arms shipments to Iran, and provided various forms of military assistance, including facilitating the Iranian air strike against Iraqi military airfields at H-3 (Al-Walid, in the Iraqi pan-handle, 50 miles east of the Jordanian-Iraqi border) in April 1981, which resulted in the destruction of 15–20 per cent of the Iraq's air force. The alliance was eventually formalized in March 1982 when a high-level Syrian delegation, headed by then Foreign Minister Abd al-Halim Khaddam visited Tehran and concluded a series of bilateral agreements on oil, trade and a secret one on military matters. Syria also subsequently shut off the flow of Iraqi oil through the IPC (trans-Syrian) pipeline to the Mediterranean, thereby reducing Iraqi oil exports by more than half-a-million barrels/day, which translated

---

[20] Patrick Seale, *Asad: The Struggle for the Middle East,* Berkeley: University of California Press, 1989, p. 357.

into losses of US$ 17 million per day (or US$ 6 billion per annum).[21]
Subsequent to Khaddam's visit, Tehran launched a series of offensives between March and May 1982, which led to the expulsion of the Iraqi army from most of the territory they had occupied in Iran. During this period, Syria deployed army units along its border with Iraq, while its warplanes periodically violated Iraqi air space. These moves unnerved the Iraqis who had to contemplate the possibility of a two-front war, and were forced to deploy army units in the east, away from the war theatre to resist the Iranian offensives.[22]

Phase Two (1982–1985)
The second phase in the evolution of the alliance was marked by close cooperation and intensive efforts to respond to new challenges not only in the Gulf region, but more importantly in the Levant. This period can be characterized as the height of Syrian-Iranian power in the region, but also paradoxically as one of lost opportunities which sowed the seeds of decline for the Syrian-Iranian axis due to the drastic shifts in the configuration of forces in the Middle East. The two allies continued their collaboration against Saddam Hussein after the expulsion of the Iraqi army from Iranian soil. A major milestone in this regard was Iran's decision to continue the Gulf war by invading Iraq in July 1982 in a bid to overthrow the Iraqi Ba'athist regime. It persisted in its efforts in the years that followed without achieving a decisive breakthrough. Hence, the conflict turned into a war of attrition and a stalemate ensued.

However, the primary arena of Syrian-Iranian collaboration and success during this period turned out to be the Levant due to new challenges that emerged on the Arab-Israeli front. Subsequent to the Israeli invasion of Lebanon in the summer of 1982, Tehran had signalled its willingness to assist its Arab ally in that theatre. After the rapid rout of the Syrian forces, as a shrewd strategist, Hafez Assad devised a two-track approach to minimize the risk of further escalation and direct military confrontation with Israel, and, at the same time, roll back the Israelis. This could be described as a 'sword and shield' strategy. The political linchpin of his strategy was Syria's special relationships with the Soviet Union on the international level, with Iran on the regional level, and with Lebanese allies on the local level. The offensive component, the 'sword', was to utilize Iran's aid and influence among the Lebanese Shiites to wage a campaign of subversion, terror, and guerrilla warfare against their mutual opponents, the Gemayel government, the Israelis and the US and French contingents of the Multinational Force in Lebanon. The defensive element, the 'shield', was to rebuild and expand Syria's conventional forces with Soviet assistance in order to deter an Israeli first strike and achieve

---

[21] Shahram Chubin and Charles Tripp, *Iran and Iraq at War*, Boulder, Colorado: Westview Press, 1988, p. 180; and Hirschfeld, 'The Odd Couple', pp. 107–8.
[22] Shahram Chubin and Charles Tripp, *Iran and Iraq at War*, Boulder, Colorado: Westview Press, 1988, p. 180; and Hirschfeld, 'The Odd Couple', pp. 107–8.

strategic parity with Israel. This strategy worked well and paid off handsomely as their opponents were dealt a series of devastating blows resulting in the Israeli retreat and the withdrawal of US and French forces by 1984–1985. The most notable ones were the assassination of Lebanese President Bashir Gemayel in September 1982, the demolition of the Israeli Defence Forces (IDF) headquarters in Tyre in November 1982, the destruction of the US embassy in Beirut in April 1983, the bombing of the barracks of US Marine and French Paratrooper contingents of the Multinational Force in October 1983, the repeated demolition of the IDF headquarters in Tyre in November 1983, and the bombing of the US embassy annex in East Beirut in September 1984. These attacks led to the withdrawal of US forces in February 1984, the scrapping of the Israeli-Lebanese peace treaty in March 1984, and the phased withdrawal of Israeli troops from most of the territory they had initially overrun between January and June 1985.

At the same time though, Iran's refusal to terminate hostilities with Iraq, and the continuation of the Gulf conflict, led to countermoves, resulting in the gradual emergence of the Iraqi-Jordanian-Egyptian axis backed by Washington and Riyadh, and the relative decline of Syrian-Iranian power in the region. Concern that Saddam Hussein might be defeated also led to a US-Iraqi rapprochement, the provision of intelligence and non-military equipment by the Reagan administration to Iraq, and eventually the restoration of diplomatic relations between Washington and Baghdad in November 1984. Concomitantly, Moscow and Paris increased their military assistance to Iraq in order to prevent an Iranian victory. Hence, by the spring of 1985, it was clear that Syrian-Iranian power had reached its limits, and was now being contained by a formidable coalition of regional and extra-regional actors.

Phase Three (1985–1988)
The third phase in the evolution of the alliance represented the most problematic period in bilateral relations, and at the same time, was quite critical in laying the foundations of a durable partnership, in other words, the long-term institutionalization of the axis. In both the Levant and the Persian Gulf, where the two allies had previously cooperated, they now developed conflicting agendas. The failure to end the Lebanese civil war (following the withdrawal of Western and Israeli forces), and Iran's continuation of the war with Iraq served to undermine the position of the Damascus-Tehran nexus. Furthermore, the two allies adopted different positions in Lebanon as the Israeli threat receded. On almost every issue in Lebanon, the two allies stood on opposite sides. The two allies had differing visions of the political future of Lebanon. Syria wanted to reform the political system and establish a stable, secular state within its sphere of influence, while Iran seemed to favour the creation of a theocratic system mirroring its own model. The rapid rise of the fundamentalist, pro-Iranian Hezbollah movement at the expense of the secular, pro-Syria Amal militia led to tensions and recurrent clashes between the two groups. In addition, during the Amal-led siege of Palestinian refugee camps between 1985 and 1987, Syria steadfastly supported its proxy much to Iran's dismay

which tried to mediate and end the confrontation peacefully.
Concurrently, in the Gulf, Iran's determination to prosecute the war against Iraq caused a great deal of concern, prompting a growing number of states to throw their weight behind Baghdad. As Tehran became increasingly isolated and the prospects for an Iranian victory faded, Assad grew ambivalent about the continuation of the conflict and seemed inclined to favour a negotiated settlement. There were other areas of contention also, such as the Syrian-Jordanian rapprochement, intermittent Syrian-Iraqi negotiations, and Syria's confrontation with the Sunni Islamic Unification Movement (Tawhid) of Shaykh Sa'id Sha'ban in the northern Lebanese city of Tripoli. However, through constant consultations, the two allies were able to prioritize their interests, resolve their differences, and redefine the parameters of cooperation during 1985–1988, thereby leading to the maturation and consolidation of the alliance. The resurgence of Iraq's power by the late 1980s as it turned the tables on Iran in the Gulf war, the gradual withdrawal of Soviet support for Syria during the Gorbachev years, the concurrent ascendance of US influence in the Middle East, and the need for the two allies to cooperate in order to stabilise the situation in Lebanon, altogether, helped cement the relationship.

Phase Four (1988–1991)
During the fourth phase, in the inter-war period between the end of the Iran-Iraq hostilities in August 1988 and the Iraqi invasion of Kuwait exactly two years later (in August 1990), Syria and Iran continued their collaboration due to Iraq's growing power and assertiveness throughout the region. By now, Saddam Hussein possessed one of the five largest military establishments in the world, and was indisputably the dominant power in the Gulf region. Bilateral cooperation was made imperative also by the formalization of the counter-axis that had emerged in the 1980s, with the creation of the short-lived Arab Cooperation Council (ACC) consisting of Iraq, Jordan, Egypt and North Yemen in February 1989.[23] The main challenge came in Lebanon, where an anti-Syrian revolt led by the commander of the Lebanese army, General Michel Aoun, provided Saddam Hussein with an irresistible opportunity to hit back at his Syrian rival by providing arms to Aoun's forces. Iran, although weak, isolated and unable to challenge Iraq in the Gulf, assisted Syria by mobilizing Hezbollah and other Lebanese groups in the conflict against Aoun, who was eventually defeated by the Syrians and their allies in 1989. Besides involvement in Lebanon, Iraq pursued an activist foreign policy by assisting Mauritania in its conflict with Senegal, aiding the Khartoum government in its efforts to crush the rebellion in southern Sudan, encouraging the unification of North and South Yemen, maintaining an inflexible stance in the peace negotiations with Iran, holding joint military exercises with Jordan, and making inflammatory statements threatening Israel.[24]

---

[23] For a good analysis of the ACC, see Curtis R. Ryan, 'Jordan and the Rise and Fall of the Arab Cooperation Council', *Middle East Journal*, 52(3), 1998, pp. 386–401.
[24] Joe Stork and Ann Lesch, 'Background to the Crisis: Why War?', in *The Persian*

During the 1990–1991 Kuwait crisis, Iran, which had been exhausted after eight years of war with Iraq, stayed out of the fray and remained neutral, while Syria joined the US-led coalition in order to cut down Saddam Hussein and reap the benefits of being on the side of the victors, including George H. W. Bush's promise to resolve the Arab-Israeli conflict. There was some speculation at the time that the Tehran-Damascus nexus was falling apart due to a thaw in Iranian-Iraqi relations, but this did not turn out to be the case. In fact, during the crisis, Hafez Assad visited Tehran and received assurances from the clerical leadership that Iran would maintain its neutrality and abide by UN-imposed sanctions on Iraq. Both sides also took a further step to consolidate and institutionalize their alliance by establishing the Joint Higher Syrian-Iranian Cooperation Committee, chaired by their respective vice-presidents and foreign ministers. The aim of this body was to forge closer political, economic and military ties between the two sides through regular consultations.

Phase Five (1991–2003)

Following Iraq's defeat in the 1991 Gulf conflict and end of the Cold War that same year, Syria and Iran preserved their links for four major reasons. First, they maintained and expanded their political, military and economic relations in view of the dominant position of the United States in the region and the world with the gradual retreat and eventual dissolution of the Soviet Union, and the rapidly changing political landscape of the Middle East and the uncertainties that it brought. Second, Damascus considered the nexus with Tehran to be a vital instrument for advancing its interests in the Arab-Israeli conflict and peace talks. Syria needed Iran in order to promote its objectives in Lebanon, by exercising influence and control over Hezbollah and encouraging its fighters to attack Israeli forces in the self-declared security zone in southern Lebanon between 1991 and 2000. It also aimed to play the 'Iran card' in the peace negotiations with the Israelis and Americans in order to regain the Golan Heights. Damascus considered the nexus with Tehran to be a vital instrument for advancing its interests in the Arab-Israeli conflict and peace talks. Third, as long as Saddam Hussein remained in power, the two allies, particularly Iran, believed the maintenance of the alliance to be essential in order to keep Iraqi power in check. Fourth, starting in 1991, the two allies undertook a joint programme to acquire the capability to manufacture ballistic missiles domestically. Towards this end, they also sought technology transfers and assistance from Russia, China, and North Korea. This could be attributed in large part to Iraq's success in using surface-to-surface missiles against Iran in the Iran-Iraq war, and against Israel in the Kuwait conflict. In the Syrian case, this was also motivated by Israel's overwhelming superiority

---

Gulf War: Views from the Social and Behavioral Sciences, Herbert H. Blumberg and Christopher C. French (eds), Lanham, MD: University Press of America, 1994, p. 21 and Amatzia Baram, 'Calculation and Miscalculation in Baghdad', in *International Perspectives on the Gulf Conflict 1990-91*, Alex Danchev and Dan Keohane (eds), Basingstoke, England: Macmillan Press Ltd, 1994, p. 26.

Iran and Syria: An Enduring Alliance 281

in conventional and non-conventional weapons. Tehran along with Pyongyang helped build missile production facilities in Syria for example in Hama and Aleppo.

Eventually, the support for Hezbollah in order to make sure that Israel paid a price for the continued occupation of the self-declared security zone and the Golan Heights paid off handsomely. An increasingly effective guerrilla campaign mounted by the Lebanese movement throughout the 1990s culminated in the Israeli withdrawal from Lebanon in May 2000. This was the first time that Israel withdrew from occupied territory without signing an agreement. Concomitantly, between 1991 and 2000, Damascus participated in US-brokered peace talks with Tel Aviv in a bid to regain the Golan Heights in exchange for peace and recognition of Israel. However, this process did not bear fruit. Washington tried to corner and isolate Iran during much of the 1990s under the dual containment policy. Although expectations emerged for a thaw in US-Iranian relations during the early years of Mohammad Khatami's presidency, this proved to be a false dawn as the reformist president demonstrated his lack of resolve and courage to take on the more hard-line elements within the regime which were opposed to any rapprochement with the United States. Perhaps, the most detrimental aspect of Syrian-Iranian policy during the 1990s was the support both states provided to varying degrees for Islamist movements such as Hamas and Islamic Jihad. Although one could be sceptical whether the Oslo process would have indeed borne fruit at the end of the day, the suicide attacks undertaken by extremists, especially those targeting Israeli civilians, contributed significantly to destroying trust and confidence and any prospects for success in the peace negotiations.

Phase 6 (2003 to Present)
Finally, in the sixth phase, since the US-led invasion and occupation of Iraq, cooperation between the two allies has increased markedly. Syria and Iran viewed the overthrow of Saddam Hussein by US-led forces in April 2003 with ambivalence. On one hand, both welcomed the toppling of their longtime foe. On the other hand, the speed of the military victory initially raised fears that they could be the next targets in the Bush administration's 'war on terror'. However, once it became clear that Washington faced major difficulties, and was becoming bogged down in Iraq, there was a degree of relief in Damascus and Tehran. The two allies are still concerned about the prominent US military presence in the region, but over the past several years, they believe US power and influence have begun to wane. Iran has tried to maintain and cultivate close ties with all the major Iraqi political parties and militias, particularly the Shiite ones, in order to ensure that Baghdad will not assume a hostile stance towards it.

Overall, the partnership was reinvigorated by the 2003 US-led invasion of Iraq and the Bush administration's indifference to become engaged in order to resuscitate the Syrian-Israeli and Palestinian-Israeli tracks of the peace process. A clear sign of this was when Syrian Prime Minister Muhammed Naji al-Utri on a visit to Iran in February 2005 declared that the two partners were presenting a 'united front' against the challenges they faced in the Middle East.

With regard to the 2006 crisis in Lebanon, irrespective of whether the war had been planned by either or both sides, one thing is for certain: once the hostilities started, the United States found it expedient to prevent a speedy end to the conflict in the UN Security Council for more than one month, calculating that a sustained Israeli ground, sea, and air assault on Lebanon lasting several weeks would weaken and hopefully destroy Hezbollah, thereby, depriving the Syrian-Iranian camp of one of its major trump cards in the regional power struggle against Washington and Tel Aviv. From the US perspective, the destruction of Hezbollah would have also paved the way for possible military action against Iran if the dispute over Tehran's nuclear programme was not resolved politically on terms that Washington found advantageous and favourable. This is because potential Hezbollah retaliation against Israel serves as a trip wire for US military action against Iran and Syria. It is noteworthy that in a premature, but telling statement during the conflict, then US Secretary of State Condoleezza Rice confidently asserted, 'We are witnessing the birth pangs of a new Middle East.'[25]

In terms of who emerged as the victor in the 2006 war, although Hezbollah leader Hasan Nasrallah claimed victory, in the greater scheme of things, it was not so much Hezbollah that won, but Israel that lost. Tel Aviv set high benchmarks for victory, including the freedom of the two Israeli soldiers seized at the outset of the conflict and the annihilation of Hezbollah. However, it fell short of its stated objectives. Hezbollah was weakened, but at the same time, it demonstrated enormous resourcefulness and resilience during the fighting, particularly in the realm of electronic warfare (EW), and in the immediate aftermath of the conflict with its recovery, rehabilitation, and reconstruction efforts. It should be underscored that subsequent to the month-long war, Hezbollah gained enormous popularity and support among the masses in the Arab-Muslim world. In July 2008, Hezbollah scored a major symbolic victory when it exchanged the bodies of the two Israeli servicemen for five Lebanese prisoners, most notably Samir Qantar, and the remains of 199 others. In addition, two months earlier, in May 2008, the Doha agreement which ended an eighteen-month-long political deadlock in Lebanon, marked a significant gain for the pro-Syrian camp led by Hezbollah. As a result of the accord, the Hezbollah-led opposition secured 11 cabinet posts which would enable it to veto any cabinet decisions, something they had been demanding all along.

Although the anti-Syrian March 14 movement led by Saad Hariri fared well in the June 2009 parliamentary elections in Lebanon, subsequent events and the December 2009 visit of Hariri as the new prime minister to Damascus were clear signs that Syria and Hezbollah could not be ignored and had to be accommodated. There would have to be consensus building and compromise

---

[25] Rami G. Khouri, 'New Rules for the Middle East', *The New York Times*, 26 May 2008.

by the new government in order to overcome the political paralysis that had plagued Lebanon since the elections.

Looking at more recent events, it remains to be seen whether the Obama administration's policies towards Syria and Iran will yield substantive results. Although the prospects of a military strike on Iran have decreased markedly after the publication of the US National Intelligence Estimate (NIE) on Iran's nuclear activities since December 2007 (which concluded that Tehran had abandoned its nuclear weapons programme in 2003), tensions still remain high. One cannot completely dismiss the prospect of at least aerial strikes on Iran. At the same time, the likelihood for major advances on the Palestinian-Israeli track of the Middle East peace process seems remote.

Overall, Israel's failure to deliver a knockout blow against the Syrian and Iranian-backed Hezbollah movement in the 2006 Lebanon war, the absence of any major progress in the Arab-Israeli peace process, Washington's preoccupation with the Iraqi and Afghan imbroglios, and the volatility in international oil markets magnified Syrian and Iranian influence and diminished Washington's room for manoeuvre in the Middle East. However, this does not mean that the Syrian-Iranian axis is on the ascendant again. Although both countries are defiant, both are also on the defensive, particularly in view of the unrest in Syria since 2011 and the harsh Western sanctions imposed on both countries. It seems unlikely that the political and strategic stalemate in the region can be broken any time soon. Much also depends on how the situation in Iraq, Afghanistan, and Lebanon evolve, and the policies of the Obama administration.

The Changing Structure and Balance of Power in the Syrian-Iranian Alliance

In terms of the shifting balance of power and the evolution of the power structure in the alliance, a great deal has changed since its inception three decades ago. During the 1980s, Syria was the dominant partner, whereas now Iran enjoys a more influential position. For 29 years (from 1976 to 2005), Syria was the more dominant player in Lebanon because, in addition to its proximity, it maintained a sizeable military presence in that country. However, since Syria's military withdrawal in 2005 and the prominence of the pro-Iranian Hezbollah movement in Lebanese politics, this is no longer the case. In addition, during the 1980s, Syria's importance in Arab and regional politics was magnified by the fact that Egypt had been banished from the Arab fold after the 1979 Camp David Accords, and Iraq was entangled in a conflict with Iran. Damascus also proved very adept at using proxies to fight its battles during this period. While Iran engaged Syria's Ba'athist rivals, Hezbollah and other Lebanese groups were mobilized to fight the Israelis, and the pro-Syrian Amal militia besieged the Palestinian strongholds in Lebanon. In the words of one astute Lebanese observer at the time: 'Syria fights Iraq with Iranian blood, the Palestinians with Amal blood, and Israel with Lebanese blood.'[26]

Furthermore, while both countries had poor relations with the United States, Syria, unlike Iran, enjoyed the political, military, and economic backing of the Soviet Union until the late 1980s when bilateral relations cooled markedly under Mikhail Gorbachev. During the Iran-Iraq conflict, Syria served as a conduit for arms shipments from both the East and West to Iran. Tehran's dependency became particularly great after the deterioration of relations with Moscow in 1982, and Washington's efforts to impose a worldwide arms embargo on Iran from 1983 onwards (known as Operation Staunch). As we all know though, necessity is the mother of invention. Therefore, Iran began to develop its own arms industry during the 1980s, and already by the 1990s, it had taken the leading role in joint efforts with Syria to develop ballistic missiles. Today, Iran exports arms to Syria, and moreover, finances Syrian arms purchases from Russia, Belarus, North Korea and other states. During the 1980s, Iran also needed the alliance with Syria in order to prevent becoming isolated in the Middle East, and to dispel pro-Iraqi propaganda that the Iran-Iraq war was an Arab-Iranian conflict. Following Iraq's invasion of Kuwait, Iran mended fences with many Arab countries, including Jordan, Saudi Arabia, Tunisia, Morocco, and Mauritania to name a few. Prior to the outbreak of the Arab spring, Iran enjoyed widespread popularity among the Arab masses.[27] Until recently, Tehran's power and prestige had been enhanced also by its political posturing on the nuclear issue, relatively high oil prices on international markets, and the commitment of US forces in Iraq and Afghanistan where Iran had the capacity to make the situation even more problematic for Washington and its allies.

Conclusion

In general, recent developments have diminished the prospect of full-scale conflict between the Syrian-Iranian camp and its opponents. However, this does not necessarily mean that the two sides will engage in dialogue and negotiations in order to resolve differences. At present, the United States has very little leverage over Syria and Iran. Overall, both countries have been able to stave off isolation in the post-Cold War era. Although they have not always been successful in steering events in a desirable direction in the Middle East, their ability to thwart the ambitions of actors such as Iraq, Israel, and the United States cannot be ignored. In this respect, the achievements of the Syrian-Iranian alliance over the past three decades have been quite impressive. Irrespective of how much longer the partnership endures, it has left its imprint on the modern Middle East politics. For the foreseeable future, Syria and Iran will continue and perhaps intensify their cooperation in view of the regional situation and the challenges that may lie ahead.

---

[26] Judith Perera, 'Assad's Secret War', *The Middle East*, August 1985, p. 17.
[27] Robert Baer, *The Devil We Know: Dealing with the New Iranian Superpower*, New York: Crown Publishers, 2008, pp. 155–57.

Chapter 17

Iran and the Twenty-First Century 'Persian world': A Tajik Perspective

Frédérique Guérin

Contemporary Iran is heir to a rich Persian-language literary culture which is shared in varying degrees by the populations of West, Central, and South Asia. From the nineteenth century on, this area has been profoundly altered by European imperialist policies, reshaped into modern, national entities, and fragmented between rival geopolitical spheres of interest. Although the traditional position of the Persian language in the region has vastly declined,[1] the cultural references carried by the Persian literary heritage have been resilient throughout the region. Besides, modern varieties of Persian are today official languages in Afghanistan (Dari) and Tajikistan (Tajik), and remain widely spoken in regions of Uzbekistan (Samarqand, Bukhara and Surkhandaria) and in northern Pakistan.

In the midst of a profound geopolitical restructuring in the heart of Eurasia since the disintegration of the Soviet Union, reference to a shared cultural legacy has emerged as a soft power tool of Iran's contemporary foreign policy and is used to increase regional influence. Afghanistan and Tajikistan stand out in this policy, as they form with Iran the contemporary 'Persian-speaking world'. While Afghanistan and Iran had continuously maintained close, if not always easy, relationships since the autonomization of the Afghan kingdom in the early eighteenth century, Tajikistan, as well as the other new states of post-Soviet Central Asia, were newcomers to Iranian external politics, and their encounter turned out to be all but straightforward. Iran's cultural diplomacy met with genuine enthusiasm in Tajikistan at the turn of the 1990s (1988–1992), an enthusiasm which, however, promptly cooled down with the start of a civil war in that country (1992–1997), a conflict in which Iran played an active role. Even so, only ten years after the end of the civil war, the streets of Dushanbe, the Tajik capital, were covered with Iranian flags to celebrate the

---

[1] See Bert G. Fragner, *Die Persophonie: Regionalität, Identität und Sprachkontakt in der Geschichte Asiens*, Berlin: Das Arabische Buch, 1999.

official visit of Iranian President Mahmoud Ahmadinejad on the occasion of the first Persian-speaking summit held in March 2007. Ever since then, Tehran and Dushanbe have proactively sought to promote political, economic, and cultural ties between the two countries and are trying to rally Afghanistan's President Hamid Karzai to their vision of an integrated Persian world. The three heads of state have met four times in the past three years, in high-level Persian summits that led to the signature of a number of cooperation agreements. In the latest of these trilateral summits, President Ahmadinejad went so far as to suggest the creation of a security alliance similar to NATO between the three Persian-speaking countries, leading some analysts to wonder, most often very sceptically, about the possible emergence of a pan-Iranian alliance.[2]

Very few scholars have competently tried to analyse the interplay between domestic, regional, and international dynamics, and between long-term cultural history, contemporary national identity, and the making of foreign policy in greater Central Asia. Mohammad-Reza Djalili has been a precursor and a leading expert in this matter. A respected scholar in both Iranian studies and international relations, Professor Djalili at once realized the tremendous geopolitical shift happening in Iran's backyard following the dissolution of the Soviet Union, as well as the complexities of the reconnection between the Islamic Republic of Iran and the Central Asian states. From the early 1990s on, he set out to raise awareness among his students of international relations of the critical geopolitics of greater Central Asia, and his efforts were met with enthusiasm. He also organized a series of conferences in Geneva aimed at fostering scholarly debate and research on the geopolitics of Eurasia.[3] He prolifically contributed innovative studies on the reconnection of the region with its neighbours,[4] and produced the most comprehensive and incisive study

---

[2] Roman Muzalevsky, 'The "Persian Alliance" and Geopolitical Reconfiguration in Central Asia', *Eurasia Daily Monitor*, 7 (161), September 2010, available at: http://www.jamestown.org/programs/edm/single/?tx_ttnews[tt_news]=36799&tx_ttnews[backPid]=27&cHash=2438778ab3 (accessed 6 June 2011).

[3] The first conference was devoted to the then little-known and troubled independent Republic of Tajikistan in December 1993. The contributions were published in a volume in French and English. *Le Tadjikistan à l'épreuve de l'indépendance*, Geneva: Publications HEI, 1995, co-edited with Frédéric Grare, translated and published in English in 1998 as *Tajikistan: the Trials of Independence*, Richmond: Curzon, 1998, co-edited with Frédéric Grare and Shirin Akiner. Other conferences addressed the following issues: 'Le Caucase postsoviétique: La transition dans le conflit' (1994); 'The OSCE and the Multiple Challenges of Transition: The Caucasus and Central Asia' (2003); 'The Illusions of Transition. Which Perspectives for Central Asia and the South Caucasus?' (2004); Le monde turco-iranien en question (2008). They all led to similarly titled publications.

[4] 'Caucase et Asie centrale: entrée en scène et recomposition géostratégique de l'espace', *Central Asian Survey*, 13, 1994, pp. 7–17; 'Moyen-Orient, Caucase et Asie centrale: des concepts géopolitiques à construire et à reconstuire?', (with Thierry Kellner), *Central Asian Survey*, 19, 2000, pp.117–40; 'New Foreign Policies for New

of the geopolitics of Central Asia,[5] well before the world's news agencies turned their attention to Central Asia following the 2001 September attacks in New York City. As an Iranist concerned with the position of Iran in the twenty-first century, Djalili has dedicated specific attention to Iran's policy in Central Asia and more specifically to the contemporary Iranian world.[6] In a 2002 article, he skilfully drew the contours of the 'Iranian spiritual universe' while revealing the complex and fragmented nature of this geo-cultural area in modern times.[7]

The author of this article has incommensurably benefited from Djalili's intellectual work on the modern encounter between Iran and Central Asia, and the piece presented here is a modest contribution to the area of research. This chapter aims to contribute to a better understanding of the current geopolitical developments taking place within the Persian-speaking world by studying the position of one of its components, the Republic of Tajikistan. The geo-cultural inclination of Tajikistan towards Iran is often taken for granted, without giving proper consideration to the geopolitical worldview that is being elaborated by its ruling elite. Although it is difficult to gauge to what extent this perspective will take hold in the broader society and will be maintained through time, it is undoubtedly useful to bring this element into the equation when examining the developments taking place in the modern Persian-speaking world. In order to do so, this chapter will first review the current state of the Persian world before presenting the Tajik geopolitical discourse which, given the lack of reference to past experience of statehood, is to a great extent based on a constructed geopolitical mythology. Finally, it will look at the latest developments in the relations between Iran and Tajikistan and conclude with some remarks on the implications of this relation for the potential re-emergence of a Persian-speaking geopolitical area in the twenty-first century.

The Persian World

Tajikistan and the Contemporary Persian World

The Persian world is a concept which refers to the geo-cultural area where the Persian-language literary culture has played a central role. This area, called *Iran-zamin* (Iranian lands), extends far beyond the borders of

---

States: Transcaucasia and Central Asia in the International Arena', in *The OSCE and the Multiples Challenges of Transition*, Farian Sabahi and Daniel Warner (eds), London: Ashgate, 2004, pp.13–36.
[5] *Géopolitique de la nouvelle Asie centrale. De la fin de l'URSS à l'après-11 septembre*, Paris: PUF, 2001–2003 (with Thierry Kellner).
[6] 'L'Iran face aux développements en Transcaucasie et en Asie centrale', *Cahiers d'études sur la Méditerranée orientale et le monde turco-iranien (CEMOTI)*, 16, 1993, pp. 245–55; 'Téhéran face à l'Asie centrale', *Nouveaux Mondes*, 4, 1994, pp. 175–90; 'In Search of New Friends : Iran and Central Asia', *World Affairs*, 1, 1997, pp. 102–15.
[7] Mohammad-Reza Djalili, 'Un monde iranien aux multiples identités', *Boèce. Revue romande des sciences humaines*, 3, 2002, pp. 33–46.

contemporary Iran into Anatolia, Kurdistan, the Caucasus, Central Asia, and Mesopotamia.[8] In addition to the Persian language, this area has been fashioned by two pervasive cultural elements: Islam and the process of ethno-cultural intermingling with Turkic peoples, which started as early as the fifth century and became overwhelming from the eleventh century onwards.[9] The 'Iranian world' therefore greatly overlaps with what has been identified as a Turko-Persian Islamicate œcumene.[10]

Although the history of the Persian world is one of ethno-cultural encounters and cross-fertilization, recent history has contributed to the fragmentation of what used to be a more or less coherent cultural continent. The sixteenth century is often conceived as a milestone in the fragmentation of the Persian area with the adoption of Twelver Shiism as the state ideology by the Safavid dynasty (1501–1722). This event generated a durable political and cultural singularization of the Iranian state and complicated the relations between the 'heretic' empire and its Sunni neighbours (the Ottoman Empire, the Uzbek khanates, and the Mughal Empire) but it did not put an end altogether to cultural and intellectual exchanges between Khorasan, Transoxiana, and the Indian subcontinent.[11] Much more divisive has been the colonial penetration of European powers in the nineteenth century. Intense competition between the British and Russian empires in the heart of Eurasia resulted in the division of the region into distinct geo-cultural areas, the reification of artificial political borders, and the emergence of profoundly transformed collective identities. The European imperial rivalry cut off the Indian subcontinent (turned into British colonies) and Central Asia (conquered by Tsarist Russia) from each other and from Iran, generating in the process the arbitrary definition of the Afghan state as a buffer zone. Traditional socio-political organization was fundamentally altered by colonial policies and by the introduction of the European national ideology in the twentieth century. Following the Bolshevik revolution, Central Asia and the Caucasus were

---

[8] For a more elaborated discussion of the definition of Persian lands, see Xavier de Planhol, 'Lands of Iran', *Encyclopaedia Iranica*, online edition, 2004, available: http://www.iranica.com/articles/iran-i-lands-of-iran (accessed 27 May 2011).

[9] For an excellent presentation of the process of Turkicization of Central Asia and Iran, see Yuri Bregel, 'Turko-Mongol influences in Central Asia', in *Turko-Persia in Historical Perspective*, Robert L. Canfield (ed.), Cambridge: Cambridge University Press, 1991, pp. 53–77; and Xavier de Planhol, *Les Nations du Prophète: Manuel géographique de politique musulmane*, Paris: Fayard, 1993, pp. 479–678.

[10] Robert L. Canfield, 'Introduction: the Turko-Persian tradition', in *Turko-Persia in Historical Perspective*, Robert L. Canfield (ed.), Cambridge: Cambridge University Press, 1991, pp. 1–34.

[11] Robert McChesney, '"Barrier of heterodoxy": Rethinking the ties between Iran and Central Asia in the 17th Century', in *Safavid Persia: The history and politics of an Islamic society*, Charles Melville (ed.), London: I. B. Tauris, 1996, pp. 231—67; and Maria Szuppe, 'Circulation des lettrés et cercles littéraires: entre Asie centrale, Iran et Inde du nord (XVe-XVIIIe siècle)', *Annales. Histoire, Sciences sociales*, 59(5), 2004, pp. 997–1018.

divided into ethno-national Soviet republics in the 1920s and national specificities were emphasized throughout the Soviet period. In South Asia, the introduction of the national ideology not only contributed to end colonial rule in the subcontinent, but also led to a bloody partition of the subcontinent along religious and national lines. Persia, which Iranians themselves had always called 'Iran', underwent an authoritarian reform process which aimed at turning the country into a European-type nation-state. The policy involved the official renaming of the country as Iran and elaborating a rather restrictive definition of the nation which glorified the 'Aryan', pre-Islamic past, rejected as negative 'external' influences that had altered the 'purity' of Iranian identity, and came to consider the surrounding regions as a mere cultural backyard of the historical Iranian empire.

The introduction of national definitions of the self and the writing of new historiographies based on ethno-national, linguistic, and territorial criteria have profoundly altered the geopolitical and geo-cultural meaning of the centuries-old Persian cultural area. As Ahmad Karimi-Hakkak puts it:

> Each segment of a once-coherent culture had been trying to help itself to as much of the cultural heritage as it could afford (...) Nationalism and the modern idea of the nation-state presented a distorted and fragmented view of that culture to the world at large, with little perceptible cultural coherence.[12]

Today, the notion of a Persian world is related to Iran's imperial history and is sometimes referred as *Iran-e bozorg* (Greater Iran). Afghanistan and Tajikistan are two countries that speak 'national' variants of the Persian language, Dari for the former, Tajik for the later, and that claim legacy over the Persian heritage in Central Asia. The way these two countries will position themselves with regard to the idea of a Persian world and will relate to Iran remains the object of considerable uncertainty. The two countries are both extremely unstable and vulnerable to external influences and are located at the crossroads of different geopolitical areas. They are both characterized by internal fragmentation and confronted with the challenge of consolidating the national idea among their population. It is therefore interesting to follow the current rapprochement between Tajikistan and Iran and try to understand the type of geopolitical outlook being developed in Tajikistan, the newest of the three countries.

Tajikistan's Geopolitical Mythology

Tajikistan was created ex-nihilo in 1924 in the context of the national delimitation of Russian Turkistan by the newly established Soviet government. Given the profound intermingling of Turkic- (mostly Uzbek-) and Tajik-speaking populations, the Tajik state was initially designed as an

---

[12] Ahmad Karimi-Hakkak, 'Iranica Heirloom: Persian Literature', *Iranian Studies*, 31, 1998, p. 528.

autonomous republic within the Republic of Uzbekistan.[13] To accommodate nationalist reactions among Tajik representatives who complained against the injustice of the initial project, Tajikistan became a full-fledged Soviet republic in 1929.[14] However, the belated territorial claims articulated by Tajik representatives were not satisfied and the Republic of Tajikistan remained located for most of its parts on the isolated, mountainous, and unruly eastern terrains of the former emirate of Bukhara. Substantial Tajik minorities were left outside the Tajik Republic, as were the two historical centres of Persian culture in Central Asia, the cities of Bukhara and Samarqand. Throughout the Soviet period, Tajikistan remained the poorest republic of the Soviet Union. The development of the country's economic infrastructure was designed to suit the Soviet Union's economic needs and did not involve consideration for national sustainability. As a consequence, Tajikistan has become heavily dependent on Uzbekistan in terms of energetic resources and transportation networks, and therefore highly vulnerable to Uzbek political influence. The territorial configuration of the Republic of Tajikistan not only deprived the country of a viable territorial basis on which to build a national project, it also created a deep-rooted hostility towards Uzbekistan, held responsible for the loss of what would come to be considered as Tajik historical lands.

Nevertheless, Soviet institutional, linguistic, and educational policies contributed to shaping the contours of Tajikistan and ascertaining the content of Tajik nationality. Under Soviet tutelage, the ethno-cultural definition of the Tajik nation was carefully distinguished from the other Persian-speaking populations outside the Soviet area. The official codification of the Tajik language emphasized the difference between the Persian of Iran and the Dari of Afghanistan, and the shift to the Cyrillic script in 1940 further contributed to the cultural estrangement of the Tajik population from the classical and modern Persian heritage.[15] Even so, Tajik intellectuals who were obsessed with the need of compensating for their country's material deprivation and cultural isolation in a Turkic-speaking environment found in the Soviet

---

[13] The process that led to the nationalization of the Uzbek and Tajik ethnicity and the delimitation of two ethnonymic republics is too complex to be recounted here. Detailed and well-documented analyses can be found in Bert Fragner, 'The Nationalization of the Uzbeks and Tajiks', in *Muslim Communities Re-emerge*, Andreas Kappeler, Gerhard Simon, Gerog Brunner (eds), Durham: Duke University Press, 1994, pp. 13–32; Arne Haugen, *The Establishment of National Republics in Soviet Central Asia*, Hampshire/New York: Palgrave Macmillan, 2003; Paul Bergne, *The Birth of Tajikistan: National Identity and the Origins of the Republic*, London: I.B. Tauris, 2007; Francine Hirsch, *Empire of Nations: Ethnographic Knowledge and the Making of the Soviet Union*, Ithaca: Cornell University Press, 2005; and Terry Martin, *The Affirmative Action Empire: Nations and Nationalism in the Soviet Union, 1923–1939*, Ithaca: Cornell University Press, 2001.
[14] This decision was also, if not mostly, strategic. The creation of a Persian-speaking Republic could serve as a foothold for Soviet propaganda in the wider Persian-speaking world.
[15] Muriel Atkin, 'Tajik National Identity', *Iranian Studies*, 26, 1993, pp. 151–58.

academic disciplines of orientalism, history, or ethnography the intellectual resources to claim ownership over the whole Persian heritage of greater Central Asia. Understanding the way this heritage was appropriated is more than a mere academic exercise: it is important because it has had practical consequences for the development of a national ideology since independence, and influences the way Tajikistan positions itself in the international arena.

Tajik official historiography was brought forward in the 1970s by the influential Tajik scholar and statesman Bobojon Gafurov (Ghafurov), first secretary of the Tajik Communist Party (1946–1956) and head of the Moscow Institute of Oriental Studies (1956–1977). His most complete work on Tajik history, *Tajiki. Antique, Ancient and Medieval History* (Moscow, 1972),[16] has been instrumental in shaping a geopolitical mythology which a) introduced a historical antagonism between Tajik and Turkic (especially Uzbek) nations; b) linked the fate of the Tajik nation to the Russian people and c) recognized a strong ethno-cultural connection with the contemporary Iranian nation while emphasizing the distinct and equally prestigious contribution of the two Iranian peoples to the civilizations of Eurasia.

Ethnographic debates that informed the making of ethno-national republics in Central Asia in the 1920s have generated a durable ontological insecurity among the Tajik intelligentsia. Tajik leaders who supported the creation of a Tajik republic in the 1920s had to justify the existence of a Tajik nation against Uzbek claims that the Uzbek and Tajik peoples formed one single nationality speaking two languages, that most of the Tajik-speaking populations were in fact Uzbeks who had been Persianized during periods of Western Iranian influence in Transoxiana, and that direct remnants of East Iranian populations were restricted to the mountainous regions of the Pamir range and nowhere close to form a nationality. Proving the fallacy of this line of argument, which had brought the 'Tajik people' close to ethno-cultural assimilation within the Uzbek nationality, became an existential battle for several generations of Tajik academics to this day. Using the legacy of tsarist aryanophile orientalists,[17] Tajik historians sought to demonstrate through historical and ethnographical research that the Tajik people were indeed the direct heir of the most ancient inhabitants of the region, the Aryans, and the leading ethnic component of the refined culture that flourished in the oases of Central Asia. They argued that their East Indo-Iranian forebears formed a Central Asian endogenous population at the origin of the specific urban sedentary civilization of Bactria and Soghdia and had coalesced to form the Tajik people under the Samanid dynasty (819–999). After this golden age which saw the development of a high culture based on the New Persian language, the Tajiks lost their state, their lands, and their culture to successive waves of Turkic invaders.

---

[16] It is now an acknowledged fact that Gafurov's main work on Tajik history was ghost-written by the Russian orientalist Boris A. Litvinski.
[17] Marlène Laruelle, 'The Return of the Aryan Myth: Tajikistan in Search of a Secularized National Ideology', *Nationalities Papers*, 35, 2007, pp. 51–70.

This ethnographic account of the Tajik people led to the emergence of the notion of 'historical Tajikistan'. The cradle of this mythological land was 'Aryana', a vast region stretching across Eurasia from the Altai Mountains in the east to the Carpathian Mountains in the west. The political contours of the historical state of the Tajik people were later drawn by the Samanid state, considered to be the first manifestation of Tajik statehood. This geopolitical mythology directly clashed with Uzbek national historiography since it laid claim to most of what constitutes the territory of modern-day Uzbekistan. It has contributed to a profound animosity between scholars of both nations, which has reached extreme levels since independence. State-sponsored Tajik historians have overtly accused Uzbekistan of perpetrating a cultural genocide over the Tajik population, citing arguments such as the decline of the number of Tajiks in the population census carried out in the Uzbek republic, and the linguistic policy promoting Uzbek in Tajik-speaking areas. The perceived Uzbek expansionism which culminated during the Tajik civil war with the direct military involvement of Tashkent in the conflict, gave additional arguments to Tajik intellectuals to foster the image of the Uzbek as the eternal enemy.[18]

This 'enclave mentality' has led the Tajik leadership to view Russia as benefactor and protector of Tajik interests. Official historiography endorses the civilizing role played by Russia in the history Tajikistan. For all its shortcomings and 'bourgeois' pitfalls, Russian colonization is thought to have brought some aspects of modern development to the region, paving the way for the transition from capitalism to socialism. Soviet Russians are then praised for enabling the Tajiks to recover their own statehood in 1929 and saving them from cultural assimilation within the Uzbek nationality.[19] In the official historiography, Tajikistan is indebted to the Russian people who enabled the new state to join the community of civilized nations through massive and generous education and industrialization policies. To counterbalance the *de facto* Russian cultural domination over Eastern nationalities within the Soviet Union, Tajik intellectuals have emphasized the common Indo-European origins that have supposedly connected the fate of both peoples through history. Tajiks and Russians are thought to have common Aryan ancestors who had to fight against the same barbarian assaults and whose fate ended up diverging because of the massive penetration of Turkic tribes in the Central Asian steppes. By extension, the Aryan filiation claimed by Tajik intellectuals also serves to connect the Tajik nation to the wider and

---

[18] On the representation of Uzbeks as the malign other, see Anita Khudonazar, 'The Other', Working Paper Series, Berkeley Program in Soviet and Post-Soviet Studies, 2004. On the Uzbek military role in the Tajik civil war, see Stuart Horsman, 'Uzbekistan's involvement in the Tajik civil war 1992–1997: domestic considerations', *Central Asia Survey*, 18, 1999, pp. 37–48.

[19] The injustice of the national delimitation is blamed on local pan-Turkists who are thought to have manipulated figures and scientific evidence to influence soviet Russian leaders.

supposedly more civilized family of European nations. For the same purpose, Tajik historiography has also continuously stressed the outstanding cultural achievements of the Tajiks' ancestors and their contribution to the greatest world civilizations, including the European. This theme has been overwhelming since independence, with anniversaries of antique cities and jubilees of great 'Tajik' figures such as Ibn Sina (Avicenna), al-Khorezmi, al-Farabi, and even Zoroaster, succeeding one another. The aim is not only to boost people's pride in their national past, but also to change the image of contemporary Tajikistan in Western countries from one of an isolated, obscure nation to one of an open, progressive, and civilized nation ready to recover its place in world history.

If Russia remains portrayed as a benevolent nation in newly published history textbooks and as a strategic partner in official discourse, the unity of fate between the two nations has been seriously questioned in the last two decades. The Soviet invasion of Afghanistan in 1979 has antagonized large portions of Tajik society and intelligentsia and irreversibly challenged the traditional geo-cultural positioning of Tajikistan in the (post-) Soviet area. Tajik citizens who participated in the Afghan war, mostly as translators and interpreters, rediscovered how closely connected culturally they were with the Afghan people and how inimical the country to which they belonged was to their Persian-speaking brethren. This event spurred an elite-led movement of revalorization of the Persian identity of the Tajik people during Perestroïka and the early days of independence. In 1989, under pressure from the street, a law was passed making Tajik the official language of the republic and renaming it *Farsi-Tajik* to emphasize that Tajik was the same language as Iranian Persian. The revalorization of the Tajik language was the most consensual item of the agenda put forward by the nascent opposition movement gathering urban elites and religious leaders, who joined in a coalition demanding a profound re-evaluation of Tajikistan's cultural identity and geopolitical position that would bring the country closer to the Muslim and Persian world. Among the former, which constituted the national-democratic movement, many championed an exaltation of Tajiks' Aryan identity reminiscent of pre-revolutionary Iranian 'Achaemenid nationalism'. The latter favoured promoting the Islamic elements of Tajik identity and, despite being of Sunni obedience, used many Iranian slogans from the Islamic revolution to articulate demands for the establishment of an Islamic state in Tajikistan.

The outburst in 1992 of a civil war between regional networks fighting over the redistribution of power in post-Soviet Tajikistan and the internationalization of the conflict with the political and military involvement of Uzbekistan, Russia, and Iran, somehow reinforced the traditional geopolitical mythology within the new leadership that won the war. During the Tajik civil war, Uzbekistan supported the northern faction, a region which is physically more integrated with Uzbekistan than with the Tajik territory, which had been politically close to Tashkent throughout the Soviet period, and which threatened to secede during the short-lived government formed by the 'Islamo-democrat' opposition in 1992. Uzbekistan is reported to have intervened militarily, supplying air and ground forces to the Popular Front fighting the regional factions supporting the opposition. Tashkent was utterly upset by the political manoeuvre that at the conclusion of the war brought to power Emomali Rakhmon(ov), a representative of the rival southern faction who thereafter played an ambiguous role in the peace negotiations that led to a power-sharing agreement with the Islamic and democrat opposition. Tashkent was accused of supporting two uprisings in 1997 and 1998 in the north of the country led by renegade Colonel Makhmud Khudoberdyev, an ethnic Uzbek and a commander in the Popular Front from the Northern faction. Following this sequence of events, Uzbekistan was confirmed in the role of expansionist power intending to swallow the Tajik nation into the Uzbek state. This reinforced the need for securing a protecting shield against the perceived pan-Uzbek threat among the friendly nations of 'Aryan' stock.

Russia was called upon during the Tajik civil war to play the role of pacifier. It is telling that both the opposition and government forces turned to Russia to arbitrate their conflict and put an end to armed conflict. Russia was therefore the major external player in the Tajik civil war. It was the leading force of the CIS peacekeeping force deployed in Tajikistan between 1993 and 2000, and *de facto* provided the national defence forces of the Tajik government with crucial help, most importantly by maintaining a military base on Tajik territory – a base that still exists today. Not only has Russia been considered the guarantor of Tajikistan's political stability and territorial integrity after the civil war, it has also remained the main economic partner of the impoverished country as well as an influential chaperon in the conduct of Tajik foreign policy. Nevertheless, the traditional image of Russia as a protective shield and a civilizing partner has been seriously eroded in the last decade by three main factors: the tragic fate of the Tajik economic migrants in Russia, working without legal status in terrible conditions and falling prey to racist crimes; the improvement of Russian-Uzbek relations to the detriment of Tajikistan in regional geopolitics; and the disappointment towards the level and nature of Russian investments in Tajik economy. With the intervention of the international coalition in Afghanistan in 2002, Tajikistan has been on the forefront of the 'war on terror' and has gained strategic value. This enabled Dushanbe to gain some leverage in its relations with Russia, as was revealed in the dispute over Russian military presence in the country in 2004, and to look for alternative strategic partners, Iran being one of them. Finding new partners proves to be all the more critical in that relations with Uzbekistan have kept deteriorating in the past decade. Tashkent has mined its border with Tajikistan (and Kyrgyzstan) following terrorist attacks in the Uzbek capital in 1999 and has continually imposed a harsh border regime, seriously constraining the transit of goods and peoples to and from Tajikistan. Conflict over energy supplies, a long-standing dispute between the two countries, has escalated in recent years with Tajikistan's stated desire to fulfil ambitious plans to construct massive hydroelectric dams that will give the possibility to Tajikistan to control the amount of water flowing into Uzbek agricultural fields.

Iranian involvement in the Tajik civil war on the side of the Islamic opposition initially dampened Tajik leaders' enthusiasm for a quick reconnection with the outer Persian world. However, the positive role played by Iran in the inter-Tajik peace negotiations (1994–1997) and the subsequent pragmatic, ideology-free, and overall benevolent policy followed by Tehran in Tajikistan did much to improve the relations between the two countries and lay the ground for the establishment of an ever-expanding cooperation throughout the 2000s. We now turn to assessing the modalities of this cooperation and the remaining serious challenges to the establishment of a durable strategic relationship.

Tajikistan and the Persian World: An Axis in the Making?

Cultural Cooperation

Projects in the field of cultural cooperation are the most promising but they also constitute a serious test to the so-called Persian brotherhood. Tajikistan has developed a rather clear ethno-national positioning within the Persian world. Based on the official historiography developed by Bobojon Gafurov in the 1970s, Tajikistan has positioned itself as a member of the Persian family with its own specific ethnogenesis and cultural legacy. Tajiks are presented in official accounts, printed in Iran in Cyrillic and Persian scripts, as the heirs of the Eastern Iranian civilization of lower Central Asia, which formed endogenously, pre-dates the Achaemenid civilization, and has actually contributed many original elements to West Iranian culture. In the same fashion, emphasis is put on the fact that New Persian, in which the most refined literary works of the Persian culture were produced from the tenth century onwards, was developed in the oases of Central Asia and from there spread to the Western Persian lands. Reversing the perspective on the flux of cultural influences within the Persian world, Tajikistan seeks to indigenize its Persian identity, and lay the ground for a relation with Iran that is based on mutual respect for ideological and cultural differences.

At the same time, this vision of Tajik identity remains an élitist one and needs to be made popular through a nationwide and international cultural policy which Dushanbe cannot afford and cannot sell to foreign investors either. Tehran has a specific role to play here. Although Tajik national ideology can sometimes be controversial for the Iranian intelligentsia, it offers innumerable opportunities for cultural cooperation. Tajikistan's official programme aimed at internal and external consumption does meet to a certain extent the objective of Iran's foreign cultural policy of promoting the knowledge of Persian language, culture, and history in order to improve the

Islamic Republic's image abroad.[20] Tehran is therefore the main sponsor of Tajikistan's policy in the field of culture and education. Tehran and Dushanbe have signed many agreements ranging from teachers' training, scholarly exchange, and media cooperation to the holding of conferences, national festivals, and the publication of books. Tajikistan and Iran are now planning to create a joint Academy of Sciences, Arts and Literature[21] and to open Centres of Iranian Studies in every Tajik university. The way the Persian heritage will be approached by Tajik and Iranian teachers in these centres will be an interesting test for the stated project of promoting a Persian-speaking Union.

Economic Cooperation

Tajikistan is in dire need of new economic partnerships and foreign investments. Iran has a substantial financial capacity, which can be channelled through political relations because of the close links between the state and the economic actors. This contrasts with Western governments, which have limited leverage over national and international private companies and tie their aid to political reforms. Iranian businessmen are now well established in Tajikistan and bilateral trade between the two countries has risen steadily from US$ 40 million in 2000 to US$ 200 million in 2010, making Iran one of Tajikistan's five top trading partners. An important goal for Tajikistan is to find reliable investors who can sustain their commitment to support strategic projects that are geopolitically sensitive. In that area too, Iran presents a specific advantage.

The Islamic Republic has reportedly become the main foreign investor in 2010 with a total investment of US$ 65 million, for the first time surpassing Russia.[22] But what makes Iran an important new investor for Tajikistan is not only the volume of those investments, but mostly their strategic nature and the political commitment behind them. Tehran is proactively supporting Dushanbe's infrastructure projects aimed at opening new transportation routes, thereby reducing Tajikistan's over-dependence on Uzbekistan's transportation network. Iran has financed and carried out (although with serious technical shortcomings) the construction of a road under the Anzob pass bypassing Uzbekistan and connecting Dushanbe with the country's northern areas all year round. Tehran has also started investing in the

---

[20] See also Nadia von Maltzahn's chapter in this volume.
[21] Ariel Farrar-Wellman and Robert Frasco, 'Tajikistan-Iran Foreign Relations', *IranTracker*, 7 July 2010, available at: http://www.irantracker.org/foreign-relations/tajikistan-iran-foreign-relations#_ftnref19 (accessed 27 March 2011).
[22] Rasoul Shodon, 'Iran reportedly the largest investor in Tajikistan in 2010', *Asiaplus*, 25 January 2010, available at http://news.tj/en/news/iran-reportedly-largest-investor-tajikistan-2010 (accessed 4 September 2011).

construction of roads and railways connecting Tajikistan and Iran through Afghanistan and further to China.[23]

Iran is also emerging as a key investor in Tajikistan's energy sector, another critical area for Tajikistan which is experiencing recurrent energy crises and depends on Uzbekistan for its energy provision. The first Iranian offer to enter the sector in the early 2000s was countered by Russia, but Tehran has since then proven to be consistent and credible in supporting Tajikistan's ambitious hydroelectric plans. Iran started the construction of Sangtuda 2, a hydroelectric plant on the Vakhsh River which is expected to be completed in September 2011. Unlike Russian investments in the construction of the powerful power plants of Roghun and Sangtuda 1, the terms of the Iranian investment agreement will ultimately give Tajikistan ownership over the energy infrastructure. Most importantly, Iran stands out as a foreign investor because of the political stance Tehran is ready to adopt in defence of Tajik interests in the bitter energy and transportation conflicts that oppose Tajikistan and Uzbekistan. While Russia is revising the initial plans agreed upon for the construction of Rogun dam to satisfy Uzbek demands, Iran stood firm in support of Dushanbe during the blockade imposed by Tashkent on freight shipment, carrying construction material towards Tajikistan during the summer of 2010. Iran's backing of Tajikistan is a strong political positioning, as it risks alienating Uzbekistan, which is a strategic regional player and a more important economic partner for Iran than Tajikistan.[24] Yet this stance may well be a long-term position. Iran has announced that it is considering realizing three additional hydroelectric projects, one in Aini on the Zeravshan River, and two in Nurabad on the Hingob River, projects that were initially to be carried out by China until Beijing decided to pull out under Uzbek pressure.

Iran's investments in Tajikistan's energy sector are not only aimed at supporting the country's energy self-sufficiency, but also at linking the energy sectors of the three Persian-speaking countries by supporting electricity exports from Tajik power plants to Afghanistan and Iran. Iranian investments in Tajikistan are expected to continue to grow and diversify in the coming years.[25] They are part of wider regional design aimed at integrating physically and economically the contemporary Persian world and could become a concrete factor bringing the three Persian-speaking countries closer together.

---

[23] Iran is currently completing the Shagon-Zighar road, which is part of Tajikistan's Dushanbe-Kulob-Darvoz-Khorog-Kulma-Karakorum highway system considered as vital to Tajikistan's transportation network.

[24] Roman Muzalevsky, 'Iran Maneuvers Uzbek-Tajik Squabbles', *ISN Insights*, March 2011, available at http://www.isn.ethz.ch/isn/Current-Affairs/ISN-Insights/Detail?lng=en&id=127172&contextid734=127172&contextid735=127166&tabid=127166 (accessed 4 September 2011).

[25] A private Iranian company has signed a contract to build a cement factory in the southern Khatlon province, as well as a coal power plant for an amount of US$ 500 million.

This regional plan is critical for Tajikistan, which needs to open new routes through the long southern border that it shares with Afghanistan. Giving more cohesion to this area is also in line with Tajik geopolitical culture, which seeks to escape its enclave position within the Turkic world, and join in a new, Persian family. However, technical, financial, and political obstacles to this pan-Iranian economic policy are considerable, and Iran still has to demonstrate that it has the capacity to realize its ambitions.

Security: A Factor of Disunity or Rapprochement?

The volatile security situation in (and around) Afghanistan remains a stumbling block for the development of economic and political cooperation between Iran and Tajikistan, and *a fortiori* for the emergence of an integrated Persian area. Continuing instability in Afghanistan hampers the development of infrastructure and trade through Afghanistan. Drug trafficking is a major concern for both Tajikistan and Iran, the latter reportedly having the highest rate of drug addiction in the world. Both Tajikistan and Iran are making huge efforts to establish tight border controls, Tehran going so far as to erecting a wall on its Afghan border, a move which is unlikely to facilitate the development of trade in the area—nor the establishment of confidence and friendly relations between the two countries. In addition to that, the massive involvement in the Afghan conundrum of a great variety of international actors under the leadership of the United States further complicates attempts at designing long-term projects between the three countries. The presence of US troops in Afghanistan, Central, and South Asia is a primary security concern for Iran, and the establishment of an inimical pro-Western regime in Kabul is one of Tehran's greatest fears. Allegations of Iranian support for armed combatants fighting the coalition in Afghanistan are highly plausible, but such support is hardly acceptable for Dushanbe, which is concerned with the spill-over of armed militancy onto its own territory.

Yet Iranian influence in Afghan politics makes Tehran not only part of the problem, but part of the solution as well. Tajik leaders are highly aware of this fact, having themselves experienced both the negative and the positive role this regional power can play in the stability of their own country. Security concerns related to the situation in Afghanistan may therefore play in favour of cooperation with Iran in the field of security. Dushanbe and Tehran share a long-term interest in establishing friendly and mutually beneficial relations with Afghanistan. The establishment of a partnership over regional security issues has also the potential of providing some leverage to each country, both having highly constrained external policies—although for different reasons.

Tajikistan's national security rests almost entirely on its strategic partnership with Russia. Moscow's political stance in the Uzbek-Tajik dispute is raising serious concern in Dushanbe and encourages Dushanbe to look for alternative security arrangements. Iran's isolation on the international scene and determination to counter American's presence in its immediate neighbourhood makes Tehran eager to establish strong partnerships with countries in the region. For now, military arrangements between Tajikistan and Russia prevent Dushanbe from entering into a proper military partnership with Iran, but the two countries are displaying their will to establish closer ties in the field of security. In May 2010, the ministers of defence of the two countries signed a memorandum of understanding to increase their military cooperation, particularly in the field of personnel training and weapons production. In return, Dushanbe has declared officially on several occasions that it supported Iran's 'peaceful nuclear programme'. Tajikistan was also the first country to back Iran's request for membership in the Shanghai Cooperation Organization (SCO), an intergovernmental security organization founded in 2001 that comprises China, Russia, Uzbekistan, Kazakhstan, Kyrgyzstan, and Tajikistan. Given Russia's mild reaction to evolving Iran-Tajik security ties, its own expanding military collaboration with Tehran, and its seemingly favourable stance towards Iran's joining the SCO, the trends towards the two Persian-speaking countries entering into a strategic relationship seems to have the potential to expand.

Ideological Divergences

The biggest obstacle to a long-term relationship between Tajikistan and Iran remains the ideological nature of the Iranian government. The Tajik leadership is heir to a radically secular Soviet outlook and has always been weary of Iran's ideological influence in the religious sphere. Since the presidency of Mohammad Khatami, Iran has abandoned its ambition of exporting the revolution to Central Asia and has downplayed religious overtones when interacting with the Sunni, secular countries of the region. While this shift in the official policy has contributed to restoring some amount of confidence among the Tajik leadership, ideological divergences have not disappeared altogether in as much as the Islamic Republic of Iran is not a monolithic body but a complex structure of powerful organs capable of exerting ideological and political influence beyond Iranian borders. Tajikistan remains therefore extremely cautious of the potential religious influence that Iranian actors might exert within Tajik society, and recent reports of growing numbers of Tajik citizens converting to Twelver Shiism, mostly in the south of the country, have raised alarms in Dushanbe.[26] This might be the reason behind the recent official order to dismiss several dozens of pupils from an Iranian school in Dushanbe,[27] and contribute to Tajikistan's continuing

---

[26] F. Kabirov, 'Tadzhikistan na tret' uzhe shiitskiy... ili iranskiy? (In Tajikistan, already 30% of the population is Shiite... or Iranian?)', Centrasia.ru, 22 December 2010, available at:
http://www.centrasia.ru/newsA.php?st=1293039240 (accessed 23 February 2011). This figure is no doubt exaggerated but shows the genuine concern about this phenomenon in Tajikistan.
[27] 'Tajiks, Afghans To Be Dismissed From Iranian School In Dushanbe', *Radio Free Europe/Radio Liberty*, 27 December 2010, available at
http://www.rferl.org/content/article/2260752.html (accessed 15 January 2011).

reluctance to lift the visa regime and increase the number of flights between the two countries.

Dushanbe's alarm about reported conversions to Twelver Shiism is in fact adding to a broader concern about the penetration of competing ideologies within Tajik society, and first of all the increase in followers of non-traditional, potentially radical, Sunni schools of thought. The declaration of 2009 as the year of Imam Azam Abu Hanifa and the adoption by the national parliament in March of that year of a new law on religion which mentions the 'specific role of the Hanafi branch of Islam' in Tajik society is an important shift from the government's official position, which had always refused to give prominence to a specific religion, given the secular nature of the State.[28] This reveals the sense of urgency to counter the rise of foreign Islamic ideologies. The forcible repatriation in November 2010 of Tajik students undergoing religious education in several Muslim countries, including Iran,[29] is another indication of the government's fear of foreign religious influence being imported in Tajik society. The restrictive policy being applied on religious education abroad is therefore not specifically targeting Iran. Indeed, the Iranian and the Tajik leaderships share a similar concern towards the rise of Sunni Salafism in Central Asia (so-called 'Wahhabism') and Tehran is reportedly willing to support the Tajik government in promoting a local, traditionalist or Sufi version of Islam within the population.[30] Iran itself is confronted with hitherto unknown levels of armed violence in the south-eastern predominantly Sunni province of Sistan and Baluchistan carried out by Jundollah, a Baluchi Sunni opposition group.[31] Although the grievances articulated by the movement concern mostly ethnic and religious rights, Tehran seems concerned about potential links between its internal opposition and Islamist fighters operating on the Afghan-Pakistan border.

Conclusion

Tehran and Dushanbe have joined efforts in recent years to promote the image of a dynamic 'Persian world' on the international scene and have become the

---

[28] Fakhriddin Kholbekov, Iskandar Aliev, 'Tajikistan's New Religion Law Sparking Questions', *RFE/RL Watchdog*, 2 April 2009, available at http://www.rferl.org/content/Tajikistans_New_Religion_Law_Causing_Controversy/1601529.html (accessed 12 May 2011).

[29] Edward Lemon, 'Tajikistan: Dushanbe Forcing Students Abroad to Return Home', *eurasianet.org*, 29 November 2010, available at http://www.eurasianet.org/node/62460 (accessed 15 January 2011). In Iran, Tajik students compelled to leave the country were receiving religious education in Sunni madrasas in the province of Sistan and Baluchestan.

[30] Sébastien Peyrouse and Sadykzhan Ibraimov, 'Iran's Central Asia Temptation', *Current Trends in Islamist Ideology*, 10, 2010, available at
http://www.currenttrends.org/research/detail/irans-central-asia-temptations (accessed 15 January 2011).

[31] See Stéphane A. Dudoignon's chapter in this volume.

vocal promoters of the establishment of a 'Persian-speaking Union' which would involve Iran, Afghanistan, and Tajikistan. The celebrations of Nowruz, the Persian New Year, have been the occasion to organize trilateral summits between the presidents of the three countries for the past three years. The Persian-speaking leaders have signed a number of agreements on these occasions to promote cooperation in the fields of trade, security, transportation, energy, and culture. Some proposals have been made that seem totally unrealistic, such as the creation of a common currency, or the establishment of a military alliance. But projects in the field of transportation and energy, although difficult to realize and hardly viable economically, represent a real chance for the landlocked and underdeveloped republics of Tajikistan and Afghanistan.

Clearly, the stabilization of Afghanistan and the evolution of international politics in this country will be the main factors influencing the developments of such a 'pan-Iranian' project. Until Afghanistan is able to take control of its own destiny, position itself with regards to its Persian heritage, and develop some sort of Afghan national identity, the political and cultural concept of 'Persian world' will lack consistency.

For now, Tajikistan and Iran are steering the process because they share common interest in this regard. Yet, the ideological abyss that separates post-Soviet secular Tajik leaders and religiously orientated Iranian officials is not about to vanish, unless one of the two states experiences a change of regime. Indeed, the uncertain future of the regimes in both countries may well turn out to be the most critical factor in the bilateral relations in the years to come. The lack of legitimacy of the regimes in power is currently a factor that plays in favour of a rapprochement. Emomali Rahmon and Mahmoud Ahmadinejad, two leaders that are contested domestically and on the international scene, find mutual benefits in extending one another political support. Yet, such short-term political interests will not be enough to establish a sound basis for the long-term rapprochement of the three Persian-speaking countries. Indeed, it is difficult to imagine the emergence of a modern, integrated, pacified Persian world, based on a shared regional vision, when the worldview of the population of each of its national components is so fragmented, and when their leaderships are so contested and lack a vision for the development and national cohesion of their *own* respective countries, let alone the wider Persian world. Popular unrest is to be expected in the three states, and that will have a profound influence on regional dynamics within the contemporary Persian world.

List of Contributors

Ali Ansari is Professor of Iranian History & Director of the Institute for Iranian Studies at the University of St Andrews, and Associate Fellow of the Middle East Programme, Royal Institute for International Affairs (Chatham House). He is the author of *The Politics of Nationalism in Modern Iran* (2012); *Crisis of Authority: Iran's 2009 Presidential Election* (2010); *Iran Under Ahmadinejad*, Adelphi Paper, (January 2008); *Confronting Iran: The failure of US policy and the roots of mistrust* (2006); *Modern Iran since 1921: The Pahlavis and after* (2007); *Iran, Islam & Democracy - The Politics of Managing Change* (2006); and has recently been appointed Editor of the Cambridge History of Iran, Volume 8 (The Islamic Republic).

Denis Bauchard is a consultant in international relations. He is presently Senior Fellow for North Africa/Middle East at the French Institute of International Relations (IFRI) in Paris. A former president of the Institut du monde arabe in Paris, he was Ambassador of France to Canada (1998–2001) and Ambassador of France to Jordan (1989–1993). He was Chief-of-Staff to the Minister of Foreign Affairs, Hervé de Charette (1996–1997) and Assistant Secretary at the Ministry of Foreign Affairs, North Africa and the Middle East (1993–1996). He was appointed as Minister Plenipotentiary in 1987, served as Deputy Assistant Secretary at the Ministry of Foreign Affairs (1982–1989) and was Financial Counsellor at the French Mission to the United Nations (1978–1981). He has published and edited several books, most recently *Le nouveau monde arabe: enjeux et instabilités* (2012), and is a contributor for several newspapers (*Le Monde, Le Monde diplomatique, Politique Etrangère*) and websites (IFRI, Grotius, Boulevard Extérieur).

Houchang Esfandiar Chehabi is a professor of international relations and history at Boston University. He is the author of *Iranian Politics and Religious Modernism* (1990); principal author of *Distant Relations: Iran and Lebanon in the Last 500 Years* (2006); editor of *Robert Michels, Political Sociology, and the Future of Democracy* by Juan J. Linz (2006); editor of *Persian Literature and Judeo-Persian Culture: Collected Writings* by Sorour S. Soroudi (2010); co-editor, with Alfred Stepan, of *Politics, Society, and Democracy: Comparative Studies* (1995); co-editor, with Juan J. Linz, of *Sultanistic Regimes* (1998); and co-editor, with Vanessa Martin, of *Iran's Constitutional Revolution: Popular Politics, Cultural Transformations and Transnational Connec-*

tions (2010). His main research interests are Iranian cultural history and the politics of islands.

Thierry Coville is a professor of economics in Novancia, a Business School belonging to the Chamber of Commerce of Paris, and Research Fellow at IRIS (French research centre for international and strategic studies). He was a research fellow in the French Institute of Research in Iran from 1991 to 1994. He worked as an economist in the Centre of Forecasting of the Paris Chamber of Commerce from 1996 to 2006. He was also the editor-in-chief of the magazine of the Paris chamber of Commerce specialized on international affairs, Accomex. He has published a large number of articles on Middle East affairs and on international economics and finance. Among his books are *L'économie de l'Iran islamique: entre ordre et désordres* (2002) and *L'Iran: la révolution invisible* (2007). He is also a consultant for firms interested in Middle East markets.

Stéphane A. Dudoignon is a Senior Research Fellow in the CNRS (in the Centre for Turkic, Ottoman, Balkan & Central Asian Studies, Paris) and an Associated Scholar at the University of Amsterdam. Since 2008 he has been the Director of the Central Eurasian Reader bibliographical journal (Klaus Schwarz Verlag, Berlin). An historian of Islam in modern and contemporary Central Eurasia, he devotes the bulk of his work to the social history and hagiography of the religious personnel of Islam in Soviet Tajikistan, to the role of the Baloch in the twentieth and early-twenty-first-century revival of Sunni Islam in Iran, and to the social functions of Islam in the Volga-Ural regions of Russia during the late Tsarist period. In parallel, since 2009 he has been conducting research on the national instrumentations of Soviet Oriental studies in the former republics of the USSR. S. A. Dudoignon is also a translator of modern and contemporary literatures from Russia (Evgenii Grishkovets, Mikhail Yelizarov), the Caucasus (Jelil Memmedguluzade), and Central Asia (Barzu Abdurazzoqov, Bahmanyar, Chulpan).

Narsi Ghorban is currently the Managing Director of Narkangan Gas To Liquid International Company. He is also the Chairman of Doran Energy and the Director of the International Institute for Caspian Studies (IICS). He is currently the secretary to the Environment and Energy Commission of the International Chamber of Commerce (ICC-Iran). He received his BSc from the American University of Beirut. He also holds an MPhil from Brunel University, UK, and a PhD in Petroleum Economics from the University of London. Dr. Ghorban has been an independent energy consultant in the UK and Iran since 1979, in which position he has consulted for several organizations and international oil companies. He has also worked with the Organization of Petroleum Exporting Countries (OPEC), the Institute for International Energy

Studies, and a number of companies engaged in oil, gas and petrochemicals business in the Middle East. He is a fellow of the Energy Institute (IE) London, a member of the Royal Institute of International Affairs (RIIA), London, a member of the International Institute of Strategic Studies (IISS), London, a member of the Iran Association of Energy Economics (IAEE), Tehran. Dr. Ghorban has published many articles and papers in various international journals.

Jubin Goodarzi is an assistant professor at the International Relations Department at Webster University, Geneva, and has been a consultant on Middle Eastern affairs with the United Nations since 1996. He has worked with a number of US and UK research institutes and foundations, including the Center for Strategic and International Studies (CSIS) in Washington, DC, the Royal Institute of International Affairs (Chatham House) in London, and the Ford Foundation in New York. Dr. Goodarzi is author of *Syria and Iran: Diplomatic Alliance and Power Politics in the Middle East* (2009), and numerous articles and book reviews on the international relations of the Middle East.

Frédérique Guérin received her PhD in History and International Politics from the Graduate Institute of International and Development Studies in Geneva. Her doctoral research examined the interaction between nation-building and foreign policy making in post-Soviet Tajikistan. From 2003 to 2007 she worked as the scientific coordinator of the Islamic-Secular dialogue project in Tajikistan. Frédérique Guérin is now a Research Fellow at the Geneva Centre for Security Policy, where she focuses on the role of cultural factors in international security.

Homa Katouzian is a social scientist, historian and literary critic. He is the Iran Heritage Research Fellow, St. Antony's College and Member, Faculty of Oriental Studies, University of Oxford. He is also editor of Iranian Studies, Journal of the International Society for Iranian Studies. He taught Economics at the Universities of Leeds and Kent at Canterbury (UK) 1968-1986 when he decided to devote all his time to Iranian studies. He was a fellow of the School of Historical Studies, Institute for Advanced Study, Princeton, 2001, Visiting Professor of Sociology, University of California, San Diego, Spring 1990, Visiting Professor of Economics, University of California, Los Angeles (UCLA), 1985, Economic Consultant, UNCTAD, UN, Geneva, 1982, etc. He has published widely both in English and Persian. His English books include *The Persians, Ancient, Mediaeval and Modern Iran* (2010), *Sadeq Hedayat: His Work and His Wondrous World* (ed., 2011), *Sa'di, the Poet of Love, Life and Compassion* (2006), *State and Society in Iran: the Eclipse of the Qajars and the Emergence of the Pahlavis* (2006) and *Musaddiq and the Struggle for Power in Iran* (1999). His research interests include Iranian history, comparative history, sociology of history, and modern and classical Persian literature.

Thierry Kellner is a lecturer at the Université Libre de Bruxelles (Department of Political Science) in Belgium. His main research interests include Chinese foreign policy (especially relations with Western Asia), the foreign policy of Iran (especially with Asian Countries) and the evolution of Eurasian geopolitics. His latest book, co-authored with Mohammad-Reza Djalili, is *Histoire de l'Iran contemporain* (2010).

Farhad Khosrokhavar is a Professor at the Ecole des Hautes Etudes en Sciences Sociales (EHESS) in Paris, France. His main fields of study are Iranian society after the Islamic Revolution and Islam, in particular its radical forms in Europe and the Middle East. He has published 17 books, three of which translated in nine different languages and more than 70 articles, in French, in English, and in Persian. He has been a Rockefeller Fellow (1990), has given conferences in different European and American universities (Saint Antony's College at Oxford, Princeton, NYU, Columbia, UCLA, USC, Stanford, Harvard, Yale, Texas University at Austin...). He was a Yale Visiting Scholar in 2008 and a Harvard Visiting Scholar in 2009. His latest books are: *Muslims in Prison: a comparative perspective between Great Britain and France* (with James Beckford et Danièle Joly) (2005); *Suicide Bombers, The New Martyrs of Allah* (translation from French) (2005); *Quand Al Qaeda Parle: témoignages derrière les barreaux* (2006); *Inside Jihadism: Understanding Jihadi Movements Worldwide* (2009); *Etre jeune dans le pays des ayatollahs* (in cooperation with Amir Nikpey) (2009); and *Jihadist Ideology: The Anthropological Perspective* (2011).

Nadia von Maltzahn is a Research Associate at the Orient-Institut, Beirut. She completed her DPhil in Middle Eastern Studies at St Antony's College, University of Oxford, and her main research interests lie in cultural policy, modern history, and international relations, with a particular focus on the Middle East. She is the author of *The Syria-Iran Axis: Cultural Diplomacy and International Relations in the Middle East* (2013).

Alessandro Monsutti is Adjunct Professor and Director of Research of the Programme for the Study of Global Migration at the Graduate Institute of International and Development Studies in Geneva. Trained as a social anthropologist, Monsutti has conducted multi-sited research since the mid-1990s in Afghanistan, Pakistan and Iran to study the modes of solidarity and cooperation mobilised in a situation of conflict and forced migration. He is the author of *War and Migration: Social Networks and Economic Strategies of the Hazaras of Afghanistan* (2005).

List of Contributors 307

Mehdi Mozaffari is a professor in the Department of Political Science, University of Aarhus, Denmark and the head of the Centre for Studies in Islamism and Radicalisation (CIR). He has been a visiting scholar at different universities (Geneva, Grenoble, Sorbonne, MGIMO /Moscow) and a senior fellow at Harvard University. He is the author, co-author and editor of a number of academic books, including *Globalization and Civilizations* (ed.) (2002); 'Mega Civilization: Global Capital and the New Standard of Civilization' in *The New Millenium* (2000), *FATWA: Violence and Discourtesy* (1998), *Authority in Islam: From Muhammad to Khomeini* (1987); *Security Politics in the Commonwealth of Independent States* (1997). His most recent publication is *Western Totalitarianism: A Reminder* (2011).

Firouzeh Nahavandi is a professor at Université Libre de Bruxelles, Belgium, where she also directs the Research Centre for International Cooperation and Development (CECID). She has more than 20 years' experience of teaching and research in mainly two areas. First in development theories and second in socio-political development of non-Arab Muslim countries, including Iran, Afghanistan, Pakistan and the Central Asian states. She currently also focuses on women studies in the Islamic world. Her main publications are : *Aux sources de la révolution iranienne, contribution à une sociologie politique des révolutions* (1988); *L'Asie du sud-ouest, Afghanistan, Iran, Pakistan* (1991) ; *Culture du développement en Asie* (1997); *Globalisation et néolibéralisme dans le tiers-monde*, (ed.), (2000) ; *La question de l'Islam et de l'Etat à l'aube du XXIe siècle* (co-editor with Paul Claeys)(2001); *Repenser le développement et la coopération internationale: Etat des savoirs universitaires* (ed.)(2003); *Mouvements islamistes et politique* (2009); and *Du développement à la globalisation* (2009).

Arzoo Osanloo is an associate professor at the University of Washington's Law, Societies, and Justice Program. She holds a JD from American University (1993) and a PhD in Anthropology from Stanford University (2002). Formerly an immigration and asylum/refugee attorney, Osanloo conducts research and teaches courses focusing on the intersection of law and culture, including human rights, refugee rights and identity, and women's rights in Muslim societies. Her geographical focus is on the Middle East, especially Iran. She has published in various journals, including *American Ethnologist, Cultural Anthropology* and *Iranian Studies*, and is the author of *The Politics of Women's Rights in Iran* (2009). Her current project considers the Islamic mandate of forgiveness, compassion, and mercy in Iran's criminal sanctioning system, jurisprudential scholarship and everyday acts among pious Muslims. She currently serves on the Executive Board of the Middle East Section of the American Anthropological Association.

Walter Posch is a Research Fellow at the German Institute for Foreign and Security Policy, Berlin. He received his PhD in Iranian Studies from Bamberg University, Germany; he has been Middle East Analyst at the National Defence Academy in Vienna (2000--2004), and Research Fellow at the EU Institute for Security Studies in Paris (2004--2009). The focus of his research is on Iranian domestic politics, foreign policy of the Islamic Republic of Iran, with a particular interest on the Islamic Republic of Iran's security apparatus, as well as the Ottoman-Safavid conflict.

Clément Therme is an Associate Fellow at the Centre d'analyse et d'intervention sociologiques (CADIS) at EHESS in Paris and a Research Fellow for the Programme for the Study of Global Migration at the Graduate Institute (Geneva). He has also taught in the Department of Politics, Languages & International Studies at the University of Bath. His articles have appeared in *Politique étrangère*, *Maghreb-Machrek* and *Politique américaine*, and he is the author of *Les relations entre Téhéran et Moscou depuis 1979* (2012).